THE
BATTALION

The Stackpole Military History Series

THE AMERICAN CIVIL WAR
Cavalry Raids of the Civil War
Ghost, Thunderbolt, and Wizard
In the Lion's Mouth
Pickett's Charge
Witness to Gettysburg

WORLD WAR I
Doughboy War

WORLD WAR II
After D-Day
Airborne Combat
Armor Battles of the Waffen-SS, 1943–45
Armoured Guardsmen
Army of the West
Arnhem 1944
Australian Commandos
The B-24 in China
Backwater War
The Battalion
The Battle of France
The Battle of Sicily
Battle of the Bulge, Vol. 1
Battle of the Bulge, Vol. 2
Beyond the Beachhead
Beyond Stalingrad
The Black Bull
Blitzkrieg Unleashed
Blossoming Silk against the Rising Sun
Bodenplatte
The Brandenburger Commandos
The Brigade
Bringing the Thunder
The Canadian Army and the Normandy Campaign
Coast Watching in World War II
Colossal Cracks
Condor
A Dangerous Assignment
D-Day Bombers
D-Day Deception
D-Day to Berlin
Decision in the Ukraine
Destination Normandy
Dive Bomber!
A Drop Too Many
Eager Eagles
Eagles of the Third Reich
The Early Battles of Eighth Army
Eastern Front Combat
Europe in Flames
Exit Rommel
The Face of Courage
Fatal Decisions
Fist from the Sky
Flying American Combat Aircraft of World War II
For Europe
Forging the Thunderbolt
For the Homeland

Fortress France
The German Defeat in the East, 1944–45
German Order of Battle, Vol. 1
German Order of Battle, Vol. 2
German Order of Battle, Vol. 3
The Germans in Normandy
Germany's Panzer Arm in World War II
GI Ingenuity
Goodwood
The Great Ships
Grenadiers
Guns against the Reich
Hitler's Nemesis
Hold the Westwall
Infantry Aces
In the Fire of the Eastern Front
Iron Arm
Iron Knights
Japanese Army Fighter Aces
Japanese Naval Fighter Aces
JG 26 Luftwaffe Fighter Wing War Diary, Vol. 1
JG 26 Luftwaffe Fighter Wing War Diary, Vol. 2
Kampfgruppe Peiper at the Battle of the Bulge
The Key to the Bulge
Knight's Cross Panzers
Kursk
Luftwaffe Aces
Luftwaffe Fighter Ace
Luftwaffe Fighter-Bombers over Britain
Luftwaffe Fighters and Bombers
Massacre at Tobruk
Mechanized Juggernaut or Military Anachronism?
Messerschmitts over Sicily
Michael Wittmann, Vol. 1
Michael Wittmann, Vol. 2
Mission 85
Mission 376
Mountain Warriors
The Nazi Rocketeers
Night Flyer / Mosquito Pathfinder
No Holding Back
On the Canal
Operation Mercury
Packs On!
Panzer Aces
Panzer Aces II
Panzer Aces III
Panzer Commanders of the Western Front
Panzergrenadier Aces
Panzer Gunner
The Panzer Legions
Panzers in Normandy
Panzers in Winter
Panzer Wedge, Vol. 1
Panzer Wedge, Vol. 2
The Path to Blitzkrieg

Penalty Strike
Poland Betrayed
Red Road from Stalingrad
Red Star under the Baltic
Retreat to the Reich
Rommel's Desert Commanders
Rommel's Desert War
Rommel's Lieutenants
The Savage Sky
Ship-Busters
The Siege of Küstrin
The Siegfried Line
A Soldier in the Cockpit
Soviet Blitzkrieg
Spitfires and Yellow Tail Mustangs
Stalin's Keys to Victory
Surviving Bataan and Beyond
T-34 in Action
Tank Tactics
Tigers in the Mud
Triumphant Fox
The 12th SS, Vol. 1
The 12th SS, Vol. 2
Twilight of the Gods
Typhoon Attack
The War against Rommel's Supply Lines
War in the Aegean
War of the White Death
Warsaw 1944
Winter Storm
Wolfpack Warriors
Zhukov at the Oder

THE COLD WAR / VIETNAM
Cyclops in the Jungle
Expendable Warriors
Fighting in Vietnam
Flying American Combat Aircraft: The Cold War
Here There Are Tigers
Land with No Sun
MiGs over North Vietnam
Phantom Reflections
Street without Joy
Through the Valley
Two One Pony

WARS OF AFRICA AND THE MIDDLE EAST
Never-Ending Conflict
The Rhodesian War

GENERAL MILITARY HISTORY
Carriers in Combat
Cavalry from Hoof to Track
Desert Battles
Doughboy War
Guerrilla Warfare
Ranger Dawn
Sieges
The Spartan Army

THE
BATTALION

The Dramatic Story of the
2nd Ranger Battalion
in World War II

Col. Robert W. Black

STACKPOLE
BOOKS

Published by
STACKPOLE BOOKS
5067 Ritter Road
Mechanicsburg, PA 17055
www.stackpolebooks.com

Maps designed by Mike Bechthold
Cover design by Wendy A. Reynolds

Printed in the United States of America

10 9 8 7 6 5 4 3 2 1

ISBN (paperback): 978-0-8117-1273-6

The Library of Congress has cataloged the hardcover edition as follows:

Black, Robert W.
  The battalion : the dramatic story of the 2nd Ranger Battalion in World War II / Robert W. Black.— 1st ed.
      p. cm.
  Includes bibliographical references and index.
  ISBN-13: 978-0-8117-0184-6
  ISBN-10: 0-8117-0184-0
  1. United States. Army. Ranger Battalion, 2nd. 2. World War, 1939–1945—Regimental histories—United States. 3. World War, 1939–1945—Campaigns—Western Front. I. Title.

  D769.312nd .B63 2006
  940.54'1273—dc22
                                        2006008711

To Julie Rankin Fulmer,
daughter of Lucy Lolli Rankin and T/5 Richard Rankin,
Company A, 2nd Ranger Battalion,
for her dedicated work to preserve the memory of the Rangers.

Table of Contents

Prologue

June 6, 1944, 0700 hours. In the mobile headquarters his officers had dubbed "The Circus Wagon," Gen. Dwight D. Eisenhower lay in bed. Eisenhower was exhausted, but unable to sleep. The evening prior he had visited the 101st Airborne Division as they prepared to board their aircraft for battle. He had demonstrated full confidence before his men, as a commander should, but predictions were that the invasion of Normandy would take a heavy toll on Allied troops. The staff knew he had written a statement in the event of success, but only Eisenhower knew about the alternate message he had prepared in case of failure. Typically and properly, he would take full responsibility for defeat, knowing that was a ticket to oblivion. To an onlooker, General Eisenhower seemed calm. Before him was an open book, a western, but Eisenhower was not reading. He was waiting. His mind was on the great task he had been entrusted with: "You will enter the continent of Europe and, in conjunction with the other United Nations, undertake operations aimed at the heart of Germany and the destruction of her armed forces."

Eisenhower raised his eyes to an operation map of Normandy. By this time, the paratroopers and glider troops would have landed. His eyes wandered along the British and Canadian beaches of Gold, Sword, and Juno and the American beaches of Omaha and Utah. Between the two American beaches stood a towering promontory: Pointe du Hoc, a cliff one hundred feet high that jutted like an arrow-

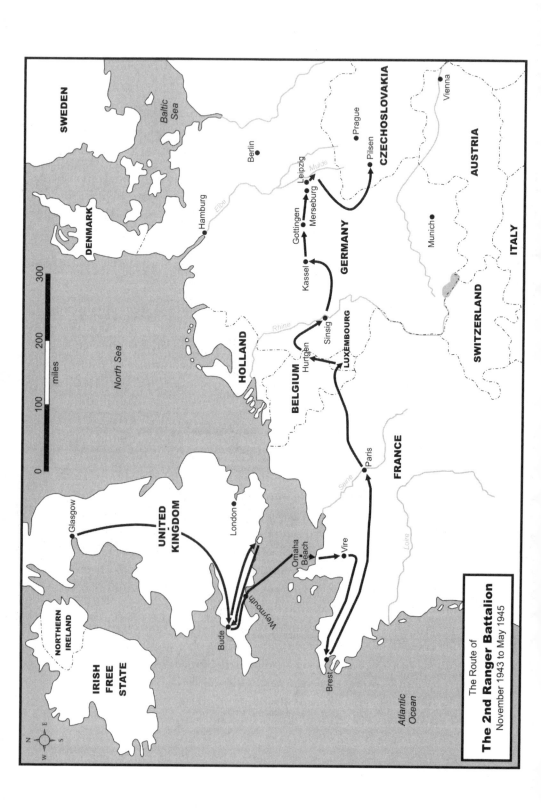

SWEDEN

DENMARK

Baltic Sea

Hamburg

Berlin

CZECHOSLOVAKIA

Vienna

Prague

Pilsen

Leipzig

Mulde

Merseburg

Göttingen

GERMANY

AUSTRIA

Munich

Kassel

Rhine

Sinsig

Hürtgen

LUXEMBOURG

SWITZERLAND

ITALY

HOLLAND

BELGIUM

North Sea

miles

0   100   200   300

FRANCE

Paris

Seine

UNITED KINGDOM

Glasgow

London

Loire

Weymouth

Bude

Omaha Beach

Vire

NORTHERN IRELAND

IRISH FREE STATE

Brest

Atlantic Ocean

N
W   E
S

The Route of
The 2nd Ranger Battalion
November 1943 to May 1945

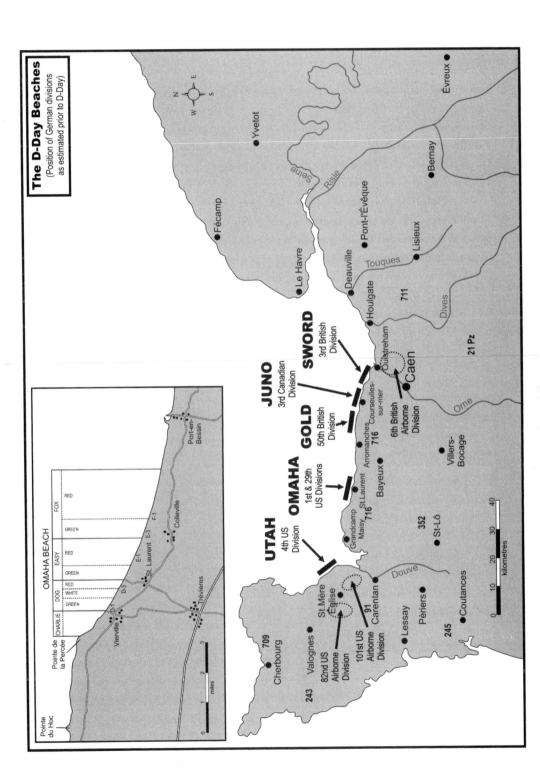

The D-Day Beaches
(Position of German divisions as estimated prior to D-Day)

N
W — E
S

Seine
Risle
Yvetot
Fécamp
Le Havre
Deauville
Pont-l'Évêque
Houlgate
Touques
Lisieux
Bernay
Évreux
Dives
711
21 Pz
Caen
Ouistreham
Orme
Villers-Bocage
Courseulles-sur-mer
716
Arromanches
Bayeux
716
352
St-Lô
Grandcamp
St Laurent
Maisy
Douve
Carentan
Périers
Lessay
Coutances
245
91
St Mère Eglise
Valognes
Cherbourg
709
243

SWORD
3rd British Division

JUNO
3rd Canadian Division

GOLD
50th British Division

OMAHA
1st & 29th US Divisions

UTAH
4th US Division

6th British Airborne Division

82nd US Airborne Division

101st US Airborne Division

0 10 20 30 40
kilometres

OMAHA BEACH

Pointe du Hoc
Pointe de la Percée
Port-en-Bessin
Colleville
St. Laurent
Vierville
Trévières

FOX EASY DOG CHARLIE
RED GREEN RED GREEN WHITE GREEN RED
F-1 E-3 E-1 D-3 D-1

0 1 2 3
miles

head into the English Channel. Atop the cliff was a plateau, the location of a German battery of heavy guns that could interdict the assault force while it was still some twelve miles from land, and strike either of the American landing beaches. The all-volunteer 2nd and 5th Ranger Battalions were intent on eliminating those guns. Three companies of the 2nd Battalion would climb the cliffs and lead the way. There were many who thought the mission was madness, but Eisenhower believed in the Rangers and the Rangers believed in themselves.

Crowded into British LCAs (Landing Craft Assault), the men of Dog, Easy, and Fox Companies, 2nd Ranger Battalion, followed their guide boat through a watery world of sound and fury. The battleship *Texas*, cruisers, and destroyers were pounding the shore. Allied aircraft were zooming overhead, their wings and fuselages painted in alternating black and white stripes for recognition. The distant shore was shrouded in smoke, haze, and bursts of flame. In the boats, fatigue weighed heavily on the men. Few had slept soundly on what might be their last night. They had all been aroused around 0300, and an hour later had left their ships in the assault landing craft. Though heavily weighed down with equipment and weapons, the men were tossed about by seas that threatened to sink their small craft. Though few had eaten heavily, sea sickness was rampant. Men stood to empty their stomachs over the side of LCAs or vomit on each other, then retched in empty agony.

Trapped in the tossing craft, the tense emotion of the men was like an electric charge. They were committed to the mission and wanted to get on with it, but things were going wrong. A key officer had to be relieved the night before the invasion. One of the LCAs had already sank, throwing its men into the cold waters of the English Channel where they screamed or begged for help no one could stop to give. At 0630 the Rangers should have been landing at the base of the Pointe du Hoc, but they had been led in the wrong direction. Now their only option to get to the cliff was to travel parallel to the shore. The bullet splashes and concentric rings arising in the water made it clear that they were within range of German guns. A landing craft was hit by German fire. The men could now see German soldiers running along the cliff top of Pointe du Hoc looming ahead of them above a booming surf and narrow beach. Bullets of the vaunted German MG-42 machine guns splashed in the water and rang on the hulls of the landing craft.

With a centuries-old warrior heritage, these American Rangers had endured the most difficult training that man could devise to overcome the greatest challenges of the enemy and nature. Now their battle would begin. The payoff was at hand. As the ramps went down, some men thought of the words they had heard each time they were tempted to complain: "You volunteered."

DEFINITIONS
Battalion
"Unit composed of a headquarters and two or more companies . . . it may be part of a regiment and be charged with only tactical functions, or it may be a separate unit and charged with both administrative and tactical functions.

"A battalion has no such unity as a battleship but is a complex organism that maneuvers ordinarily on a front a mile or more in width, includes a variety of specialized weapons, and often has attachments of engineers and tanks to provide greater tactical flexibility. In jungle or hedgerow fighting, the battalion frequently exists only as a mechanism to coordinate, perhaps with the greatest difficulty, the separate engagements of companies, platoons or even squads."

Ranger
An American Ranger is a highly trained volunteer who has the courage, confidence and ability to spearhead attacks and invasions and to operate behind enemy lines. Rangers are select troops who excel in intelligence gathering and are the masters of the ambush and the raid. To develop knowledge, stamina and strength of will, the Ranger is trained, tested, and proven in the most trying circumstances. Rangers lead the way and they do so understanding that "It is all in the heart and the mind." In training, Rangers are taught that they can accomplish anything and are expected to.

World War II Phonetics
Clarity is critical in military radio communications; therefore, letter codes are used. These phonetics become part of military conversation

and infantry companies are often referred to by their phonetic identifier. In World War II the phonetic alphabet was as follows:

A   Able
B   Baker
C   Charlie
D   Dog
E   Easy
F   Fox
G   George
H   How
I   Item
J   Jig
K   King
L   Love
M   Mike
N   Nan
O   Oboe
P   Peter
Q   Queen
R   Roger
S   Sugar
T   Tare
U   Uncle
V   Victor
W   William
X   X-Ray
Y   Yoke
Z   Zebra

CHAPTER ONE

Camp Forrest, Tennessee
April 1–September 4, 1943

Oh, this is number one, and the fun has just begun,
Roll me over, lay me down, and do it again.

—*World War II song*

B ATTALION . . . TENCH . . . HUT! Boot heels slammed together as more than 500 officers and men came to attention. Toes were turned out at a forty-five-degree angle—legs straight without locking the knees. Backs were stiffened, chests thrust out, stomachs pulled in, and hips level. Their heads were erect, eyes facing directly to the front. Each man's arms were positioned at his sides and his fingers joined and curled, thumbs lined up with the seams of his trousers. It was Thursday, April 1, 1943—April Fool's Day, but no one was joking. A group of volunteer soldiers had come together at Camp Forrest, Tennessee, to form the 2nd Ranger Infantry Battalion.

The spring of 1943 represented a turning point in World War II. German Army Group South under Field Marshal Erich von Manstein was counterattacking at Kharkov in the Soviet Union while German U-boats menaced the Allied convoys of the North Atlantic. The war was no longer one-sided. The Russian winter had cost the Germans heavily. American and British bombers were striking Germany, while the British 8th Army and the American II Corps under Gen. George S. Patton attacked the Germans in Tunisia in North Africa. In the Pacific, the Americans had successfully concluded the Guadalcanal campaign and had completed the Burma Road to bring much-needed supplies to the Nationalist Chinese fighting the Japanese Army.

It was clear that the United States and Great Britain intended to invade the European continent, and the planning and troop buildup to accomplish this was underway. The 2nd Battalion, though it didn't know it yet, would play a significant role in that invasion.

In World War II, a battalion of an infantry division consisted of 37 officers and 857 enlisted men. Napoleon once said, "God is on the side of the big battalions," but Ranger battalions are few and small in number. At full strength, the 2nd Ranger Battalion rolls would carry only 27 officers and 484 enlisted men. It was not expected that the battalion would maintain those numbers for very long. This battalion was destined to go in harm's way and face heavy casualties.

The men of the battalion would train, eat, sleep, shower, and face danger together, bonding to a degree that few others would. They would enter into battle in Normandy on June 6, 1944, to lead the way across the hell of Omaha Beach, climb the cliffs, and destroy the guns of Pointe du Hoc. At Brest they would capture a German fortress and the great guns of the Lochrist battery. They would fight through the hedgerows of France, in Belgium, Luxembourg, and on into Germany. They would endure and bleed, and many would die in the mud and snow and horror of the Hürtgen Forest. They would fight as part of Gen. Courtney Hodges's 1st Army, Patton's 3rd, and Gen. William Simpson's 9th, and when the announcement of the end of the war in Europe came, they would be all the way across Europe in Pilsen, Czechoslovakia.

Of the 997 men who would earn the Combat Infantry Badge with the battalion, 158 of them would be killed in action or die of wounds. Receiving the Purple Heart medal were 758 wounded. Some wounded were so hurriedly evacuated that an additional unknown number of Purple Hearts were awarded at the hospitals. Some men escaped wounds caused by bullet or shell, but some wounds that do not qualify for a medal can still disable a man for life. The battalion was awarded a United States Presidential Unit Citation, the French Croix de Guerre with Silver Gilt Star, and two British Military Medals as well. Men of the battalion were awarded nineteen Distinguished Service Cross medals and eighty-one Silver Stars. An estimated 150

Bronze Star medals for valor were won, and two men received the Soldier's Medal for saving others from drowning.

When the war was over, most of the men went back to civilian life, some going to college under the GI Bill. They became businessmen, lawyers, doctors, engineers, auctioneers, and postmasters. They married and raised families. Some were still in the service when the Korean War began, and again donned their uniforms to serve.

When the battalion came together in 1943, it was made up of young men who had come of age in the economic despair of the Great Depression. Resilient and self-sustaining, they had worked through the hard times at any job they could get. They had been laborers, waiters, miners, embalmers, salesmen, barbers, farmers, and musicians. One, who of necessity lived frugally, was a poet. Some had served in the National Guard. Only a few had been Regular Army. Some of the volunteers had been part of the Civilian Conservation Corps (CCC). Those who had been part of this key Depression-era government program had done much to improve the land, clearing the waste from forests and building roads and parks. While living under military discipline in the camps, they learned to stand at attention and march, how to make up an army cot, and live among groups of other men. Their training did not include firing weapons, but the men of the CCC had a head start on being soldiers when World War II came along.

The men of the battalion came from many cities and towns across the country, big places like Miami, Detroit, and Philadelphia, but mostly little places like Homer City, Pennsylvania; New Prague, Minnesota; Seymour, Texas; Rich Hill, Missouri; and Frostproof, Florida. They came from throughout the Army, primarily infantry units such as the 29th, 76th, and 80th Divisions, but also armor, artillery, cavalry, and the U.S. Army Air Corps. Some had served a previous hitch in the Army or Marines. All had completed basic training. They would endure the most difficult training, gradually becoming hardened, eliminating the physically and mentally weak as well as those who could not function as part of a team. More than 50 percent of the volunteers who assembled on April 1, 1943, would not go into combat with the battalion. They would ask to be relieved and quickly sent off, or orders would arrive dispatching them elsewhere.

Facing a common challenge, the men began to know each other, to draw close and develop trust. Many had unusual histories. William

"L-Rod" Petty was from Georgia, a farm boy whose father brutally beat him, on what Petty described as a "fairly regular but unpredictable basis."[1] The beatings ended when Petty was fourteen, and he repelled an assault by swinging a pick mattock at his father. The elder Petty fled but the son's hatred never left. When his father died, Bill Petty spit on the casket.

Petty was beginning his junior year at the University of Georgia when war intervened. He was bright but argumentative. Several of his front teeth were missing from an altercation when a member of the football team flattened him. Petty could hate with a passion, hold a grudge indefinitely, and resented most of those in authority over him. Unable to please his father, Petty expected perfection in himself and others. He was acerbic, courageous, would fight anyone win or lose, and a superb shot. He cared deeply for those in his charge and made every man under him feel important. He would become the soul of Fox Company.

In time, Petty would form a deep friendship with Herman "Herm" Stein, whom he referred to as his "Pet Ape," the nickname stemming from Stein's remarkable ability as a climber. Born on Staten Island, New York, Stein's affluent family life changed rapidly when his father lost his fortune in the Great Depression.

Petty and Stein were in Capt. Otto Masny's Fox Company. Masny was tall and rangy and the men called him "Big Stoop" after a cartoon character. The nickname was not derogatory—Masny's men respected him; they could talk to him, and Petty remembered beginning a conversation with the words, "Goddammit, Big Stoop . . ."

Leonard "Len" or "Bud" Lomell was Brooklyn born but raised in New Jersey. He completed college at Wesleyan in Athens, Tennessee, in June of 1941. After Pearl Harbor he attempted to get into West Point or Annapolis, but learned that he did not have a birth certificate and had been adopted. Before the legalities could be resolved, he was drafted and sent to the 76th Infantry Division where he became a platoon sergeant. Lomell then attended a two-week Ranger school and was one of the 60 out of 200 men to complete the course. Offered the chance to be first sergeant of Dog Company, 2nd Ranger Battalion, Lomell accepted. Dog Company had originated as a unit of hand-picked volunteers from the 76th Infantry Division. It was the only company that would arrive at Camp Forrest intact.

A close friend of Lomell was Jack Kuhn who hailed from the railroad center of Altoona, Pennsylvania. A four-year stint in the National Guard horse cavalry had prepared him for active service. Drafted in March of 1942, Kuhn was stationed at Fort Meade, Maryland, when he heard about the Rangers. He volunteered and joined Dog Company.

Frank South and William "Willie" Clark first met on the firing range during Basic Training at Fort Jackson, South Carolina. South was eighteen and a raw recruit. Clark was older, had been in the service prewar, and was a T/4 (wearing the three stripes of a sergeant with a "T" underneath). Basic training was a refresher for Clark, who delighted in giving advice to South. While living in tents on the firing range, South received word that his mother was coming to nearby Columbia, South Carolina. South requested a pass but, given his location on the firing range, was naturally turned down. When South complained to Willie Clark, the more experienced man tried to trick him into getting his butt chewed. Clark told South to see the chaplain and all would be well. Believing Willie, South did so and received commiseration prior to being hauled before the battalion commander. The officer informed South that being instructed to see the chaplain was an old army joke, and he had been had. As he was a man with a heart, the officer allowed the pass. South informed Clark that his joke had not worked, and Willie complained, "The damn Army is turning into a bunch of pansies for Chrisakes!"[2]

Willie and Frank were part of a six-man group that volunteered for the Rangers on completion of basic. Carrying the exalted rank of T/4, Willie got the men in shape by short stints of close-order drill, a minimum of calisthenics, long smoke and rest breaks under shade trees, and escape and evasion to the post exchange for beer and ice cream. When he was displeased, Willie would require that everyone, including himself, put on his gas mask and double-time around the training area. Trying to run while wearing a gas mask is an exercise in misery. South found that if the diaphragm was taken out of the mask, a man could breath easily. He informed all the volunteers of this, but not Willie Clark. The next gas mask run was spirited with Clark practically run into the ground. When Willie learned the cause and the perpetrator, Frank South got KP (Kitchen Police) duty. In time, the two men found mutual interests and became close friends.

It was fitting that these Rangers and their comrades should begin their training at a camp named for Confederate lieutenant general Nathan Bedford Forrest. Forrest was known in the Civil War as "the Wizard of the Saddle." This military genius began his career as a colonel of a regiment of Mounted Rangers. Forrest believed in attacking and felt the key to success on the battlefield was to relentlessly hammer his opponent. Forrest called that "bulge" and said that "five minutes of bulge is worth a week of tactics."[3]

Camp Forrest was 85,000 acres of sandy hills patched over with scrub oak, pine, and brush located southeast of Nashville, Tennessee. The sand was ubiquitous—it rode the wind, curled into funnel shaped "dust devils," and settled in clothing, bedding, weapons, food, and water. The sand should have provided good drainage when the rains came, but its companion was a red soil that became a thick glutenous mud miring men and vehicles.

The initial battalion commander was Lt. Col. William C. Saffarans, who had been commandant of the two-week Second Army Ranger Training Course. Saffarans was a good officer, but the needs of the service quickly sent him off to run a jungle school in Hawaii.

The initial days were spent in Camp Forrest's, Block 19 barracks area where the volunteers received physical examinations that were based on paratrooper requirements. Many men were failed at this point. Some did not even receive a physical as they were identified as having been kicked out of their former units. One soldier who came from the Desert Training Center got off the train at Camp Forrest, saw the wife of the commander of Camp Forrest, and propositioned her. He and other easily recognized undesirables were marched to the station, put on a train, and returned to those who had sent them.

Men hated standing in line for administration, equipment, food, and shots. They endured triple typhoid, tetanus, and other inoculations with aching arms and then marched to battalion supply where they were issued clothing and equipment. Each man received two sets of fatigue (field) and khaki uniforms, socks, and underwear. Because the men were expected to be hard on clothing in training, one set of fatigues had been previously worn by other soldiers. These hand-me-downs were shabby and despised by the men. The second set of clothing, which was new, was not to be used but kept in barracks bags, called "B Bags." These were olive drab or blue laundry bags with a draw string that would be stored in the company area until the unit had completed training.

There was much confusion. The battalion supply section worked around the clock and after the work day men would be called to stand in line for hours only to be issued a pair of shoe laces. In each company they began to draw lots by tent, and the men in the losing tent stood in line for the rest, who scattered like quail for the nearby town of Tullahoma, a PX beer, or their cots.

There was only one kitchen, and it seemed like a man could starve to death in the long chow line. Since the cooks were inefficient, men at the tail end of the line got the slops. When the cooks blew the whistle for chow, the men began to shout comments on the ancestry of the cooks, their sexual preference, and bodily appearance. Some men preferred a more direct approach and cursed the hash slingers face to face. Ranger John Burnett of Easy Company was on KP peeling potatoes and scrubbing pots and pans. The menu called for lamb, but Burnett read the packing labels and found they were being served goat meat from Idaho. Dysentery raged. The primitive food service conditions made it difficult to keep utensils clean, and greasy trays in an army chow line are passports to loose bowels. Paper plates were tried, but as the food was little more than a watery "slum," the food ran right off. At formations the first sergeants would command, "Fall in," and as the roll was called, men would fall out without command to sprint for the latrines.

The men of the battalion were formed into companies. There were six assault companies designated A through F—phonetically they would be called Able, Baker, Charlie, Dog, Easy, and Fox companies—with each consisting of three officers and sixty-five enlisted men. The six assault companies were organized with a company headquarters consisting of a captain as company commander, a first sergeant, a company clerk, and a messenger/grenadier, and two identical rifle platoons. The platoons were commanded by a first lieutenant, and platoon headquarters consisted of a staff sergeant platoon guide, a T/5 (corporal with a T under the rank) sniper, and a PFC (private first class) messenger. Each platoon had two identical rifle sections and a special weapons section (60mm mortar) headed by a sergeant. Each rifle section had a sergeant in charge of an assault squad and a light machine-gun section. A corporal squad leader and four riflemen comprised the assault squad of the rifle section. They were supported by the light machine gun section carrying one M1919A4 .30-caliber light machine gun. The primary weapon of the battalion was the .30-caliber M1 rifle. In battle, the weapons carried are tailored to the mission, and men are often allowed latitude in the choice of weapon. Thompson submachine guns and Browning automatic rifles (BARs) were included in the mix with many men carrying .45-caliber pistols and fragmentation grenades as well.

Supporting the assault companies was a headquarters and head-quarters company. The battalion is the first level of organization where the commander has a staff of officers. In World War II battalions normally included an executive officer as second in command, an S-1 Personnel officer, S-2 Intelligence officer, S-3 Plans, Operations and Training officer, and S-4 Logistics officer. The senior representative of the enlisted men was the sergeant major. The battalion commander and his staff would form the headquarters, and two officers and ninety-four enlisted men would make up the personnel, supply, communication, transportation, IO (intelligence and operations), mess, and medical elements of headquarters company.

Soldiers did not use the phonetic name "How" for headquarters company. Because riflemen frequently refer to anyone they believe is two yards back as rear echelon, it was known as "Hindquarters Company." The job of the assault companies was to fight. Headquarters company sent the assault companies' medics, radio operators, wire men, and vehicle drivers as needed and provided ammunition, supplies, and food. Rangers operate on the principle that they will often be surrounded by the enemy, and there were no rear echelon or supposedly "safe" jobs in the battalion.

On April 11, the men occupied an area they called "Tent City," one mile northeast of the Camp Forrest barracks area. The green tents were pyramidal in shape with six enlisted men to a tent sleeping on canvas cots. Each officer had a smaller tent to himself. The gear was stowed under the cot and clothing hung from a triangle-shaped device that surrounded the center pole of the tent. The first tent in line was the orderly room, the domain of the company commander, first sergeant, and company clerk. The orderly room tent could be identified audibly by the clickity-clack of a typewriter pounding out the ever-changing rosters and morning reports.

The open space to the front of the tents was called the company street. At the head of the company street was the cook shack and at the foot was the communal latrine. For washing up, most cleanup was done from water in a steel helmet or a tin basin supported by four pegs in the ground. To take a shower meant walking a mile to a location where other soldiers lived in barracks. If these soldiers were kind, they would permit the would-be Rangers to shave and shower in comfort. The battalion commander and staff rated more permanent structures. Battalion headquarters was in a tar-paper shack and the supply section in an old barn. It was unseasonably rainy and cold for the first two weeks in Tent City. No matter where they went, the rain found them. The company streets were ankle deep in mud. Lt. James W. "Ike" Eikner, the communications officer, scrounged a generator and provided lights. Whoever serviced the generator was excused from training, so there were many volunteers, except for Saturday when the men hoped for a pass to go to town.

Initially there were no radios in the battalion. They had EE-8 field telephones but no wire. Eikner and his men put on their climbing belts and made midnight requisitions as they went up telephone poles in the area occupied by the Military Police and the Women's Army Corps Detachment. There was confusion about who would command. Several officers temporarily held the position of battalion commander. Spirits soared when the men heard that Maj. Charles "Monk" Meyer, West Point Class of 1937, would take over. Meyer was small, agile, and gutsy. His nickname, "Monkey," had been courteously shortened to "Monk." Despite his diminutive 143 pounds, Monk Meyer had been a star football player at the U.S. Military Academy. In 1935 he was the hero of the Army-Navy game, throwing three touchdown passes, and the same year tied heavily favored Notre Dame with a forty-yard touchdown pass. As a career officer, some men said Monk saw the battalion as a dead-end job and that he drove through the area in a jeep and promptly left. Whatever the reason, Meyer showed up at Tent City, but was just as quickly gone.

At this point, the battalion were Rangers in name only, volunteers preparing to take the two-week Ranger training course established by Lt. Gen. Ben Lear, commander of the Second U.S. Army. Rangers are not developed in two weeks, but a rough assessment can be made on determining who should not be Rangers. The orientation officer informed the men they would learn the doctrine of "Rangerism—the doctrine of a personal fight, a brain and brawn fight, an ingenious American fight, and a carefully thought-out dirtier fight that will top the instinctive and naturally dirty fight that the blond, square-head, self-appointed supermen, that the undersized, slant eyed yellow 'Nips' wage against us on two fronts today . . . no country will accept a challenge, a real threat or a dare faster than America. And no country will take hold of a job and do it better and faster than America will—once she starts."[4]

To begin the shakedown, the men were required to complete a three-mile march in thirty-seven minutes, a five-mile march in one hour and a nine-mile march in two hours. The marches would be done with full equipment including rifles, combat packs, and gas masks. Those who could not complete the march were transferred out. There were many who gave up. When it wasn't raining, the Tennessee sun seared a lasting memory on those who stayed.

The men were not permitted to drink water from their canteens during the marches. Maj. Lionel McDonald, Monk Meyer's replacement, and his executive officer, Maj. Wesley L. Rogerson, were elderly men, believed to be Indiana National Guard officers who at one time were state policemen. These officers rode in a jeep and drank water when they wished. The junior officers and men hated the sight of these supposed leaders riding while the men marched and wished the jeep would run out of gas. Lt. Stan White of Able Company recalled that a man yelled from the ranks, "Hey, major, what are you going to do when the jeep runs dry?"[5]

In May, the preliminaries included a seventy-mile march accomplished over a period of three days. Following compass headings, they marched part of the route by road and part overland. Some quit on the first day. At nightfall, while the battalion medics treated blisters and sprains and the men prepared to sleep on the ground, the two majors returned to Tullahoma to be with their wives.

The march made the volunteers realize how important the medics were. The medical section was a part of the battalion headquarters company. The section consisted of a doctor and fifteen enlisted men. During the life of the battalion, thirty men would pass through the medical section. In battle, eighteen of them would earn the Purple Heart for sustaining wounds, and seven medics would be wounded more than once. Frank South and Willie Clark had been trained as medics. At Camp Forrest they and other 2nd Battalion medical aid men became practiced at jabbing an arm or buttock with a hypodermic needle or treating a wide variety of sprains and blisters. The medics administered aspirin for almost any ailment. For colds, they concocted a mixture of terpene hydrate and flavoring, such as sugar, codeine, and alcohol. The more alcohol the better. On weekends when they could not leave Camp Forrest, officers and enlisted men would report to sick call hacking and coughing, complaining of cold in the chest and requesting a large dosage of cold medicine.

The junior officers of the battalion led the training. Infantry officers are both leaders and teachers and their classrooms present varying challenges. The platoon leader of 1st Platoon, Easy Company, 2nd Lt. Ted Lapres, was fresh from Officers Candidate School. Such officers had to bear the indignity of being called "ninety-day wonders." Lapres wanted to test the skills of men who had only completed basic training. Pvt. Duncan Daugherty was told to "fix bayonet" and attack Lieutenant Lapres, who would then demonstrate how an unarmed man can defend himself against a charging enemy. Daugherty was reluctant to follow the order. Lapres assured the young soldier that he could take care of himself, and the two men squared off. Lapres crouched with hands spread to his front—Daughtery with rifle butt at his side and bayonet pointed at the lower part of his opponents throat. Shuffling forward, Daughtery made the standard thrust of the bayonet which Lieutenant Lapres sidestepped and brushed aside in masterful fashion. Unfortunately for Ted Lapres, he had forgotten that the thrust is only step one of the bayonet drill. If the attacker misses with the point of the bayonet, step two is to swing the rifle butt forward and deliver a telling blow. Following the drill, Daugherty swung the metal-tipped end of his rifle in a sweeping arc upward into Lapres' testicles. When he had sufficiently recovered, his groin if not his pride, Lapres complimented Pvt. Daugherty and departed the area. A sergeant carried on with the presentation of the class on hand-to-hand fighting.

In Easy Company, Daugherty and Private Richard "Hub" Hubbard had been assigned to the same tent and became buddies. Daugherty

was from Detroit and Hubbard was from Addyston, Ohio, a small town
on the banks of the Ohio River. The two men went to Tullahoma to
see a movie. They wanted dates, but in Hubbard's words, "There were
60,000 men after 200 girls."[6] Hubbard could not understand why a soldier who could get a beer at the post exchange (PX) for ten cents
would go to Tullahoma and pay $1.25. True, PX beer was 3.2 percent
alcohol and beer downtown was about 7 percent, but twelve Army
beers for the price of one civilian brew seemed good economics.
Daugherty and Hubbard were among many Rangers who were sending money home for their families and had to pay deductions for
insurance and war bonds. After the Tullahoma experience they stayed
close to camp. Going swimming was a principal relaxation.

On June 2, Capt. Dean H. Knudson arrived from the 1st Ranger
Battalion. Knudson had fought in Africa at Kasserine Pass and Faid
Pass and took part in the superb El Guettar raid where men of the 1st
Rangers used their knives and bayonets on the Italians and Germans.
Because of his battle experience, Knudson was assigned temporarily
as S-3 (Plans, Operations, and Training officer). While the men of the
battalion stood at attention in the hot sun Knudson looked them over
with distaste and snarled, "Rangers? . . . BULL SHIT!" Knudson's
pep talks were filled with horrific tales of long distance marches in
deep sand under the broiling African sun. He spoke with nostalgia of
skin worn off the soles of the feet and blood sloshing in the boots.
Knudson proclaimed that discipline in the 1st Battalion was so tight
that when a few men made an unauthorized night visit to an Arab
town, Maj. William O. "El Darbo" Darby ordered the entire battalion
to make an all-night march with full equipment. Listening to "Blood
in the Boots" Knudson, the men of the battalion were mightily
impressed.

On June 7 the two-week Ranger School began. In full combat
gear with packs and weapons, the men marched to and from training
areas. These were forced or speed marches, the men hustling along
the roads and trails. A twenty-five mile march had to be completed in
eight hours. These marches would continue for fifty minutes, after
which there would be a ten-minute "smoke if you got 'em" break. In
ten minutes men could get off their feet, lean back against the pack,
smoke a Camel or a Lucky, elevate weary legs, massage the feet, pop a
blister, or nap. Then it was, "On your feet, we're movin out." Captain

Knudson marched with the battalion, standing in a jeep as it rolled along beside the sweating men and roaring out to them that they must "Shape up or ship out!" The word was passed that Knudson had ruined his feet in Africa, and because he was a Ranger who had seen the elephant and heard the song of the bullet, he was forgiven.

The weekly cycle of speed marches increased from five to nine miles, and a distance march normally was twenty-five miles in length. Speed increased with the men marching at four, five, then six miles an hour. Easy Company claimed they covered fifteen miles in two hours. The men of headquarters company also made the marches. Lt. "Ike" Eikner and his communications section marched six and a half miles in an hour. Eikner was twenty-eight and had a heart condition he was concealing and thought he'd die on the march, but he wasn't going to quit.

Eikner was a son of the old south, born in Aberdeen, Mississippi, on December 7, 1913. His ancestry had roots in the Jamestown settlement of 1607 and featured fighting men throughout the history of America. One, Joseph Vesey, had been a lieutenant serving under John Paul Jones in the Revolutionary War. Vesey later became a privateer and kidnapped and seduced the beautiful Malay Princess Mai. Ike Eikner was a distant descendent of that union. Ike worked for Southwestern Bell Telephone in Houston, Texas, and was celebrating his birthday when the Japanese attacked Pearl Harbor. Drafted in March 1942, he attended Benning School for Boys (Officers Candidate School), was commissioned in November, and was with the 80th Infantry Division as a communications officer when he volunteered for the Rangers.

In addition to speed marches, about nine miles from Tent City was an area that included a cliff with a vertical face estimated at ninety feet. The men were to use ropes to descend the cliff and then climb a hill on the other side. The first man to descend on the rope fell from the cliff face and lay writhing in pain at the base of the cliff. How to extract a man from such a predicament had not been thought out, and it took an hour to deliver the soldier into an ambulance. Until better medical evacuation procedures were developed, the cliff descent was postponed, and the men speed-marched back to Tent City. Piper Cub aircraft buzzed the column. Selected Rangers were on board as observers, and they dropped sacks of flour, simulating bombing. Men took cover, sprinting for the gullies. One ambulance and one Ranger received direct hits. Though the butt of many jokes, the flour-coated man had the consolation that it was not high explosive. The Tennessee sun came out in all its fury and canteens were empty of water. The march home saw men fall by the wayside, men who would not be Rangers.

The distance marches were accomplished at what was called the "Flexion Step," a half-walk, half-run gait. It was less difficult for those with long strides. The short-legged man had to dog-trot to keep up the pace. The marches were also a means of transportation to and from the training areas. The training included calisthenics with never-ending sit-ups and push-ups. The Army called the starting position of the push-up "the front leaning rest position," which is a joke. It is not a restful position. Men said it was likely devised by some sergeant from the coal fields of Pennsylvania or Kentucky whose mammy kept him in check by bellowing, "Drop and give me twenty!"

After they stretched out their muscles, the men moved beside logs fourteen feet long and as thick as a telephone pole. On various commands, six men, working in unison, raised the log waist high and then over the head to one shoulder, and lift the log over the head to the other shoulder, continuing this in repetition. The logs were heavy, and if the men did not work in unison, heads got rapped and skin was torn from hands and shoulders. It built muscles as well as teamwork and was inexpensive. The United States government had plenty of logs.

The marches, the calisthenics, and the logs were preliminary to last-man-standing drills. These drills were conducted in pits, which were log-rimmed, three-and-a-half feet deep and forty feet square with a ten-inch cushioning of sawdust that was packed hard by rain. The surface resembled a cement pad, and the sawdust was alive with wood ticks. Here in the pits it was every man for himself, squad against squad, or platoon against platoon. One platoon would enter the pit and the second would go in after them. It was no holds barred with kicking, gouging, biting, and groin grabbing preliminary to the violent heave which threw the other man out. These actions continued until only one man remained standing in the pit.

Another pit drill called "Capture the Captain" was based on throwing out the opposing platoon's lieutenant or platoon sergeant. The leaders took position in opposite corners of the sawdust pit. Their platoons tried to defend them while getting to the other platoon's leader and throwing him out. Men delighted in pounding the young officers who fought back with fury. Shoulders and arms were dislocated and bones broken. It was individual and team spirit at work. Each man came to believe he was the best soldier of the best squad of the best platoon of the best company of the best battalion in the United States Army, which was, naturally, the best army in the world.

The men of the battalion devised their own physical games. In crossing barbed wire entanglements, one man would hold his combat pack across his stomach and throw himself over the wire apron. The rest of the men would then run across his back. This led to a spontaneous sport called "Barbed Wire." During breaks, if a man was found lying on his stomach, every man who was able to reach him would run over his body.

As the weeks went by and the men hardened, they began to yearn for a break in the regimen. If they had a pass, the men would do their best to get cleaned up, walking from Tent City to the other units' barracks to take a shower and then sweating under the sun as they walked back. When they were ready to go to town, they would suddenly be called to a formation. Junior officers and men would be required to take their "B Bags" and form a long line at Battalion Supply. Man by man they would have their B Bag equipment inventoried to be certain they had not used anything they might need if the battalion was suddenly shipped out. The timing of these inspections was, in soldier talk, "chickenshit."

For the single junior officers and some of the enlisted men who had cars, a pass meant heading for Chattanooga, Tennessee (population 130,000). Nine miles south of Chattanooga was Camp Oglethorpe, a large training base for the Women's Army Auxiliary Corps (WAAC, later WAC). The young women were part of a generation that did not have "The Pill." They were taught that pregnancy out of wedlock brought shame, ostracism, and financial disaster. War, however, changed things. With dying young a strong possibility, healthy men and women lived for the moment.

One of the great love stories of the battalion was Bill Klaus and Olive Smith, whom Bill called "Smitty." They where high school sweethearts at Sussex, New Jersey. On December 7, 1941, they were in Bill's 1933 Plymouth convertible listening to the radio when the word came of the attack on Pearl Harbor. Bill left his job at Dupont for the Army in June of 1942. On December 31, 1942, when Bill had a short leave, they celebrated the incoming New Year by getting married. Bill Klaus was in the 76th Infantry Division at Fort Meade, Maryland, when he volunteered for the Rangers and became a charter member of the battalion. After a short stint with Dog Company, Bill went to Able and in time he would become the first sergeant of that company.

Some men settled for a bottle. Capt. Cleveland Lytle, commander of Able Company, was a much respected, tough, spit-and-polish officer. On duty, Lytle was a hard-charging leader whose favorite cry was, "We're heading for pay dirt!" Off duty, he was a heavy drinker. Platoon leader Lt. Stan White would stay sober and serve as driver as Lytle and a British commando officer, a liaison officer to the Ranger School, made the rounds of the bars.

Since they lacked transportation, most of the enlisted Rangers went to Tullahoma, a manufacturing town located two miles west of Camp Forrest. Tullahoma's population had been less than 5,000 people before the war, but construction workers, civilian government employees, and dependants of soldiers had brought the population to over 60,000. It was almost impossible to book a room at the King or Horton Hotels, where rates were the outrageous price of $5.00 to $10.00 a day. The houses, apartments, or tourist homes available would strip a soldier of his pay. Tullahoma was a typical soldier town with specialty stores where a soldier could purchase a gaudy sateen pillow usually fringed and bearing the American flag or the word "Mother." There were pawn shops, tailors, tattoo parlors, and hole-in-the-wall restaurants where men from the north were served something called "grits." There were the inevitable bars and bar girls.

The watering hole for the battalion was a large establishment divided into two sections: "the Hub" and "the Wheel." The Hub was for couples, and the Wheel was for singles. The Rangers ended up at the Wheel. They could drink, meet girls and dance, or listen to the jukebox. The men were grateful for the women who came to the Wheel, though they called soldiers "Sugah." The jukebox cost a nickel a song and contained the big band sounds of Glenn Miller, Benny Goodman, Artie Shaw, and Harry James. They danced to Miller's "In the Mood," drank beer, griped, sang "Don't Get Around Much Anymore" and "Pistol Packin' Momma," and tried to get past first base.

Because the United States government was going to great effort to teach the soldiers to be aggressive, they frequently fought. The only people at hand to fight were other Americans.

There were other units stationed at Camp Forrest, including the 633rd, 755th, and 827th Tank Destroyer Battalions. In one incident the tank destroyer (TD) men had been the first at the Wheel and were reluctant to surrender their turf. The TDs, as the Rangers called them, affronted Ranger pride, and fists flew. A TD sitting at a table with his friends insulted one of the smaller of the Dog Company Rangers who was passing on his way to the latrine. The Ranger attacked the entire table of TDs. Other Rangers joined the fray and drove their opponents from the bar. The TDs retreated to the Horton Hotel, where they were eventually discovered and hammered again.

Taxi cabs were few in number, but they were the easiest way to get back to Camp Forrest. On one occasion a cab arrived and a group of TDs got in one side of the cab while the Rangers entered on the other side. The fight occurred inside the vehicle. While the taxi driver stood by wailing at the damage to his vehicle, the TDs were thrown out. Whenever a fight occurred, the military police would be called, but they frequently became additional victims. Ranger officers called off their men and the damage was reimbursed.

Some Rangers would inspire fear in other soldiers just by their appearance. Lt. Ike Eikner described three of his warriors: "T-Sgt Jack Roach, tall and agile, little scar on his cheek and always ready for action; T-Sgt John Koepfer, about six feet and 220 with the look of a mad gorilla; T-Sgt Joe Zimkus about 5 feet 10 at 250 pounds and with the look and disposition of a constipated bull dog. Nobody, and I mean nobody, messed with these guys."[7]

The 2nd Ranger Battalion would go to war with men like these.

CHAPTER TWO

Rudder

Why, man, he doth bestride the narrow world like a colossus.
— *William Shakespeare,* Julius Caesar

The rugged training was getting the men in shape, but the battalion was lacking something vital. Morale was low. The battalion needed leaders with personality who genuinely cared about the welfare of the men. The 2nd Ranger Battalion finally gained its personality on June 30, 1943, when Maj. James Earl Rudder assumed command.

Each morning, one of the officers would go forth at 0600 to take the report after the reveille roll call. The senior officers of the battalion rarely showed up, so the lieutenants frequently went casual. On one occasion, 1st Lt. Ralph Goranson was not fully uniformed when he strolled down to take the report. A jeep carrying a powerful-looking officer with major's gold leaves rolled up beside him. "Who the hell are you?" boomed the officer. Goranson popped to attention and snapped off a salute, "1st Lt. Ralph Goranson, sir!" he responded. "How the hell am I supposed to know what you are?" snarled the major. "Get your ass back to your quarters and put on your rank insignia and then get over to that formation . . . and you better not be late!"[1]

That was Rudder. The battalion had a twelve-mile speed march that day, and Rudder made it with them. That evening, Lieutenant

Goranson was told to report to the battalion commander for an interview. Goranson found Rudder in his tent with his boots off. Rudder was cutting off his socks, which were soaked in blood, and bandaging his feet. Goranson had the feeling that Rudder would be on the next march and the one after that. He was right.

Rudder stood six feet tall and weighed about 220 pounds of muscle and bone. His massive chest made him seem taller, and behind his back the men called him "Big Jim." He was born in Eden, Texas, on May 6, 1910, the son of a prosperous farmer. He played center on the Texas A&M football team and graduated in 1932, and he was commissioned through the superb Army Reserve Officer Training Course there.

Communication is the soul of motivation; Rudder was especially gifted at both. Because he was mentally and physically tough, he could back up his orders. He was coaching football at John Tarleton Agricultural College at Stephenville, Texas, when he was called to active duty. In 1941 he served as a rifle company commander and as a student at the Infantry School at Fort Benning, Georgia. A year later, he was a battalion executive officer with the 83rd Infantry Division at Camp Atterbury, Indiana, and attended the Army Command and General Staff College. In early 1943 he served as assistant G-3 (division-level Plans, Operations, and Training officer) of the 83rd before he came to the Rangers.

Rudder was a Texan through and through. Since Ike Eikner had relatives in Texas and had worked there, Rudder would engage him in conversation. "Ike, what in the hell is wrong with this outfit?" He asked, not favorably impressed with what he saw. Eikner responded, "Sir, we have a bunch of gung-ho youngsters who've had their fill of routines and want to get on with the business end of this war. There is a discipline problem—you will need to tie a knot in some tails."[2]

Under a hot Tennessee sun, Rudder gathered the battalion and seated them in a circle. He spoke with authority. "I've been sent down here to restore order and get going with realistic training. Now let me tell you, I am going to work your asses off and before you know it, you're going to be the best trained fighting men in this man's army. Now with your cooperation, there will be passes from time to time when you have the time. I'll grant as many leaves and passes as I can. If I don't get your cooperation, we'll still get the job done, but it will be a lot tougher on you. Now if such a program does not appeal to you, come up to the office, and we will transfer you out. So much the better for you and us. Any questions?"³

It was a "play ball with me or I'll jam the bat where the sun don't shine" kind of speech that athletes and soldiers understand. Training was intensified. Lt. Sid Salomon, who was a charter-member platoon leader of Charlie Company, said of Rudder's command of the battalion, "He put it together and made something of it."⁴

Rudder saw no value in deliberately treating the men as animals. He worked them hard, but fair. They ran "police" calls back and forth, picking up every scrap of paper and cigarette butt until their area was clean. From then on, whatever post the battalion held, it left its area in better condition than when it arrived. Rudder initiated gripe sessions during which any man of any rank could air his views and make suggestions. The sand and dysentery of Tent City were not conducive to good morale, so within a week of his arrival, Rudder had the battalion moved to barracks on 28th Street in Camp Forrest. These barracks had showers, and Rudder worked on improving the quality of the food. Cooks were rotated to cooking schools and sent again or transferred out if the food was not up to standard. Rudder even sent an officer, 1st Lt. George Williams, the commander of headquarters company, to the Camp Forrest Cooks and Bakers School to ensure a qualified mess officer was on hand.

Rudder's opinion of the disgraceful state of uniforms was, "Class X clothing is for class X soldiers!"⁵ Tattered hand-me-downs were discarded, and new clothing was issued to the men. Rudder intended to accomplish his mission of making the battalion a unit capable of taking on the most hazardous tasks, but within that mission he was watchful of the welfare of his men.

Rugged training continued. The men would be formed in two lines, about ten paces apart, facing one another. Rifles with bayonets affixed were thrown back and forth as quickly as possible. Self preservation required men to be agile. Only one man missed his catch, the bayonet going through his foot.

Demonstrations of hand-to-hand combat followed, and practice would take place in the sawdust pits under the watchful eye of sergeants from the 1st Ranger Battalion. Frank South was standing in front of Willie Clark when the instructors called for volunteers. Clark put his hand over South's head and pointed downward, vigorously volunteering South. The instructors said, "Good, now we have two men here," as South and Clark were dragged into the pit. "Now for the first throw!" the instructors shouted, and they hurled the two around as though they were rag dolls. "This is how you do an overhead throw," followed by, "this is how you do a choke hold!" proclaimed the happy instructors. The experience left the bruised Frank South with an understanding of what he had to learn. However, it did little to sober Willie Clark, whose insolence, quick wit, and penchant for practical jokes would not always serve him well.

The sound of a whistle brought the men hurrying into formation, and they moved on the double to a "blitz" course. This course required the men to sling a rifle with fixed bayonet over their shoulder, run and grab a swinging rope, and "Tarzan" across a water-and-mud-filled ditch while a sadistic soul threw lighted charges of dynamite that exploded in showers of mud. After letting go of the rope, the men leaped and grabbed a ladder-like device and swung hand-over-hand to the other side. Upon landing, the soldiers unslung their rifles and ran forward to bayonet a dummy. The next rope swing in the course was over barbed wire.

The men followed this by climbing and sliding down a rope, and scaling and leaping from a wall. Their subsequent crawl through concertina wire featured bullets whizzing overhead, as well as more dynamite explosions. Almost at the "enemy position," the soldiers butt-stroked and bayoneted another dummy. Signaled by the whistle, the men speed marched to the firing range, where they practiced on .45-caliber pistols, M1 or M2 rifles, BARs, Thompson submachine guns, .30-caliber light machine guns, and 60mm mortars.

Missing a target on the firing range meant seeing a soldier in the pits beneath the target wave a red flag known as Maggie's Drawers, back and forth. It shamed a man to have it waved at him. Individual shooting records were kept and publicized. From the many expert riflemen, two snipers per company were selected and given additional training with the Springfield .03 rifle. The men of the battalion fired until their shoulders were sore, knowing that all of these weapons would have to be cleaned at night.

They practiced standing in foxholes throwing the serrated 20-ounce cast iron fragmentation grenades. Pull the pin, let the handle pop, and five seconds later the grenade explodes with a bursting radius of thirty yards. Throw the grenade too quickly, and the enemy might throw it back. It is also not good to be late when throwing a fragmentation grenade. Throwing the armed grenade a good distance away is also advisable. Frank South had one slip from his hand as he prepared to throw from a foxhole. Fortunately the grenade landed outside the hole and there was time to yell, "Get down!" a recommendation that was quickly followed by all men in the other holes.

There were classes on demolition, bayonet, and knife fighting. Night exercises were a part of the regimen. In the darkness, the men ran assault courses and practiced sliding on their backs under low-strung barbed wire while machine-gun fire, normally on a ratio of three ball to one white or red tracer, split the air above their heads. The tracers looked like hoses spraying in color. Headquarters company under 1st Lt. George S. Williams frequently played the role of the enemy attempting to ambush the assault company patrols. These exercises usually ended at 0200 hours, and reveille came at 0545.

To provide realistic training for war means putting men into dangerous situations where some will be injured and some may be killed. Men were exposed to frequent live-fire exercises, to explosives, and to tanks running over their foxholes in order to be properly prepared for what they would encounter on the battlefield. Casualties in training were expected. Sgt. Joe Camelo of Dog Company blew his hand off when he held on to a demolition charge too long. Ranger Antonem and Lieutenant Worzocna, also of Dog, were seriously injured when working on a booby trap that exploded. Lt. F. M. Phillips, the commander of Charlie Company, was crossing a stream on a rope when an oversized demolition charge blew him up and finished his Ranger career. 1st Lt. Ralph E. Goranson of Chicago assumed command. The dead were buried with honor, the injured were sent to hospitals, and the men of the battalion got the training they needed.

They also learned a few new songs. The men of the battalion came from a singing generation. When permitted, they sang the easy songs of soldiers. On marches the companies vied with each other to gain the title of "The Singingest Company." In the barracks at night, the men would break out the guitars. Lou Lisko, an ex-steel worker from western Pennsylvania, was in Ike Eikner's communications section. Lisko was one of the best of the guitar players. He knew the songs of the Depression, the songs of young men on the hard roads looking for any form of honest work. This was a railroad generation, when young men were called by the mournful wail of steam locomotives whistling for a grade crossing. They sang "I've Been Working on the Railroad," "The Wreck of the Old 97," and "The Wabash Cannonball." They were young men who, in the words of the Jimmie Rogers Depression song, were "Waiting for a Train." They had never dreamed it would be a troop train.

Major Rudder was informed that the battalion would participate in a review for senior officers of the Second U.S. Army. The meager time available to practice fell in the afternoon under a burning sun and on a windswept practice field. As the men marched, clouds of choking dust arose about them, coating their sweat-soaked bodies and uniforms. Over and over in practice, the battalion moved into position and passed in review while men spit dust and gasped for breath. The men felt the rehearsal was overdone, especially since they had to march three miles to the field where the event was held. Discipline began to unravel. There was griping and sloppy performance in the ranks that was noticeable to visiting officers. Rudder was reprimanded for the inefficiency of his unit.

Furious that his men had let him down, Rudder marched the battalion at attention for the three miles back to the cantonment area and stood them even taller. "You have performed disgracefully. You bring shame on yourself and me. There is no place in this battalion for a man who won't give his entire self for the betterment of this organization." Rudder closed his remarks by saying, "If any of you don't like the way I'm running this outfit, come on down to see me and we'll settle it man to man!"[6] Rudder's words had the desired effect. The men knew they had a commander worthy of the name Ranger.

Rudder expected the battalion to excel in all things. There would be no more sloppy marching, and he held dress retreat parades four nights a week. Barracks were inspected on Saturday mornings and officers held evening schools for the non-coms. The men were routinely reminded of the reasons for rigorous training, as they were frequently informed of the progress of the war. If there were complaints about the hardships, the standard response was, "You volunteered." Unlike many commanders who kept their distance from the troops, Rudder talked to the men frequently. "First, I'm going to make men of you," he said, "then, I'm going to make soldiers of you and, then, I'm going to make Rangers of you."[7]

Rudder played military musical chairs, switching NCOs and officers from company to company to get the leadership that he wanted. He required every leader had to know the name of the men who served under him. This was difficult on Rudder and the company commanders, but they worked at it. At the squad and platoon level, not to know your men by name meant no weekend pass issued. By mid-July 1943, Jim Rudder had gauged the quality of the men in the battalion and a housecleaning of undesirables was underway. The malcontents and the shirkers were removed. After four months of training, men understood what was expected of them. At least half of the men in the battalion quit or were removed.

Some of the men Rudder wanted to transfer fought the move. Rudder planned to transfer L-Rod Petty because he was missing his front teeth. Petty assured Rudder that he did not want to bite Germans to death, just shoot and bayonet them. Petty was allowed to stay.

From April through June, the battalion had transferred out and replaced 21 officers and 309 enlisted men. In July, 8 officers and 212 men departed. In August, only eight officers and fifteen men were transferred. Some of those dismissed were good men who would do well elsewhere, but they didn't have what it took to be Rangers. On August 3, five officers and sixty-eight enlisted volunteers arrived from the 100th Infantry Division. Most of these enlisted men were transferred out, but four of the officers would become distinguished members of the battalion: 1st Lt. Richard Merrill, 1st Lt. Sidney Salomon, 2nd Lt. William Moody, and 2nd Lt. Gerald W. Heaney. The selection process was ruthless. Of the sixty-five initial volunteers who entered Easy Company, fourteen would complete the training and go overseas with the battalion. Only six of those men remained in the company when Germany surrendered in May 1945.

As fast as men were being transferred out, other volunteers were coming in, and in large numbers. The U.S. Army was in full support of Ranger recruitment. The program was widely advertised and Rudder made frequent recruiting trips, including visiting the 79th, 100th, and 106th Divisions, making personal selections from the many volunteers. Rudder also recruited men for the 5th Ranger Battalion, which would be activated on September 1, 1943.

Training was now conducted under the buddy system. The men of the battalion lived, trained, traveled, and played as two-man teams, contributing to the overall company mission. B-rations would be issued to a company and each man would be given an item of food, a can of fruit, a loaf of bread, or a piece of meat. An assembly area, normally about fifteen miles from base camp, would be designated. The buddy team would be required to find their own way to the assembly area and bring their contribution to the company food supply. When the company was assembled and fed, an exercise would take place that would take the company to another location. When the exercise was concluded, the two-man buddy teams were required to find their own way back to base camp.

Speed marches continued, averaging ninety minutes for a 7.5-mile course. "Blood in the Boots" Knudson departed for another assignment. His final speech highly praised the battalion.

CHAPTER THREE

Fort Pierce, Florida:
Scouts and Raiders School
September 4–15, 1943

Water, water every where,
And all the boards did shrink;
Water, water every where,
Nor any drop to drink.

—*Samuel Taylor Coleridge, "The Rime of the Ancient Mariner"*

On September 4, 1943, the battalion said farewell to Camp Forrest and Tullahoma. In pouring rain they boarded a Southern Railroad troop train en route to attachment at the United States Naval Amphibious Training Force, Fort Pierce, Florida. There were many schools there and the battalion was scheduled for an eleven-day course of instruction at the Amphibious Scouts and Raiders School. Most of the assault company Rangers rode in coach class. The medical section, including Frank South and Willie Clark, found themselves in first-class bedroom cars, served to them on trays by uniformed stewards. The men played cards, read, wrote letters home and dozed while listening to the click and clatter of the steel wheels on the steel rails and the mournful cry of the steam engine whistle.

Whether in coach or first class, on arrival at Fort Pierce at 0800, September 5, the soldiers uniformly shouldered their weapons, packs, and duffle bags and disembarked from the train. There were a band, dignitaries, and a few of the local belles to welcome the men, but the public address system, which had worked well three hours before, emitted nothing but squeaks and snarls. The welcoming ceremony was given up, and the men staggered under their heavy loads toward waiting trucks, which hauled the men away to Hutchinson Island. En route, they had a brief and distant view of the town of Fort Pierce. They were soon looking at sea, sun, and sand in quantity greater than desired. Bundled pyramidal tents awaited erection. The first duty was to rapidly establish their camp. The advance party had staked out the limits of each company street. The kitchen and latrines had been erected and sump holes dug. It was hot and humid and a multitude of Florida bugs were about, but working in ten-man crews, the battalion tents were up in less than an hour. Mosquito netting hung around each of the cots. Some of the men had "Flit" guns, horizontal cans of insecticide with a pump handle on top. The mosquitoes drank the insecticide like beer. The tent sides were rolled up in hope of a breeze from off shore but it was a forlorn hope. The bottles containing alcoholic refreshment were buried in the sand under the tents. No Ranger officer would look there—they had their own sand to hide their bottles.

The Amphibious Scouts and Raiders School was a joint Army-Navy project with Army captain Lloyd E. Peddicord serving as commanding officer and Lt. (jg) John J. Bell as the officer in charge of the naval element. Both officers knew their subject. Peddicord was an up-from-the-ranks officer. During the North African landings on November 8, 1942, he had taken command of a Navy scout boat, led it through the darkness to the mouth of the Sebou River, and brought landing craft to their destination under fire. The Navy wanted Peddicord to get the Medal of Honor, but the Army had already awarded him a Silver Star and would not go through the administrative hassle to change it. Several of the Navy instructors had been awarded the Navy Cross for their actions in North Africa.

At the time of their attendance at Scouts and Raiders School, the vital mission which the men of the battalion would perform had not yet been determined. The battalion trained to be versatile, to conduct raids on enemy coasts, to gather intelligence or confirm intelligence reports, or to accurately fix the location of invasion beaches in advance of landing forces.

Marched to the lecture hall, the men of the battalion were informed by Captain Peddicord that they were expected to complete a fifteen-day course in eight days. They knew they were headed for water when life belts were issued.

Hutchinson Island was a colorful scene of green tents on white sand beside a pink ocean. Despite orders to the contrary, men took advantage of nightfall for a swim in the off-color water. They were soon scrambling out of the water and yelling "Medic!" The tides had brought an invasion of jellyfish to the waters of Fort Pierce.

Florida abounds in nature's little pests. Because the blood-sucking sand flies were so prevalent, they became part of the training. Each morning after reveille, the Rangers would stand at attention stripped to their shorts while the sand flies feasted on them. No one dared to be the first to move and after a time they accepted the bites. The men trained on the beach, running and practicing hand-to-hand combat or jujitsu, as it was called at the time. The leaders were unsparing in these fights, yelling at the men to "Get tough!" If the men had been involved in night training until 0200, they began boat training at 0900; otherwise, after sand fly and PT formations, training commenced at 0800.

They learned to swim wearing life belts and carrying weapons, and then without life belts. The primary boat used for training was an inflatable tube type constructed of rubberized fabric. The boat was twelve feet long and five feet at its widest point, at the beam. There were ten separate air-filled compartments so that even if most of the compartments were destroyed the boat would not sink. Four carrying handles, two on each side, were cemented to the boat. The Rangers were formed into seven-man crews, with three paddlers on each side of the boat and an officer or noncommissioned officer in charge of each boat. Training included climbing down cargo nets from a mock-up transport ship. They practiced inflating and deflating rubber boats as well as getting in and out of them rapidly on dry land. All boats and crews were positioned offshore and by platoon were signaled to come to shore under the watchful eyes of the instructors. The platoon was then ordered back into the boats to repeat the exercise.

The platoon was taken several miles out into the Atlantic Ocean, where they practiced deep-water emergency action when the boats turned over at sea. In order to pass this requirement, the men had to turn the boat over, then right it without losing weapons or paddles. All Rangers were required to swim but some could do it better than others. The reality of turning the rubber boat over in deep water panicked some and amused others. No one ever let a brother Ranger drown, but it was fun to "watch him go down a couple of times."[1]

When using the rubber boats, men sat astride the rubber tubes with their outside legs in the water. The deep water operations often were done at night. "It's hell out there," opined a Navy instructor, "You never know when a shark or a barracuda might come along and take off a leg."[2] The men of the battalion did not encounter such denizens of the deep but the jellyfish stung with fury inside their clothing. The men practiced at sea without sight of land, finding their way to shore by compass. They became familiar with Jack and Jim and Coon Islands, the Fort Pierce inlet, and landmarks such as the casino and the Coast Guard Station. Performing surf landings, they would come to shore by day or night, catch a breaker, and ride it to the beach. Becoming quite adept at this, they tried to bring the boat in to land with a thump on the coral rock on the beach. If they did not make it, the boat piled up on the rocks, flesh was torn, and some ribs were cracked.

Lt. Ted Lapres, leader of the 1st Platoon of Easy Company, successfully brought a rubber boat to the edge of a breakwater and unloaded his boat team. The boat was not moored and when Lapres tried to step from the boat, it began to drift away. Lapres had one foot on the breakwater and the other foot on the edge of the drifting boat. As his legs spread wider, Lieutenant Lapres began to resemble a chicken wishbone about to be torn apart. The men hurried to help, but as Ranger Richard Hubbard reached out, Lapres tumbled into the water. A towering wave arrived and drove the unfortunate lieutenant out of sight. The boat team stood on the edge of the wharf and in time Lapres burst to the wave-tossed surface looking for anything to vent his wrath upon. Dick Hubbard had the misfortune of being the first man Lapres saw. "God damn you, Hubbard," yelled Lapres, "you pushed me!"[3] Ted Lapres was a good officer and a reasonable man when dry. The boat team eventually convinced him of Hubbard's innocence.

When there were accidents, the Navy fretted not over the men, but damage to the boat. For the men, coming ashore meant stripping off the clothes and rubbing sand over the body to reduce the sting of the jellyfish, which immediately attracted the sand flies.

The training went on day and night, often in stormy seas and heavy surf. By the fourth day, men were caught sleeping while paddling. At the Fort Pierce inlet on Coon Island, a mock up was constructed where the battalion could practice techniques to disembark from ships and come down cargo nets onto the British-made Landing Craft, Assault (LCAs). These boats were designed to carry thirty men and the Ranger assault companies were organized so that a platoon could fit into one LCA. At night, the assault companies would make beach landings while Headquarters Company set off demolition charges and flares.

There was no time for relaxation and some men gave up scarce and precious minutes of sleep to write letters home by candlelight. Olive "Smitty" Klaus, now pregnant, wrote Bill everyday. The war made their lives uncertain and put their plans on hold, but it was fun to write about what it would be like when they were together again.

The relentless training continued. The Navy contingent liked what they saw in the battalion and several Navy Scouts and Raiders School instructors requested permission to join the Rangers. Transfer between services was not an option and their request was denied. On September 10, 1943, the battalion was alerted to prepare to move to either Boston or New York on October 10. Rudder and his battalion staff had been at work for days planning the graduation exercise dubbed "Plan Surfboard." The mission was to come in by sea and make a night attack on the town of Fort Pierce, which, per the exercise, was in German hands being used as a submarine base. Reconnaissance was followed by briefings, and at dusk on September 13, the attack began. The battalion would land over a mile-and-a-half-wide front with a ten-minute interval between companies disembarking. Scouts went in first and set up colored lights visible only from the sea to guide the incoming boats to their landing points. Coming in from sea, Able Company would guide their craft toward a steady red light, then once ashore capture the waterworks, airport, and Highway No. 1. Baker would come in toward a steady white light and secure the yacht basin and power plant. Baker had a special squad headed by Capt. George Williams of headquarters company. Williams had made claim that he had knowledge of power plants and would accompany the raiding party to keep the power plant in operation. His claim to power plant expertise raised eyebrows among his men, but Williams was actually a professional engineer in civilian life. Charlie honed in on a steady blue light. They would capture the Burston and Fort Pierce hotels which for exercise purposes were German Navy Headquarters. Dog would search for a steady yellow; Easy, a blinking white. These two companies would seize the area designated as the submarine base. As battalion reserve, Fox honed in on a blinking red and Headquarters a blinking green light and took up positions ashore.

The Navy sentries and city guard had been told of the exercise, but they were caught by surprise. Rangers vaulted the high wire fence at the power plant and took control. Assault teams climbed to the top of buildings and set up machine guns covering the streets. With all objectives taken, Major Rudder visited the naval commandant, who grimly declared the exercise concluded.

On the ninth day, September 14, the battalion rested and had passes to Fort Pierce, where they could find women and beer. The men of the battalion were lean now, a rollicking, roaring band. Their release generated what a battalion document termed "a general exhilaration of spirit." So general, so exhilarating, and so spirited was this release that at the request of local authorities and the commandant, the battalion was subsequently confined to quarters.

CHAPTER FOUR

Fort Dix–Camp Ritchie–
Camp Shanks–the Ocean Voyage
September 16–November 30, 1943

When I was at home, I was in a better place,
but travellers must be content.

—*William Shakespeare,* As You Like It

The long line of olive drab trucks arrived early on September 16 to carry the men to the Fort Pierce railhead. Ranger Richard Hubbard said the moves were usually "hurry up and wait," but that would not happen leaving Fort Pierce. It was evident that those in authority wanted the Rangers gone. A Southern Railways train waited on a siding, the steam engine huffing as it prepared to roll. World War II was the last great fling of the American railroads. Rail travel had been in decline since 1917 when a man named Henry Ford decided to put wheels under everyone. It took the vast dimensions of World War II to necessitate the use of every form of rolling stock and locomotion the United States could muster. The time of the great steam engines had been passing as the diesel locomotives came on line, but with the outbreak of war the steel dinosaurs that were the steamers came back from the scrap yards with a roar. As the men of the battalion heard the conductor yell "BOARD!," the whistle shrieked and the giant drive wheels spun. This was a true troop train, bare metal frames and hard seats, an instrument of the devil and devoid of comfort.

The destination was Fort Dix, New Jersey. A majority of the men were from New York, Pennsylvania, and New Jersey, and there was a sense of anticipation as the train rolled north. They knew they were headed overseas, bound for war, but there was a good chance that they would get some time at home. They would see their families and, for many, have a chance to hold the girls they loved.

The train pulled into the Fort Dix railyard at 0800 hours on September 18. A fall chill was in the air and the northern men who had grown accustomed to the heat of southern camps shivered as they gathered their gear. They were soon sweating as they marched under heavy loads to never-popular wooden-sided pyramidal tents. The day was spent in the now familiar routine of setting up the camp along previously staked out company streets. The most popular addition of tenting in the north was a pot-bellied stove that kept the interior of the tents comfortable. As a result of some good work by the advance party, the battalion had two kitchens serving hot food.

Fort Dix, New Jersey, was heaven after Camp Forrest and Fort Pierce. There were PX beer and USO dances. Fort Dix was pass and leave heaven for the men. For those who had cars, gas was fifteen cents a gallon. Bus service was convenient and the bars and flesh-pots of Wrightstown, Trenton, Philadelphia, Baltimore, and New York City were close by. Rudder gave them two days' leave. Trenton was big and handy; the battalion had a dance there and the jitterbug kings showed off their routines. Places in Trenton named "The Pirate Ship," "The Herby Derby," and "Murphys," became Ranger hangouts. Patriotism was at a high level among the civilian community. The patriotism of young women was particularly important and appreciated.

Training resumed on September 19 and was built around platoon and company firing problems. The exercises were prepared by the battalion and consisted of performing "dry run" no-ammunition problems, followed by performing the same problem with live ammunition. One squad laid down a base of fire while the other moved, then they alternated the process.

They continued to hone their rifle and machine gun skills and practiced throwing live fragmentation grenades, but training with crew-served weapons was now part of the regimen. They became skilled with the heavier 81-mm mortar. The Rangers surprised artillery officers when they were more effective at shelling a hill with their mortars than a 105mm howitzer artillery battalion stationed at Fort Dix.

A weapon despised and quickly discarded by the battalion was the British .55-caliber Boys antitank rifle. This shoulder-fired, bolt-action brute weighed in at thirty-six pounds and was five feet, four inches long. The recoil had the kick of an Army mule. Men fired it from the prone position and flinched while pulling the trigger. Rangers claimed the recoil would create a trench as the gunner was driven backward. By 1943 the effectiveness of firing the Boys antitank rifle against a German tank was described as "You bet your life." For an antiarmor weapon, the men much preferred the 2.36-inch rocket launcher called a "bazooka." The weapon was named after a jury-rigged musical device used by popular comic Bob Burns.

There were many senior officers who remembered the horror of gas warfare in World War I, and gas-mask training was now standard. They underwent the gas chamber drill, which required going into the gas chamber, donning the mask, then being required to remove it, and standing steady while the room filled with tear gas. With tears streaming from their eyes, gasping and hacking, they were allowed to return to fresh air. It was hell being the last man in the formation in the gas chamber.

There were Saturday morning stand-by-the-foot-of-the-cot inspections, where the blanket had to be pulled tight enough to bounce a quarter. There were training films on the horrors of venereal disease. The men watched and thought, "The hell with the VD, let me at that one in the short skirt."

The *Why We Fight* series was also shown. There was no media touting equal opportunity for German and Japanese opinion. Propaganda was straightforward during World War II. There was a war to be won and there was no concern for calling the Germans, Italians, and Japanese names. They were Goddamn Krauts, Nazi bastards, Wops, and Yellow Japs, and seeking understanding of their point of view was not part of the program.

Men were still being cut from the rosters and transferred to other outfits. Though they had survived a grueling process that would have made them leaders in many units, the 2nd Ranger Battalion documents called them "undesirables," and they were sent off. The assault companies had an extra platoon leader in case of injury or failure; these were now cut and it was a hard process. The company commander made his choice of what officer must go. Ralph Goranson said, "It was hard for me and it was hard for him." It helped that there was additional time to make the choice. The movement date of the battalion had been changed from October 10 to October 27.

Not all was going well. There were problems with the medical section of the battalion. The enlisted men were competent, but a series of medical officers proved unworthy and were transferred out.

The man who joined the battalion at Fort Dix on September 24 and made the 2nd Ranger Battalion Medical Section was Dr. Walter Block. In civilian life, Block was a forty-year-old pediatrician. He wanted to be a paratrooper, but his wife, Alice, begged him to keep his feet on the ground. Block convinced her that the Rangers had something to do with trees and that was okay by her. As a doctor, he was a no-nonsense man devoted to maintaining the health and mission of the battalion. On duty, Doc Block made the speed marches with the rest of the battalion and off duty he did countless push-ups to toughen his body. Ike Eikner described Walter Block as "an officer who was at one and the same time physician, soldier and gentleman." Block would not tolerate what he considered slipshod performance and could cut a throat almost as well as he could sew one.

With Block's arrival, his fifteen-man Medical Section became separate from but supported by Headquarters Company. One aid-man (private or private first class) medic would be attached to each of the assault companies; the remaining nine served in the battalion aid station under Block or were dispatched to the assault companies as needed.

On September 28, two officers and two NCOs left the battalion for the port of embarkation at New York City. They would form the advance party of the battalion for its arrival in England. Their departure signalled to the men that their time in the homeland was drawing short.

At a battalion formation on September 29, Rudder informed the men that five-day furloughs would begin the following day. The timing would be fortunate for Bill Klaus as his wife Olive gave birth to their daughter Carol Lynn on the day of the formation, and Bill was promptly home. Lt. Sid Salomon's second platoon of Charlie Company had the best platoon score and Dog Company had the best company performance on the firing ranges. Rudder awarded these men an extra day of leave. The companies would take turns going on furlough, and those who were returning or awaiting their turn to go would train seven days a week. It was by this device that Rudder was able to meet his training requirements and yet give his men a break. It was another example of caring for the men. Individual company photographs and a battalion photograph were taken at this formation. Up to this time the men had worn the red and white "2" that was the Second U.S. Army patch. At the formation, Rudder awarded to each of the men five of the newly-approved Ranger shoulder insignia. To men in proud units, symbols of identity such as patches, are important.

The new Ranger insignia had been designed by Lt. Joseph Smudin, a cavalry officer who had served as battalion S-2 at Camp Forrest. Smudin's design was forwarded to the War Department and approved on July 16, 1943. The insignia consisted of a horizontal blue diamond with the word "RANGERS" superimposed thereon, with that word and the edging of the insignia in yellow gold. The blue diamond was a colorful symbol, but it had problems. First, it was a generic symbol. The patch did not identify the battalion to which the man belonged and by September of 1943 there were already five proud Ranger battalions (the sixth would not be formed until September 1944). Second, the patch looked much like the symbol of the Sun Oil Company, which supplied a gasoline called "Sunoco." Later, when men began to wear it, other soldiers called out "Blue Sunoco" when they saw the insignia and fights ensued.

Rudder knew the insignia was lacking unit pride. The battalion photograph taken at Fort Dix, New Jersey, in October 1943 showed the seated Rudder with a three-foot-wide copy of the insignia at his feet. It has been changed so the identification "2nd" appeared above the word "RANGERS" and "BN" appears below it. No one in the army had bothered to check with the 1st Ranger Battalion to learn if they had a symbol of identity—they did have one, and all the Ranger battalions of World War II would later adopt it.

While some companies were on home leave, the remainder continued training. A distant objective designated as an enemy supply dump would be assigned to each assault company. These objectives and the routes to them often included moving off the Fort Dix training areas. For the first three days of the exercise, the two platoons of an assault company would be on their own and assigned the mission of reconnoitering a different route to the objective. On the fourth night, the two platoons would reassemble with the company headquarters at a prearranged assembly area and assault the objective. Headquarters Company again supplied the enemy force. They were supplied with some D rations, but were expected to forage off the countryside. That foraging instruction was not made clear and soon local farmers began to complain to the police and military authorities about missing of chickens. An angry, red-faced Rudder gave his men hell and, if a chicken forager was identified, he paid for the bird—there were few who paid.

The speed marches continued, but a new wrinkle was added. The battalion now marched and crawled over and through sewer pipes, junkyards, and barnyards, and wriggled through thickets of brush. The battalion staff delighted in finding the most slime-covered, offal-filled, stinking challenges.

Another motor move began at 0400 hours, October 21, 1943. Again, the long line of olive-drab $2^{1}/_{2}$-ton trucks, the clanging of dropped tail gates, the clambering under loads of equipment, and the helping hands reaching downward as men struggled to get aboard. This time the destination was the War Department Military Intelligence Training Center at Camp Ritchie, Maryland, for the final War Department test before shipment overseas.

The former National Guard camp was now a place where opposition forces included those who spoke German or Japanese. Maps that were written in the language of the enemy and contained their symbols were used, and mock enemy vehicles helped men identify the shapes they would see in combat. The men could practice street fighting in small towns that had been constructed to resemble those in France and Germany.

The training scenario had enemy forces overrunning the critical terrain known as Hill X and in position to continue to threaten the line of defense for the Americans. A friendly division was being rushed to the area, but would not be in position to counterattack until the following morning at 0900. The mission of the battalion was to retake Hill X by 0830 and set the stage for the divisional counterattack. The enemy included infantry and a unit of horse cavalry.

After the umpire briefing, a command reconnaissance was conducted. Rudder issued his command guidance and the staff worked up his options. When his decision was made, Rudder issued his orders. The battalion would infiltrate the enemy outpost line and make a surprise attack on Hill X. Charlie Company would infiltrate to the right of Hill X while Easy Company infiltrated to the left. When Charlie and Easy companies were positioned on the flank or rear of the enemy position, Able, Dog, and Fox Companies would cross a railroad that served as a line of departure and make a frontal assault. These five companies would kick off the attack at 0830 on October 22. Baker Company would initially be in reserve and would patrol to screen the battalion command post. The attack would be coordinated by SCR300 radio. Company commanders made their reconnaissance and briefed the men who were dispersed in the apple orchard. Each man was issued a card with his name, rank, and serial number. If a man was ruled killed or wounded, the card would be taken from him by the umpires.

Rudder's plan hardly fitted the military maxim of KISS ("Keep It Simple, Stupid!"). His direction amounted to a double envelopment combined with a frontal attack being made over a wide front. This would have been a difficult arrangement to coordinate in daylight, and this attack was being made on a moonless night. Control problems developed promptly. The soldiers had to traverse a steep and heavily forested 2,200-foot ridge. Radio contact between the battalion and the companies was lost. Rudder had moved to a forward command post (CP) that was soon under attack by an enemy patrol. Headquarters Company manned the perimeter until Baker Company reinforced and the enemy was repulsed.

The Ranger situation was deteriorating. Major Rudder and his staff no longer had control over the battalion. To save the exercise, it would be necessary for the companies to carry out their missions independently.

Ralph Goranson led Charlie Company to the right and penetrated the enemy outpost line. Without being noticed, Goranson made it to the right rear of the objective, set up his machine guns, and caught the enemy rear security force by surprise. Horses and men were taken, and the umpires ruled the enemy force "annihilated." Charlie Company then began to climb Hill X. They found themselves facing a clifflike 2,000-foot slope. The night ascent put every free-climb skill the men had learned to the test. A sergeant later said, "If the men had seen how steep that cliff really was, they wouldn't have even attempted to scale it."[1] Though exhausted, Charlie Company reached the top, set up a perimeter defense, and sent patrols to contact Easy Company.

As the other companies made contact with the enemy, Rudder moved forward to regain contact. The only information that he had came from prisoners. In this exercise, some of the enemy were dressed in German uniforms and spoke German. Rudder took a small party to re-establish control. In the process the party was ambushed, and Rudder barely escaped capture.

At 0830, the individual company commanders followed their orders and launched their attacks. Able, Baker, Dog, and Fox swept in from the front, and Charlie and Easy hit the enemy in the rear, with Easy overrunning the enemy command post. Within minutes the exercise was successfully concluded, and the difficult task of reassembling the Battalion and getting it back off the treacherous slopes was underway. The men looked forward to their first hot meal in fifty-four hours.

Camp Ritchie was an important experience for the battalion. The difficulties of control, using line-of-sight radios in difficult terrain, were brought clearly into view. More would need to be done to assure that the battalion commander had the means to influence the action. It was obvious that the small-unit leadership had performed with skill. The long hours of training paid off. They had continued the mission, as Rangers should, and prevailed.

That afternoon, the battalion was trucked to the Intelligence School drill field. Platoon by platoon, the men traveled through a round-robin demonstration of German and Japanese equipment, viewing enemy weapons, mines and booby traps, equipment, and uniforms. At one station, some of the Rangers were required to clear a path through a German minefield that contained numerous booby traps. Elsewhere, other Rangers had the opportunity to fire German weapons. For the first time, they heard the reports of the German Mauser Kar 98K rifle, the Machinenpistole MP38, and the MG34 and MG42 light machine guns. The bolt-action, five-shot Mauser rifle did not impress the Rangers. The American M1 rifle was clearly superior. The German MP38 was like the American carbine, a good weapon in the sense that it was easy to carry, but like the carbine the MP38 lacked energy. The German MG34 and MG42 machine guns were another matter. In World War II the MG42 (named for the year of its introduction) was the finest machine gun in any army in the world. Its *brrrrrrrp* represented the spitting out of up to 1,550 rounds per minute. The eleven-man German squad was organized to support and protect the fire of this machine gun, and two ammunition bearers were dedicated to each gun.

It was cold, but with hot food in the belly and a successful experience behind them, the mood of the battalion was upbeat. While waiting for the trucks, the men built great campfires and gathered around them singing. Rudder was delighted with the performance of his men, and the higher-ups were pleased with Rudder, promoting him to lieutenant colonel two weeks later.

The crisp air of November 1943 found the battalion at Fort Dix, New Jersey, readying for overseas shipment. The preparation of a unit for combat is an exacting process with a thousand details that must be checked and rechecked. Officers learn that giving an order is 1 percent of that effort, supervising to insure it is properly carried out is the other 99 percent.

When the last clean-up was finished and breakfast complete, the battalion formed in the company streets, shouldered all equipment, and marched a mile to the railyard. The train ride was brief and they were soon back at Camp Shanks, the final place of preparation for overseas movement.

Thirty-seven officers and 536 enlisted men had been tested, found wanting, and been transferred out of the 2nd Ranger Infantry Battalion. The 25 officers and 488 men who remained were going to England fully aware that the shakedown process would continue.

The battalion traveled by truck on 49th Street in New York City to Pier 90 where the giant passenger liner *Queen Elizabeth* was waiting. Merely getting to the gangway was a major operation. Loaded down with weapons, full field packs, and duffel bags, soldiers climbed steep stairs and traversed lengthy corridors to the embarkation station. At the foot of the gangway officers waited with rosters. As last names were called, men responded with first names, were checked off, and proceeded to climb to the ship. "Petty!" called the officer (no mumbling here). "William!" was the response. "Stein!" . . . "Herman!," "Jones!" . . . "Ivor!," "South!" . . . "Frank!," "Webb!" . . . "Morris!" Loud and clear like gunshots on a still morning, the men sounded off and shouldered their heavy gear onboard to an aft compartment on the main deck. Ranger William F. Weber had guard duty and narrowly missed seeing his father. The older Weber had delivered soda to the vessel, but all civilians had cleared the ship prior to troop boarding.

The officers had staterooms, but there was little comfort since eight officers occupied a room designed for two people. The enlisted men's sleeping area had once been the cocktail lounge of the great vessel. Now the bones of beauty were still visible, but the ship was cloaked in wartime grey. The lounge where the rich once refreshed themselves in comfort was filled with four-tiered canvas bunks.

There was no choice location. The man on the top bunk had to climb. Everyone else had the sag from the bunk above, hanging inches from their nose. Of course, not all of the battalion would endure such discomfort. Medic Frank South recalled, "No eight-tiered bunks for us. We had cabins again, and essentially free run of the ship. Willie, another medic, and I berthed in the ship's surgery. We had nice beds, a hot-(sea)water bath and all the amenities."[2] The *Queen Elizabeth* departed from New York harbor at 1700 hours on November 23, 1943. In the wars of the twentieth century, departing American soldiers sailing to war tended to remember two significant objects—if going to the Pacific, it was the Golden Gate Bridge of San Francisco; if departing from New York City, it was the Statue of Liberty. The Rangers joined other soldiers who lined the rails of the *Queen Elizabeth*. At age nine John "Whitey" Bakalar of Able Company had seen the Statue of Liberty as an immigrant from his native Czechoslovakia. Now Bakalar was going back to Europe as an American soldier. As they lined the ship's rails, each man had his private thoughts, and there were many who wondered if they would ever see the Statue of Liberty and their homeland again.

Sporting the newly acquired silver leaf of a lieutenant colonel, Rudder called the battalion officers and key NCOs together in what had once been the luxurious officers' lounge. "I've been appointed Provost Marshall for the trip," Rudder said with a wry grin, "and the battalion will serve as military police."[3] The assemblage took the news with grim humor. The leaders knew the men of the battalion had been "familiar" with the MPs at Camp Forrest, but that relationship had been more violent than instructive.

Mission assigned, the orders went out. The liner was separated into sections named red, white, and blue. The assault companies were detailed to act as deck security. This included directing the flow of traffic during boat drills, clearing troops from the deck areas when the ship was traveling in blackout, hurrying troops to muster, and keeping them out of officers' country and the nurses' and WAC areas. There were 15,000 servicemen and women on board and many of them were curious. There was so little space that tiers of cots had been built into the ship swimming pools and troops occupied the cots sleeping by shift. The Ranger insignia had been removed prior to departing Fort Dix, and their identity remained a secret. There was nothing about the uniform to reveal the men of the battalion, but a badge that was emblazoned with "MP" and the firm command "That's off limits!" served as authority.

Headquarters Company had the worst duty. They had to maintain order in long chow lines. It took five shifts for each feeding and the troops were assigned different colored mess cards that told them when they could eat. Sailors were not accustomed to standing in lines on board ship and were the most quarrelsome. Most of the Rangers hated the military police duty. They disliked taking away the liberties of other soldiers. Policing the chow line meant listening to an endless stream of complaints. British food was being served, not American. Thanksgiving Day was observed at sea and the men looked forward to the American tradition of turkey with all the trimmings. What they got was greasy pork.

Conversations with troops of various other units were frequent, but the Rangers' identity was not disclosed. A long, lanky infantryman said to Ranger Bill Stivison, "I heered there wuz commandos on this boat, but I ain't never seen none."[4]

A grey ship on a grey ocean, the *Lizzie*, as the great ship was affectionately called, traveled alone without escort warships, relying on speed to escape the prowling U-boat wolf packs of German admiral Karl Doenitz. No matter their size, the sea is not impressed with the ships of man. The huge liner buried its bow in towering waves, rolled and shuddered, and was tossed about. Most of the passengers were landsmen unfamiliar with sea-going travel. They clung to the ship rails and vomited.

After gaining their sea legs, the men had leisure time to play cards, read, and talk. The talking was critical. In training, they were always on the go—they knew what each man was capable of and a capsule overview of his history, but there was little time to hold real conversations. Off duty they wanted a woman, a drink, or both. Going to war by ship, they had time to talk of experiences or hopes and dreams. They had time to get into each other's heads and hearts. Few of them had wanted to be soldiers. The tide in the affairs of men that Shakespeare had written about had put them here. Events beyond their control had shaped their generation and their destiny. The cards which they had been dealt included an economic depression followed by the largest global war in history—it was their lot. They had made it through the depression and now they were getting on with meeting the challenge of the war.

For seven days the *Queen Elizabeth* made this winter voyage and for six days the ship's clocks were turned forward one hour at 0100 hours. Bodily clocks went askew. Men saw their sleep going behind them in the wake of the ship. It was a week of washing in salt water and living in the same clothes. There was a brief scare one night as the ship made a sudden turn. Men thought the cause might be a submarine. In Headquarters Company the rumor spread that a wolf pack of thirty U-boats had formed an arc-shaped ambush. Only the numbers were wrong. Capt. Duke Slater learned that radar had revealed three blips spread out ahead on the surface. The British had also broken the German naval code and picked up the transmissions of the submarines. The speeding liner spun on its wake and avoided the trap.

Had the *Queen Elizabeth* or *Queen Mary* been torpedoed, the loss of life would have been horrific and the effort necessary to deliver troops to England revamped. The invasion of Europe would have been delayed. Speed triumphed, and as the great screws churned a white wake, the *Queen Elizabeth* was soon back on course. The day following the submarine scare, a four-engine Sunderland flying boat with British red, white, and blue roundels on the wings flew over the ship, and morale soared as a connection was made with their destination.

In the chill morning light of November 30, those on deck could see snow-covered mountains against an azure sky. Soon, green forests and great warships lying at anchor were in view. Ghost-like but majestically, the *Queen Elizabeth* made her way into the Firth of Clyde and dropped anchor. A vast flock of seagulls surrounded the ship. "Welcome to Scotland," they seemed to cry, as a bitter wind swept in and battered the men with rain and hail.

The Rangers were the last to leave. As they departed down the gangway, an army of cleaning women marched up, attacking the mess left by the troops in a coordinated assault that would have warmed the heart of any general.

CHAPTER FIVE

England, Preparations for Invasion December 1, 1943–June 5, 1944

I am not come forth to find difficulties but to remove them.

—Adm. Horatio Nelson

On the morning of December 1, 1943, the men of the battalion boarded ferries heading to the docks of Greenock, Scotland. Again shouldering their weapons and equipment, the battalion moved to a vast warehouse/staging area where those who had time for a nap found the floor more comfortable than the steel cots. Newly promoted Capt. George Williams, the supply officer, headed a fifty-man detail drawn from each of the companies who remained at the *Queen Elizabeth* to bring the heavy equipment, extra weapons and supplies from the ship.

"Load up. We're moving out," was the cry. Another march, this time to the Greenock train station. In the fading light of evening, the men loaded onto a train of coaches. Trains were a favored target of strafing aircraft so no light could be shown. Drawn blackout curtains isolated the men from the surrounding world as the locomotive huffed its way to momentum. The swaying hours passed with some men seeking sleep on non-reclining seats and others engaged in the inevitable pinochle and poker games.

With the dawn, the curtains were opened and the men of the battalion saw their first glimpse of the manicured English countryside. At

Exeter they had a firsthand view of the effects of German bombing. The train sped through the hills of south England and on to the open plains of the west, arriving at the station of Bude, Cornwall, in the early afternoon of December 2. Much to their surprise and delight, a band greeted the men on arrival; it was the band of the American 190th Field Artillery, a 155mm howitzer battalion whose duty it was to play for the newcomers. The unit that the band represented, however, was not overjoyed with the presence of the Rangers, as they represented competition for the single women.

Bude is a summer coastal resort town on the southwest foot of England. Bude Bay is on the Celtic Sea and the town lays just south of the mouth of the wide Bristol Channel. The weather is temperate year round—temperate for England, that is. Rain and chill wind frequently buffeted the town from the open sea across the downs.

In a world at war, Bude was an outpost of peace. The prewar population of about 5,000 had been swelled by refugees from the German bombings who went to Bude for safety. Bude was a quaint, quiet place of row and beachfront homes, cobblestone streets, and thatched and tile roofs. The town had numerous pubs, a fish and chip shop, and a theater where the single film changed twice a week. There was a small lounge for servicemen at the Anglican church where the Rangers could have tea and a cherry tart or ginger cookie, and in these quiet surroundings a letter home could be written. The River Strat runs through Bude and the seacoast features the Upton cliffs that the Rangers could practice climbing. The men were not aware that these cliffs looked very much like those off the Normandy coast of France.

There was no formal military camp at Bude for the Rangers. The battalion's advance party had made the billeting arrangements working with the Bude-Stratton Urban District Council. The men were divided into groups and then led to private homes throughout the town. The homeowners were paid a small stipend during winter months to house them.

The homeowner was required to provide sufficient space and ventilation. Rooms had to contain at least a carpet, rug, or mat, a chair, a table, and lighting. A bed could be provided, but if not, the Ranger used army-issued bedding. Soldiers were entitled to hot water for washing and shaving and at least one hot bath per week if possible. If the bath could not be provided the stipend was reduced by a penny a day. Every Ranger had to keep his room clean, make his own bed, observe blackout regulations, and conserve light and fuel. No meals were required to be provided by the host family.

There was a wide range of hosts and accommodations. Some men found themselves living in working-class neighborhoods, while others boarded with people of means. John "Whitey" Bakalar roomed with a family that had a beautiful daughter. The young woman was dating an Englishman who was a conscientious objector. When Bakalar moved into her home, the girl became furious that an American would come across the ocean to fight the Germans and her boyfriend would not. She dismissed the Englishman. Bakalar's friends thought that he had won her hand, but the immigrant American soldier and this English girl were just friends who understood that freedom has a price.

T/5 Dick Rankin and S/Sgt. Fred Culbreath of Able Company roomed with Jack and Martha Blight at 4 Killerton Road. The Blights were representative of the kind people of Bude. Jack Blight was a mechanic. The Blight's food was strictly limited as Britain was on an austerity program that made American rationing look like luxury, but they and most of the English hosts gave freely to the American soldiers who lived in their homes. Some of the men were treated to breakfast in bed. The men of the battalion quickly learned that this kindness often came at the cost of the host family going hungry. Men began to say, "Thank you, but I could not eat another bite and, oh, by the way, I happen to have this can of cocoa in my package from home. Can you use it?"

From the locals, the men learned that they were strangers in a foreign land that spoke English, not American. When they arrived at Bude, not one man in ten knew that a "flicker" was a movie. They were unaware of the term "loo," but they soon learned to crap in them. A British female host would ask "What time do you want to get knocked up tomorrow?" It took some time to understand that meant being awakened.

Colonel Rudder and his staff set up headquarters at the aging Links Hotel. The staff had been hard at work planning the training program. A formation was held at which Rudder informed the men of his expectations regarding their conduct. Rudder had been given full authority to further hone his battalion strength, and additional men and officers were transferred while other applicants were interviewed. Capt. Pete Staples had been with the battalion since its activation and was serving as battalion executive officer. Staples had a fine reputation, but Rudder wanted a more experienced second in command. Staples was transferred out, and Maj. Max D. Schneider, who had been promoted from his assignment as a company commander with the 1st Ranger Battalion, arrived to serve as the battalion executive officer. Max Schneider was an important addition to the battalion, a capable and combat-experienced officer who would play a significant role in future events.

The advance parties of the various companies had many tales to tell the newcomers. Lieutenants Heaney and Dahan and Rangers Philip Robida and Mack Styles had arrived in England on October 19. The Rangers were assigned to the U.S. First Army, the senior headquarters. However, that headquarters had not arrived in England. With no one to report to and little to do, the two officers and two enlisted men sought to become more familiar with the English. They gave themselves six weeks of consecutive three-day passes to London.

The enforced good life was only temporary. Heaney and company knew they would soon return to a routine of log drills and speed marches. Lieutenant Heaney decided to keep them in shape by doing speed marches through the English countryside. As the part of their air defense system, the English had a multitude of barrage balloons raised above their land. The finned blimp-like balloons had cables suspended beneath them that would tear the wings from any German bomber that had the misfortune to fly into them.

In wartime England, there were instances where a woman might be drafted into the service before a man. The barrage balloon units could be staffed by the often young and lovely girls of the Women's Auxiliary Air Force (WAAFs). As Heaney and his trio marched past a barrage balloon unit, the women had finished work for the day and were nude from the waist up, washing their upper bodies. In an effort to spare the ladies embarrassment, Lieutenant Heaney ordered his men to "double time." Apparently, Heaney did not hear his own order as his feet went up and down while running in place, and his neck seemed to be in a strain. His comrades claimed that he was two hundred yards behind when they finally got his attention.[1]

Getting men to a formation from tents or barracks is easy—getting them to work on time from their civilian homes took some doing. Rudder told the men that reveille would be at 0630 and all should be in formation at that time, or the following morning reveille would be at 0615, and so on. Rudder's instruction was unworkable, since some of the men had such a distance to hike that they had a far earlier wake-up than other men. When reveille was being held at 0500, Rudder decided mass punishment was not a good option. The policy was changed so that only offenders received punishment, consisting of a two-hour hike with full field pack and weapon at night after regular training. The companies had special wake-up parties that rounded up their habitual latecomers.

The S-3 section (plans and operations) worked up a training program and the word went out. The first week was devoted to getting the men to the peak of physical fitness. It was back to the familiar routine. After reveille and the morning roll call, there were calisthenics and speed marches, as much as twelve miles carrying full equipment. Training in scaling heights began on the rugged Upton Cliffs of Bude. Familiarization classes were held for British customs and uniforms and equipment of the British Army. A formal retreat formation was held four times weekly and every man's gear and billet at whichever home he stayed was inspected by battalion officers on Saturday mornings.

Browning automatic rifles were issued, and the battalion S-3 section established firing ranges on land requisitioned by the British government. Most of the weapons in the battalion came from World War I. When loaded with its twenty-round magazine, the Browning automatic rifle (BAR) weighed over twenty-two pounds. The BAR sang in a deep bass that rumbled at a cyclic rate of 550 rounds per minute. Anyone who has ever carried a BAR never forgot the brute. Heavy and cumbersome, it was devastating when working, but subject to frequent jams. The BAR, the light machine gun, the Thompson submachine gun, and the 60mm and 81mm mortars were weapons from World War I. Only the carbine, the magnificent M1 rifle, and 2.36-inch rocket launcher were products of World War II.

The Ranger training had now reached the testing phase. On December 17, several officers and men left the battalion on detached service to take part in British Commando raids on the coast of France. Of these Rangers, 1st Lt. Morton "Big Mac" McBride of Dog Company got ashore. McBride and his commando comrades were taken cross-channel by gunboat. While still invisible to coastal observers, they changed to a small cockle-shell type craft to make the night run to shore. At the landing point, the cliff was vertical. While several of the commandos rowed the boat away from shore, the remainder moved to the cliffs. Only McBride and three of the British were able to make the climb, moving inch by inch through the stygian darkness and barbed wire entanglements which the Germans had on the cliff face.

On the cliff top, the four men assembled and began to move inland. The moon, which had been covered by clouds, appeared in full brilliance. Some distance away but coming toward the edge of the cliff was a line of German soldiers, spread out with fixed bayonets on their Swastika-stamped Mauser rifles.

McBride and the commandos made as fast a descent as the wire would allow and lay quietly in the dark shadows of the cliff face while the suspicious Germans thoroughly searched the cliff top. As dawn approached, the men signaled their small craft back to shore. They then endured a ten-mile row through swells while using a direction finder to make contact with the low-silhouette gunboat that was lying out of sight of the French coast.

Over time, new officers joined the battalion. Among the arrivals was 1st Lt. Robert Edlin. No one called him Robert—it was always "Bob." Edlin was born in Evansville, Indiana, one of seven children raised in a family during the hard times of the Great Depression. Edlin knew about hard-working farm life, about pitching hay and shocking wheat.

In 1939, at age seventeen, Edlin joined the 152nd Infantry Regiment of the Indiana National Guard. On December 1, 1940, his unit was activated. In 1942, Edlin graduated as a ninety-day wonder from Officers Candidate School at Fort Benning. By 1943, he was in England with the 112th Infantry of the 28th Division. He spent several months at a British Battle and Commando School. Being disgusted with what he saw as a lack of spirit in his division, he volunteered for the Rangers. Edlin was accepted by Lytle and Rudder and was assigned to Able Company as leader of 1st Platoon. Edlin had been a boxer and would put on the gloves with any of his troops. The men quickly gained respect for his leadership and his fists. He would go up against anyone, and the men who beat him were above his weight class. 1st Sgt. Henry "Steve" Golas of Charlie Company pounded Edlin, but Golas had done a previous hitch in the Navy and been Pacific Fleet middleweight boxing champion.

As training progressed, Major Schneider, the battalion executive officer, Capt. Harvey Cook, the intelligence officer (S-2), and Capt. George Williams, the supply officer (S-4), left for London and a visit to Combined Operations Headquarters at Whitehall. The purpose of the visit was to plan raids on the coast of France. They would later be joined by Lieutenant Colonel Rudder.

The men had other pursuits. It was soon said that British girls wore "utility underwear . . . one Yank and they're down." So many English girls were getting pregnant by Americans that a British comic noted, "In the next war, you will only have to send the uniforms."[2]

In the week prior to Christmas, there was the usual physical training and assault practice. With the 190th Field Artillery Battalion nearby, the opportunity for the Rangers to practice infiltration and the artillerymen to practice security was at hand. The gunners were going on field maneuvers on December 20 and the Ranger S-2 (Intelligence) section tracked them, penetrated the security, and plotted the locations of several of the guns. On Christmas Eve, the 190th was still on their maneuver. Baker Company Rangers slipped through the artillery security, took breech blocks out of all the howitzers, and let the air out of the tires on the big guns. That was enough for the 190th commander, who promptly cancelled the joint exercise.

Christmas 1943 was for most men their first Christmas away from their homeland, and for all a Christmas away from family, wives, children, and other loved ones. The men of the battalion quickly formed a special relationship with the people of Bude, one that extended to the many children of the town. In their earliest days at Bude, the men of the battalion had decided to host a Christmas party for the local children. Living under Britain's wartime austerity program, the little ones seldom saw oranges or pineapples, cookies, gum, or candy. The men saved these items from their rations or from packages from home. A dance hall in Bude was obtained and decorated, complete with a Christmas tree. On Christmas Eve, the battalion hosted seven hundred children who gorged themselves on sweets, watched cartoons, and snuggled up to the big Rangers.

Three days after Christmas, the men of the battalion began to scatter by company, moving on various dates to various locations where they trained with British commandos.

The men of the battalion were now experts in many of the arts of destruction and death. Explosives were a specialty; they knew how to render an artillery piece ineffective, drop a bridge, or fell trees to block a road. They could cut telephone poles with explosive charges to sever communication. The pranksters among them delighted in constructing makeshift noise-making devices from the primer caps that were used to set off TNT charges. These homemade fireworks would be placed in a buddy's equipment or his bunk. It was a form of self-devised training and they became wary before they picked anything up.

Across the English Channel, other men worked feverishly as well. Though he boasted of an "Atlantic Wall," Adolf Hitler had expected that the German string of victories would continue, and men who garrisoned the defenses on the coast after the fall of France were sent east to the Russian front. Hitler's fighting generals knew the Allied buildup in England had purpose, but it was not until November 1943 that Hitler issued Directive 51, which gave priority to the defense in the west. Generalleutnant Wilhelm Richter wrote that "two years [1942 to 1944] had been lost during which time nothing or just simple field positions were constructed." Field Marshal Erwin Rommel was sent to inspect the defenses and his report was grim. Much needed to be done.

Before the work could be accomplished, the German High Command had to agree on a strategy. Keenly aware of Allied airpower and its ability to interdict reinforcements, Rommel wanted to fight it out on the beaches and said, "Either we repel the invasion within the first eight hours or the campaign in France is lost." Field Marshal Gerd Von Rundstedt felt that it was impossible to defend all the beaches of France. Von Rundstedt wanted to hold strong mobile forces away from the coast and counterattack at whatever point the invasion came. Von Rundstedt's position was "the invasion would have to be stopped by D plus 2 and five additional armored divisions with freedom of movement would be needed."[3]

Both views contained logic, but the strength of one was the weakness of the other. Adolf Hitler became involved and held four of the Panzer (armored) divisions under his own control while parceling out the rest. Rommel's strategy was adopted, leaving Von Rundstedt without a single tank division.

A successful amphibious invasion required three phases: lodgement, buildup, and breakout. The Americans, British, and Canadians studied their maps to determine the best places for landings, and the Germans did the same. The Nazis employed a large pool of construction workers called the Todt Organization under the leadership of Albert Speer. The group was named after Dr. Fritz Todt, the famed engineer who had designed and built the autobahn. Todt died in 1942, but by 1944 already more than 1.5 million workers began construction of formidable coastal defenses.

The cliffs, reefs, and tidal range of the Normandy coast greatly limited the number of areas suitable for a major amphibious assault. Studying their maps and engineering and reconnaissance reports, Allied planners selected a forty-mile stretch of coast with intermittent beaches. What would become known as "Omaha Beach" was about 7,500 yards of shore naturally formed into a slight crescent shape and fronted by a tidal flat that gently sloped landward. At low tide large stretches of beach from waters' edge to shore would be exposed to view. The British and Canadian beaches and the American Utah Beach were backed by terrain that was relatively flat. Behind Omaha Beach were bluffs with steep ascents reaching one hundred feet in height. The bluffs were near the beach and melded into cliffs on the distant flanks.

The German defenders also recognized that this beach was a possible landing site and began to plan countermeasures. The German defense was calculated on the attackers coming ashore at high tide. That assumption was based on the belief that from the attackers' viewpoint, a low-tide assault would require men to cross long stretches of up to three hundred yards of open beach before getting to the German positions. High tide would bring Allied troops closer to their objectives.

The German officer corps knew the trade of war. A high-tide landing allowed for a multitude of obstacles to be hidden beneath the water. Skilled military engineers supervised the placement of 3,700 obstacles on Omaha Beach. Steel beams were welded into hedgehogs and ramps and placed underwater to rip the hulls of landing craft. Trees were cut in the Foret de Cerisy, some twelve miles distant.

Because of fuel shortages, these were hauled by horses, sawed by hand, and dug into the beaches as waterproof mine-tipped obstacles to landing craft. Metal, concrete, and wood "dragons' teeth" were installed. The Germans laid 10,000 mines. Obstacles were often topped with antitank Tellermines. The *Schutzendosenmine,* called the "shoe mine" by the Americans, was a small antipersonnel mine shaped like a small box. These were designed to blow off the foot of the man who stepped on them. There were eighty-five German machine guns covering Omaha Beach. Many of the mine fields were sheltered by barbed wire intended to trap men, holding them beneath the death-dealing fires of fourteen pieces of artillery ranging from 37mm to 88mm and six mortar positions.[4] The bunkers and pillboxes were often sited to fire down the line of any units coming ashore and protected from observation and fire from the sea. Naval historian Samuel Eliot Morison wrote, "Altogether, the Germans had provided the best imitation of hell for an invading force that American troops had encountered anywhere. Even the Japanese defenses of Tarawa, Peleliu, and Iwo Jima are not to be compared with these."[5]

The German effort was not without problems. Allied bombings hampered the work. Tide silted the obstacles, requiring them to be dug out. April storms washed some obstacles away and wrecked others. Mines were ruined or exploded by water and had to be replaced. The work was endless and hampered by over-organization. Oberstleutnant Fritz Ziegelmann, chief of operations for the 352nd Division, wrote, "The Headquarters of the Air Forces, Navy, Todt Organization and fortress engineers worked parallel to each other, but often also in opposition." There was competition for supplies. Ziegleman gave, as example, the Luftwaffe building a radio-direction-finder station in concrete, while the infantry heavy-weapons crews that protected it had to settle for digging earthen positions in holes that encountered sub-soil water.[6]

Along the French coast from Gatteville to Le Havre, the Germans positioned batteries of captured artillery. The fixed German defenses in the so-called Atlantic Wall relied heavily on captured artillery, and eighteen batteries of primarily French and German with some Czech weaponry were employed. Seven of these batteries were 155mm French-made guns. Problems with ammunition and spare parts for the wide variety of guns existed but, as the guns were in a positional defense and the Germans intended to win at the beaches, ammunition could be stockpiled in advance.

Both German and Allied military planners saw the Pas-de-Calais area as the best spot for the invasion. Hitler believed the blow would fall in Normandy, with the port of Cherbourg as the prize. Hitler's generals pointed out that the Pas-de-Calais area was the shortest route for an invasion force coming from England, and there were good ports that, when captured, would serve as the funnel through which Allied supplies would pass. Though he ordered a build-up in Normandy, Hitler went along with his generals' decision that Calais was the best spot for the invasion. The German generals keyed their defense to Calais. The Allies went elsewhere.

As early as August 1943, the Allies made the decision to land in western Normandy at the base of the Cotentin Peninsula. The assault would unfold across a forty-mile front from the Orne River to beyond the Vire Estuary. Choosing the date was more complicated. The English Channel had a stormy reputation, tides differed over the broad front, and moonlight was required for the airborne operations. Despite differing conditions on American, British, and Canadian beaches, the landings had to be made at approximately the same time to avoid defeat in detail. Many options were considered, including landing in darkness and landing under cover of smoke; both of these choices were rejected because of control problems. Gen. Norman Cota, speaking at the Assault Training Center on June 2, 1943, referred to a concept of forming an assault division with Ranger battalions and attached support units hitting the beach first to establish the lodgement; then infantry and armor divisions would come as a follow-on force. However, this option was rejected. The 1st Infantry Division was the only combat-experienced unit the Americans had that was available for the invasion.

It was clear to Allied planners that there was no room for maneuver. This would be a frontal assault into fortified positions. To many officers who had studied the American Civil War, the situation was reminiscent of Burnside's assault at Fredericksburg, Pickett's at Gettysburg, and Hood's at Franklin, none of which were successful. Now the defenses were even more formidable and only the chill waters of the English Channel would be at the backs of the American soldiers.

American general Dwight D. Eisenhower assumed command of the Allied effort after the invasion site had been selected. Eisenhower made important changes—beefing up the available force to 2,876,000 men and increasing the number of assaulting divisions from five to nine. Forty-five divisions, 4,000 ships, and 12,000 aircraft were ready for use. The German generals, having fifty-eight divisions and 2,000 tanks available, felt confident they were equal to the challenge.

British general Bernard Law Montgomery planned the invasion. Montgomery was a master of the set-piece battle, approaching it like a chess master and thinking several moves ahead, he was careful to have each step well planned. The Allied Army would make the initial attack with nine divisions, going in over five beaches. The British and Canadians would attack on the Allied left over beaches named Gold, Sword, and Juno. On the right, the Americans using V and VII Corps would attack over beaches named Omaha (the Vierville-Colleville area) and Utah (the Madeleine area). The Western Naval Task Force would be composed of Assault Force "O" (Omaha), Assault Force "U" (Utah), and a follow-up Force "B," which would follow in Force "O" on Omaha Beach.

Gen. Omar Bradley would head the American land effort as commander of the U.S. First Army. His Navy counterpart was Adm. Alan Kirk, commander of the Western Task Force. General Bradley had Maj. Gen. J. Lawton Collins in command of VII Corps, heading the Army forces assaulting Utah Beach, with Rear Adm. D. P. Moon as his Navy counterpart. Maj. Gen. Leonard Gerow would command V Corps, assaulting Omaha Beach, and Adm. John L. Hall would head Assault Force O, with the mission of getting Gerow's men ashore in France and assisting them.

The Rangers were part of General Gerow's V Corps. Gerow had the mission of securing a Normandy beachhead between Port-en-Bessin and the Vire River. The initial American assault by Gerow's corps at Omaha Beach would begin at 0630 and cover a 6,000-yard-wide front between Vierville and Colleville. This assault would be made by Maj. Gen. Clarence Huebner's 1st Infantry Division which had battle experience in North Africa and Sicily. The 1st Division would be reinforced and have four infantry regiments beefed up by attachments of armor, artillery, and engineers to form Regimental Combat Teams (RCTs). In addition to its own 16th and 18th Infantry

RCTs, the 1st Infantry Division would have the 115th and 116th RCTs of Maj. Gen. Charles Gerhardt's 29th Infantry Division. General Huebner would command the assault. However, as the move inland was made and follow-on forces came in, he could quickly revert to command of his own 1st Division while General Gerhardt assumed command of his 29th Division. Thus unity of command would be maintained with a single division commander during the assault phase, but that would quickly flow into a two-division front. Huebner also had command of the Provisional Ranger Force (2nd and 5th Battalions). The follow-on force at Omaha (Force B) included the 2nd Infantry Division.

During the first week of March, Colonel Rudder became a "Bigot," that word being the code identification for those who were in the know about the invasion of Normandy. Rudder later said that when Gen. Omar Bradley told him what the battalion was expected to do, "I thought he was kidding." Bradley was not kidding. On March 15, Rudder and his S-2 officer, Capt. Harvey Cook, left for Plymouth, England. Secrecy precluded the troops from knowing the purpose of Rudder's absence, but they correctly speculated that Rudder was being briefed on what role the battalion would play when the bullets began to fly. Rudder and Cook were being provided with Bigot information on the enemy, weather, and terrain at the objective area as well as planning for the battalion mission.

Four miles to the west of Omaha Beach was a triangular point of land jutting into the English Channel called Pointe du Hoc, which was guarded by sandstone cliffs that ranged from sheer to overhanging and were 85 to 117 feet high. Beneath these cliffs, the beach was narrow, rocky and pounded by a relentless surf. At the top of the cliff, the land was flat as a table top, an ideal location to position artillery that could dominate the landing beaches.

On top of the point, in the closing months of 1943, the Germans began constructing a fortified coastal battery of six 155mm guns captured from the French. Though frequently called "howitzers" in U.S. Army reports, the artillery of Pointe du Hoc were not high-angle-of-fire howitzers, but long-barreled guns with a famed reputation. In World War I, the Germans were outreaching French artillery with their 150mm guns. To counteract this, the French had developed by 1917, and improved in 1918, the *Grande portee (GP)* Filloux, Saint-

Chamond 155mm (6.1-inch) gun. "GP" means "great range." Filloux was the designer, and Saint-Chamond was the manufacturer. Approximately twenty feet long, the gun and its carriage weighed some 26,000 pounds.

With the improved ammunition of World War II, the guns could throw a ninety-five-pound shell over a range of approximately twelve miles, covering the approaches to Omaha Beach and providing the ability to wreak havoc on the oncoming invaders. There was also sufficient range to disrupt the effort to land at Utah Beach. Located at First Army map coordinates 586938, the guns of Pointe du Hoc were in position and manned by the men of oberleutenant Brotkorb's 2nd Battery, 1260th Artillery Battalion. The battalion was commanded by Maj. Paul Fredrichs at Arromanches. The 1st Battery, also equipped with six French 155mm guns, was to the east at Riva-Bella. The 3rd Battery was at Mont Fleury with Russian guns. The 4th Battery at Longues to the east was a *Marine Kusten Batterie* (navy coastal battery) and had four Czech-made 150mm guns in a heavily fortified position. The battalion front covered 15.5 miles, and battalion headquarters was 19.3 miles from the guns at Pointe du Hoc, with communications primarily by landline.[7]

Though an Army Coast Artillery Battalion (*Heerskustenartillerie-abteilung*), the 1260th was part of a defense under the command of Adm. Theodor Krancke, who had command of both German army and navy batteries as long as they were firing on targets at sea. If the targets of the battalion were on land, control would revert to the army. Krancke had designated the word *Grosslandung* ("large landing") to be broadcast if the Allies came ashore. All German naval units were to attack, and coast artillery batteries were to engage.[8] The fight had to be won at the shoreline.

The guns of Pointe du Hoc were the only German battery that had the capability to reach offshore and strike the mother ships, destroy the incoming landing craft, and also wreak havoc on both Omaha and Utah Beaches. This unique ability made these guns critical to the German defense and their destruction vital to the success of the Allied invasion. In the Neptune plan for U.S. First Army, there were 330 enemy battery positions to be dealt with, and number one on the list were the guns of Pointe du Hoc.[9] So threatening was the Pointe du

Hoc battery that, to protect the transports from their fire, Admiral
Kirk decided to unload the troops eleven miles out at sea.[10]

Initially, the Germans intended to leave the six guns in open
emplacements which would give them a 360-degree range of fire.
Experience with Allied air power elsewhere prompted a change of
plans. Early in March, the Germans removed two guns from the open
positions and began to build casements. Hedging their bet, the Germans decided to leave guns 1 and 6 in open positions with an all-
around arc of fire. Because of the restriction of the protective walls of
reinforced concrete approximately nine feet wide, case-mated guns
would be able to traverse only 120 degrees. Guns 2 and 3 would be in
casemates facing at a 40-degree angle covering the Omaha Beach
approach while guns 4 and 5 would be in casemates facing at a 330-
degree angle covering Utah Beach.[11]

By March 8, 1944, photo-reconnaissance missions flown by twin-
boom P-38 aircraft revealed that work was moving forward to casemate two gun positions. Allied planners reasoned the work would
continue to protect the remaining four, so leaving nothing to chance,
they decided to attack the guns of Pointe du Hoc from the land, sea,
and air.

Pointe du Hoc had been designated as Air Force target number
4901W/J/101 and the junction of the Vierville/Grandcamp road and
a road leading to the gun positions selected as the main point of
impact (aiming point) for the bombs. Bad weather in mid-April
delayed bombing, but preliminary "softening-up" attacks on the
Pointe du Hoc battery began on April 25, 1944. Most of the work
would be done by 9th Air Force twin-engine medium (B-26) or light
(A-20) bombers. A total of forty-eight tons of bombs were dropped in
this attack.

To avoid revealing Allied intent, bombing attacks had to be scattered and made to seem part of a much broader program. For every
bombing mission flown against the invasion area, two such missions
were flown elsewhere. On May 22, the Ninth Air Force mediums
again carpeted Pointe du Hoc with bombs. This time it was the 323rd
Bomb Group of the 98th Bomb Wing that came in two boxes, each
consisting of sixteen B-26 aircraft. Fighter aircraft—a squadron of P-
38 Lightnings from the 367th Group—flew top cover as the first box

came over the target at 11,840 feet altitude. Each bomber was carrying two 2,000-pound bombs. Lt. Col. R. B. Pratt was at the controls of the lead plane, while the navigator-bombardier, 1st Lt. J. W. Price, peered through his bomb sight. All aircraft in the box would release their bombs when Price, the most experienced bombardier in the box, made his drop. Seeing the lead bomber drop its ordnance was the only signal that mattered.

The Air Force rated their strikes as good, fair, poor, or gross. Colonel Pratt rated the strike of his box as "fair." Most of the pilots were not cheered by their results, but Lieutenant Brown thought his bombs struck home near number 2 gun position. He was correct.

Oberstleutnant Fritz Ziegelmann wrote, "During these last days of May repeated bombing attacks were also made on the army coast battery on the Pont du Hoc (3rd Battery, 1260th) and the positions of the 3d Bn., 1716th A. Regt., causing the loss of half of the guns, as well as on the direction finder stations of the Air Force and the Navy. Therefore, these stations could only be used to a limited extent." On Pointe du Hoc, one of the gun positions was struck and the artillery piece disabled.[12]

Back in England, British commando planners worked with Rudder in the development of a plan to accomplish the land portion of the mission. Significant assistance was rendered by Lt. Col. T. H. Trevor, who had led Number 1 Commando and was an authority on cliff assaults. Trevor joined the planning effort in early December 1943, where his experience and ability were invaluable.

The initial concept was to land the Rangers at Omaha Beach in the second wave, move inland, then advance four to five miles along the coastline and attack the battery from the southeast landward side. That technique had been tried during an attack on the Pointe Matifou Battery at Algiers in North Africa and, though only light opposition was encountered, the overland move took too long to prevent the battery from engaging the invading force.

The planners next examined an approach from the opposite flank at Grandcamp, some two miles west of the battery, and attacking eastward toward the guns. Aerial photos revealed that the Germans were preparing defenses against an attack from the landward side against the battery. Near Grandcamp the Germans had flooded low areas, thus forcing an attacker to come over open terrain and up slopes into a "killing ground."

There were no beaches near Pointe du Hoc. The topography of the coast west of Omaha Beach to Grandcamp consisted of cliffs ninety to one hundred feet high. It became obvious to the planners that as attacks on the left and right were not feasible, the attack must be made in the center by way of climbing the cliffs. Aerial photos and intelligence reports revealed that the Germans felt the towering cliffs and the pounding sea were a natural defense against a seaward attack and the main thrust of their defense was against attack from inland. Still, the cliffs were not barren of defense and the attack would have to be made under fire. Some officers considered the mission suicidal. The Navy intelligence officer on Admiral Hall's staff said, "It can't be done. Three old women with brooms could keep the Rangers from climbing that cliff."[13]

The great advantage of going up the cliffs was that if 200 men could be put up the ropes these attackers would be on the objective and in position to quickly eliminate the guns before they could wreak havoc on Omaha and Utah Beaches. If the assaults were made up both the east and west side, the Rangers could attack in a pincer movement. The big "if" was making it up the ropes under enemy fire and then reducing the formidable defenses of the battery. In addition to the attack on the guns of Pointe du Hoc, Rudder was given a mission at Pointe de la Percee, overlooking Omaha Beach, three miles to the east. In the event the 1st Battalion, 116th Infantry, could not force the Vierville draw, Rangers would climb the nearby cliffs to flank the German positions there. To accomplish his mission, Colonel Rudder organized the two Ranger battalions into three elements designated Force A, B, and C. Force A and C would be used on Pointe du Hoc, and Force B, which consisted of Charlie Company, would attack Pointe de la Percee.

Force A would consist of Dog, Easy, and Fox Companies of the 2nd Ranger Battalion. They would be the assault force at Pointe du Hoc, landing within three minutes of the lifting of close support fire. Easy and Fox would land on the eastern (left) side of the Pointe and

Dog Company would land on the west. The three assault companies would then climb the cliffs. Dog Company had the mission of destroying the three western guns, numbers 4, 5, and 6. Easy Company would eliminate the observation post and gun 3, and Fox Company would destroy guns 1 and 2. After the guns were eliminated the three companies would assemble while one platoon of Easy would remain on the Pointe to serve as security for the Headquarters group. Dog, Fox, and the remainder of Easy Company would then move about 1,000 yards inland to the coastal highway, cross it and set up a blocking position on this main German line of communication between Grandcamp-Isigny and Vierville, holding it until linkup with the 116th Infantry of the 29th Division was accomplished. If the attack on the Pointe was successful, the message "Praise the Lord" would be sent. If the attack failed, a message clear to a generation of pinball machine players would be sent: "Tilt."

Force C would comprise Able and Baker Companies and some Headquarters elements of the 2nd Ranger Battalion and the Ranger Group, and all of Max Schneider's 5th Ranger Battalion. If the initial assault on Pointe du Hoc was successful and they heard "Praise the Lord," Force C would land at Pointe du Hoc and follow up the cliffs.

If the assault failed and the guns were not eliminated by H-hour plus 30 minutes (0700), Able and Baker Companies of the 2nd Battalion would land at H plus 60 minutes (0730) and the 5th Ranger Battalion five minutes later in the eighth and ninth waves going in on Dog Green Omaha Beach. Using Able and Baker Companies of the 2nd as front and flank security and keeping the 5th Ranger Battalion intact, Force C would then move overland to Pointe du Hoc to destroy the guns.

To the German planners, climbing the cliffs to attack the guns was an impossible mission. The Rangers were intent on proving them wrong.

The U.S. Army understood that history would be in the making and wanted the lessons to be recorded. Teams of skilled historians from the War Department Historical Branch were sent to England. The men on these teams came from the history chairs of America's leading universities. Lt. Col. Charles Taylor, executive officer of the historical branch, had been professor of medieval history at Harvard University. Taylor would record the Ranger actions during the invasion of Normandy. Taylor's assistant was Sgt. Forrest Pogue, who had a Ph.D. in history, had studied in Paris, and was skilled in French. Pogue would record much information on Omaha Beach.

The Allied invasion would fall upon that portion of the French coast defended by the German 84th Corps under Generaloberst Freidrich Dollman, whose headquarters was at le Mans in Normandy. Dollman had seven infantry divisions and three Panzer (armored) divisions to defend or have available to reinforce the French coast from the Orne River to the northeast corner of Brittany. When the Rangers went ashore to eliminate the guns of Pointe du Hoc, they would encounter elements of two German divisions, the 352nd and the 716th.

Initially, Generalleutnant Wilhelm Richter's 716th Infantry Division was thinly spread, responsible for defending thirty miles of the French coastline from the Vire to the Orne Rivers. This unit had been in Normandy since 1941 and many of its best men had been sent to fight in Russia. The 716th contained a high percentage of foreign nationals, some of whom joined voluntarily and others who were conscripted. At the height of Nazi power, Hitler's spokesmen preached the doctrine of a united Europe led by Germany. They enrolled over 100,000 men from Spain, Holland, Norway, Belgium, and France in western Europe. In the east, men from countries oppressed by the Soviet Union joined the German army. Large numbers of Cossacks volunteered and nearly 100,000 from Ukraine. Georgia, Finland, Latvia, Lithuania, Estonia, Rumania, Bulgaria, and Poland also volunteered. Both the SS and the Wehrmacht had battalions, regiments, and even divisions of men who were not German. Many joined from hatred of the Soviet Union. By 1944 whatever luster these men had seen in the German cause had dulled. From eastern or western Europe, for most of these men, the primary motivation for fighting was fear of what would happen to them if they lost the war and survived it.

Many of the German-born soldiers in the 716th were considered elderly by infantry standards. A thirty-year-old rifleman is known as "Pop" in an infantry platoon, but elderly German soldiers had been trained well. In the 1920s, Gen. Hans von Seeckt had the mission of building a German Army under the stern restrictions of the Versailles Treaty of World War I. The Germans have a great love for the outdoors. From 1933 onward, German children joined the *Jungvolk* similar to the American or British scouting movement, but with military overtones. Step by step the young progressed through the Hitler Youth and Labor Corps with their final destination the military services. Meanwhile, under the Versailles restrictions, Seeckt developed a concept by which every rifle company could provide the leadership for a regiment. Every man was trained to assume duties several ranks above them when mobilization came. Combat arms officers were not only expected to be courageous, but to repeatedly demonstrate that courage in battle. By June of 1944, the German Army had been at war for nearly five years and knew the work. In Germany the soldier was honored, patriotism and courage were revered, and initiative in battle expected. It is myth that the German soldier was an automaton. German troop leadership—*Truppenführung*—taught that "simple actions logically carried out will lead most surely to the objective." Furthermore, the first criterion in war remains decisive action. Everyone, from the highest commander down to the youngest soldier, must constantly be aware that "inaction or neglect incriminate him more severely than any error in choice of means."[14]

In October of 1943, the German Army suffered severe defeats on the southern front in Russia. These losses forced a reorganization of German infantry divisions in France and Belgium. The depleted 321st Infantry Division was sent to the area of St. Lô in France. Recruits, many of whom were seventeen and eighteen years old, arrived and the 321st with similar remnants of the 258th Infantry Division and the 546th Grenadier Regiment were reconstituted as the 352nd Infantry Division. The 352nd had as its symbol a white shield trimmed in red featuring a black horse leaping a black hurdle. In the upper lefthand corner of the shield was the number 352. The shield was not worn as a shoulder or helmet insignia but was used on some vehicles and tactical signs. The division was commanded by Generalleutnant Dietrich Kraiss who had commanded a division on the Russian front. Though its home station was designated as Hanover, Germany, and many of the new recruits came from that region, for all practical purposes the 352nd was born in France.

Oberstleutnant Fritz Ziegelmann, chief operations officer of the 352nd, noted that about 50 percent of the officers of the new division had seen battle in the east. Training was hampered by shortages of equipment, ammunition, fuel and food. The weakened physical condition of the young recruits showed that the war was taking its toll on the German food supply. Milk was needed, but could not be obtained through supply channels. Zeigelmann credited local French farmers for selling milk to the Germans.[15]

The 352nd was a 1944-type division consisting of about 12,000 men, including about 1,500 auxiliary volunteers (*Hiwis*) from the domains of the Soviet Union. The three grenadier (infantry) regiments were the 914th led by Oberstleutnant Ernst Heyna, the 915th under Oberstleutnant Ernst Myers, who would be killed in action, and the 916th commanded by Oberst Ernst Goth. Each regiment had two grenadier battalions, and each battalion had four numbered companies, 1 to 4 for the 1st Battalion, 5 to 8 for the 2nd Battalion. The division was organized into combined-arms teams called *Kampfgruppe*, each containing one grenadier regiment, one artillery battalion, one pioneer (engineer) company with elements of signal and supply, and command and control elements from division headquarters. It was planned that four of the grenadier battalions would be equipped with bicycles.

By March 1, 1944, the 352nd was filled out in personnel and equipment. Having no specific orders as to destination, the 352nd had trained to fight on the Eastern Front. Oberstleutnant Ziegelmann was not satisfied with the division's state of training, which was still at the small-unit level and had not reached the level of exercises as battalions and regiments. His complaints in monthly reports to his seniors were ignored. Ziegelmann wrote, "As general staff officer, one had the impression that the highest authorities had no other concern but to be able to report at the earliest time that another division brought up to full strength was available."

On March 15, 1944, 84th Corps ordered the 352nd forward to the coast, thus bringing more troops into the crust of the German defense of the beaches. The frontage of the 716th was shortened with the result that the majority of their defense would be on beaches that the British intended to attack. One regiment of the 716th Infantry Division—the 726th Grenadier Regiment less its 2nd Battalion—

would come under operational control of the 352nd Infantry Division and remain in position to occupy coastal installations and form small counterattack contingents in the area that would become known as Omaha Beach.

Allied intelligence failed to discover the move of the 352nd to the coast and continued planning under the impression that this powerful division was twenty miles inland in the vicinity of St. Lô. The Allies did not know until hours before the invasion that one of the best divisions in the German Army had moved to the Normandy coast—by then it was too late to change the plans. The Germans believed French resistance forces tried to get the message through by carrier pigeon, but the Germans were well aware of that technique and shot pigeons along the entire coast. A soldier of the 716th was credited with using a shotgun to bring down two birds carrying the message of the move of the 352nd.[16]

Work on the German defenses proceeded with maximum energy. Oberstleutnant Ziegelmann noted that on average the German soldier worked nine hours daily on the defenses and spent three hours in training. The frenetic pace wore down the physical strength of the men.

Believing that the Allies would not attack Pointe du Hoc from the sea, the Germans stationed approximately eighty-five men of Oberleutnant Brotkorb's 2nd Battery, 1260th Artillery Battalion, to man the battery and 125 infantry of Oberst Korfes's 726th Grenadier Regiment to protect it. The primary orientation of the infantry was to prevent an attack from the landward side. The inland defense included barbed wire and minefields that were by covered by machine gun fire and a 20mm antiaircraft gun position. Two additional 20mm antiaircraft guns were placed on the flanks of Pointe du Hoc as well as several machine guns. The antiaircraft (flak) gun crew consisted of Air Force personnel and, as part of Herman Goering's Luftwaffe, was somewhat aloof from the army. With the exception of those manning cliff-side machine-gun positions, most of the German infantry was inland. Having made the decision that the cliff of Pointe du Hoc would not be climbed, the thorough German planners hedged their thinking by rigging 200mm or larger ready-to-explode shells from naval guns on the sides of the cliff. A tug on a pull-type firing device would ignite a short fuse to send the cliff wall crashing down on those below.

The observation post and critical ranging equipment were manned by artillery men and men of the Luftwaffe and German Navy. New ranging equipment was secured for the battery, but it was too large to place in the completed observation post so it was moved to a 20mm antiaircraft emplacement to the west. As the Germans had planned to keep the gun battery on Pointe du Hoc, they provided well-protected underground quarters there for the artillerymen. These and all positions on Pointe du Hoc were connected by trenches and tunnels.

To the eastern rear of Pointe du Hoc was the town of Vierville and farther west in the Omaha Beach sector was the town of Grandcamp. This area was defended by elements of the 726th Infantry Regiment minus one battalion. An inland road passed behind Pointe du Hoc and continued behind Omaha Beach westward past the operational boundary between the U.S. First and the British Second Armies. After destroying the guns, blocking this road would serve as an easily identifiable objective for the Rangers.

To improve the odds of success, Allied heavy and medium bombers were let loose on the German defenders. The Germans called the fighter-bombers that pounded them from the air *Jagdbombers* and nicknamed them *Jabos*. The Typhoons of the British and Canadians and the P-47 Thunderbolts of the Americans were especially dreaded. American fighter aircraft were known to attack even a single soldier on the ground.

The April and May bombings brought home the strength of Allied airpower to the defenders of Normandy. Four batteries along the coast seemed to be most exposed. One of the guns of Pointe du Hoc was disabled by bombing, so the Germans decided to move the guns to alternate locations. For the 2nd Battery, 1260th Artillery, on Pointe du Hoc, this created a major problem as they possessed only one tractor to move their five remaining heavy (10–14 ton) guns. These were taken inland, a French farmer recalling three of the guns being moved past his house in one night.[17]

Because of the difficulty of turning the heavy guns around, the Germans were faced with deciding where to point the guns. Should they face east toward the beach that the Americans would call Omaha, or west toward what would become Utah Beach? German planners recognized that the Allies needed a significant port to effect a buildup of forces. A landing in the Vire River area west of Pointe du Hoc would facilitate the capture of the harbor and port city of Cherbourg. So they decided the western beaches (Utah) needed first priority. The guns were well sited to do ranging fires in the Vire estuary while an alternate fire plan was being developed for Omaha.

Experts in deception, the Germans constructed false guns of telephone poles on Pointe du Hoc to hide the removal of the 155mms. Allied intelligence had some indication that the guns had been moved, but they could not find the new location, and it appeared from aerial photo reconnaissance that they were still in position on the Pointe.

Unaware of these changes, the honing and recruiting process of the battalion continued as officers were transferred to other units and new officers joined the battalion. Capt. Edgar L. Arnold was recruited by Max Schneider. The two men had known each other since high-school days in Shenandoah, Iowa. Arnold took command of Baker Company.

Unlike the Rangers of the 1st, 3rd, and 4th Battalions who had a British chaplain, the 2nd and 5th obtained an American chaplain from an artillery unit. Father Lacy was a short, rotund, Roman Catholic priest from Boston, Massachusetts. Ivor Jones described Lacy as "one magnificent human being. He took care of Catholics, Protestants, Jews, and Arabs."

Bill Darby, famed founding leader of the 1st Ranger Battalion, was a redleg artilleryman who had to have his cannon. El Darbo's four 75mm guns mounted on half-tracks were named after the aces in a deck of cards and had done yeoman service for the 1st Ranger Battalion at the Chiunzi Pass in Italy. Rudder had long wanted to fill out his Table of Organization and Equipment with a cannon section of his own, and on March 4, 1944, he got his wish. Seventeen enlisted men who knew the half-track and were trained on the 75mm gun came to the Rangers from the 3rd and 5th Armored Divisions.

On March 26, Maj. Max Schneider left the battalion to become commander of the 5th Ranger Battalion. Capt. Cleveland Lytle was appointed battalion executive officer in his place. The last three days of March 1944 were given over to a battalion exercise to test the ability of the companies to work as a team, the ability of the staff to coordinate activities, and Headquarters Company to support them. Carrying full equipment, the men marched forty miles cross country, frequently deploying to attack, while other forces sought to ambush or delay the movement.

Communications officer Ike Eikner welcomed Capt. Jonathan H. Harwood of the Army and Lt. P. C. Johnson and Lt. Kenneth Norton of the Navy. These officers and twenty-three enlisted men who came from the 293rd Joint Assault Signal Battalion formed the shore-fire control party. They and the destroyer USS *Satterlee* would train with the Rangers during amphibious exercises. A forward observer from the 58th Armored Field Artillery, 1st Lt. Carl M. Johnstone, was also attached to the battalion. The 58th was a half-track-mounted 105mm howitzer battalion with the mission of providing direct support to the 116th Infantry, to whom the Rangers were attached. The 58th Artillery had seen service in North Africa and Sicily. These soldiers were experienced gunners who had trained with the Navy. They had the knowledge and the equipment to communicate from shore to ship and adjust naval gunfire support.

April 1, 1944, was the first birthday of the battalion. The enlisted men put on a comedy skit in which they parodied the events of the last year and their leaders. It was all taken in good grace. Big Jim Rudder proved he could laugh at himself, and Capt. Cleveland Lytle made a short speech in which he said, "Characters! Brother, we got 'em." The word "characters" became part of the battalion lore, a title the men cherished.

Three days into April, the battalion left Bude for the Braunton Assault Course in North Devon County and south of the Bristol Channel. To many it was the hardest week of training they were to endure. Each company was divided into two thirty-man teams. Working under the critical eye of British commando instructors, the men practiced breaching barbed wire defenses and using shaped charges and flame-throwers to destroy bunkers.

The final test was at Baggy Point, a promontory on which the British had duplicated the German fortification and trench system of the French coast. Under supporting fire, the Rangers were required to go up the cliffs and eliminate the defenses. Rudder was delighted with the performance of his cannon section led by Lt. Conway Epperson and Lt. Frank Kennard, as their men put 75mm rounds through the pillbox view slits at 1,000 yards.

Rudder had made decisions on how to employ the companies to accomplish his D-Day mission, and the training began to reflect those decisions. On April 9, Dog, Easy, and Fox Companies, under the command of Capt. Duke Slater, took a train to Swanage on the west coast of the Isle of Wight. There on the high cliffs of Alum Bay and the adjoining Needles, the men were introduced to a wide variety of cliff-assault equipment. They practiced ascending the cliffs by free-rope climb, toggle rope, and various types of ladders.

They practiced with a specially equipped mortar that would fire a rope and grapnel up and over a cliff 200 feet high. The grapnel was effective at digging into an assortment of surfaces and provided the rope stability for the men to make the climb. They practiced using steel ladders which came in four-foot sections and linked together in building-block fashion to the desired height. There were rope ladders and smooth ropes. Men were often hurt when they undertook these dangerous cliff-climbing experiences. On an eighty-foot cliff, Ranger Glen Sacha of Dog Company was nearing the top when a man climbing above him loosened a large rock. Although Sacha was wearing a steel helmet, the rock struck him directly on his head and smashed the rifle he had slung on his back. Torn from the rope, Sacha plummeted more than sixty feet into the sea below. When he was pulled from the water, he was unconscious. Critically injured, he was rushed to a hospital where his life was saved, but he would not return to his company. A new arrival who was seen going through Sacha's pockets was fortunate to escape with his life and was immediately dismissed from the battalion.

Climbing and rappelling the faces of cliffs had become routine. In Easy Company, Duncan Daugherty stood with his back to the edge of an eighty-foot high sloping cliff while he lustily complained to his comrades that he should have joined the paratroops instead of the Rangers. "We have to walk to our objective while paratroopers fly," said Daugherty. "We have to climb cliffs. All they have to do is stand with their backs to the open door of the aircraft, lift their helmets in farewell, and step backward." Carried away by the force of his logic,

Daugherty stepped backward and disappeared from view. Rushing cliffside his horrified friends saw him rolling and bouncing en route to the beach far below. Although the men believed the fall would injure or kill him, Daugherty managed to snag enough brush and stone on the way down to complete his impromptu journey sitting on the sand. Daugherty looked upward at the anxious faces of his friends and shouted, "Watch that first step. It's a bitch!"

The M1919A4 light machine guns were proving troublesome in cliff climbing. At Swanage the company replaced many of their machine guns with Browning automatic rifles. Though heavy, the BAR could be taken up a rope or rope ladder by one man and quickly put into action.

Meanwhile, Pointe du Hoc had been designated as Air Force target number 4901W/J/101 and the junction of the Vierville/Grand-camp road and a road leading to the gun positions selected as the main point of impact (aiming point) for the bombs. Bad weather in mid-April delayed bombing but preliminary "softening-up" attacks on the Pointe du Hoc battery began on April 25, 1944. Most of the work would be done by Ninth Air Force twin-engine medium (B-26) or light (A-20) bombers. The medium B-26 bomber could carry 4,000 pounds of bombs, and the light bomber A-20 could accommodate 2,000 pounds.

While Dog, Easy, and Fox trained in cliff climbing, Able, Baker, and Charlie were on the water practicing over-the-beach assaults with the 5th Ranger Battalion. All company commanders now knew their missions, and the training was geared to the invasion of Normandy. On April 27, Able, Baker, and Charlie were trucked to Staging Area D-1 near Dorchester in the County of Dorset, beside the English Channel. The companies of the battalion were assembled to participate in a pre-invasion exercise code-named "Fabius I." Designed to rehearse and test Assault Force "O," the Fabius I troop list included the V Corps assault troops from the 1st and 29th Infantry Divisions, the supporting engineers and attached units including independent tank battalions and Rangers. Over 20,000 men were involved.

As it was the mission of both the 2nd and 5th Ranger Battalions to destroy the guns of Pointe du Hoc, a command structure that unified the efforts of the two battalions was needed. On May 9, 1944, a Provisional Ranger Group Headquarters was activated, commanded by

Lieutenant Colonel Rudder. Maj. Richard Sullivan of the 5th Battalion would serve as executive officer. The Provisional Ranger Group staff was drawn from officers of both battalions but did not move as a team until loading out for the invasion. Within the Provisional Ranger Group the two battalions operated in conjunction but independently. Group Headquarters was scarcely noticeable to the men in ranks. While the plans were honed, the assault companies of both battalions continued to train.

One of the more unique aspects of their training was in the DUKW, a $2\frac{1}{2}$-ton amphibious truck. These were mounted with 100-foot power ladders "borrowed" from the London Fire Department by some very persuasive British commando officers.

The vehicle could come in from the sea, adjust the inflation of its tires to the beach, park on the beach, set four jacks, and run its power ladder up the cliff. The ladder was not just for climbing. Two Vickers machine guns were mounted at the top with extra drums of ammunition. Every third round was a fiery tracer allowing the gunner to see the strike of the bullets. The gunner was partially protected by a shield of half-inch steel plate and wore a belt which held him to the ladder. Since both machine guns could be fired simultaneously, a considerable amount of firepower could be delivered. The gunner would ride the ladder up and open fire when he reached the top of the cliff. Ike Eikner developed a throat microphone that allowed the gunner to communicate by radio, freeing his hands to operate the machine guns.

Two of the vehicles would be brought together. Their ladders extended 100 feet in the air and touched each other in an inverted V. Every man in the 2nd and 5th Ranger Battalion would climb one ladder to the top, swing over to the other ladder, and descend. This was done with full equipment, including 81mm mortar base plates and tubes. John Raaen recalled "the tops of the ladders swung in the wind. To cross over from one to the other you had to wait for the ladders to swing close enough to cross." Raaen felt the ladders could swing fifteen feet apart and the experience was frightening.

Each DUKW had a seven-man crew consisting of a driver, ladder operator, gunner, and four jack men. Each of the cliff assault companies, Dog, Easy, and Fox, provided the men to operate one DUKW. A fourth vehicle had a crew from the various companies. When all four vehicles were assigned, the men named them Swan I, II, III, and IV.

The Rangers were as ready as they would ever be. Weapons and equipment were checked and double checked. The steel helmets of the battalion had at horizontal orange diamond (lozenge) painted on the rear with the number 2 in the center. The 5th Ranger Battalion had the same orange lozenge but with the number 5. Officers had a vertical white bar superimposed over the lozenge while noncommissioned officers wore a horizontal white bar.

All passes were stopped, the camps were sealed, and intelligence and operational briefings were intensified. The men knew where they were going and what they would be facing. They studied maps, aerial photographs, and sand table and rubber mockups of the terrain. They knew the sign and countersign when challenging someone coming into their position. They knew the type of artillery they were going to find and how to destroy it. They knew the German soldier and how to use his equipment and weapons. They knew the tides, the beaches, the cliffs, and the locations of minefields. Each man understood his individual mission and that of his buddy. They knew the mission of the squad, section, platoon, company, and battalion and that of the 116th Infantry. Ranger Morris Prince of Able Company wrote, "We became so familiar with the terrain that every man could have maneuvered over this land blindfolded, although never having seen that piece of ground." Oberstleutnant Fritz Ziegelmann of the 352nd would note at the end of the first day of battle that the Americans had "good maps, sketches and views of the field of view of the attacker."[18]

During their limited remaining free time, many men wrote letters, and each of these had to be censored by an officer to be certain no classified information was revealed. S/Sgt. Lawrence Johnson knew a girl who had moved to Paris before the war and felt that in some unknown fashion mail would get through to her. Johnson wrote a letter making a date to see the girl in late June. Lt. George Kerchner censored the letter and refused to let the letter pass as written. He returned the letter to Johnson, telling him to delay the mail until after the Rangers were in France.

Each man was issued twenty dollars in French francs for use in case of emergency. The dice and card games began. In Fox Company, T/5 Charles Vella was the ultimate winner with dice, capturing over $1,200 in French currency. This amount was more than he had ever seen in his life. There was no room for Vella's funds in the light combat packs which the men would carry ashore, so Vella packed his money in the larger backup packs that would be brought ashore later with Sgt. Regis McCloskey's ammunition boat.

PFC George "Bill" Mackey of Easy Company took a different approach with his winnings, giving it to his friends PFC Paul Medeires and PFC William Bell. The two men protested, but Mackey had a premonition of death and said, "No, I won't be needing it. You fellows have a drink on me when you reach Paris."[19]

When it came time to dress for the invasion, much latitude was granted. Often this was done after the company talked it over. Some men wore the Ranger diamond insignia on their uniforms and some did not. Some officers left their helmet rank insignia painted in white while others painted it in black or covered the rank with mud. Few wore assault vests. Some reported wearing khaki uniforms and field jackets. Many spoke of clothing impregnated against chemicals. This clothing was discarded as soon as possible once in battle. The Rangers were also authorized to wear Corcoran jump boots. To the airborne soldier, this was heresy. The Corcoran was the mark of those who went into battle by air. When it came to the Rangers, however, a few fights settled the issue and the Rangers kept their jump boots. As for their weapons, no one covered them with pliofilm (a plastic-like covering), as was done in some following waves. The men knew that in the assault they would not have time to remove the coverings.

On June 3, 1944, the men of the battalion left Area D-5. Singing en route, they were trucked down by the sea at the Weymouth Esplanade to board their landing craft. Dismounting, they marched along the quay. Able Company led the battalion in a column of twos.

In the 1920s and 1930s, there was a popular writer of romantic historical fiction named Rafael Sabatini. His novels were full of flashing swords and daring. One of his biggest hits was *Scaramouche*, the opening lines of which were: "He was born with the gift of laughter and the sense that the world was mad." Those words could well have been written as a description of Ranger Bob Edlin of Able Company. As they marched, Edlin counted cadence to keep his men in step. He noticed that Rudder, his mind on other things, was not in step with the rest of the men. Edlin decided to have some fun.

In Army lingo, Edlin knew he would have his "butt in the wringer" if he yelled, "Hey colonel, you're out of step!" so he used the old soldiers' trick of "everybody but!" In his best command voice, Lieutenant Edlin ordered, "Everybody but Colonel Rudder . . . change step, HARCH!" The command was executed flawlessly, but the men knew the reason and laughed. Everyone, including Big Jim Rudder, enjoyed it.

LCAs (Landing Craft, Assault) were waiting dockside to take the men to the mother ships. At Weymouth, Edlin boarded LCA 626 and was recorded as the first man to board a landing craft for the invasion of Europe.

Commander Stratford Dennis, Royal Navy, was captain of HMS *Prince Charles* and commander of Assault Group 0-4 homebased in Portland. Dennis had the responsibility of taking the Rangers to the debarkation area ships designated LSI (Landing Ship, Infantry) and of getting them ashore in his assault flotillas of LCAs. Able, Baker, and Charlie Companies, with some Headquarters personnel, boarded *Prince Charles* whose Assault Flotilla 501 used LCAs numbered 401, 418, 421, 441, 458, 626, 750, and 1038. Dog Company with one platoon of Easy were on the SS *Amsterdam*, Assault Flotilla 522 with LCA numbers 668, 858, 860, 861, 862, and 914. Fox Company with the other Easy Company platoon and headquarters personnel boarded the SS *Ben My Chree* (Manx for "girl of my heart"), Assault Flotilla 520 with LCA numbers 722, 883, 884, 887, 888, and 1003. All battalion vehicles, including the ladder carrying DUKWs and 75mm cannon-mounted half-tracks of the cannon platoon, were on Landing Craft, Tanks (LCTs). The 5th Ranger Battalion boarded HMS *Prince Leopold*, Assault Flotilla 504 with LCAs 550, 568, 570, 571, 622, 623, and 1045, HMS *Prince Baudouin* with Assault Flotilla 507 with LCAs 521, 554, 577, 578, 670, 863, and 1377, and SS *Princess Maud* with Assault Flotilla 519 and LCAs 649, 662, 837, 843, 857, and 882. The *Maud* was a reserve ship, and its six boats were to be used to replace any other LCA in Assault Force 04 that might become disabled before the LCAs departed for the assault. None of *Maud's* boats were needed by the Rangers, so they were shifted to the *Empire Javelin* to carry elements of the 1st Battalion, 116th Infantry. Of the forty LCAs that would head toward Normandy in these flotillas, eleven would be lost in action, eight from the 2nd Ranger Battalion ships, and three from the ships of the 5th Ranger Battalion.

The invasion was scheduled for June 5, since that was a date when low tide came soon after dawn and, after a night with a full moon, would assist an airborne landing. It was critical to come into the

beaches in daylight when the vast number of craft could avoid colli-
sion, and the coxswains could see the exposed obstacles. The rising
tide of approximately a yard per minute would float free any stranded
landing craft. It was all carefully thought out, but bad weather
forced postponement. June 6 would be the date remembered in
history.

While the Rangers boarded their ships, the bombers continued to
attack. On June 4, forty-two Havocs, twin-engine light bombers of the
409th and 416th Bomb Groups of the 97th Bomb Wing, struck Pointe
du Hoc. Unfortunately, with the guns already moved, the bombing
had little effect.

On June 5 at 1630 hours, the battalion sailed for war. There was
plenty of time for introspection. Assault Squad Leader Sgt. L-Rod
Petty gave considerable thought about leadership. Petty had reached
twenty-two years of age in May 1944. He was only three or four years
older than the men of his squad, but overcoming the hardships of his
life had given him maturity and confidence. When he snarled at his
men about something they did wrong, it was in the hope of saving
their lives.

PFC Garness Colden asked to talk privately with Petty. Standing by
the ship's railing the night before the great invasion, Colden revealed
that he had a premonition that he would be killed in battle. His concern was for his father whom he loved deeply. Petty, who hated the
sire who had so mistreated him, could only marvel at such love
between a father and a son. He promised Colden that if he survived
and Colden did not, he would visit the young soldier's father and tell
him of the love his son carried unto death. The two men shook hands
on it.

Father Lacy held an all faiths prayer service. "Tonight I want you
all to pray—but tomorrow I will do all the praying for you. What you
will be doing is a prayer in itself, and you won't have time to spend on
your knees."[20]

Maj. Cleveland A. Lytle, however, thought they would need more
than prayer. Assigned by Rudder to lead Dog, Easy, and Fox Companies in their assault on Pointe du Hoc, Lytle felt the attack on Pointe
du Hoc was suicidal and unnecessary. He'd heard rumors that the
French resistance had reported the guns had been moved.[21]

On the *Ben My Chree* the night of June 5, a group of officers got together to celebrate Joe Rafferty's shipboard promotion to captain. Rafferty had replaced Cleveland Lytle as Able Company commander so Lytle was present as well. Whiskey had found its way aboard or was obtained from the ship's officers. As the alcohol took hold, Major Lytle began to loudly condemn the mission. When the medical officer Capt. Walter Block tried to restrain him, Lytle punched Block. Several officers were needed to restrain Lytle as he was taken below. Colonel Rudder relieved Lytle of command of Force A.

With Lytle gone, Rudder had a serious problem. Lytle's role could not be assigned to one of the company commanders as they had their own units to lead. Rudder's responsibility was for both the 2nd and the 5th Ranger Battalions, and his proper station was wherever he could best control and support the actions of both. He had planned to go ashore with Max Schneider and Force C.

Now, Rudder would personally lead the attack of Dog, Easy, and Fox Companies on Pointe du Hoc. As a result, when the action began, he would be out of communication with the command ship *Ancon* or with Col. Charles D. W. Canham, the commander of the 116th Infantry, to which the Rangers were attached. He would be unable to coordinate the actions of all parts of his force and to look after the needs of all of the Rangers for fire support and ammunition.

Bob Edlin was kind to Lytle in his memoir, *The Fool Lieutenant*, and "figured . . . the Lord made it happen the way it did." It should be noted that no one believed that Maj. Cleveland Lytle was a coward. In fact, he would later prove himself in battle by winning a Distinguished Service Cross with the 90th Infantry Division. However, on June 6, 1944, Lytle would not go ashore.

As the Rangers dealt with this eleventh-hour command change, vast fleets of Allied aircraft took wing with two thousand fighter planes from 171 American, British, and Canadian squadrons and 1,400 transport aircraft (including gliders) lifting the American 82nd and 101st and the British 6th Airborne Divisions toward their objectives.

An additional 1,333 heavy bombers and 800 medium bombers filled the night sky to attack targets from the mouth of the Seine to Cherbourg. The mission of the heavy bombers was to eliminate German gun batteries covering the American and British beaches, including the guns of Pointe du Hoc. The RAF after-action report noted, "The St. Pierre (Pointe du Hoc) battery was considered the most dangerous of all."[22]

Naval gunfire in the V Corps zone was scheduled to begin at 0550 hours and be lifted three minutes prior to the troop landing. It would be provided by the battleships *Arkansas* and *Texas*, three cruisers, eight destroyers, and a great number of smaller craft, 40mm gun and rocket ships. Everything that could fire from the sea, including tanks and artillery heading for shore, were positioned to fire en route to the beach. The hope was that surviving Germans would be hindered from using fighting positions during the invasion.

The *Arkansas*, two French light cruisers, and destroyers would fire on the eastern Omaha beaches in support of the 1st Infantry Division. Of great interest to the Rangers was the 27,000-ton battleship *Texas*. Commissioned March 12, 1914, it had served largely on convoy duty in World War I and in 1942 had supported the North African campaign. Among its armament the *Texas* carried ten 14-inch guns and twenty-one 5-inch guns. If all went well, the *Texas* might save the Rangers a lot of pain and suffering.

The skill of American, British, Canadian, and other Allied seamen was tested and not found wanting in the cross channel movement as some 5,000 vessels of varying size proceeded through the darkness toward their assigned position. *Texas* was led by destroyers and the British cruiser *Glasgow*. By 0300 hours on June 6, 1944, Capt. C. A. Baker, USN commander of the *Texas*, had his ship in position and anchored 11.8 miles from the coast awaiting dawn. At 0424 the *Texas* heaved anchor and moved to the bombardment area 12,000 yards off shore. By 0530 she was anchored, her port (left) side to the beach, and great batteries prepared to fire. In addition to fire-control parties on the beach, the *Texas* had seventeen American naval pilots flying British Spitfire aircraft to locate targets, adjust fire, and assess battle damage.

The sleek destroyers prowling the flanks and standing close to shore were part of Desron (Destroyer Squadron) 18, commanded by Capt. Harry Sanders, USN. Those destroyers most important to the Rangers were under the command of Sanders's deputy, Cmdr. W. J. Marshall, who led Destroyer Division 36, including HMS *Talybont* and the USS *Satterlee, Harding, Barton, Thompson,* and *O'Brien.* Commander Marshall was initially aboard the *Satterlee.* Had the captains of some of these destroyers laid their hands on the signal officer who gave them their radio call signs, they likely would have strangled him. *Satterlee* was "Wimpy," *Harding* was "Cookie," and *Thompson* was "Dagwood." Only *Barton* as "Big Boy" and *O'Brien* as "Irish" had radio call signs fitting for a warrior. Regardless of their designations, the blazing guns of these American warships were about to enter history in the waters off Omaha Beach and Pointe du Hoc.

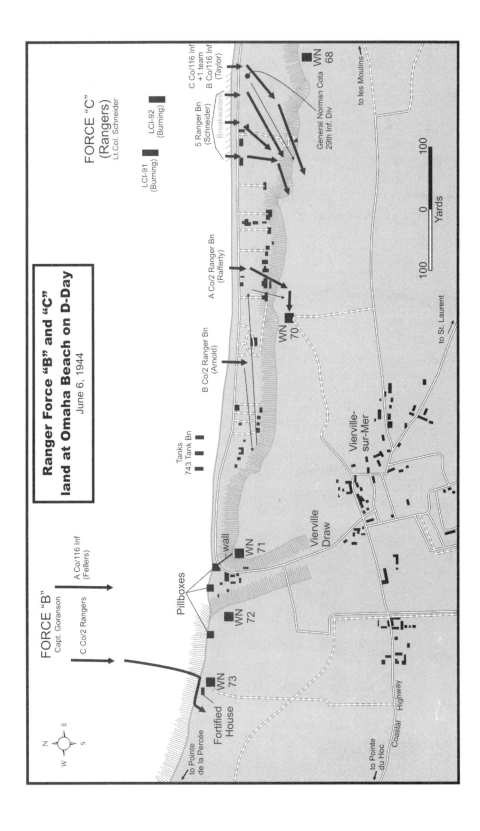

**Ranger Force "B" and "C"
land at Omaha Beach on D-Day**
June 6, 1944

FORCE "B"
Capt. Goranson

A Co/116 Inf
(Fellers)

C Co/2 Rangers

FORCE "C"
(Rangers)
Lt.Col. Schneider

LCI-91
(Burning)

LCI-92
(Burning)

N
W   E
S

to Pointe
de la Percée

Fortified
House

WN
73

to Pointe
du Hoc

Coastal Highway

to St. Laurent

Vierville-
sur-Mer

Vierville
Draw

WN
72

WN
71

wall

Pillboxes

Tanks
743 Tank Bn

B Co/2 Ranger Bn
(Arnold)

A Co/2 Ranger Bn
(Rafferty)

WN
70

Breakwaters

5 Ranger Bn
(Schneider)

C Co/116 Inf
+1 team
B Co/116 Inf
(Taylor)

General Norman Cota
29th Inf. Div

WN
68

to les Moulins

Yards
100   0   100

CHAPTER SIX

Normandy, D-Day, June 6, 1944

He that outlives this day, and comes safe home,
Will stand a tip-toe when this day is named.
—*Shakespeare,* Henry V

The Germans had lost the battle of the sea as well as the battle of the air. Now would come the battle of the land. From horizon to horizon, the waters of the English Channel were filled with ships great and small. Stately battleships and powerful cruisers moved into position. Sleek corvettes and destroyers, the hunting foxes of the sea, carved the water that foamed white at their bows. Overhead, fleets of bombers and fighters thundered toward France. The rails of troop ships were lined with waiting, watchful men to whom all this pomp and pounding was but an overture to their entry onto the stage of history.

Morale soars when soldiers see the enemy being shelled. The preliminary "drenching fire" was breathtaking. At 0550 the 14-inch guns of the *Texas* opened fire on the relatively small area of Pointe du Hoc, the great ship leaning sideways in the water from the force of the blast. Long tongues of fire flew from the muzzles. Those nearby felt the air sucked from their lungs, and smaller vessels and their crews shuddered from the shock. The *Texas* was firing over the head of many landing craft, and to men therein it seemed as though freight trains were rumbling above them. In support of the landing at Pointe

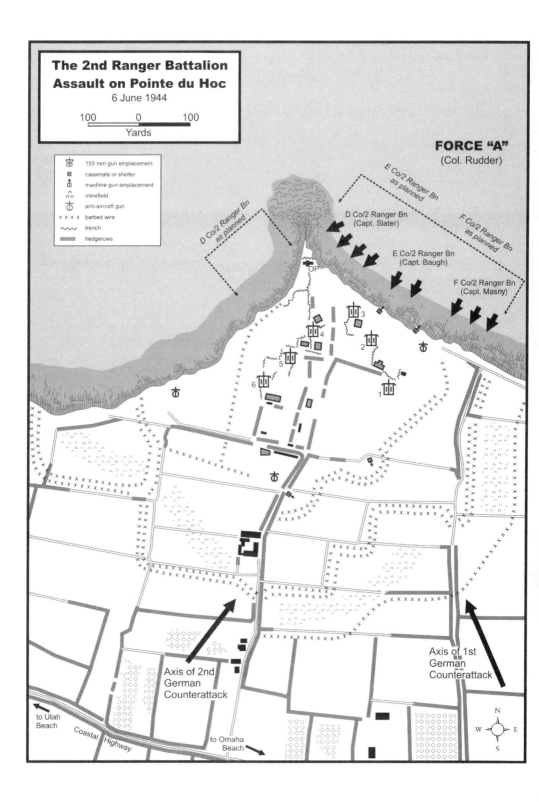

The 2nd Ranger Battalion
Assault on Pointe du Hoc
6 June 1944

100   0   100
Yards

FORCE "A"
(Col. Rudder)

155 mm gun emplacement
casemate or shelter
machine gun emplacement
minefield
anti-aircraft gun
x x x x barbed wire
trench
hedgerows

D Co/2 Ranger Bn
as planned

E Co/2 Ranger Bn
as planned

F Co/2 Ranger Bn
as planned

D Co/2 Ranger Bn
(Capt. Slater)

E Co/2 Ranger Bn
(Capt. Baugh)

F Co/2 Ranger Bn
(Capt. Masny)

OP

3
4
2
5
6
1

Axis of 2nd
German
Counterattack

Axis of 1st
German
Counterattack

to Utah
Beach

Coastal Highway

to Omaha
Beach

N
W E
S

du Hoc, the *Texas* would fire 690 shells from its 14-inch batteries, and another 272 rounds of 5-inch ammunition aimed primarily at Omaha Beach targets.

H-Hour, the time set for Dog, Easy, and Fox Companies to land, was at 0630. At 0610, sixteen twin-engine B-26 medium bombers of the 99th Air Wing, 391st Bomb Group, swept in to unload their deadly cargo.

Over Omaha Beach the crews of heavy bombers felt the rush of air entering the planes as bomb-bay doors opened. Airmen trained and skilled at daylight bombing found themselves in dim light with cloud cover beneath them. The decision was made to delay the bomb release from five to thirty seconds to ensure troop safety. From a technical aspect everything went well, but the delay in timing meant the bombs fell inland as much as two miles behind the German positions.

The LCT(R) rocket ships arrived as planned and at 0629 there was an enormous *woosh* as the rockets fired. The sound was dramatic but of little tactical value as the rounds fell short into the water. As the rockets roared, DD (duplex drive) amphibian tanks from the 741st Tank Battalion launched 6,000 yards from shore. Most found the heavy seas too strong for the canvas shields, and twenty-nine tanks were sunk, some with the loss of their crews. All of these failures were contributors to the horror that would be endured by the infantry and engineers tasked to clear the beach obstacles.

In the Channel, the mother ships carrying the 2nd Ranger Battalion pointed their bows toward Normandy. The men were well trained, proud, and physically and mentally ready for combat. As youths, many of the men of the battalion had read the classic romances. They knew of Arthur, Lancelot, and Ivanhoe, D'Artagnan and the Three Musketeers. All the heroic characteristics portrayed in those great tales of adventure were found in the men of the 2nd Ranger Battalion.

Aboard the *Prince Charles* in the dark hours of the morning of June 6, 1944, ten miles off the Normandy coast, the Ranger missions began. Capt. Ralph Goranson led his men in reciting the Lord's Prayer. Then Goranson said, "Give 'em hell!" and the loading of the landing craft began. On the *Prince Charles*, the boats hung from davits, and British seamen lashed planks from the boat deck to the landing craft to form small bridges. The men were accustomed to carrying heavy loads, but as resupply on the beach was uncertain they were

burdened with ammunition and rations for five days. This created a
heavier and bulkier load than they had carried in training. Assisted by
British sailors, the men walked the planks in darkness.

At 0430 Charlie Company was lowered away. The British-made
LCAs were capable of landing a four-man crew and thirty-seven men
in eighteen inches of water. Forty-one feet, six inches long, the craft
had a wooden hull but was armored on bulkheads, sides, and the
decked-over troop well. There was a wooden bench on either side
where men sat facing the interior. A third bench ran the length of the
center of the craft which men straddled facing the bow. Armed with a
Bren gun and two Lewis guns, the LCA was well armed, could travel
at seven nautical miles per hour, and had a low silhouette.

Force B consisted of Charlie Company commanded by twenty-four-
year-old Capt. Ralph E. Goranson with Lt. Bill Moody as 1st Platoon
leader. They were in LCA 418. Lt. Sid Salomon and his 2nd Platoon
were in LCA 1038. Charlie Company had a dual mission: to eliminate
enemy positions at Pointe de la Percee, and then to go overland to
Pointe du Hoc to rejoin the battalion. With cliffs up to ninety feet
high, Pointe de la Percee was three miles east (left) of Pointe du Hoc
and occupied the eastern (right) flank of Omaha Beach. From Pointe
de la Percee, German artillery and automatic weapons could fire down
the length of Omaha Beach. The plan on Dog Green, the right "Dog"
section of Omaha Beach, was to have Company B of the 743rd Tank
Battalion come ashore at 0625 hours in tanks configured to operate
on land or water. At 0631, Company A of the 116th Infantry would
land, and at 0633 men of the 146th Engineer Combat Battalion and
Charlie Company of the 2nd Ranger Battalion were to land. Succeeding waves would then land at five- to ten-minute intervals.

When the ramps were lowered on the LCAs, the platoon leaders
would lead the way. Lieutenants Moody and Salomon would be the
first men off their craft. With the overall responsibility of the company, Captain Goranson was seven or eight men back in the unloading process on LCA 418. In each boat, the platoon sergeant was the
pusher, the last man off.

Goranson felt a justifiable pride in his company. These men
would never quit. In the boats were two Rangers who had once been
first sergeants of Charlie Company. They were busted for off-duty
infractions, had not sought transfer, and were now going ashore as

riflemen. One of the men on LCA 418 was Sgt. Walter Geldon of Bethlehem, Pennsylvania. June 6, 1944, was his third wedding anniversary.

The seas ran high, and the landing craft were tossed about. The men had been offered breakfast prior to leaving the ship. Most had eaten sparingly, but a few gorged themselves. The incessant rise and fall of the waves soon had men searching for the paper "barf" bags they had been issued. The bags were quickly filled, and men began to vomit in their steel helmets. Sea water was coming into the landing craft threatening to swamp them and barf and bail became a repetitious and nauseous combination. As they drew closer to shore, the skies lightened with the dawn. Soon, concentric, donut-shaped impressions were being made in the waters about them. The realization came that these were shells from German artillery and mortars landing nearby. Next came the singing of machine-gun bullets ricocheting off the hull.

Low tide at Omaha Beach was at 0530, an hour before the assault began. During the hour prior to the assault, the tide would rise $1\frac{1}{2}$ feet, the waters moving only 100 feet toward the shore. From 0630 to 0730 hours, the tide would rise $6\frac{1}{2}$ feet and the average width of the beach that the men must cross would decrease from 300 to 150 yards, but that would not occur for one hour. Under fire the men of Charlie Company had to cross a beach nearly the length of three American football fields.

Sunrise was at 0558. However, there is that period known as BMNT (Beginning Morning Nautical Twilight) that has been defined as the time a white thread can be distinguished from a black thread. In this dim light Captain Goranson and the men of Charlie Company could see the dark shapes of the landing craft of Company A, 116th Infantry, slightly to their left front. The landing craft were led by guide boats to a point some 18,000 yards from the mother ships and 4,000 yards from shore. This was the line of departure where the landing craft would begin to fan out to make the final run to shore. The location was identified by small patrol craft positioned on line.

The German defensive deployment included strongpoints (*Stutzpunkt*) that were often of battery size or larger. Pointe du Hoc— number 75 in the defensive plan—was such a position. The *Widerstandsnest* (WN) were smaller-caliber gun positions, usually squad or

platoon in size, equipped with machine guns and mortars. There
were fifteen of them at Omaha Beach, which the Allies numbered
east (1st Infantry Division sector) to west (29th Infantry Division sector) as WN60 to WN74. Direct-fire artillery and antitank guns were
sited to fire down the beach from reinforced concrete casements that
were shielded from fire and observation from the sea. Machine guns
were in the casements and/or in positions on the bluffs where they
were accompanied by mortars. Artillery forward observers were
located at WNs to direct the fires of artillery positioned to the rear. All
fires were interlocking, even those of high-caliber guns. Even the
dreaded 88s used crossfire on Omaha Beach.

WN71, WN72, and WN73 were located at the Vierville draw.
WN71 was on top of the bluffs and consisted of a series of bunkers
and firing positions connected by trenches. On the side of the cliff
overlooking the draw were concrete machine-gun emplacements.
Nine machine-gun, two mortar, and one artillery position were
located at WN71. WN72 (today a U.S. National Guard monument)
was a massive structure housing an 88mm gun that fired eastward
down the beach. This position also included a 50mm gun with flexi-
ble fields of fire as well as machine guns. WN73 held a 75mm gun
that, like the 88 at WN72, fired eastward and covered the length of
Omaha Beach. On the cliff top were bunkers, trenches, a fortified
house, eight machine guns, and two mortar positions. These were the
German positions that would be faced by men of Company A of the
116th Infantry and Charlie Company of the 2nd Rangers. Charlie's
objective would be the elimination of WN73.

To the left front (east) of the Rangers, the men of the 741st and
743rd Tank Battalions were in the first wave of landing craft with the
mission to take up positions at the water's edge and cover the landing
of the infantry that followed close behind. In the eastern (16th
Infantry) sector of Omaha Beach, only five tanks of the 741st reached
the beach. In contrast, naval officers in the 116th Infantry zone
brought their LCTs to Dog Beach through the hail of fire that caused
several to sink. Steering onto the beach, these gallant men unloaded
thirty-two tanks of the 743rd Tank Battalion along the width of their
sector of Omaha Beach.

Though supporting naval gunfire was heavy, the Germans placed
the leading craft under a withering fire. Because of sunken landing

craft, only eight of the sixteen tanks in Company B of the 743rd Tank Battalion made it to shore. With most of their officers dead or wounded, the surviving tankers laid down supporting fire from the edge of the beach. They in turn were picked off by German gunners. American tanks sank or were destroyed by the dozens. After the action, General Gerow reported the V Corps loss of seventy-nine tanks on Omaha Beach.[1]

At about 0636, the men of Company A, 116th, landed on Omaha Dog Green. This company, which had been under heavy fire on the way in, found itself in the jaws of hell. One boat foundered, and another was ripped apart by the German fire. When the ramps were lowered, the men in the lead were mowed down. Trying to escape the horror, heavily equipped men jumped over the sides and into water that was frequently over their heads. In one boat, all thirty-two occupants were killed. All officers and most of the noncommissioned officers of Company A, 116th, were casualties. Beaten down, the survivors tried to find shelter behind obstacles or in the water.

Confusion on the part of other units contributed to the suffering of Company A, 116th. G Company, which was to land to the left of Company A, drifted east and landed about 1,000 yards away. In their sector of the beach, the remaining tanks of Company B of the 743rd Tank Battalion and Company A, 116th Infantry, received all the initial attention of the German defenders. Around 0645, nine minutes after the ramps dropped for Company A of the 116th, Charlie Company of the 2nd Rangers came ashore into the meat grinder of Omaha Charlie.

German machine guns, mortars, and artillery tore into the small Ranger company. LCA 418 with Captain Goranson and Lieutenant Moody's 1st Platoon was hit by enemy mortar or direct artillery fire on the ramp. By the time Goranson exited, the ramp had been blown off and two other explosions ripped the craft. Men tried to escape by climbing over the side and dropping into the water.

Death stalked the beach as the ramps dropped and Rangers struggled ashore. Some fell beneath a German machine gun firing directly into the boat, but the men kept moving. This was not the flamboyant charge so frequently depicted in war films; chilled, seasick, and numb with horror they found on the beach, the Rangers struggled through soft, wet sand that mired their boots. About every hundred yards on the beach were poles topped with two pieces of crossed wood painted different colors. These were "Mortar Markers," locations of pre-registered fires from which the German gunners had only to traverse right or left to shell the beach accurately.

The Rangers were volunteers and honed by training to a razor's edge. That added motivation and training enabled them to do what the brave men of Company A of the 116th had been unable to do— keep moving inland. Sid Salomon remembered men of the 116th looking up in surprise as Salomon and his men went past. All the months of physical training, the log drills, the speed marches, the cliff climbing, the boat drills, and the weapons and demolition instruction came together at Omaha Beach in the words, "Get off the beach! Go forward!"

Of the sixty-eight Rangers in Company C of the 2nd Ranger Battalion, nineteen were killed on the beach, including Sgt. Walter B. Geldon, making his third wedding anniversary his last. First Sgt. Henry "Steve" Golas paused when he saw men cringing under the fire. "Get your ass off this beach!" shouted Golas then moved forward only to fall dead before the curtain of German fire. Thirteen more Rangers were seriously wounded, and five were lightly wounded in crossing the almost 300 yards of exposed beach at low tide. Those who survived kept moving while the wounded crawled behind them.

T/5 Jesse Runyan, a BAR gunner, was shot in the groin and lost the use of his legs. Despite his wounds, Runyan continued crawling forward pushing his weapon in front of him, firing as he went.

As the craft carrying Lt. Sid Salomon, leader of 2nd Platoon of Charlie Company and his men went in, a man not intentionally seeking to be humorous exclaimed, "They're firing on us!" The fire he heard was light in comparison to what was coming. The Germans had the boat zeroed in but wanted to fire into the men, which required waiting until the ramp dropped. Lt. Sid Salomon was the first man off. It took a moment for the German machine gunner to adjust his aim, and Salomon jumped to the right into waist-deep water. The second man, Sgt. Oliver Reed, jumped left and was hit. Reed fell in the water and began to slide under the ramp. As bullets churned the water, Salomon grabbed Reed by the collar and dragged him to the beach.

A German mortar put a shell into the midst of the men behind him. Blasted off his feet by concussion and with a shrapnel wound in his back, Salomon thought his life had come to an end. He attempted to remove the operations map from his assault jacket in order to pass it to Sgt. Charles Kennedy, his platoon sergeant, but as sand began kicking up in his face from bullets playing about him, Salomon got up and moved forward. When he reached the base of the cliff, medic Robert Lambert removed Salomon's field jacket and shirt. He dug shrapnel from the flesh and put sulfa powder on the wounds. After Salomon put on his shirt, he joined his men in climbing the ninety-foot cliff. When he reached the top, he found only nine men left in his platoon.

S/Sgt. Oliver Reed still lay on the beach where Salomon had dragged him, along with another wounded Ranger, PFC Nelson Noyes. Both men had a clear view of the carnage. Three tanks came ashore and were promptly knocked out by German fire. Naval gunfire was hammering the German positions. Noyes saw an American tank struck by a shell and burst into flame. A wounded crewman came out of a hatch with his clothes ablaze. The soldier manned the .50-caliber machine gun and fired on the Germans until he slumped dead over the gun.[2]

Crossing the beach, Ralph Goranson felt the burning wind as he took bullets through his first-aid packet, canteen, pack, and clothing. The impact of the slugs spun him around as he went forward. Nine bullets penetrated his gear, but none touched his flesh. Goranson reached the sea wall and was lying prone when Mike Gargas yelled, "Mashed potatoes! Mashed potatoes!" Goranson looked at the excited man, "What the hell are you talking about?"

"Right between your legs!" screamed Gargas. Goranson looked down at a German concussion potato-masher-type grenade with the fuse smoking. He swung his legs outward and hunched up, and the grenade exploded without causing him harm.

The surviving Charlie Company Rangers reached the base of a cliff. Goranson looked left and saw Lt. Bill Moody. Moody yelled, "Plan Two?" Goranson knew the 29th Division units had not broken through, thus Plan One was not an option. Goranson held up two fingers and yelled, "Right." Moody nodded and with Sgt. Richard Garrett, Sgt. Julius Belcher, and PFC Otto Stephens went along the beach about 350 yards until they found a crevice in the cliff face. Stephens led the way, pulling himself up by driving his bayonet into the cliff face. At the top of the cliff, he secured a rope which others could climb. Lieutenant Moody followed and at approximately 0700 hours reached the top with Stephens. The two Rangers drew fire from a fortified house, but moved along the cliff top, with Moody shouting down directions to Goranson and the remainder of the Rangers. They carried lengths of rope approximately ten feet long with a loop at one end and a cross bar at the other. Moody and Stephens fastened some of these at the top of the cliff and lowered them. With the aid of these toggle ropes, the other men of Charlie Company began to climb. Within minutes, the majority of the company was on top of the cliff. No unit has a better claim to being first on the high ground at Omaha Beach than Charlie Company of the 2nd Ranger Battalion.

Though few in numbers, Ranger buddy teams set about reconnoitering the cliff top. On the high ground to the left of the Rangers was the fortified house now badly beaten up by naval gunfire. Ranger reconnaissance patrols found that this farmhouse was tied in with German strong points protecting the exit from Omaha Beach to Vierville. Though the house was not part of his mission, Goranson saw the impact it and the Germans in the trenches behind it were having on Omaha Beach. By this point Charlie Company had been joined by some twenty men of B Company of the 116th. Goranson immediately set up a support position while Lieutenant Moody and six Rangers cleared the stone house. Though driven off their emplacements several times, the Germans knew the trench system and continued to infiltrate back to their fighting positions.

Goranson placed a BAR gunner from the 116th in a German machine-gun position on the cliff top where the soldier had an excellent field of fire. He soon called Goranson to inform him that he was seeing some soldiers in the distance, but he could not tell if they were German or American. Goranson looked through field glasses and saw Germans. The BAR opened fire and dropped two at 400 yards. Later in the day Goranson returned to check the position. The BAR operator was carving the twelfth notch in the stock of his weapon.

On top of the cliff, Lieutenants Moody and Salomon shared a shell hole while peering over the rim to examine the trench system to their front. As the two men lifted their heads above the hole, Bill Moody was killed by a German bullet and fell against Salomon's shoulder. Salomon yelled, "Let's go!" to the others and charged up and out of the shell hole for the trench line. Once inside the trench, they found it ran along the edge of the cliff and contained a dugout. Salomon signaled his men to stop and threw a grenade through the open door. When the grenade exploded, Salomon and his men leaped in front of the opening and sent a hail of bullets into the interior and then hurried onward.

In the German trench system, the Rangers often had the advantage of surprise. As they ran along the trench, they found a German bunker where a machine-gun crew was placing enfilade fire on the beach. Sgt. Julius Belcher kicked open the rear door of the German position and threw a white-phosphorus grenade inside. As the badly burned Germans poured out of the position, Belcher killed them.

Lieutenant Salomon and his men next came upon a German 81mm mortar section firing on the beach below and killed the crew, improving the odds of survival for those still coming ashore. Salomon then put his men into a defensive position and awaited much-needed reinforcements.

FORCE A EN ROUTE TO SHORE

Tidal current played a major factor in navigation during the D-Day landing. The pull was so strong that supporting destroyers were required to steam into the current to maintain station. At least one guide boat at Omaha Charlie drifted off station. Currents, smoke, morning haze, and the tension and confusion of battle all contributed to the fact that many units along Omaha Beach had landed to the east of their planned objectives.

Aboard the LSIs (Landing Ship, Infantry) *Ben My Chree* and *Amsterdam,* Dog, Easy, and Fox Company Rangers of the 2nd Battalion (Force A) were awakened at 0230 hours. Thirty minutes later, those who wanted breakfast had two small pancakes. Dr. Block cheerily described this as "the last meal."[3] Around 0400 the men were loaded into the assault landing craft which formed up astern of Motor Launch (ML) 304, and two escorting gun boats. Behind the LCAs were LCTs of the U.S. 18th Flotilla and commanded by Lt. Chet Roundy. LCT 46 was carrying the four DUKWs, Swan I to IV with their London Fire Department ladders. Sgt. Richard "Hub" Hubbard of Company E was on Swan II admiring the painting on the side of the bridge of the LCT. The ship was nicknamed "Iron Mike" by its crew, who had painted a muscular arm and hammer on the bridge.

Critical to bringing the Rangers to the correct landing sight were the actions of the British-manned guide boat that would lead the landing craft. At 0430 hours Motor Launch 304 led out and began what should have been an hour-long trip to shore.

The Fairmile Motor Launch (ML) was a versatile craft similar to an American PT boat. Made throughout the British Empire, MLs weighed between seventy-nine and eighty-five tons, were 112 feet long, and had a beam (width) between seventeen and eighteen feet. The MLs could operate in less than five feet of water and had served as sub chasers, torpedo boats, minesweepers, and rescue boats, and had taken commandos on raids. For the invasion of Normandy, MLs acted as navigational leaders to guide the landing craft to their objectives. Armed with a 3-pounder gun forward of the pilot house, one twin and one single 20mm Oerlikon, and two machine guns, they were small and deadly ferrets of the sea.

ML 304 of the 11th ML Flotilla was under the command of Lt. Colin Beever, Royal Navy Volunteer Reserve, whose mission was to lead the Rangers to Pointe du Hoc. It was a difficult task as the tide was running strongly to the east and much of the voyage would be made in darkness and strong wind. Beever was plotting his course based on radar and Q.H.2, a radio system that used intersecting beams to determine location. At 0530 both navigational systems were determined to have failed. Lieutenant Beever then attempted to set his course by dead reckoning and visual recognition. He counted on the German battery at Pointe du Hoc to be firing, thus revealing its location, but the cliffs were shrouded in smoke, and the high-explosive pounding of naval gunfire was changing the appearance of the land.

As with Charlie Company, the cold spray soaked the men of Dog, Easy, and Fox Companies in the LCAs. The constant toss and heave of the small boats turned over stomachs. It was the biggest amphibious invasion in history with thousands of ships and planes in view. It was a sight to remember, something to tell the grandchildren. But many men did not see it, since they were face down heaving out the contents of their stomachs.

Without his navigational aides, Lieutenant Beever led the flotilla in the wrong direction, guiding them to Pointe de la Percee some three miles to the east of Pointe du Hoc—this despite the fact that the HMS *Talybont*, a British destroyer, reported that the strike of the shells from the battleship *Texas* could clearly be seen on Pointe du Hoc. At the line of departure 4,000 yards from the beach, LCT 46 was ordered to stop, and the four DUKWs wallowed into the water. The mission of the DUKWs was to follow the LCAs and position themselves to support the climb. Twenty-five-year-old Sgt. Bill Stivison called Capt. Duke Slater on his SCR 536 radio and gave the code word "Splash," indicating that the DUKWs were in the water. Stivison also had the responsibility of notifying Slater if any of the DUKWs were put out of action, broadcasting "Erase 1, 2, 3, or 4," depending on which DUKW was disabled or sunk.

As daylight revealed the shoreline, Colonel Rudder became uneasy about the direction that Lieutenant Beever's craft was taking. Though Rudder was senior officer, getting the Rangers to the correct landing point was a navy responsibility. Lieutenant Beever was in charge of this portion of the mission and no army officer had the authority to overrule him. As the minutes passed, Rudder increasingly believed they were going to the wrong beach.

At 1,000 yards from shore, Colonel Rudder, who was riding in LCA 888, the lead landing craft, ordered his coxswain to change course. The British sailor protested but Rudder was adamant and the course correction was made. When the reason for the correction was made clear, Lieutenant Beever turned the flotilla for the westward run. On board Swan II, Hub Hubbard saw Easy Company 1st Sgt. Bob Lang give a thumbs up as his LCA sped by. By now the landing craft were close to shore, so close that Lieutenant Commander Baines, captain of the HMS *Talybont*, would write, "Their course from Raz de la Percee along the shore to Pte. du Hoc was suicidal."

HMS *Talybont* had been on station between the American destroyers *Satterlee* and *Thompson*, firing on Pointe du Hoc since 0550. It was 0630 when the LCA course correction was noted. The DUKWs would be running a three-mile gauntlet of German fire, and the slow-swimming amphibians (five miles per hour in water) were especially vulnerable. To the German observers on shore, the ladder-carrying DUKWs likely resembled floating artillery and therefore choice targets. At 0640 HMS *Talybont* saw bullet strikes from two German machine guns on or around the three rear DUKWs. *Talybont* could see the impact but could not pinpoint the location from which the enemy was firing. Lieutenant Commander Baines brought the *Talybont* close to shore and opened fire with 4-inch guns and 2-pounder pom-poms on the cliffs.

The *Talybont* action reduced the German fire, but soon after Swan II passed Pointe de la Percee, the fire of other automatic weapons again struck the amphibian. The engine stopped and Sergeant Hubbard shouted to the coxswain to raise the hood and make repairs. The coxswain pointed to bullet holes and replied, "You fix it." The whiplash of German 20-millimeter fire was cracking the air and smashing into the drifting vehicle.

The men tried to get the frame of the ladder between them and the shore, but the DUKW kept turning on its axis, resulting in a life or death game of musical chairs as men moved around the craft seeking cover. Three men aboard were casualties. Duncan Daugherty was seriously wounded from a bullet in the chest that collapsed a lung. Another Ranger appeared to be dead. An LCA went by, ignoring their calls for help. A second LCA stopped and rescued the men of Swan II and returned them to the mother ship. The coxswain who saved them was berated for not continuing on with his mission. The men of Swan II were evacuated to a hospital in England.

About 0640 hours, LCA 860, carrying Capt. Harold "Duke" Slater, commander of Dog Company, and Lt. Morton McBride, began to take on water, slowed, stopped, and began to sink. Slater shouted, "Abandon ship! Abandon ship!" Having no choice, two officers and seventeen men of Dog Company and the LCA crew did so as they sought to shed equipment and activate life preservers.

With Swan II out of operation, Bill Stivison raised his radio to call Captain Slater to inform him "Erase 2." What Stivison heard was Duke Slater's radio operator yelling over the net, "We're sinking! We're sinking! We're sunk!" There could be no stopping the flotilla. Slater attempted to keep the men together, but the high waves drove them apart and the numbing cold of the water put them in shock. One life preserver failed to activate and, unable to shed his equipment, a man screamed in desperation and sank; another tried to swim ashore and disappeared. S/Sgt. Norman Miller, T/5 Thomas Mendenhall, PFC

Harold Lester, T/5 Raymond Riendeau, British seaman William H. Pusey, and Army photographer PFC Kegham Nigohosian drowned. Riendeau had been rated the best swimmer in the battalion, but Lt. Morton McBride saw Riendeau's lifeless body drift past. The survivors would be in the water over an hour and a half, suffering from hypothermia and the ingestion of large quantities of salt water before being rescued.[4] Despite pleas to be placed on a landing craft to Omaha Beach, they were taken to a hospital ship and then to England. Slater and the other survivors would not rejoin the battalion for nineteen days.

Several of the supply craft, carrying among other things the Rangers' packs, were also experiencing difficulty staying afloat. As water began to swamp his craft, Sgt. Regis McCloskey of Fox had no choice but to throw packs overboard, including those containing T/5 Charles Vella's money and Sergeant Frederick's teeth, thus earning him their consummate anger. One supply craft, LCA 914, foundered. Cries for assistance rent the air as terrified men struggled to remove heavy equipment and inflate life jackets. Unfortunately, there could be no stopping for those men in the chill water, and the cries turned to screams of despair. Ranger Francis J. Connelly of Easy Company and PFC John D. Oehlberg of Dog Company were among the Americans who died along with British seamen Donald Harris, John McCoy, and Wilfred Grosse. PFC John Riley of Dog Company was the only man to survive the sinking of LCA 914. The remaining nine landing craft and supply boats of Rudder's Force A moved toward shore in a double column, the intent being that those in the rear would speed up to form an assault line as the beach was approached.

On the narrow beach below the cliffs of the French coast, the anxious eyes of Pvt. Leonard Goodgall and Sgt. Raymond Crouch followed the progress of the Ranger flotilla. Goodgall and Crouch were members of Company I, 506th Parachute Infantry Regiment, 101st Airborne Division. The night before, they had hobbled toward the waiting rows of twin-engined C-47 aircraft, weighed down by the needful burden of parachutes and equipment. In the assembly area, there was always the adjusting of the harness straps that held tight against the inner thigh. Paratroopers were very careful that their testicles not be caught under the canvas harness when they got the violent shock of the parachute opening. Around 2200 hours on the night of June 5, they sped upward into the darkness. By 0105 hours on the morning of June 6, the stream of troop-carrying aircraft had passed over the Channel Islands and was nearing the coast. "Stand up and hook up!" yelled the jumpmaster. Goodgall stood and snapped his static line to the cable, the combination that would pull his parachute open as he fell toward earth.

Goodgall remembered, "Suddenly, all hell broke loose." German antiaircraft fire hit the plane, the right engine caught fire, and the plane shuddered and dived, throwing him to the floor. The aircraft leveled, then took another hit. The green light came on near the side door, the pilot's signal for the jump to begin. Only the first four men were able to exit. As Goodgall's parachute snapped open, he saw three other parachutes and the burning C-47 falling toward the sea. The USS *Thompson* reported seeing a burning aircraft go down. Goodgall could see the outline of the cliff, but there was water beneath him of unknown depth. Pulling down on two of the web risers from his harness, Goodgall was able to slip-spill air that allowed him to angle toward the Normandy coast. A few feet made the difference between life and death. When Goodgall landed and cleared his harness, he was in less than two feet of water. He made the narrow beach and met his friend, Raymond Crouch. The paratroopers tried to climb the cliffs but could not. With shells and bombs bursting on the cliffs, they waited until they could see the landing craft of the Rangers. They then followed along the shoreline to find the place where their fellow Americans would come ashore.[5]

Though Rudder's Force A Rangers were now headed for Pointe du Hoc, valuable time had been lost. The naval supporting fire was timed to lift at 0625, five minutes before the planned Ranger touchdown. The error in direction made the landing of Dog, Easy, and Fox Companies over thirty minutes late, giving the Germans time to reorganize and man their defenses. It also meant it would delay the signal to the remainder of the 2nd Ranger Battalion and the 5th Ranger Battalion to land at Pointe du Hoc.

At 0700 hours, Rudder's nine Force A landing craft and three DUKWs were approaching the east side of Pointe du Hoc. The assault plan had called for Lieutenant Colonel Schneider, with the eight follow-on Ranger companies, to wait until 0700 for the signal to come in behind Rudder's force. If no signal was received by 0700, Schneider was to land at Omaha Dog Beach and move overland to destroy the guns of Pointe du Hoc. Knowing how critical reinforcement could be to the three assault companies, at 0700 Schneider delayed ordering his flotilla to lay-to offshore. Schneider waited beyond 0700, anxiously hoping for the signal that a successful landing had been made. 1st Lt. Ike Eikner, communications officer for the battalion, had alternate means of communication, including radio, visual signals, and carrier pigeons. The plan included mortar flares to be fired from the top of the cliffs as a signal for Schneider to close on the beach, and a series of radio code words Eikner developed.

With the landing craft of the three companies coming in on the east flank of Pointe du Hoc instead of approaching the tip from the front, the original plan to land on both sides was no longer realistic. Rather than have Dog Company, which because of a sunken boat was now short twenty Rangers, attempt to do a U-turn, Rudder made the decision that the three companies would go on line and all would land on the east flank of the Pointe.

Captain of HMS *Prince Charles* and commander of Assault Group 0-4 was Royal Navy Commander Stratford Dennis. It was his responsibility to dispatch Force C to the proper destination, either Pointe du Hoc if the success signal was received, or Omaha Beach if climbing the cliffs failed. The capability of communication existed between HMS *Prince Charles* and ML 304, but until 0630 (H-Hour) radio silence was being maintained. The naval code word "Crowbar" (touchdown) was to be reported by ML 304 when the Rangers landed at Pointe du Hoc, and "Bingo" (success) when they climbed the cliffs.

It was not until 0709 that "Crowbar" was heard. Commander Dennis knew only that the Rangers were now on the beach at Pointe du Hoc. Pacing the deck, he waited for the radio success signal while lookouts searched in vain for alternate pyrotechnic signals. After waiting an agonizing forty-five minutes without receiving word, Dennis made the painful decision to follow the secondary plan and send Force C ashore at Omaha Dog Green.

OMAHA CHARLIE BEACH

On top of the cliffs near Omaha Charlie, Captain Goranson saw a boat carrying men coming ashore in the fourth wave. Sending a messenger to them, he was soon joined by some twenty men of Company B of the 116th, who also came up the ropes. As the Rangers cleared out an enemy bunker, Goranson left behind a man from the 116th to keep the Germans from getting back into it.

WN73, the strongpoint that Company C was now ready to engage, was a key point in the German defense scheme covering the D-1 exit to Vierville. Though few in number, officers and noncommissioned officers in Charlie Company led their men into the German trenches and began a series of small, personal actions that disrupted the German defense. Using concealed routes of approach, the Germans reinforced from Vierville and fought hard to hang on to their strong point. Though not of sufficient strength to dislodge the enemy, Goranson's party kept moving through the trenches, picking off German troops, and destroying mortar and machine-gun positions which they came upon. The door of a position would be kicked or blown in, and white phosphorus grenades thrown inside. When the wounded and burned Germans ran out, the Rangers killed them. In this fashion sixty-three Germans perished. One German was taken prisoner.

About 1430, Captain Goranson took a patrol west to reconnoiter Pointe de la Percee. As the Rangers arrived, they saw gunfire from a destroyer eliminate the German positions. Another destroyer saw the Rangers and, mistaking them for the enemy, opened fire. A forward observer on the beach saw the error and called off the naval gunfire. Two Rangers were wounded by the 5-inch guns of the destroyer and another concussed so badly that he had to be stopped from walking off the cliffs.

POINTE DU HOC

As they moved closer to shore, Force A, comprising Dog, Easy, and Fox Company landing craft, began to peel off into position to land along a strip of rocky beach approximately 500 yards long and 30 yards wide. On the right flank, landing from right to left, were LCAs 861, 862, 888, and 722. These four craft carried Easy Company and Rudder's command element. Dog Company, with LCAs 668 and 858, was in the center, and the three LCAs numbered 887, 884, and 883 carrying Fox Company were on the Ranger left.

Covering a frontage of some 500 yards, the nine landing craft touched down on the east (left) side of Pointe du Hoc. Pounded by bomb and shell, the thirty-yard-wide strip of beach was deeply cratered. These holes, combined with heaps of earth and stone torn from the cliff face, presented obstacles to the landing.

The first craft to land and the third from the left was LCA 888, carrying Colonel Rudder and much of his command element, plus men of Easy Company and four men of Headquarters. Touchdown was between 0705 and 0708. The Germans could be seen on the cliff top. Sgt. Domenick Boggetto opened fire with his BAR and shot a German soldier, whose body fell from the cliff. The remainder of the Germans disappeared from view, only to return and begin firing down into the Dog Company boats and showering them with grenades. As with other boat teams, Rudder's party embarked into deep bomb craters, whose clay sides were slick and difficult to escape from. The grapnels were fired, but as their ropes were wet, none reached the cliff top. Under fire, Rudder's command group reached the cliff wall, where the command post was established in a small cave. After a restless night, paratroopers Goodgall and Crouch of the 506th Parachute Infantry joined up with the Rangers on the narrow beach. They were taken to join Rudder, who told them to stay with him; days would pass before they saw their parent unit again.

While automatic-weapon fire was received from the flanks, it had been a busy morning aboard the USS *Satterlee* (DD626). Its skipper, Lt. Cmdr. Robert W. Leach, USN, of Orange, Massachusetts, had first trained his guns on Pointe du Hoc at 5,000 yards at 0548. *Satterlee*, along with the *Texas* and other support ships, lifted fires at 0625. Because of ML 304's misdirection, Rudder's Rangers failed to arrive at the Pointe on schedule. Now that they were there and in trouble, the *Satterlee*'s close-support training kicked into gear. Cmdr. W. J. Marshall, who was on the bridge at the time, ordered the ship in closer. With fire roaring in its boilers and guns blazing, the *Satterlee* sped toward Pointe du Hoc.

Aboard the drifting DUKW Swan II before their rescue, Hub Hubbard witnessed the charge of the *Satterlee* and called it "the most daring thing I've ever seen. That boat was at flank speed. The bow wave was as high as the main deck. The ship was so close in shore it appeared to be only a few feet off the beach. *Satterlee* was followed by ML 304, its 3-pounder barking and with a sailor standing amid ship firing 20mm shells at the cliff edges."[6] Lieutenant Beever was disoriented, but not a coward. His swift craft sped close inshore and put twenty rounds of 3-pounder and 1,000 rounds of 20mm fire into the German positions.

Though the *Satterlee* herself was hit by enemy machine guns, she was firing four 5-inch guns and lashing the cliff tops with the fire of two twin 40mm and two single 20mm guns. A large section of the cliff broke free, falling around Rudder, who later observed he "had the living hell scared out of him" by the avalanche.[7] Lieutenant Eikner was knocked flat. As Eikner looked skyward, he saw the face of a young German soldier peering down at him from the clifftop. Eikner dragged his weapon from the earth, aimed at the German, and pulled the trigger, but the weapon was fouled with dirt and would not fire. Struggling to clear the weapon and expecting to be shot, Eikner glanced up at the cliff top. The German was gone.

HMS *Talybont* had been shelling other targets and saw that the *Satterlee* was doing well. Lieutenant Commander Baines wrote in the *Talybont* log: "U.S.S. *Satterlee* was giving close support and I decided not to interfere." At 0728, radio communication was established with the Rangers' shore fire-control party. From then until the evening of June 6th, the log of the *Satterlee* is a repetitious recital of "commenced firing" and "ceased firing, target destroyed." A U.S. Navy report stated: "The longest interval between salvos during the day was a twenty-minute pause when the crew tried to eat K rations. Before they finished, the Rangers had again called for shelling and the meal was interrupted."[8]

Rangers firing from landing craft and beneath the cliff added to the action, and the cliff-top Germans were driven from view. A German machine gun firing from the east (left) and sited to enfilade the beach continued to shoot with particular effectiveness. Under this rain of fire, the Rangers struggled in surf and wet clay to get to the cliff face.

On the extreme right, LCA 861, carrying Easy Company commander Capt. Gilbert "Sammy" Baugh and 1st Platoon leader Ted Lapres, came in near the tip of Pointe du Hoc and went aground about twenty-five yards from shore. Three or four Germans were standing on the cliff top firing down at the Rangers. As Easy Company Rangers leaped from the front of the craft, men in the rear fired on the Germans, driving them from sight. The Germans then began to throw grenades over the edge of the cliff, and two men were wounded. All six boat-mounted, rocket-propelled ropes were fired without any reaching the cliff top. Baugh, Lapres, and the Easy Company men then used hand-fired rockets, and several grapnels finally caught. Captain Baugh was severely wounded in the hand as he began to climb the ropes.

PFC Harry Roberts, one of the best climbers in Easy Company, ascended the rope hand over hand, bracing his feet against the steep slope and walking up the cliff face. Twenty-five feet up, the rope gave way and Roberts fell. Another rope was fired and Roberts climbed the cliff face again in what he estimated as forty seconds. As he reached a small niche under the cliff edge, a German soldier cut the rope. Roberts caught the rope and tied it to a picket post for barbed wire. The weight of the next man pulled the rope free, leaving Roberts temporarily stranded. Shells and bombs had collapsed the cliff face and a mound of stone and clay enabled other Easy Company men to throw a line to Roberts. Going over the cliff edge, Roberts did not see any Germans. He then lay over the rope to secure it as Lieutenant Lapres and four other men climbed up. Following Ranger procedure, the six men immediately moved to attack their objectives, which were the fortified German observation post at the tip of Pointe du Hoc and gun position 3. Approximately ten minutes had passed since their landing craft had reached shore.

Below the cliff face, five Easy Company Rangers from LCA 861 were waiting for a chance to climb the rope. Suddenly the cliff face above them exploded and a cascade of earth and rock fell, partially burying PFC Paul Medeiros. With his friends' help, Medeiros broke free. The men were surprised to see the rope still in place. All five quickly reached the top and found that the other men from their craft had gone on. They did the same.

Easy Company's LCA 862 with Lt. Joseph Leagans was the second landing craft from the left to land. T/5 John Burnett fired a rocket-propelled rope, then went off the ramp in hip-deep water. Two of the six ropes fired from LCA 862 caught and held. Leagins, S/Sgt Joseph Cleaves, and T/5 Victor Aguzzi went up the ropes. They waited in a shell hole until T/5 John Burnett and another Ranger joined them. They then started for the German observation post and number 3 gun position. Other Easy Company men and those of the naval shore fire-control party swarmed up the ropes after them.

Twenty yards to the left of Rudder, LCA 722 came in with fifteen men from Easy Company. Also on 772 was British lieutenant Ronald F. Eades of the Royal Navy Volunteer Reserve. Eades was accompanying Lt. Col. Thomas Trevor, the six-foot-four-inch-tall British commando who had led the efficient #1 Commando in the invasion of North Africa and who also happened to be the commanding officer of the Thames Yacht Club, Knightsbridge, London.

Trevor, a swagger stick tucked under his arm, walked about the beach calmly, talking to the men and encouraging them. As he walked, he used a stutter step, a long step, a short step, and a side step here and there to throw off a sniper's aim. It didn't work. A sniper put a bullet through Trevor's helmet but only bloodied his head. The action enraged Trevor, who discarded the disfigured helmet. He had the wound bandaged and continued to walk the beach, cursing the Germans and encouraging the men.

Heavier equipment soon began to make it to shore and on up the cliff as mortar tubes and baseplates were hauled up by 0745. LCA 722 carried communications equipment, including the SCR 284 radio and two carrier pigeons. Despite coming to land on the edge of a crater, the Rangers brought the equipment ashore and T/4 Charles Parker and other communications men carried the heavy radio to cliffside and promptly had it working. While on leave at a London hotel some months before, PFC John Sillmon of Easy Company told a friend that he would not be going to Paris, that he would be wounded in the invasion and would go home. Coming in on LCA 722, Sillmon was wounded three times on the run to shore and twice during landing. Despite five wounds, Sillmon survived and went home to Kannapolis, North Carolina.

T/5 Edward Smith "walked" up the rope and reached the top within four minutes of landing. Smith was soon joined by Sgt. Hayward Robey who carried a BAR. The two men saw Germans off to their right throwing grenades over the cliff edge. Robey lay prone in a shallow niche and fired two magazines (forty rounds) at the Germans. Three of the enemy fell and the rest dove for cover.

First Sgt. Leonard Lomell of Dog Company came in on LCA 668. As Captain Slater's craft had foundered, there were only two LCAs from Lomell's company left. The original plan had been for Dog Company to be the only unit to land on the west (right) side of Pointe du Hoc. As a result of the error by guide boat ML 304, Rudder was now bringing Dog Company in on the east side of the Pointe, the left flank of Easy Company, and in the center of the Ranger landing. Lomell's craft encountered boulders torn from the cliff face and was forced to drop the ramp before reaching the narrow beach. The men had to swim about twenty feet to shore with their equipment.

Not a man to shy from discipline, Lomell had taken action against a subordinate sergeant during the training phase. In anger, the man had said words to the effect that they would soon be in combat and sometimes officers and noncommissioned officers got shot by their own men. As he struggled to shore from LCA 668 carrying his weapons, a box of rope, and a hand projector rocket, Lomell's side was grazed by a bullet. Behind him was the man whom he had disciplined. Furious at what he thought was an attack on his life, Lomell went after the man, who angrily denied the charge. Medic Bill Geitz pulled Lomell away, saying he had seen the German who fired the shot. Lomell apologized and went about his duties. The two men later became close friends.

All of the ropes for Lomell's group of Dog Company men were on an overhang and climbing was difficult. While German potato-masher grenades came sailing down from the cliff top, Lomell had sections of extension ladders brought ashore. Using high mounds of debris as a base, he and most of his men went up on ladders, with only two climbing the toggle rope. As Lomell went over the cliff, he saw Capt. Gilbert Baugh, Easy Company commander, clutching a .45-caliber pistol in a mangled hand. Lomell continued on his mission telling Baugh that he would send back a medic if he saw one.

Lt. George F. Kerchner had boarded LCA 858 as leader of 1st Platoon of Dog Company. Now, with the sinking of Captain Slater's craft, Kerchner found himself acting company commander. On the way in to the beach, Kerchner's men frantically bailed to stay afloat and three men were hit by machine-gun fire. The ropes were wet and, when fired in series, only one of the six ropes, a hand line, got over the cliff and held. The men ran a gauntlet of fire from German gunners but, fortunately, the rope was in a crevice that gave shelter from flanking fire. Within fifteen minutes, all of the men were at the top of the cliff. Dog Company had the western gun emplacements 4, 5, and 6 as their objectives. The first men up the cliff put a stop to the German grenade throwing and again in small groups headed for their objectives.

Fox Company had as their objectives eastern guns 1 and 2, and the machine-gun position at the eastern edge of the cliff. The change in landing plan had crowded Fox Company out of its intended landing area, and the boats came in farther east. At the time, no one noticed. Two men were wounded coming in on LCA 887 and men saw the first two ropes fired fall short. Despite the skilled steering of a cool-headed British coxswain, they had grounded just short of a water-filled bomb crater. Lt. Robert Arman, the Ranger boat team commander, and his men wrestled to shore the other four boat-mounted rockets, their ropes, and grapnels. Set up on shore, the rockets could not be fired because of a missing lead wire. T/Sgt. John Cripps, platoon sergeant of 2nd Platoon, stood close to the rockets, joining hot wires and exploding the rockets in turn. Each time a rope-carrying rocket was fired, the flashback burned his skin and kicked up sand and gravel which tore into his face. Bullets were falling around Cripps's feet, but he would not quit. The four ropes caught and held. Cripps was in pain, his face burning. Medic Frank South treated the wounds and Sergeant Cripps went on with his duties. Everyone who saw Cripps's action was in awe of his courage, but his only recognition for that action would be that his comrades never forgot it.

Lt. Jacob "Bangelore Jake" Hill would be first off Fox Company boat LCA 884. At the rear of the boat was Capt. Walter Block, battalion surgeon, and two aid men, Otto Bayer and Frank South. Three medics were distributed among other landing craft. All of the medics were carrying expanded medical kits. The last man to exit the craft would be Frank South, who was carrying the largest of the kits and described himself as "a walking aid station."[9] Mounted on a mountain-pack board and likely weighing seventy pounds, the load included plasma, sulfa-based antibiotics, drugs, surgical instruments, suture material, and still more bandages. South had about fifty feet of $\frac{3}{8}$-inch line tied to the pack board and coiled on top. If the beach was under heavy fire or he had to drop it in the surf, South could drop the pack board, then, when he reached the shelter of the cliff, pull it after him.

The military social position of the medical aid man rises in proportion to his proximity to combat. Men were aware they might soon need his services and joked to cover deeper concerns. "Hey doc, if the lieutenant and I get hit, you know who to take care of first—let him lie there." A recently married Ranger complained that the army did not issue bullet proof jock straps and asked if South could get him one. South suggested the man borrow an extra steel helmet and carry it over his crotch.

LCA 884 was under heavy enemy fire and three men were wounded before they came ashore. The boat grounded on the edge of a shell hole filled with water shoulder high. When fired, four of the six ropes held, but each rope lay in a position clearly exposed to German fire. Pvt. William Anderson tried to go up one, but the climbing angle was bad and he could not make it. Lieutenant Hill then took his men over to use the ropes of Captain Masny's craft.

Staying on the beach, Block set up his aid station and a Red Cross flag in a protected spot. During the landing the three Ranger companies had fifteen men wounded and one killed. Frank South heard the repeated calls of "Medic!" and worked his way up and down the beach. Most of the men with critical wounds were treated by Doc Block, but the medical aidmen were kept busy as well. In the Fox Company area, Frank South treated 60-millimeter mortar crewman Bill Walsh who was shot through the neck, and worked on twenty-six-year-old Sgt. Leon Otto, who had been shot in the stomach. It was South's first experience with an abdominal wound. He administered as much morphine as he felt Otto could tolerate, dressed the wound, and got Otto on a litter keeping him as warm as possible. Otto was begging for water. South knew that water would be deadly and had to deny the plea. Otto was taken off the beach to a destroyer, but died on board.

On board LCA 888, Sgt. L-Rod Petty had no idea that the ML 304 had been leading them in the wrong direction and felt it was a very clever feint. While waiting to get to shore, Petty passed around a dollar bill and had the other Rangers sign it. The men on LCA 888 also sang "Happy Birthday" to Sgt. Thomas F. "Red" Ryan, who turned twenty-two on June 6. As they neared shore, they began trading fire with Germans on the cliff, and as the ramp went down in waist-deep water, they struggled ashore. Petty had loaded his pockets with tobacco for his curved stem pipe and extra ammunition for the BAR. When the ramp went down, Petty jumped into the water and went to the bottom of the shell crater before surfacing and struggling to shore through light automatic-weapons fire. Petty was one of the fastest climbers, and he soon found one of the ropes that Cripps had fired and started up. He was wet and the rope was wet, but Petty was making good progress and was about forty feet up when the grapnel began to give way. Petty began a slow descent. To his right, Bill McHugh was climbing another rope and, seeing Petty in difficulty, jokingly called, "Hey L-Rod, you're going the wrong way!" Petty began to shout curses at the rope, at McHugh, and at the world-at-large, but his difficulties were not over. When he reached the bottom of the rope, Petty found Doc Block working on wounded a few feet to his right. Captain Block looked up and yelled at Petty to quit fooling around and get up the rope. Petty shouted, "Go to hell, captain— what does it look like I'm trying to do? You do your damn job and I'll do mine." Petty quickly found another rope and in short order was on top of the cliff. In a very rare occurrence for Bill Petty, he later apologized to Block. Petty felt he had been wrong, the feeling reinforced by the knowledge that it is not good policy for a combat man to be out of favor with the battalion surgeon. On top of the cliff, Petty found his squad and promptly moved off. He soon found he had walked into a mine field.

The extreme left landing craft and last to reach shore was LCA 883, carrying Fox Company commander Capt. Otto Masny, platoon leader Lt. Richard Wintz, and his boat team along with Lt. G. K. Hodenfield, a reporter for the soldier newspaper *Stars and Stripes*. Masny and his men were fortunate that a jutting portion of the cliff shielded them from German enfilade fire. Masny had observed coxswains on some boats dropping ramps and firing the rope rockets before touchdown. Masny ordered the men not to fire the rockets until the boats landed. The result was that LCA 883 made a dry landing, the ropes went up and over the cliff and five of the six boat-fired ropes held. Movement up the ropes was smooth except for the free climbers. Wintz was one of these and found the wet and muddy rope difficult to climb hand over hand and the cliff face so slick that footholds could not be found. Wintz was exhausted by the time he reached the top, but he took six men and headed off for the objective.

The Fox Company Rangers soon came under fire from a German 20mm antiaircraft gun. Not knowing that in the separation and confusion of battle that this was the third attempt to eliminate the gun, Lieutenant Wintz decided to attack. Sgt. Charles Weilage had a 60mm mortar set up in a crater, and Wintz planned to use that to support his assault. The attack began, but after two men were wounded, the effort was aborted because of a mistaken message to Wintz that he was to withdraw. Now a messenger came from 1st Sergeant Frederick that company commander Otto Masny wanted the gun destroyed. Once again Lieutenant Wintz began his attack only to have it cancelled by a radio message from Colonel Rudder that naval gunfire would be employed on the target.

Navy lieutenant Johnson of the shore fire-control party had radio communication with the USS *Satterlee* and was adjusting the fires of the gallant ship. At 0816 *Satterlee* commenced firing her 40mm guns and delivered what observers remembered as seven salvos from her main battery of 5-inch guns. At 0837, twenty-one minutes after opening fire, the section of cliff that had concealed the German position was blown away and the *Satterlee* ceased fire. Naval reports claimed that the destroyers were closing to within 1,500 yards of their targets, close range for naval gunfire. The *Satterlee's* deck log shows the ship closed to within 200 yards of Pointe du Hoc, then anchored in sixty feet of water where she would continue giving fire support to the Rangers until that evening. With 70 percent of her ammunition used, *Satterlee* was relieved by Lt. Cmdr. A. L. Gebelin's USS *Thompson* (DD627), which had been firing on targets in the vicinity of Pointe de la Percee.[10] At 1904 hours on the evening of June 6, 1944, the *Thompson* commenced firing in support of the Rangers.

By 0713 Lieutenant Eikner and his communications team of Rangers Lou Lisko, Charles S. Parker, and Stephen Liscinsky had set up the SCR-300 radio and were trying to establish communications. About 0725 Eikner radioed the code word "Tilt" to Schneider's force and received an acknowledgment. Who acknowledged is unclear. On Schneider's part, there is no indication that the message was received. Unable to establish contact by SCR-300, Schneider's communications personnel set up their SCR-284 on board the headquarters LCA without success. Guide-craft radios were inoperable, and even the loud hailer failed. At 0715 Schneider's force received an unintelligible message. The only word that could be understood was "Charlie."

While Schneider's Force C was coming in to shore, Rudder's Force A climbed the cliffs of Pointe du Hoc. Within five minutes of landing, Rangers were on top, and within thirty minutes of touchdown, all Dog, Easy, and Fox Company Rangers, except some headquarters and mortar personnel, had joined them. What they saw bore no relation to what they had prepared for. All the study of maps and aerial photographs, all the hours spent poring over sand tables and mock-ups had given the Rangers a knowledge of every position, trench, and path—now none of it was recognizable. The preliminary bombing and shelling had torn the landscape apart. Great chunks of cliff had been blown away and boulders hurled into the sea. The face of Pointe du Hoc had been torn wide open. Shell holes impeded the landing of the DUKWs and some LCAs on the beach and became underwater traps where men could drown. Objectives could scarcely be recognized, but there was also an advantage. The shell and bomb craters were ideal cover for the men to use in their rapid advance to search for the guns.

Though the climbing of the cliffs has captured the imagination of the public, it was the manner in which the Rangers conducted themselves on reaching the top that best shows their uniqueness. Ranger tactics stressed rapid movement by small groups. From the first man up the rope, the aggressive spirit of the Ranger was demonstrated. There was no hesitancy, no waiting until all the men of their squad, platoon, or company reached the summit; as men came up the ropes, they went over the edge, formed into small parties, and moved out. An estimated twenty separate parties of Rangers quickly assembled at the top of the cliff and headed toward their objectives.

This initiative on the part of the Rangers compounded the problems for the German defense. Though not haphazardly, the Rangers were attacking everywhere. Each man was trying to accomplish what he knew had to be done. As the small groups encountered one another, they merged together, flowing inland ahead of everyone else.[11]

Under harassing fire from the observation post and some German positions to the west, the small parties of Rangers searched out their objectives only to find the casemate and the open emplacements destroyed and the guns missing. In their place were faux guns made out of wooden poles.

At the tip of the point, E Company men engaged the large observation post that had escaped damage and whose occupants were firing at the Rangers with a machine gun and small arms. Sgt. Charles Denbo and PFC Harry Roberts crawled into a trench within range of the OP and threw four grenades, three of which made it through the observation and firing slits. The machine gun stopped firing, but small arms continued, and Denbo was hit in the head. Lt. Ted Lapres came up with four men, including Sgt. Andy Yardley who was carrying a 2.36-inch rocket launcher. Yardley's second shot went through the vision slit into the OP. As the German fire ceased, Yardley was left to guard the front of the OP while the rest went around the rear.

Meanwhile, without knowing of each other's presence, another element of Easy Company was attacking the observation post from the opposite side. Lt. Joseph Leagans, Sgt. Joseph Cleaves, Technician Fifth Class Thompson, PFC Charles H. Bellows Jr., and Cpl. Victor Aguzzi were in this group. They had succeeded in driving under cover a German who had been throwing grenades over the cliff. Thompson heard the Germans making radio calls so he shot the radio antenna off the top of the OP. Sergeant Cleaves was wounded when he stepped on a mine, Lieutenant Leagans and Technician Fifth Class Thompson headed inland with Bellows covering, and Aguzzi remained to cover the rear entrance to the OP. As they had no demolitions with them, the Rangers guarded the front and rear of the OP and waited for the Germans to come out.

Easy Company's Sgt. Clifford Smith and Sgt. Hayward Robey reached the top of the cliff and saw some six Germans nearer the point throwing grenades down on the climbing Rangers. Robey dropped into a depression and fired two twenty-round magazines from his BAR. Three of the Germans went down. The remainder fled into shelters. Joined by PFC Frank Peterson, the three Rangers continued on their mission.

At the top, Lomell moved off with about twenty-two men of his 2nd Platoon. Lt. George Kerchner's lst Platoon was in the second Dog Company boat team. Most of Kerchner's platoon went up a single rope. As they reached the top, small groups went after the guns. Within fifteen minutes of landing, the Dog Company Rangers had climbed the cliff and were moving on their assignment.

That most of the rope rockets had functioned was the key to the success of the Rangers' aggressive assault. Less fortunate were the ladder-equipped DUKWs. The deep shell holes hindered them in gaining a footing on the beach. A greater problem was the small stones which covered the beach to a depth of several feet. One Ranger described movement on this beach as trying to gain traction on a deep pile of roller bearings. Forced to remain in the water, the DUKWs were buffeted by the surf and their ladders were ineffective. Sgt. William Stivison climbed to the top of one of these swaying ladders to fire the machine guns mounted at the top while German tracers whipped past him.

Photographer Lt. Amos Potts was astounded at the damage that the bombing and shelling had done to Pointe du Hoc. When the DUKWs could not land to put up their ladders, Potts had to go through the water and all his extra film was ruined. Potts shot what film he had left in the camera, then assisted in tying supplies to ropes to be hauled to the top of the cliffs before he climbed a rope and joined Rudder's command group.

Scarcely pausing, the Rangers now pressed on to the second phase of their mission, that of moving inland to block the Vierville-Grandcamp coastal road, preventing German movement along it and interrupting communications between the German units engaged at Omaha and Utah Beaches.

Those last up the ropes hurried to join their companies. As groups merged, the movement inland began to develop along two axes, with Dog and Easy Company elements moving from the Point to the highway and men of Fox Company moving parallel to the east of Dog and Easy.

At 0745 Colonel Rudder moved his command post from the base of the cliffs at Pointe du Hoc to a shell crater at the top. Dr. Block followed suit with his aid station. Medic PFC Charles Korb had been shot in the hand, and Block left Korb on the beach to care for the seriously wounded who needed evacuation and could not be taken to the top.

Rudder did not have control of the battalion or the battle at this time, and to compound his problems, he had no communication with higher headquarters. Still, Rudder did all he could to survey the battle area and bring order, his very presence providing confidence to the men.

Rudder had given Capt. Otto Masny of Fox Company the job of collecting men to organize a defense of Rudder's command post. Communication between Rudder and Masny and other key points of the perimeter was primarily by field telephone with wire laid across the ravaged terrain although much of the wire equipment, including the switchboard, was at the bottom of the English Channel with LCA 914. Meanwhile, the Germans continued infiltrating the area through the maze of trenches, and the area had to be cleared again and again.

OMAHA BEACH

Despite the slaughter on Omaha Dog Green, succeeding waves of infantry and engineers had continued to land. Men of the 146th, 149th, and 121st Engineers valiantly tried to clear paths through the obstacles in a tide that was rising faster than anticipated. The engineers were shot down in large numbers. Coming in behind Company A of the 116th and Company C of the 2nd Rangers, the men of B and D Companies of the 116th Infantry were gunned down as the ramps dropped. The situation was chaos, worsened by fire-induced shock. While some men struggled to fight, others tried vainly to seek shelter in the water or behind any object that seemed to offer protection.

Under the Force C plan to move overland to Pointe du Hoc, Able and Baker Companies of the 2nd Ranger Battalion had the mission of respectively providing point and flank security for Schneider's 5th Battalion in the attack on the German battery. Thus, Able and Baker Companies and part of Headquarters Company, 2nd Rangers, went ashore first. They landed on the boundary of Dog Green and Dog White and met a hail of German fire.

The 2nd Battalion Rangers of Force C were in six LCAs, situated from left to right: two LCAs carrying Able Company, 2nd Rangers; the

Ranger Group headquarters LCA; a 2nd Ranger Battalion headquarters LCA; and two Baker Company, 2nd Ranger Battalion, LCAs. Ramps went down at 0740. By then the bodies of dead Americans floated in the water and littered the beach. The Germans were still in their emplacements and the killing of Able and Baker Company soldiers commenced.

Before reaching shore, the LCA carrying the 2nd Platoon of Baker Company was hit by artillery or a mine-tipped obstacle that blew off the bow landing ramp. Lt. Bob Fitzsimmons was hit by the steel door, knocked unconscious by the explosion, and presumed dead. Another Ranger was wounded. Sgt. Manning Rubenstein yelled "Abandon ship!" and the men went over the side as it sank, throwing most of the men into deep water where they had to jettison their weapons and equipment to swim to shore. Machine-gun bullets laced the water as they struggled toward the beach. Sergeant Rubenstein and Sgt. Walter Fyda saw five men killed in the water. Many more men were wounded by the time they reached the sand. Lacking weapons, some went back into the water hoping for refuge from the firestorm on the beach while others struggled to the seawall.

The 1st Platoon boat ran in until stopped by steel and concrete beach obstacles, then dropped its ramp. The men started ashore jumping into the chilly water and wading through waist-deep surf and chop to the beach. Man after man fell as machine-gun fire swept the beach. Baker Company commander Capt. Edgar Arnold was hit and had his carbine shot from his hand with bullets in and through his equipment. A short distance away, Lt. Robert Brice, leader of the 1st Platoon, lay on the sand felled by a shot through the head. Arnold crawled close and tried to revive his friend, but Brice was dead. His own weapon shattered, the wounded Captain Arnold picked up Lieutenant Brice's carbine and continued across the beach. When Baker Company reached the seawall, they counted thirty men present of the sixty-eight who had been on the LCAs. The others had been trapped in the water or were killed or wounded on the beach. Among the dead were T/5 Charles Bramkamp, who had been photographed filling the role of Baker Company barber, and T/5 Elmer Olander, who was receiving his last haircut.

Attached to Baker Company, Medic Willie Clark was about the sixth man off his landing craft. Leaping into cold water up to his waist, Clark could see a burning landing craft to his left with bullets hitting the water in front of him and mortar rounds landing. He took cover behind a beach obstacle. Seeing that a mine was fastened to it, he ran to the next one until there were no more obstacles, only the open beach initially covered by about two feet of incoming tide. Clark tried to get under the water, but his gas mask and life jacket kept him on top. He tried to swim, then crawl, and then ran to get behind a tank that was stalled on the beach. Mortar rounds were falling closer so he ran for the shingle.

The beach was a charnel house of dead and dying. Clark passed a man whose face had been flattened by concussion, leaving his head looking like a flat lollipop. When he reached the shingle, Clark was exhausted and shivering with cold. He lay still for a few moments, but the tide was coming in and wounded men were drowning in it. He then jumped to his feet and began dragging men from the surging water. A German rifleman started shooting at Clark. Ranger medics did not wear the red cross on their helmets, but did wear a red cross armband that was clearly visible. Trying to help the wounded and dodge bullets made Clark angry. He thought he could see a clump of bushes on the bluff where the fire was coming from, so he picked up an M 1 rifle from a wounded Ranger and put eight shots into that area. Clark wasn't sure if he hit the German, but he was not fired on again and resumed his work. No longer trusting his armband, Clark took the red cross off his sleeve and kept the rifle.[12]

One of the first wounds medic Willie Clark had to treat was a sucking chest wound. Clark had heard about these wounds but had never seen one until now. Clark used sulfa powder on the wound. He then found a gas mask floating in the water and cut a piece of rubber from it to cover the wound. Cries for medical assistance came from all parts of the beach, and the surviving medics did the best they could. Unable to evacuate the wounded, they treated men under fire and left them in position. The dead were strewn about or lying in rows where they had fallen. Clark could tell the Ranger dead by the bloused boots. There was no shortage of medical supplies. The beach was littered with equipment, including the aid kits of dead medical personnel of the 116th Infantry. On the beach Clark met a medical officer from the 29th Infantry Division, and the two men went about the beach picking up the medical supplies and treating the wounded.

Lt. Bob Fitzsimmons had suffered a head wound and was unconscious for several hours. When he was revived, a medic treated his wound and told him he would likely loose his left eye. The medic said he could not use morphine on a head wound. Fitzsimmons was in shock and did not feel the searing pain that would come later. He found a tank traveling on the beach and climbed aboard it until he realized the tank was drawing mortar fire. Fitzsimmons got off the tank and moved closer to the bluffs. As he sought shelter, Fitzsimmons saw a U.S. Navy destroyer come so close to shore to fire at German positions that he thought the ship had beached itself.

Lt. Stan White's 2nd Platoon of Able Company came in through rough water and, as with the other LCAs, saw the water around them leap from the strike of German artillery and the kicking spurts of machine-gun fire. The boat grounded on a sand bar, but the ramp went down in chest-deep water. White struggled in to shallower water, hearing the crack of German bullets, explosions, and screams, and seeing the carnage on the beach.

Sgt. Ed O'Connor saw men ahead of him hit as they exited, so he began to run parallel to the beach to avoid being part of the larger groups of men the Germans were firing on. Turning inland and moving with his rifle at high port (held diagonally to his front), O'Connor moved inland and began to attract fire. Raised on a Wisconsin farm, he was an experienced hunter who took excellent care of his weapon and so was surprised and angry when it wouldn't fire. When he checked his rifle, he saw that a German bullet, meant for his chest, had struck near the operating rod handle, sparing his life but disabling the weapon. Seeing Lt. Stan White, O'Connor reported that his M1 would not fire. Lieutenant White gave his rifle to O'Connor and drew a .45-caliber pistol.

Adding to the chaos on the beach were the hulks of tanks from Company B, 743rd Tank Battalion. Seven tanks of the company would ultimately be destroyed on the beach by 88mm fire. Lieutenant White could see a position from which a German machine gun was raking the beach. White looked back and saw two American tanks at the water's edge with hatches closed and not firing. He ran back to the tanks and beat on the side of one without getting a response. White then ran to the other tank and again hammered on the side. A hatch opened, and White identified himself and pointed to the location of the machine gun. The tank turret swung to the right and opened fire with its main gun. German artillery promptly responded. A shell hit the tank in a sudden, violent explosion. Concussed, White remembered nothing else from the sudden shock until he found himself in a hospital.

Coming into the beach, Lt. Bob Edlin, leader of 1st Platoon, Able Company, and his men were tossed about by the waves and many men were seasick. Water was in the craft but the pumps kept it down. About three hundred yards from shore, the Germans fired on the LCA. There was a heavy belt of mine-tipped obstacles. As the coxswain began to maneuver through these, the head of the British seaman was torn off by fire. Edlin made the decision that they had a better chance by dropping the ramp and did so about eighty yards out from the beach. The water was waist deep and the interlocking fires of the German machine guns were churning the water. Edlin dove in to avoid the bullets. Three men were hit as soon as they got in the water. Through bloody water, they reached the sand from where it was fifty to seventy-five yards to the gravel shingle. Lashed with machine-gun and mortar fire, they crossed the beach. Out of a boatload of thirty-four men, only fourteen reached the shingle.

Most of the surviving Rangers continued to struggle inland but some, exhausted by the struggle to get ashore, sought to take shelter in the water or behind a beach obstacle. Capt. Joe Rafferty had successfully crossed the beach—now he made the perilous crossing back to the water. As the rapidly incoming tide swirled about his legs, Rafferty urged his men forward shouting, "For God's sake men, get off this beach!" Bill Klaus, himself wounded, saw Captain Rafferty get hit in the legs. Rafferty fell forward to his knees in the water but continued yelling, "Hurry! Hurry! Hurry or everybody's going to get killed." A second bullet then struck Rafferty in the head. Medic Robert Lambert ran to Rafferty and sat behind him in the water holding the brave officer upright. Lambert could see that Rafferty's wounds were mortal. Rafferty tried to raise his hands to his head, then died. Because Lambert had to treat other men, he released his hold, and the tide carried Rafferty's body away.

Like Captain Rafferty, Lt. Bob Edlin had made it across the beach and turned back to encourage those who were vainly seeking shelter to move forward. With Rafferty down, Edlin was now company commander. As he moved about, Edlin was hit in the left leg by machine-gun fire. As Edlin fell forward, his M1 rifle flew from his hands. Being wounded did not stop the German fire, and Edlin was again struck, this time in the right leg. Despite his own wound, Bill Klaus grabbed Edlin by the backpack and dragged him to the seawall. A "half pound" of meat had been sliced away from Edlin's left calf, and his right leg was broken by bullets. Edlin saw S/Sgt. Ted James, and the two men talked about getting wounded men who could still fight dug in at the sea wall. Edlin ordered James to take men inland with T/Sgt. John White. The men of Able Company who had made it across the beach were scattered along a front of some 100 yards, and all the offi-cers and many of the key noncommissioned officers had been killed or wounded. Even the medic, Robert Lambert, had been shot through the throat.[13] Despite this, individuals and small groups led by PFCs, corporals, and sergeants were going forward toward the bluffs.

As T/Sgt. John White reached the shingle, he heard Staff Ser-geant James and other noncoms shouting for the men who were still on the beach to keep moving forward. White could see a small group of Rangers nearby on the shingle and four others who had already crossed the road. White yelled at the men nearby to follow him. They did not hear him, so he decided that if he moved they would follow. Two of the men were hit crossing the road. Sergeant White took the remaining six men and made his way through concealing shrubbery near a beach villa. They searched the houses but found no Germans. T/5 Percy Hower saw Germans on the bluffs above and proposed sig-naling the tanks that were down on the beach to fire on them. Hower went to the roof of the house and, waving his arms, attracted the attention of a tank crewman. Using hand and arm signals, Hower was able to get the tanks to shift their fire. Meanwhile, the Germans were firing down at the Rangers. BAR man PFC Garland "Gabby" Hart was hit in the arm and the leg. White asked Hart if he wanted to remain behind, but Hart refused the offer.

The two Headquarters LCAs, one for the 2nd Battalion and one for the whole Ranger group, suffered no hits until the ramp dropped in three feet of water. Then, machine guns and mortars took their toll. The Headquarters men scattered left and right. Those that made it across the beach to the shingle were separated and functioned inde-pendently. Robert Lemin, the 2nd Battalion's sergeant major, was among those killed.

Still clutching his dead friend's carbine, Capt. Edgar Arnold ordered the Baker Company men with him across the road to a house and take shelter beyond it. Fortunately, the Germans had not placed barbed wire on the sea wall location there. Beyond the sea wall was the road, and then a stone wall with a rusting single strand of barbed wire which was likely placed by a farmer. The plan for the order of movement to get to Pointe du Hoc was for Able Company to serve as point, and Baker Company to serve as flank security for the 5th Ranger Battalion. Arnold began moving his men eastward.

Sergeant Rubenstein and a BAR man went ahead to reconnoiter the route. One man covered the movement of the other, and in leap-frog fashion they skirted the base of the bluff slope. They crawled behind shrubs, moved in bushes and screened themselves behind the shells of destroyed beach villas. After traveling about 300 yards, they were fired on by a dug-in emplacement up the slope. The BAR man returned fire and silenced the German. Continuing, they reached a point where there was no longer cover or concealment. Ahead lay open beach with three American tanks on the tidal flat below the sea-wall. Arnold ask Rubenstein to try and contact the tanks. Other Rangers assisted Rubenstein over the stone wall and began to cross over the road to the seawall. A German rifleman fired a bullet which entered Rubenstein's throat and exited from his face, and Rubenstein dropped to the road, apparently dead.

Rubenstein lay there for what seemed an hour until he decided he was not going to die. He made his way to one of the tanks and asked for a cigarette. One of the tankers tossed down a pack and Rubenstein sat on the road for a while smoking and thinking. He decided to go back down the road to the house where he had started. Sixty years later, Manning Rubenstein wrote, "When I landed on D-Day as 1st Sgt., nothing went as planned from when our craft hit a mine a few hundred yards off shore, to being in the wrong place, to meeting resistance wholly unexpected, to a situation of disaster. Yet, we eventually did what we were sent to do. All that training did pay off."[14]

Under heavy fire, Sgt. Walt Fyda of Baker Company and eight men had successfully crossed the beach to the right of Able Company and on the left of Captain Arnold's group. They arrived at a point where the seawall ended and a low dune line banked with shingle flanked the beach road. Fyda and his group had no contact with anyone and could see no other men. Crossing the road, they went through the courtyard of a small house and saw the grass burning on the slope to their front. Using this smoke and a ravine that angled to the left for cover, they made it to the top. There they met some six men from Able Company, and later Captain Arnold and his group from Baker Company.

Separated from each other, under fire and with many wounded or dead, the Able Company survivors were wrestling with command. Sergeant James thought Lieutenant Edlin had put him in charge of the company. Edlin was certain he had told Sergeant White to take over. For his part, White was worried the company had been wiped out.

White's mood improved when Sgt. Bill Courtney came down the steep bluff inland of the house. Courtney told White that he had been up on top with PFC Bill Dreher, who was still there. Courtney offered to show White the way up. White decided to look for survivors he could lead up the bluff. As White started back toward the beach, he found six more Rangers coming through the villa gate and saw more crossing the road. Now John White's spirits soared—the men were not all dead. He began gathering the Rangers who had crossed the road.

Tech Sergeant White followed Sergeant Courtney and took the men who had crossed the road up the bluff. On top, White found Sgt. Garfield Ray standing in the open and pointing with his BAR. Only twenty yards away were several German machine guns set up in firing position but no Germans were visible. White and Ray turned left to check out what appeared to be another German machine-gun emplacement. When Ray neared the position, the gunner opened fire, but because he was panicked, his shots missed. White shot at the position from the front, and the German soldier ceased firing and attempted to flee from the rear entrance of his bunker. Ray had flanked the position while White was firing. When the German ran out, Sergeant Ray killed him.

The intricate system of tunnels and bunkers allowed the Germans to take cover and suddenly reappear elsewhere firing on the Rangers. Germans fired on Bill Courtney and Bill Dreher and White returned to join the two hard-pressed men. Soon, other Rangers came up the bluff and they all went into the trenches after the Germans. White and Courtney had cleared a section of trench when potato-masher concussion grenades were thrown at them from behind, but they were not injured. Like many other Rangers, they were getting an erroneous contempt for the German grenade. White and Courtney retraced their steps and found two Germans in a hole on the slope. The two Rangers jumped in the hole with the Germans, killing them at point-blank range. Working in groups of two and three men, the Rangers began to systematically clean out the trench system, killing Germans and taking six prisoners. S/Sgt. Fred Smith was killed in this action, and two other Rangers were wounded.

White's next concern was a German counterattack. While the bluff trenches were being cleared, he moved men inland and on the flanks to forestall any effort to drive the Rangers back to the beaches. As White turned to look toward the edge of the bluff, he saw Lt. Gerald "Gerry" Heaney, the battalion assistant S-3, coming over the edge of the bluff. Heaney had more Rangers with him and men from the 116th Infantry, some of whom were carrying the impressive firepower of a water-cooled machine gun. Behind this group were the men of Baker Company. To the left, White could see the 5th Ranger Battalion moving inland. As Able and Baker Companies began to reorganize, John White paused to look at his watch—it was 0830 hours.

While the action was occurring on the bluffs, men lay wounded and dying on the beach. Near Lieutenants Edlin and Klaus was T/5 Orville Wright, who was seriously wounded, in shock, and shivering. A medic came by with a blanket on his arm that he was carrying to another man. Edlin instructed the medic to place the blanket on Wright. The man refused and started to turn away saying he had to take it up the beach. Before the man completed his turn, Edlin drew his pistol, leveled it on the man, and repeated his order. The medic treated Wright and bundled him. The mortar rounds were still falling and machine-gun bullets were striking nearby. Klaus was attempting to shelter Edlin with his body as the medic began to work on the officer and gave Edlin a shot of morphine. Klaus then began cleaning his weapon and those of the other wounded.

Fortified by the morphine, Edlin decided to go on reconnaissance. Crawling and hobbling beyond the seawall, he moved to where he could see the bluff rising ninety feet behind the beach. There was a small beach house nearby flanked by bushes. He heard Bill Dreher shout to the men on the beach, "Come on up. These trenches are empty!" followed by German automatic-weapons fire. The sound of American weapons responded until there was no further fire from the Germans.

Satisfied that his men were doing well, Edlin painfully returned to the beach, where he began to organize the approximately fifteen wounded Rangers to repel any German counterattack. An officer of the 29th Infantry Division made his way to Edlin and said, "You've done your job." Edlin bitterly responded, "Yeah, I did a hell of a job. I used up two rounds of ammunition. That's a hell of a part to play in this war."[15]

Though the machine guns were being silenced, mortars and artillery were still incoming. Edlin and his wounded companions were under fire for sixteen hours on the beach before the evacuation system caught up with them.

POINTE DU HOC

On Pointe du Hoc, the situation was chaotic with companies, platoons, and even squads separated among the torn terrain. Once over the cliff top, initial German opposition was minimal except at the observation post. As the Rangers moved inland, the advantage of surprise was no longer with them, and the German infantry, whose defense had been oriented inland, hurried to face the Rangers. The success of the battalion depended on the initiative of each man pressing forward.

Several boatloads of Fox Company were fighting a pitched battle on the left flank. Squad-size, machine-gun-equipped German elements began moving in the direction of Rudder's recently installed command post. T/5 Herman Stein and Ranger Cloise Manning fired at the German flank and dropped several at a range of forty yards. Hesitating, the Germans took cover in shell holes. Sgt. Eugene Elder was nearby with a 60mm mortar, and he opened fire at close range. As the shells began to burst around them, the Germans tried to flee. Stein described it as "a turkey shoot."[16]

Lt. Jacob Hill began to rally more men from Fox Company, one of whom was PFC William E. Anderson. Herm Stein described Bill Anderson as being "even more cocky than L-Rod Petty."[17] Anderson and his brother, Jack, were charter members of Fox Company. Jack was quiet, but Bill possessed a powerful intellect fronted by boxer's fists with the result that he went up and down the promotion ladder. He never seemed to care about rank—he simply led by personal example when the situation called for it.

Moving along hedgerows, Lieutenant Hill, PFC Bill Anderson, and the four other Rangers leapfrogged forward, with one element advancing while covered by the other. Two Rangers soon became separated from the rest of the group. Crossing an open field under fire and capturing a German eager to surrender, the four remaining Rangers crawled through a field of stubbled wheat and found cover and concealment along a hedgerow. The German machine-gun crew was not aware of the threat coming from the flank. Covered by the other two Rangers, Lieutenant Hill and Anderson crawled to an embankment about twenty-five feet from the machine gun, while the Germans were firing in another direction. Caught up in the excitement of battle, Hill, to Anderson's amazement, stood up just a few yards from the Germans and yelled, "Son of a bitch, you couldn't hit a bull in the ass with a bass fiddle."[18]

Even if the Germans did not understand Hill, he caught their attention. They began to swing the machine gun to fire on the Ranger lieutenant. Hill dropped behind the embankment, and Anderson tossed Hill a fragmentation grenade. Hill's throw was accurate, and the explosion of the grenade silenced the German gun.

As more and more Rangers arrived, they began to search for the missing guns while moving inland toward an exit road that stretched north to south from the center-rear of the Pointe gun positions to the east-west highway inland a distance of about 1,000 yards. The plan was that after the guns were destroyed, the Rangers would meet at an assembly area near the start of this road and move inland to block the highway. About thirty Rangers of Dog and Easy Companies met at the assembly area and set off for the highway.

They immediately came under fire from a group of farmhouses to the front, small-arms fire from the left, machine-gun fire from the right, and artillery. Five men of Dog Company and two from Easy Company were killed while eight men were wounded.

Despite the enemy fire and casualties, the men of Dog and Easy Companies kept moving forward. As the Rangers reached the farm buildings, the Germans withdrew. Both German artillery and American naval gunfire were falling behind the Rangers, serving as inspiration to keep moving. Beyond the farm was a flat open space, some forty yards in width, terminating in a communications trench. Though under fire, the Rangers rushed the trench, running across the open area singly or in small groups. A concrete roadblock provided temporary shelter for some Germans, but Ranger fire drove them off, and the advance continued to the next farm. Though some men were temporarily pinned down by fire, the Rangers reached the blacktop highway by 0815, only one hour and seven minutes after they had landed at the base of the cliffs of Pointe du Hoc.

The men knew that the plan called for three more companies of the 2nd Ranger Battalion and the entire 5th Ranger Battalion to be coming up the cliffs behind them. When that happened, they would be in position to attack the flanks and rear of the German defenders at either Omaha or Utah Beach. It would be some time before they learned the rest of the Rangers had been sent to Omaha Beach.

In Fox Company, Herm Stein, assistant BAR man to Sgt. Jack Richards, saw some men about three quarters of a mile away. Unable to make identification, Richards asked Stein to take a look, handing him a pair of field glasses. Stein got up on the edge of the hole, but could not make the identification either. Determined to learn if the men they saw were friend or foe, Richards climbed to the edge of the hole again. He had scarcely raised the field glasses when he slumped over. Stein pulled Richards back into the hole and found his friend had been shot in the throat. In a few moments, Jack Richards was dead. For many weeks after that, Stein carried Jack Richards's blood on his undershirt. Stein also took Richards's BAR, which he would use to great effect.

From east of Dog and Easy came L-Rod Petty, who had safely retraced his steps to get out of the minefield, and some Fox Company men. They had moved inland, running from crater to crater in short rapid bounds, then single file through mined areas. En route, the men were joined by Lt. Robert Arman. Continuing inland, the Fox Company Rangers were joined by four Easy Company men who had moved to the flank to be clear of the German artillery falling on Dog and Easy. The main body of Fox Company, consisting of about eighteen Rangers, now oriented their movement on a country lane that led to the blacktop highway.

OMAHA BEACH—FORCE C

Lt. Col. Max Schneider, commanding officer of the 5th Ranger Battalion, was the most combat-experienced officer the Rangers had. Schneider had participated in the amphibious invasions of North Africa, Sicily, and Salerno and Anzio in Italy. His knowledge, experience, and wisdom were invaluable and would contribute greatly to the success of the American effort—if he could survive the trip to the beach.

Leaving the mother ships in their landing craft, the men of the 5th Rangers experienced the same difficulties as the other. About five miles out, the boat carrying the 1st Platoon of Company F shipped water. The men bailed with their helmets, but when the water was chest high, they had to abandon the craft and were picked up by a passing LCT.

Schneider's craft was well positioned to allow him to observe and influence the action. Capt. John Raaen, commander of Headquarters Company, 5th Rangers, judged that Schneider was no more than 1,000 yards behind the two companies of the 2nd Battalion when they began their walk in hell. Learning of the carnage on Omaha Dog Green, naval officers closed that beach to landings at about 0700 hours.

Seeing that the 2nd Ranger Battalion elements of Force C were being shot up, Colonel Schneider looked at the beach area to the east (left) and saw little activity on Omaha Dog Red. Smoke from grass fires was blowing across that section of the German position and would hinder enemy observation. Stone breakwaters, a common practice to control beach erosion, ran seaward from the seawall. Schneider realized that these could provide cover from direct-fire weapons. Using hand and arm signals, he shifted the direction of his landing craft flotilla to that point.

This change of direction by Colonel Schneider was one of the key tactical decisions of the invasion. There were no soft spots in the German defense, but Schneider's quick action meant the 5th Ranger landing craft would not receive the concentrated artillery fire currently decimating Company C of the 116th on nearby Omaha Dog White and two large LCIs, numbers 91 and 92, floating nearby.

Schneider's change of course was well executed by the British seamen, who skillfully guided their landing craft through riptide and wave-tossed water and among the many mine-tipped obstacles. Touch-down of first wave craft was made at approximately 0740 primarily on Omaha Dog Red Beach. The second-wave landing craft that included Captain Raaen landed on the right of the line slightly into Omaha Dog White Beach ten minutes later. An LCA carrying the 2nd Platoon of D Company had its ramp stove in when it struck an obstacle, but the men were able to off-load over the sides. The Germans were still concentrating their heaviest fire on the larger ships. LCI 91, which carried the executive officer and alternate headquarters of the 116th Infantry, hit a Tellermine while lowering its ramp and then was hit amidships by artillery and set ablaze. Many men were seen burning as they leaped overboard. LCI 92 came in and was hit by German artillery and rocket fire just as the Rangers were crossing the beach. Looking back, 1st Sgt. Avery Thornhill of B Company saw soldiers on the two vessels waiting to disembark when German shells landed among them.[19]

When the ramps went down, the 5th Rangers landed on a front Raaen estimated at 200 yards in width. They crossed a beach of gravel and small stone and took shelter behind a log seawall. Stone beach erosion walls stretched out like fingers from the log seawall to the sea, providing cover from German fire just as Schneider hoped they would.

As the second wave of the 5th Ranger Battalion was landing, C/116th began to attack the bluff to the right front of the Rangers. Various factors were coming together that confirmed the wisdom of Schneider's choice of landing area. The smoke from the grass fires on the German positions, the log seawall, and stone beach erosion walls, the large LCIs attracting German artillery fire, and the assault on the bluffs by C/116th all contributed to the ability of the 5th Ranger Battalion to cross the beach with minimal harm.

Schneider's battalion had carefully studied the terrain in the area they were supposed to land. Now the terrain to their front presented a different look, but they were determined to press on. Schneider was getting reports from his subordinate commanders, and directing order of movement for the battalion to get through the German defense and move against the battery at Pointe du Hoc. Squad and platoon leaders were getting their men into position. Weapons were being checked and mortars were being set up to give supporting fire. Confident in his Rangers, Schneider said "Tallyho," the signal for the men to move inland to an assembly area near Vierville from which they would proceed to Pointe du Hoc.

Brig. Gen. Norman Cota came strolling up the beach. Captain Raaen jumped to his feet, ran to him, saluted, and reported, "Sir, the 5th Rangers have landed intact here and to the east about 200 yards. The Battalion Commander has ordered us to proceed by platoon infiltration to our rendezvous points."[20] John Raaen's choice of the word "intact" was a perfect fit to the situation. All along Omaha Beach the lead-wave battalions of the 116th Infantry were fragmented, shot up, and dispersed.

Satisfied, Cota then moved on to the area where Capt. Ed Luther of E Company was giving orders to his two platoon leaders. A voice behind Luther began to shout for the men to get up and move inland, which was exactly what Luther was giving instructions about and without looking around he barked, "Hey, bud! Take it easy. This is my outfit. I'll take care of it." The voice behind him shouted, "Well, you've got to get over that wall!" The angry Captain Luther yelled back, "Quit bothering my men; you'll disorganize them. The colonel's over there if you want to see him, but quit bothering me!" Just then the platoon leaders started the men over the wall. Captain Luther looked over his shoulder and saw General Cota standing to his rear. Hoping that the general would not remember him, Luther jumped the wall. His last sight of Cota was of a man with a big grin on his face, turning away to move on up the beach.[21]

Beyond the seawall on Dog White was a lateral road laced with barbed-wire entanglements on its inshore side. These entanglements were covered by frontal and flanking fire. Beyond the wire lay a stretch of flat, open land about 150 yards in length. From the flat, the ground sloped steeply upward to open bluffs. The bluffs were covered with high grass and contained gullies and depressions. On the crest were German foxholes and trenches. This was not a German strongpoint protecting a beach exit, and therefore the German defenses were not as formidable as those on Dog Green, but this was not known to the men facing the bluffs. They just knew that the attack had to be made over open ground. In a stroke of good fortune for the attackers, the dried grass was burning, and the smoke that blew eastward along the bluffs helped conceal the men from German fire.

Within twenty minutes of landing (about 0810) the 5th Ranger
Battalion had used bangalore torpedoes to blow four gaps in the wire
and move forward by platoons, sections in column with skirmishers in
line to the front much like a T formation. They crossed the flat rapidly but were slowed by the slope of the bluff and the smoke of the
burning grasses. Some men donned gas masks at this point, then
pressed on and gained the high ground, losing eight men in the
process. Looking back, Ranger Wallace Young saw Father Lacy moving calmly along the beach, helping those who didn't make it across,
though artillery rounds were falling. Young wrote, "Many of our men
at that moment came to realize God helps them that help themselves.
A good foxhole was first on the agenda and then the prayer that you
would not get hit."[22]

Capt. George B. "Whit" Whittington, B Company commander,
5th Rangers, was one of the first men to reach the top of the bluffs.
Once there, Whittington and PFC Carl Weast got behind a three-man
German machine-gun nest. As Whittington leveled his Thompson
sub-machine gun, one of the Germans glanced to the rear, saw Whittington, and began to plead, "*Bitte, bitte.*" Whittington killed the three
Germans, then said to Weast, "I wonder what *bitte* means?"[23]

After sustaining murderous fire, Company C of the 116th was also
on the move and fighting well. Both units had demolition teams at
work. Near the top of the bluff, the smoke cleared, and German mortar and automatic-weapons fire became heavy. A platoon from Company D of the 5th Rangers, led by Lt. Francis Dawson, eliminated a
key German position. The attack continued and the 5th Rangers were
joined by the survivors of Able and Baker Companies from the 2nd
Rangers, whom Schneider organized into a provisional company commanded by Captain Arnold of Baker Company.

Lt. Col. Max Schneider's mission was to get to Pointe du Hoc with
his 5th Ranger Battalion and the three companies and headquarters
elements of the 2nd Rangers. Schneider's battalion was intact when
they landed, but by the time they reached the top of the bluffs
Schneider's men were scattered and intermingled with elements of
Able, Baker, and Headquarters Company of the 2nd Rangers and
Company C of the 116th Infantry. Since Companies B and C of the
5th Rangers were relatively intact, Schneider decided to move to a
pre-planned assembly area, a road junction to the southwest of

Vierville and complete the consolidation of his force. Capt. George Whittington's Company B was ordered to serve as the advance guard with Lt. Bernard Pepper's 1st Platoon as point.

As Schneider's force attempted to pass southwest of Vierville to get to the assembly area, they encountered fierce German resistance, stalling the advance for over three hours. Schneider decided to change his route and move directly through Vierville toward Pointe du Hoc.

In Vierville they encountered snipers and tunnels that allowed the Germans to infiltrate back to areas the Rangers had cleared. Some Rangers reported encountering male and female civilian snipers. Demolitions were used on the tunnels, and the snipers were summarily dealt with.[24] A quantity of wooden bullets were found and the rumor spread that these were being used by snipers that had been bypassed. It was said that such bullets would not ricochet and caused wounds that were slow to heal. In reality, they were only practice rounds.

On the west side of Vierville, German snipers killed two men in B Company, 5th Ranger Battalion, and the company took cover. Captain Whittington and 1st Sergeant Thornhill were in a ditch behind a hedgerow deciding how to take out the snipers when a voice behind them bellowed, "Get up and start moving! We'll never win this war on our tails!" It was General Cota again.

"General, there are snipers in the trees up ahead," responded Whittingon "We're trying to clear them out. You better take cover!"

"There are no snipers!" yelled Cota.

A German bullet kicked up the dirt at Cota's feet. The general looked down and said "Well, there might be one."[25]

POINTE DU HOC

At Pointe du Hoc, Fox Company Rangers, with Sgt. L-Rod Petty scouting, reached the juncture of the lane and highway. It was now 0805. In roughly an hour since landing, the 2nd Rangers had reached their second geographical objective. Turning west and paralleling the blacktop, the F Company men encountered ineffective machine-gun fire near the hamlet of Auguay. Sergeant Petty and Sgt. William McHugh flanked a farmhouse. In the backyard, Petty was startled to see two effectively camouflaged Germans rise from the ground to his front. Petty dove forward firing his BAR, but he was so close that the barrel of his weapon was between the two Germans. The experience was nonetheless unnerving for the Germans, who shouted, "*Kamerad*," and surrendered. "Hell, L-Rod," commented McHugh, "that's a good way to save ammunition—just scare 'em to death." Two other Germans surrendered, and when they searched them, one man had a pipe tamper. "Well, I'll be damned," said McHugh, greatly angered, "it's made in the U.S." Petty broke out laughing when McHugh made the Germans do the goose-step as he marched them away barking, "*Eins, zwei, drei, vier!*"[26] While the POWs were led away, lead elements of Dog, Easy, and Fox Companies took up blocking positions to prevent German movement on the Vierville-Grandcamp highway and keep the Germans from regaining control of the point.

Over on the western flank, Lt. George Kerchener, Dog Company commander, caught up with 1st Sgt. Len Lomell and established an outpost with a BAR man and several riflemen to await the inevitable German counterattack.

Forty or fifty Germans were seen moving on the other side of the coast road. These were reserves from the 726th Grenadier Regiment being committed in an attack on Pointe du Hoc from St. Pierre du Mont. Heavily outnumbered, the Dog Company Rangers maintained fire and camouflage discipline, and the Germans passed by unaware of the Rangers.

Still searching for the guns they were tasked to destroy, the three Ranger companies sent out several patrols. In Easy Company, 1st Sgt. Robert Lang sent out a patrol led by S/Sgt. Frank Rupinski and consisting of T/5 Frank Labrandt, Ken Bargmann, and T/5 John Burnett. In Dog Company, Lieutenant Kerchner ordered out two patrols of two men each.[27] S/Sgt. Lawrence Johnson and T/Sgt. Les Arthur were one; 1st Sergeant Lomell and S/Sgt. Jack Kuhn, the other.

Lomell and Kuhn went down a country lane between two high hedgerows since it offered more cover than proceeding over open fields. They could see fresh markings on the surface of the lane, so they followed it. Lomell was in front when he looked over the hedgerow and saw the guns they had been sent to destroy. The 155mm guns were in an apple orchard, roughly 200 square feet and oriented toward Utah Beach. Ammunition and powder bags were stacked nearby, though no Germans were manning the guns. About

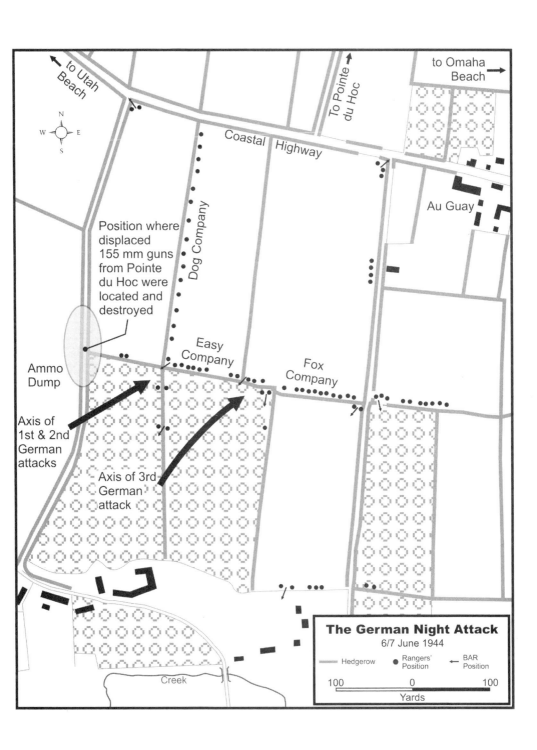

to Utah Beach

N
W   E
S

To Pointe du Hoc

to Omaha Beach →

Coastal   Highway

Au Guay

Position where
displaced
155 mm guns
from Pointe
du Hoc were
located and
destroyed

Dog Company

Easy
Company

Fox
Company

Ammo
Dump

Axis of
1st & 2nd
German
attacks

Axis of 3rd
German
attack

Creek

The German Night Attack
6/7 June 1944

———— Hedgerow   ● Rangers'
                        Position   ← BAR
                                       Position

100   0   100

Yards

100 yards away at a farm road intersection, a German officer was talking to between thirty and seventy-five men whom Lomell and Kuhn
believed to be the gun crews. While Kuhn kept watch, Lomell ignited
thermite grenades and planted them on the traversing mechanism of
two of the guns. Lomell then wrapped his field jacket around the butt
of his Thompson submachine gun and smashed the sights of all five
guns. The two men then crossed through the hedgerow and ran back
down the lane to the Dog Company position. They grabbed more
thermite grenades and went back to the guns. Dog Company sent Sgt.
Harry Fate and Sgt. Gordon Luning as messengers over different
routes to report the destruction of the guns to Colonel Rudder.
Lomell estimated the messengers departed before 0900.

Meanwhile, the Easy Company patrol dispatched by 1st Sergeant
Lang traveled in a southwest arc which appears to have brought it
onto the same road used by Lomell and Kuhn, but coming from the
opposite direction. The terrain was open fields and apple orchards
with lanes flanked by hedgerows. Near an entrance into a pasture, a
patrol member found one of the guns in an elevated position. There
were no Germans in sight. The gun Burnett found did not have a net
or camouflage over it, and there was no indication that the gun had
been in action. On opening the breech block, it was discovered that
the gun was loaded and ready to fire. To put a thermite grenade in
the open breech of a loaded artillery piece would have been suicide
since the thermite grenade had a two-second fuse. Instead, the
Rangers turned the elevating wheel to lower the gun tube to the horizontal and inserted a thermite grenade just inside the muzzle, ren-
dering the gun inoperable.

There were several small tents under some trees close to the gun
that contained the gear and personal effects of German soldiers which
the Easy Company patrol quickly looted, grabbing a camera and a
number of German potato-masher grenades. The patrol then moved
on but did not see any other guns. Beside the hedgerow-flanked lane
between their single gun and short of the position where Lomell and
Kuhn had found five other guns, Rupenski's patrol came upon the
powder supply for the German 2nd Battery, 1260th Artillery Battalion.

Rupenski set a demolition charge beside the powder bags and the
men withdrew as the powder exploded with a tremendous roar, surprising Lomell and Kuhn. Lomell recalled what happened next:

"When it blew up and we went flying and ram rods, rocks and dust and everything came down on us. We got up and ran like two scared rabbits as fast as we could back to our men at the road block. I thought it was a short round from the *Texas*. So did Jack. We couldn't even hear. But the point is, we didn't even know who did it."[28]

Capt. Ike Eikner noted that at "about 9:00 A.M. on D-Day morning two runners from Dog Company dropped into the CP (Command Post) and reported that the guns had been destroyed. About 15 or 20 minutes later a couple of runners from Easy Company reported that they had destroyed the guns. When I informed them that Dog Company had just reported them destroyed, the Easy Company fellows seemed amazed. When I reported to Col. Rudder that Easy Company was now reporting the guns destroyed, he said now we can be sure that they are really out of action and we decided to put out the message . . . that our mission was accomplished. The message went out by radio, lamp and carrier pigeon."[29]

American Rangers had accomplished what the Germans thought impossible: They scaled the cliffs, surprised the Germans and kept attacking until the guns of the most dreaded German battery opposed to the American landings at Normandy were silenced without the German gunners firing a shot.

All the Rangers who landed on June 6, 1944, the English sailors who brought them ashore, every crewman of the planes that bombed Pointe du Hoc and sailor on the ships that shelled it had a hand in bringing the mission to a successful conclusion. Recognizing the threat of the guns of Pointe du Hoc, Allied planners attempted to destroy them using the 14-inch guns of the battleship *Texas*. The destroyers *Satterlee* and *Thompson* added the shells of their 5-inch guns. The American and British Air Forces sent 76 B-17 and 115 Lancaster heavy bombers, 64 B-26 medium bombers, and 136 A-20 Havoc light bombers to destroy the guns, dropping a total of 3,264 bombs on this small patch of earth.[30] In the end, it was two American Rangers on the ground who destroyed five guns and a four-man Ranger patrol who located and took out the sixth gun.

The mystery of June 6, 1944, is why the six guns were unmanned. Simply put, it is likely the Germans never expected an attack on the cliffs. The majority of the defense of the battery was designed to stop an attack from inland, not from the sea.

There were forty critical minutes when the German gun crews could have attempted to reach their guns in the alternate positions, but they had some distance to travel over open ground from their bunkers, and men under bombardment do not know when the next shell is coming in. The earth was being ripped asunder by the 14-inch guns of a battleship plus those of a cruiser and several destroyers. Caution was definitely the better part of valor.

Back at Rudder's CP, eight P-47 fighter-bombers were called in by the naval shore fire-control party to attack a German automatic-weapons position on the left flank. When the lead plane came over, however, it appeared he was going to strike the Ranger CP. Rudder had brought an American flag ashore, and Lieutenant Eikner spread it out on the ground as a recognition signal. The P-47 pilot waggled his wings in recognition, then accurately struck his target. The flag was useful to mark the Ranger CP location from the air, but there was no guarantee of safety from friendly fire coming from the sea.

A shell fired by a fire-support vessel fell short and hit among the men, killing Army captain Jonathan Harwood and Pvt. Henry W. Genther and wounding Navy lieutenant Kenneth "Rocky" Norton of the fire-control party. Colonel Rudder was knocked down, taking a second wound after having been hit in the thigh earlier that morning, this one from splinters of concrete in his right arm. Radio communication with the Navy was disrupted. Eikner's men had established land line communication and Rudder used the field telephone to call Eikner and ask him to send litters and get communication with the ships going again.

Eikner had foreseen communication problems and had trained his men to use international Morse code. He had also secured two World War–I vintage, tripod-mounted EE-84 signal lamps. One of these was lost with the sinking of the supply craft LCA 914, but Eikner found the other was ashore and had it brought to the top and put to use. By using the blinker light and Morse code, Eikner and his men were able to maintain contact and adjust naval gunfire. Lt. Amos Potts, the photographer without film after all his was ruined coming ashore, was without a mission, so he served to aim the lamp at the ships in the Channel.

Compounding the Rangers' communication difficulties was that the Signal Operating Instructions (SOI), which prescribe the radio frequencies, call signs, and codes that authenticate messages, had been changed without the information being passed to the Rangers. As a result, Ranger transmissions were being ignored by other American units.

Beginning at noon on June 6 and lasting for an hour, Rudder had Eikner try again to establish contact with Colonel Canham of the 116th Infantry Regiment and commanders on ship. Direct radio calls were made from the SCR 300 and relayed calls using the shore fire-control SCR-284 through the USS *Satterlee*. Lieutenant Eikner also placed messages in the capsules affixed to the legs of the two homing pigeons and launched the birds skyward. The same message was sent: "Located Pointe du Hoc—mission accomplished—need ammunition and reinforcements—many casualties." The response to Rudder's request was terse: "No reinforcements available."[31]

Around 1500 the 116th Infantry responded but only to say they could not understand the Ranger message. Eiker sent the message again but no assistance was forthcoming.

While the Ranger CP wrestled with German counterattacks and communication problems, the Rangers continued to go on the attack. In late morning, Lt. Jacob Hill and Pvt. John Bacho went looking for Germans. Hill heard a German machine gun firing toward the Pointe, and the two men moved in that direction. Bacho heard sounds and peered over a hedgerow and saw about a dozen Germans on the ground talking. Though there were only two Rangers, Hill decided to grenade the Germans. Both Rangers threw fragmentation grenades over the top and dove for a ditch, but the usually reliable American fragmentation grenades failed to explode. German potato-masher grenades came sailing back over the hedge, and a firefight developed with the German numbers deciding the issue. The audacious Lt. "Bangelore Jake" Hill was shot in the chest by a machine pistol and died. Wounded in the hand, Bacho fell over Hill's body, placing his face on Hill's bleeding wound and feigning death. The Germans looked over the hedgerow and believed both Rangers were dead. At dark, Bacho made it back to the Pointe.

Ranger patrols remained active, yet no organized German defense was found. The German soldiers who were bypassed were disorganized, fragmented, and now trying to rejoin their units. The route of travel for a number of these Germans took them across a valley where Easy and Fox Companies had particularly good positions.

Sgt. L-Rod Petty found a position near a farm house that offered a clear field of fire. From this location Petty could see movement for a mile and his range of vision covered the inland roads. Though the location was isolated, Petty was allowed to remain in the location as an outpost.

Petty had a clear field of fire for his beloved BAR and it was not long before targets began to appear. Most of the Germans were coming from the direction of Omaha Beach, often traveling in groups of eight to ten men. One group of Germans were on bicycles riding close together. As they slowed to negotiate a turn, Petty swept the line with his BAR. Men and bicycles went cartwheeling. A team of horses drawing a wagon galloped into view from the farm buildings about 100 yards away trying to reach the road. The horses were being driven by a French farmer who was standing upright, lashing the animals in a scene that reminded Petty of the chariot race from *Ben-Hur*. Petty yelled, "Hold your fire!" PFC Carl Winsch Jr., responded, "Hold your fire, hell! That wagon is loaded with Germans lying down!"[32] Winsch opened fire, Petty put the automatic fire of his BAR on the wagon and the other Rangers joined in.

The German soldiers who had been trying to conceal themselves tried to leap from the wagon and find cover, but were all killed. Neither the horses or the farmer were hit, and still riding like a charioteer at the Circus Maximus in ancient Rome, the farmer and his now bloodied and empty wagon disappeared from view. Next, an unsuspecting German patrol of seven men under a noncommissioned officer came toward the Ranger position from the east. Disobeying Petty's order to hold fire until they were close, a Ranger shot the German leader at 300 yards. Petty thought the rest would scatter and fight but they surrendered.

His comrades insisted that Petty personally brought down thirty of the enemy during the course of D-Day. According to PFC Carl Bombardier, "Petty was a buck sergeant, but really took command that day. We thought he should have the Congressional Medal of

Honor for his heroics. It took six months to get him a Silver Star."[33] Petty knew he "killed some people and wounded some," but as to specific numbers, his comment was "who counts in such situations."[34] Surviving Germans were rounded up with some forty prisoners going into the bag.

In midafternoon, Herm Stein and Cloise Manning were in a shell crater trying to stay alive from an hour-long pounding by German artillery and mortars. Manning had agreed to serve as Stein's assistant on the BAR. Stein began to hear the rattle of machine-gun fire and looked over the edge of the foxhole, and he saw a German infantry squad heading toward Rudder's CP. Stein waited until the German machine-gun crew supporting the squad positioned itself forty-five yards to his front and about 100 yards from Rudder's CP; then both he and Manning opened fire, killing the crew. The surviving German riflemen immediately went to earth in shell holes.

Sgt. Murrell Stinnette, assistant mortar section leader, slid into the shell hole and asked what was going on. "We've got a batch trying to take the CP. Got a few, but the rest are hold up a little way out." Stein pointed in the direction of the Germans.

"Stay put" said Stinnette. "I'll bring up the section in the hole behind you and relay the target from the edge of the crater."[35]

After a few rounds of adjustment the Ranger mortar shells began to fall with accuracy, trapping the German soldiers. If they stayed where they were the mortar fire would kill them. If they tried to run, they would come under fire from Stein and Manning. They chose to run. Only one of the Germans was able to get far enough that he might have lived.

On crossing the seawall, Lt. Charles "Ace" Parker, commander of Company A, 5th Rangers, and his 1st Platoon, led by Lt. Stanley D. Zelepsky, became separated from their battalion. Busy with their own actions and out of communication with battalion headquarters, Parker and his men pushed on toward Pointe du Hoc. Two hours before darkness on June 6, Parker, Zelepsky, and twenty-two men of the 1st Platoon arrived at Rudder's CP. Parker had led these men to the prearranged assembly area near Vierville, but the remainder of the battalion had been slowed by heavy fighting and did not arrive. Thinking that his battalion must be ahead of him and knowing the battalion mission was to get to Pointe du Hoc, Parker set out over-

land, engaging in several firefights along the way. They captured
nearly forty German prisoners, most of whom Parker had to set free
during a heavy action in which the platoon narrowly avoided being
trapped. When Parker linked up with Rudder at around 2100 hours,
he was surprised that his battalion was not there and told Rudder he
believed the remainder of the 5th Battalion was close behind him.
Parker's men were a welcome reinforcement to the 2nd Rangers.
Lieutenant Zelepsky's platoon of 5th Rangers was soon spread out in
defensive positions.

With the coming of night, Rudder maintained his dispositions,
with some eighty men of Dog, Easy, and Fox still forward of the
Vierville-Grandcamp highway. Fox Company was on the left, Easy
Company in the center, and Dog Company on the right. Radio communication between the Pointe and the forward forces was unreliable
as equipment failed and messengers passing back and forth were
slowed due to distance and the torn earth. There was a risk of the forward force being cut off, but the blocking of the highway running
between Omaha and Utah Beaches. If Rudder pulled his advance
force back to the Pointe, he stood the risk of merely making a concentrated target for German artillery. German activity was increasing
as they recovered from the opening shock of the invasion, but no
major counterattack had developed. A third of Rudder's men were
casualties, but lightly wounded men were still fighting. The Ranger
supply of grenades and mortar shells was near exhaustion and small-
arms ammunition was in short supply. German rifles, machine guns,
and potato-masher grenades were being used by many men as the
Rangers tightened up their lines and dug in. With the exception of a
high-energy protein bar (D-Bar), the men had had nothing to eat
since leaving the mother ships. The exhaustion brought on by all they
had endured began to sap their physical strength and mental resolve.
In the CP, British commando Colonel Trevor remarked, "Never have
I been so convinced of anything as that I will either be a prisoner of
war or a casualty by morning."[36]

While the Rangers grimly held their ground, the youthful British
naval lieutenant Ronald F. Eades was living a great adventure. Hurrying about hunting snipers, Eades was mistaken for a German and a
Ranger fired on him. Eades came sliding back into the crater with Lt.
James McCullers and several Headquarters Company Rangers. Eades

lit a cigarette and said with magnificent British aplomb, "I say, fellows, I'm glad to see you do miss a shot sometimes."[37]

At the headquarters of the German 352nd Division, a boundary line was changed to facilitate an attack on the Rangers at Pointe du Hoc by a reinforced company of the 1st Battalion, 914th Panzer Grenadiers, plus available troops from the Pointe du Hoc garrison.[38] The attack was intended to begin in the afternoon, but bombing and naval gunfire was disrupting German land line communication. On the other side of the coin, however, German intelligence officers were surprised and gratified to hear many American radio communications throughout the invasion area being broadcast in clear language. Large parts of the transmissions could be understood by Germans who spoke English. The Germans were careful to encode their own radio messages, but that took time and along with disrupted communication resulted in slower coordination and delayed their counterattack on Pointe du Hoc.

Night brought a three-quarter moon and a changed landscape. Visibility had been good during the daytime, but at night the shadows of hedgerows and orchards seemed to shift. A slight breeze rustling a bush could give the effect of a moving enemy and play upon the nerves. In the foxholes, there was the feeling of battlefield isolation the Germans call *die Leere des Gefechtfeld* ("the emptiness of the battlefield").[39]

Three hundred yards inland of the highway, the Ranger survivors, about eighty-five men, consolidated and improved their positions. The Ranger position looked like an "L" with each front being about 300 yards long. Dog Company was on the right—west—and their line ran north to south, linking with Easy Company. The line then formed a right angle as the Easy Company line ran west to east, tying in with Fox Company. To provide early warning and prevent the enemy from knowing where the Ranger main line of resistance was located, several two-man outposts were placed forward of each company. Sergeant Petty of Fox Company was still on outpost with eight men over 200 yards in front Arman and Parker's positions. The other outposts were each occupied by two men and located twenty-five to fifty yards in front of the main line. Arman ordered Petty to withdraw to the main line if a German attack began.

There were no majors or colonels—indeed, no captains— available to coordinate the activities of the remnants of the three companies. Lt. Robert Arman of Fox Company was the senior officer. The other lieutenants, Kerchner of Dog Company, Leagens and Lapres of Easy, and Parker and Zelepsky of the 5th Rangers, took their initial disposition orders from Arman but after that the command structure was decentralized. Arman, Lapres, and Parker established a CP of sorts at the juncture of Easy and Fox Company on the eastern portion of the L, but there was insufficient strength to provide a reserve to counterattack enemy penetrations, and Arman was not in control in other company areas. Ammunition for the Thompson submachine guns and BARs was in short supply. Easy Company had two Thompsons and three captured German machine guns they were relying on for automatic fire.

Lt. George Kerchner, Dog Company commander, had observed enemy activity southwest of the angle where Dog and Easy Company joined. Kerchner reported this to Arman. An additional concern was the thirty to forty German prisoners the Rangers held. These were put in foxholes north of the CP and guarded by two Rangers.

Shortly before midnight, Ranger outposts in front of the juncture of Dog and Easy Companies were jarred by shouts and whistles followed by heavy German fire from just twenty-five yards in front of the Rangers' main line. At an Easy Company outpost occupied by BAR man T/5 Leroy Thompson and S/Sgt. Robert Honhart, German soldiers suddenly appeared at point-blank range. Thompson and Honhart opened fire, dropping three men. The other Germans scurried for cover and began to throw grenades, wounding Thompson in the face. Honhart took the BAR and the two men withdrew to the main line.

The German attack had come at the critical corner of the L where Dog and Easy Company joined. Lieutenant Kerchner and S/Sgt. Harry Fate had been at the point of the German attack and it appeared to them they would be overrun. If the Germans succeeded they would be in position to slice the Ranger line in half and roll up the north-south line of most of Dog Company and the east-west positions of Easy and Fox Companies. Feeling they could not contain the attack, Lieutenant Kerchner and Sergeant Fate left their foxholes and ran north along the Dog Company line. Kerchner considered taking men from the Dog Company line and striking the Germans in the flank in a counterattack, but he did not have control of the line and this was a desperate hope at best. As Lieutenant Kerchner ran north-ward along the hedgerow, he called to men to come with him, but in the gunfire and confusion only two men heard and followed. The German attack was not pressed home and was likely only a probe to draw Ranger fire and reveal their positions. As the Germans pulled back, Kerchner stayed north at the highway. All outposts except the well-forward position of Sergeant Petty were now drawn back, but the men could not find the line in the darkness and gaps developed. With Kerchner's movement there was no officer at the right angle of the Ranger line and no one from Dog or Easy was moved into the juncture of the two companies. Armed with a BAR, T/5 Henry Stecki of Dog Company and a riflemen had not heard Kerchner's call to withdraw and were now the only two men at this critical point.

Though the attack had not fallen on Fox Company, Sergeant Petty was taking plenty of rounds from a German machine gun that was ricocheting bullets off a farm roller Petty had pulled close to his position. A German attack appeared imminent, so Petty followed his instructions and withdrew his outpost to the Fox Company line. Petty with his BAR and PFC Frederick Dix with a German machine gun joined Lieutenant Arman in the vicinity of the CP while the rest of Petty's men were placed on line to the east. The German prisoners were moved farther from the CP into the center of that open field and told to dig in to protect themselves from stray fire.

Around 0100 hours the Germans of the 1st Battalion, 941st Grenadier Regiment, again struck near the juncture of Dog and Easy Companies. Enemy noise discipline was excellent and their troops managed to move within 100 yards of the Ranger positions without being heard. Suddenly, German leaders blew whistles, and men shouted their names possibly to enhance morale or to identify to their leaders their location in the darkness.

The clamor was followed by heavy machine-gun and small-arms fire, often predominantly with tracer ammunition, plus German mor-tar fire and grenades. Stecki opened fire with his BAR and, with a rapid changing of magazines, delivered a constant stream of fire for several minutes. Grenades were heard exploding, near his position. The BAR fell silent for a brief period then opened fire again. More German grenades were heard exploding then no more sound from the American position except German voices. The battlefield is often a lonely place, and darkness enhanced the feeling of being isolated. Men twenty-five yards distant did not know what had occurred. What they knew was ominous: their supply of ammunition was very low. In their holes in the earth, they clutched their weapons and strained their eyes into the night. But the Germans did not press home their second attack.

About 0300 the Germans made their third attack. This was preceded by increased mortar fire some of which fell in the area where the prisoners were located. Automatic weapons fire came into the Ranger position in high volume and the attack spread eastward. Some of the fire was believed to be coming from a German machine gun located at the angle where Stecki's BAR had gone silent.

Though the attack came in on both the Easy and Fox Company positions, the main German thrust was at the western part of the Easy Company line. The Easy Company platoon at this location was hit hard. The primary German assault massed fires intended to keep the defenders pinned down, then split the line and used enfilade fire to roll up that portion of Easy Company. There was the usual night-battle confusion about the location of both friends and enemy. Along the line Rangers were throwing captured German grenades. Sgt. Frank Rupinski was heard arguing with some Rangers that they should surrender since it was the only way they would survive. The argument closed with Rupinski yelling, *"Kamerad!"* The German infantry rolled up the Easy Company line, killing or capturing nineteen Rangers, most of whom were wounded. Lt. Joseph E. Leagens of Easy Company was among the dead.

Some of the Germans came in on the Fox Company area up the lane from the south toward Lieutenant Arman's CP, which was protected by Sergeant Robey's BAR. Sergeant Petty and S/Sgt. Frederick Dix were sent to assist, but as the German attack came in, a bullet fired by a Ranger down the line struck Dix in the helmet and stunned him.

The German machine guns seemed to be firing slightly high, and the Rangers soon found that the German soldiers were crawling toward them under this fire. Sergeant Petty and Private First Class Winsch saw a German crawling toward them, but both men were reloading their weapons, so Petty told Winsch to use a grenade. Winch dropped his rifle and rolled a grenade toward the man. The

German pushed upward to spring to his feet and the grenade rolled under his chest and exploded. The German infantry were now among the Ranger positions and men were coming out of the holes to fight hand to hand. Sergeant Petty yelled, "Down!" and as the Americans dropped, he opened fire with his BAR. Sergeant Robey joined in, and the combined fire of the BARs stopped the advance. Petty took a moment to look at the man he ordered Winsch to kill with the grenade and saw to his horror that it was an American paratrooper who had come overland and joined Fox Company.

All was confusion. No one could tell the strength of the German forces or the configuration of the remaining Ranger positions. Friend and foe were intermixed. An American came running from the west saying that Dog Company had been wiped out. Feeling they were left alone or had been bypassed, men were pulling out of position. The effect of a prolonged day of battle was telling on them. Men were exhausted and hungry, and many were wounded. Weapons fouled with heavy usage were jamming, and they were short of ammunition. The German weapons and grenades being used were effective, but their distinctive sounds added to the uncertainty of who was the enemy and who was not.

Lieutenant Arman decided to withdraw to the Pointe and told Robey and Petty to cover the withdrawal. The withdrawal was normal for this type of circumstance: it was disorganized and men ran for their lives under the protective fires of several key people, in this instance, Petty and Robey who were covering the movement with their BARs.

About 300 yards to the rear they reached the east-west blacktop road. The Germans did not pursue, and Lieutenant Arman set about reorganizing the men, seeking to determine who was missing. Arman found he had most of Fox Company, several men from Easy and none from Dog Company. Learning that Sergeant Petty was still in the previous position covering the withdrawal, Sgt. James Alexander voluntarily went back to assist. As Alexander neared Petty's position, he was captured by four German soldiers. With the immediate danger past for the rest of the men, the inevitable happened: men felt embarrassed and accused each other of pulling out. Lieutenant Parker's men of the 5th Rangers felt they had been left to fend for themselves, and men of the 2nd thought the 5th Rangers had pulled out. Men also felt anger toward others of their own units. They were exhausted, ashamed, bitter, and felt they had been unsupported. Among the dead were S/Sgt. Lawrence Johnson, who prior to the invasion had sought to mail a letter to a girl in Paris, and George Mackey, who had given his card-game winnings to his friends because of his premonition of death.

Around 0400 some forty-eight men reached the Pointe and were placed in a defensive line from gun position number 3 southwest to gun position number 5.

Colonel Rudder was told the rest of the force had been destroyed, but men had been left behind. Four were left in the Fox Company area, including Sergeant Petty, who created confusion among the Germans by opening fire in their midst, then quickly moving in the darkness to a new position. Wherever Petty went, he encountered German soldiers and minutes seemed like hours as he fled or fought as the circumstances warranted. Seeing Germans in skirmish formation he reasoned that the Rangers must be to their front so he attacked the startled Germans from the rear and ran through a gauntlet of fire, fortunately sliding into a Fox Company position. At this point Petty began to shake, and he was taken to the aid station where Doc Block gave him a pill and had him lie down on a litter in a German bunker. An hour later, the shaking had stopped, and Petty rejoined his men.

In the midst of death and destruction there was black humor. With no ammunition for their own weapons, PFC William Roberts and T/5 Albert J. Uronis of Easy Company had a German machine gun that they used on its former owners during the attack. Roberts was gunner and Uronis, who was called "A. J.," was loader. As Roberts began firing the machine gun, Uronis yelled, "I'm hit, Roberts, I'm hit!" and fell to the ground. Roberts stopped firing and turned to his friend "Where are you hit?" he asked. "Here," said Uronis groaning as he pointed to his chest. Roberts checked and found that Uronis was not wounded, he had been hit by the ejecting cartridge cases of the German machine gun and imagination had done the rest. A sheepish A. J. Uronis went back to his duty.[40]

Twelve men of Dog Company were still occupying their original positions at the roadblock. They were unaware that a withdrawal had taken place until there was too much daylight for them to move. With no other choice, the Rangers stayed under cover and maintained fire discipline all of a sudden.

The morning light revealed a grim situation at Pointe du Hoc. The remnants of the three Ranger companies numbered ninety men who could still fight, and ammunition was seriously low. The Ranger position consisted of a strip on the Pointe that was some 200 yards deep and an ideal target for artillery and mortars. Rudder's request for reinforcements had resulted in a message that "all Rangers have been landed."[41] A message sent to the 116th Infantry failed to gain permission for the 5th Rangers and the remainder of the 2nd to push on to link up.

The plan had been that the 5th Ranger Battalion and Able, Baker, and Charlie Company of the 2nd Battalion would go from Omaha Beach to Pointe du Hoc to join Rudder and Dog, Easy, and Fox Companies. High casualties during the landings intervened. The 116th Infantry of the 29th Division had suffered 341 officers and men killed during the day. A German counterattack early in the morning of June 7 threatened the position of the 29th and caused General Gerhardt of the 29th to pull off four Ranger companies of the 5th Battalion and tanks to protect Vierville, the beach exit, and the 29th Division CP.

With the mission to destroy the guns of Pointe du Hoc succeeding, the reinforcement of Dog, Easy, and Fox Companies was no longer among the highest priorities of senior army officers who had to protect and enlarge the buildup from Omaha Beach. It was hoped that the three Ranger companies could hold out, supported by naval gunfire, since it was better to have the three companies of Rangers on Pointe du Hoc overrun than to loose Omaha Beach to German counterattack. The men of the 2nd and 5th Ranger Battalion disagreed.

With the coming of dawn on the morning of June 7, Colonel Rudder found that while their position was precarious, he now had control over the battalion and could influence the defense.

Communication with the warships was vital, and Lieutenant Eikner had both radio and signal-lamp contact with the U.S. Navy destroyers that followed the USS *Satterlee* on station off Pointe du Hoc. The USS *Thompson* and then the USS *Harding* knew where the Rangers were located, and the warships had a clear field of fire.

Throughout the day the Rangers beat off increasingly weakened attempts to drive them from the cliffs. Germans still occupied the vast, concrete observation post on Pointe du Hoc, but on the afternoon of June 7, a white cloth appeared, and the eight surviving occupants surrendered. That was the good news in a situation where ammunition, food, and water were difficult to find and the principal source of weapons was those taken from the enemy.

The grim situation of the Rangers was greatly alleviated by the timely arrival of supplies. Maj. Jack Street, who had joined the Rangers at Nemours, North Africa, commanded Company G of the 1st Ranger Battalion, and served so well in Sicily, was now a staff officer with Admiral Hall. Learning of the difficult circumstances of the Rangers on Pointe du Hoc, Major Street organized a relief party. The 1st Platoon of F Company, 5th Ranger Battalion, and Lt. Frank Kennard's dismounted cannon platoon section had been fighting an independent battle on Omaha Beach and eliminated their opposition. Now available for a new mission, these men were taken off the beach, likely to the USS *Texas*. The platoon of 5th Battalion and Kennard's Rangers then boarded two landing craft carrying supplies of ammunition, water, and food and made the run into Pointe du Hoc. The men were not pleased with having to carry all the supplies to the top of the cliffs but were cheered by the welcome they received. Their arrival also meant the addition of approximately sixty men of the 5th Ranger Battalion to the defense of Pointe du Hoc. The LCVPs that dropped them off did not go back empty-handed, taking back to the *Texas* twenty-eight German prisoners and thirty-four wounded Rangers.

As darkness fell on June 7, the men of the 2nd Ranger Battalion's Dog, Easy, and Fox Companies and their comrades of the 5th Rangers still held their ground on Pointe du Hoc. At 2200 hours on June 7, Oberstleutnant Heyna's 914th Grenadier Regiment was reporting no change in the situation on Pointe du Hoc.[42] Their attacking force had not been able to drive the Rangers from the cliffs.

THE RELIEF OF POINTE DU HOC

Schneider's movement to relieve Rudder had been foiled by happenstance. Col. Charles Canham, commander of the 116th Infantry and the attached Rangers, had succeeded in getting his command group past Vierville heading for a pre-planned command post location. Canham assumed the three battalions of his regiment were fighting their way to the assembly area. When Canham arrived at his destination, he found he had no contact with his scattered troops but there were Germans nearby. With only a small group of soldiers, Canham began looking for security for his CP.

Captain Whittington and his B Company of the 5th Rangers were moving along the coastal road toward Vierville when Company C of the 116th Infantry came up on their right flank and the two companies moved forward in conjunction. About 500 yards west of Vierville German infantry in well-concealed rifle pits contested the advance with heavy small-arms and automatic-weapons fire. About 500 yards west of Vierville they encountered stiff resistance from Germans of the 916th Grenadier Regiment. Captain Whittington sent one of his platoons to flank the German position, but before they could, they encountered Colonel Canham, who cancelled the Rangers' attack and ordered them to serve as security for his CP.

Over the objections of Ranger officers, Canham stopped Schneider's advance trying to come to the assistance of Rudder's men on Pointe du Hoc. The Provisional Ranger Group was part of Canham's command and he had the authority to issue orders to Schneider. It is unclear if Canham knew that three companies of Rangers had successfully climbed the cliffs of Point du Hoc. General Gerhardt and Colonel Canham knew that Vierville must not be retaken by the Germans as it was essential the Omaha Beach lodgement remain open. Canham therefore decided to take a defensive posture and hold his ground. Greatly concerned about the condition of Rudder's men on Pointe du Hoc, Schneider pressed for plans to continue the relief movement.

A plan was devised that on the morning of June 7, a task force under Lt. Col. John Metcalfe, commander of the 1st Battalion 116th, would continue onward. Metcalfe had about 250 men of the 116th most of whom were in C Company. Added to this force were C and D Companies of the 5th Rangers and the survivors of Able, Baker, and Charlie Companies of the 2nd Rangers in a composite company. Armor was provided by eight tanks of B Company of the 743rd Tank Battalion. Maj. Richard Sullivan of the 5th Rangers was second in command of the task force. At 0800 on the seventh, movement began. Initially, scattered resistance was met and shortly after 1200 hours Metcalfe's force had reached the hamlet of St. Pierre du Mont.

Here forward progress by armor was stopped by a huge crater flanked by mine fields, and two of the tanks were damaged.

The Rangers and the infantry of the 116th continued along the coastal road until they were within a thousand yards of Pointe du Hoc when they met heavy German resistance, including a severe lashing by artillery.

Sgt. Joe Dorchak of Baker Company saw an American lieutenant of the 116th and his platoon destroy a machine gun. A lone German survivor stepped out into the open with his hands above his head. As the lieutenant moved forward to accept the surrender, the German threw a grenade he had concealed in his hands, killing the officer. The German was immediately shot down. Furious at such treachery, each soldier in the lieutenant's platoon fired a clip of ammunition into the German's body as they passed by.

As the heavy concentration of German artillery rained down on the Rangers, a brave French farmer, Maurice Lenormand, brought his horse and cart to evacuate the Ranger wounded.

Unable to push on, the Rangers and 116th were forced to withdraw to St. Pierre du Mont. Sgt. Ed O'Connor of Able Company, 2nd Battalion, found himself the last man coming back the road. As he scanned the roadside, O'Connor saw German soldiers in grey-green uniforms signaling. These Germans soon made it clear they wanted to surrender. Making motions that their hands should be on top of their heads, O'Connor motioned the Germans to him while keeping his rifle pointed at them. Soon O'Connor was happily bringing in five prisoners.

Still concerned about protection of the Omaha Beach lodgment, Colonel Canham ordered the tanks of the 743rd, Colonel Metcalfe and Major Sullivan back to Vierville for the night. Capt. John Raaen, Headquarters Company commander of the 5th Rangers was placed in charge of the Rangers and infantry that would remain at St. Pierre du Mont. Raaen called in subordinate leaders, planned his positions, and had the men dig in.

Not satisfied with sitting still while the fate of Rudder and his men was unknown, Raaen decided to send out a patrol to attempt to make contact. Raaen had been a platoon leader of Company C and knew the men well. He chose Sgt. Willie W. Moody and Cpl. Howard D. McKissick, briefed them, and sent them out into the darkness.

The next morning, Raaen learned that Moody and McKissick had returned. Hurrying to meet them, Raaen asked "Did you contact the 2nd?" "Yes, sir," was the response. Raaen asked, "What shape are they in?" Sergeant Moody handed Captain Raaen a sound powered telephone and said, "You can ask them, captain."[43] In a remarkable display of initiative the two Rangers had not only passed through 1,000 yards of enemy-held territory, they had located wire and ran a telephone line. The arrival of Moody and McKissick was greeted with joy at both ends. It was a courageous performance, and for it both men would be awarded the Distinguished Service Cross.

Not to be forgotten on D-Day were the cannon sections consisting of four old International half-tracks mounting 75mm guns. With this element was the Headquarters Company commander, Capt. Frederick O. Wilken, and 1st Lt. Conway E. Epperson and 1st Lt. Frank L. Kennard, who each headed a section of two half-tracks. The cannon-equipped half-track vehicles did not embark for the invasion with the rest of the battalion. On June 2 they departed from a hardstand parking area outside of Weymouth and joined into what Lieutenant Kennard remembered as an almost endless column of vehicles proceeding down to the loading piers. At water's edge the half-tracks were loaded on LCTs along with vehicles of the 467th Anti-Aircraft, Automatic Weapons Battalion, whose vehicles were called "Quad Fifties," as they mounted four .50-caliber machine guns that could be fired together. Epperson's tracks were on LCT 39 and Kennard's on LCT 35 both scheduled to land on Omaha Dog White Beach at H+120 (0830). However, because of the fierce resistance being put up by the Germans on Omaha, they were delayed and didn't land until 0930 and farther east than intended.

When the ramp finally went down in two feet of water, the half-tracks unloaded onto a beach that was crowded with men and equipment. As they moved toward the bluffs, German direct-fire artillery destroyed one of the vehicles. There was no exit open to get vehicles off the beach and they found they could not elevate the 75-millimeter guns sufficiently to support the Rangers who were fighting their way up the bluffs to the front.

As the leaders discussed the situation, a German shell struck home, killing PFC Frank Kosina and PFC William McWhirter and wounding Captain Wilkens and a driver.

Realizing they were sitting ducks, Lieutenant Kennard blew a hole in the wire atop the seawall with a bangalore torpedo, then attempted to climb it with a half-track. The clutch burned out in the vehicle, leaving both of Kennard's vehicles inoperable. Kennard then took his group of about eight men and linked up with Lt. John Reville's 1st Platoon of Company F, 5th Ranger Battalion, and their company commander, Capt. William Runge. The LCA carrying this platoon of the 5th Rangers and part of their company headquarters had been swamped about five miles from shore and also late in arriving. The men were picked up by a passing LCT before their craft went down and landed near Laurent-sur-Mer Beach exit at about 0900. After these men of the 2nd and 5th Battalions came together, they were pinned down for the remainder of D-Day. About 0800 on the seventh, they attacked inland and knocked out three pillboxes, killing eight Germans and capturing thirty-six. The afternoon of June 7, this independent group was taken to Pointe du Hoc by LCA. Lieutenant Epperson got Captain Wilkens and the driver evacuated and then, when the beach exit opened, was able to take the remaining half-tracks off the beach.

Along the invasion area, the German position was rapidly deteriorating. The crust of the defense was broken. The dreaded P-47s of the Americans and Typhoons of the British and Canadians wreaked havoc on German efforts to counterattack with the 21st Panzer Division. Without air support and with ammunition for artillery units growing short the Germans were finding it increasingly difficult to mount effective counterattacks. Oberstleutnant Ziegelmann observed, "Rommel's tactics, the annihilation of the enemy at sea, or its immediate repulse to the sea could no longer be employed in the sector of the 352nd Inf. Div."[44]

Meanwhile, plans had been made for an American relief force of six battalions to press on to Pointe du Hoc. The plan relied heavily on information from Colonel Rudder via the telephone provided by Rangers Moody and McKissick.

Ranger Companies B and E of the 5th Battalion would take and hold the high ground west of the sluice gate at Grandcamp les Bains. The remainder of the Ranger force and 1/116 would attack directly at Pointe du Hoc while the 2nd and 3rd Battalions of the 116th with the tanks of Companies A and C of the 743rd Tank Battalion would attack toward Grandcamp, then swing right to envelop any Germans still in the area. The attack went well, and the Rangers on Pointe du Hoc were relieved around noon on the seventh to much joy and back-slapping. The joy was short-lived, however, when the 3rd Battalion, 116th Infantry, approaching from the south, heard the sound of German weapons being fired from Pointe du Hoc. Unaware that Rangers on the Pointe had been using captured German weapons, the 3rd Battalion opened fire on the Rangers with machine guns, tanks of the 743rd Tank Battalion, artillery, and mortars. A recognition flare was fired and Rudder's American flag was displayed, but four Rangers were killed and three others wounded. An officer of Fox Company led a patrol that shut down the so-called "friendly fire." Capt. John Raaen wrote that he saw a 2nd Battalion officer jump on the deck of a tank and beat on the turret until he got the attention of the crew.

In *Pogue's War* Army historian Forrest Pogue related that Rear Adm. Carleton F. Bryant, USN, on board the battleship *Texas* heard the action and radioed Rudder. "Are you being fired on?" "Yes" came the reply. "Do you want me to put fire on them?" "No" was the reply. The Admiral thought that one over and said, "Are you being hit by friendly fire?" "Yes" came the laconic response.[45]

The linkup was accomplished and German resistance reduced. By noon on June 8, the situation was well in hand. The attacking American forces pressed on, supported by the guns of the British cruiser *Glasgow*. By nightfall, the Germans had lost Grandcamp and the battle. On Friday, June 9, 1944, Gen. Omar Bradley moved the headquarters of U.S. First Army ashore from the USS *Augusta*. Its location was the orchard where Rangers Lomell and Kuhn found and destroyed five of the guns of Pointe Du Hoc.[46]

Despite the commitment of vast numbers of men and staggering quantities of material, the success of the invasion of Europe depended upon the relatively small number of men who made the initial landings. At Pointe du Hoc the Ranger dead were laid beside a road for identification. Len Lomell would remark how "hard it was to look on the still bodies of buddies, sand and dust drifting across their faces."

Medics Willie Clark and Frank South noted the skin of the American dead had a yellowish cast, possibly because of the yellow smoke marking rounds fired by naval guns.[47]

The men of the 2nd Ranger Battalion had contributed greatly to victory in the largest amphibious invasion in history. No one has a better claim to having been the first of the invasion force to reach high ground than Ralph Goranson's Charlie Company. The action the men of Charlie Company fought on top of the cliffs and assisted by men of Company B, 116th Infantry, saved many GIs who were caught in the hellfires of Omaha Beach. Able and Baker Companies of the 2nd Rangers endured that hell on Omaha Dog Green yet continued to attack and seized the bluffs to their front. Ike Eikner's Headquarters Company provided the medics who tended the wounded and the signal service that brought the great fires of the warships on the German soldiers. Dog, Easy, and Fox Companies climbed the towering cliffs under fire, took and held the high ground, and eliminated the guns of Pointe du Hoc. Had the guns of Pointe du Hoc not been destroyed by the men of the battalion, the sands of Utah Beach may well have been soaked with significantly more blood of American youth. Able, Baker, and Charlie Companies of the 2nd Rangers and Max Schneider's 5th Ranger Battalion also had a rendezvous with history on Omaha Beach. At precisely the right moment in time, they were in position and possessed the strength to lift the invasion beyond the beaches.

The horror of the carnage on Omaha Beach seared itself on the souls of the men who fought there. In a small notebook stained with the waters of the English Channel the 2nd Ranger Battalion's S-1 (personnel officer), Capt. Richard Merrill, wrote down the numbers he would later report to Colonel Rudder. The battalion had landed with 512 enlisted men and 33 officers. Preliminary casualties numbered 247 enlisted men and 16 officers, of which 65 men and 5 officers had been killed in action.

CHAPTER SEVEN

Invasion Aftermath
June 7–August 16, 1944

Let me not mourn for the men who have died fighting,
but rather let me be glad that such heroes have lived.

—*Gen. George S. Patton*

The Allied forces had entered into the continent of Europe. For many men the beginning was also the end, but for the Rangers who survived D-Day, there were more battles to come. The casualties this small battalion suffered during the invasion were appalling. On June 8 the battalion assembled on the Isigny road and, at 1200 hours, marched to a bivouac area near the Grandcamp sluice gate. American paratroopers were scattered throughout the battle area and five of these joined the fifteen-man column of Dog Company. The road to Isigny was higher than its surroundings and flanked by open fields that extended to the town. There was no singing on this march for the men were passing the bodies of dead Rangers of the 29th Infantry Division, and Germans. As the remnant of the battalion marched past, the sun glittered from objects on some of the bodies described by one of the men as "little pinpoints of dancing light."[1] It was the reflection from the gold and silver rank insignia of dead American officers.

When they arrived at the bivouac area, it was a time for recuperation. Battalion supply vehicles arrived, and hungry and tired men were provided with ammunition, food and water, their packs, two-man pup tents, and bedrolls that had been shipboard during the invasion. They

153

pitched the tents as rain began to fall. New weapons replaced those that were damaged or lost, and machine guns were added. The necessary questions were asked and reports filled out.

With the coming of darkness exhausted men wrapped themselves in sleeping bags and were soon asleep. A single enemy bomber, what the men in all theaters of the war called "Bed Check Charlie," came overhead sending them dashing for cover, including to the nearest ditch, which they knew the Germans often mined. The aircraft roared onward dropping its bombs elsewhere, but sure enough, there were hard, round objects under several men. The only way they could tell if the mines were armed was to move, and to move chanced detonation. They laid in the ditches, sweating and talking it over. Bill Cruz of Dog Company said, "We couldn't lay there all night . . . so eventually we began to creep out of the dammed ditch. Honest, moving that few feet was a lot harder for us than that phoney bombing."[2] When daylight came, they discovered the Germans had not had time to arm the mines.

When a friend is killed, his effects are preserved and sent home to his family. Those items that are not suitable for the family are retained for use by his comrades. The men in Dog Company did not know that Capt. Duke Slater had survived. Slater's bedroll and pack included a bottle White Horse Scotch. Reasoning that at any time during the moves the bottle might be broken, Bill Hoffman rescued the liquor from Slater's gear. June 10 was Jack Kuhn's birthday and Hoffman gave him the bottle. Kuhn did not like whiskey, but he appreciated the gesture and passed the bottle around. After a while the rain, bombs, and mines did not matter.

A Baker Company patrol found the equivalent of a German post exchange that was well stocked with cognac, champagne, wine, and *Wehrmachtschnapps*. The booze patrol brought all they could carry back to the bivouac area, and things started to look up.[3]

The Army had expected high casualties among the Rangers and had replacements trained in England ready to fill the gaps. However, there were not sufficient numbers of these men, so Ranger officers went to replacement depots and made the call for volunteers. How to fill the enormous gaps left by superbly trained men who had been killed or seriously wounded and do it in a few weeks was a challenge. PFC Herbert Appel was among the volunteers. Appel had never met a battalion commander before and was surprised when Rudder talked to each new man. Appel was assigned to Baker Company, where the veteran sergeants grilled him on why he wanted to be a Ranger. He told them, "I can't get killed any deader here than in any other infantry outfit, besides, I like to have guys I can depend on next to me." He was accepted.

Officers and sergeants were moved among the companies to replace leaders lost in action and to recognize combat performance. Capt. Edgar Arnold of Baker Company became acting battalion commander until Colonel Rudder's wounds sufficiently healed for him to return to duty. There were other temporary shifts of position as Rudder's request up the chain of command for a stand-down period for retraining and refit of the battalion was denied.

Key slots still needed to be filled. With the departure of Major Lytle, a battalion executive officer was needed. Captain Rafferty of Able Company had been killed; Captain Wilkens of Headquarters Company and Lieutenant Baugh of Easy Company had been wounded and evacuated. Lt. James McCullers was moved from battalion headquarters to take command of Able Company. Lt. Sid Salomon became Baker Company commander, Capt. Ralph Goranson retained Charlie Company, and Lt. George Kerchner kept command of Dog Company, while Capt. Richard Merrill assumed command of Easy Company. Captain Masny retained command of Fox Company and Ike Eikner took command of Headquarters Company. When Rudder resumed command on June 20, Captain Arnold was made battalion executive officer.

As the Allied forces pushed inland, the American V Corps from Omaha Beach and VII Corps from Utah Beach sought to unite their effort and clear out the German pockets of resistance. The 2nd and 5th Ranger Battalions would engage in screening the V Corps' right flank in the move westward. On June 9, the battalion marched eight miles in rain to a bivouac area near Osmansville and began patrolling the next day. A French farmer came into the Fox Company area excitedly crying what the Rangers heard as *"Le boche cinq, cinq!"* The Rangers thought the Frenchman knew of the location of five Germans, and some of the Rangers went after them. When they reached the German position, the Rangers opened fire and captured a German headquarters unit, complete with payroll, killing two Germans and capturing fifty-three.

On the evening of June 11, the battalion then marched to Bois du Molay, where they became part of V Corps reserve. The men gathered in a field with Chaplain Lacy and gave thanks for survival and a remembrance of the dead and wounded. There was water available and soap. After days of living dirty the men were able to wash and shave and write letters home. The first mail call was held since departing England, and chow was being served on a regular basis. One day, a wounded cow charged into the Charlie Company area looking for revenge. S/Sgt. Maynard Priesman with a submachine gun and S/Sgt. Charlie Gross armed with an M1 rifle formed the defense. The cow was not supported by its herd, lost the engagement, and became dinner. Other animals fared better. The German army relied heavily on horse-drawn equipment, and many of horses were now roaming free. Several were rounded up, and the Ranger camps took on a distinctive Wild West flair. Willie Clark and Frank South were surprised one day by a bearded and horned billy goat that put its head over the edge of their foxhole and began to bleat. Clark and South fed the goat cigarette butts, which it devoured. The friendship dissolved when the goat snatched a freshly lit cigarette from Willie Clark's hand.

At night the German hit-and-run bombers flew overhead, and between the exploding bombs and the hammer and crash of antiaircraft guns, sleep was difficult. Most of the men built dugouts roofed by heavy logs and rested during the daylight hours.

Cigarettes were a boon to most soldiers in World War II. No one thought about cancer. Film stars touted brands of cigarettes as "easy on the throat." At the end of a long march or bitter fight, in the loneliness of the foxhole, or when a man could get a hot cup of coffee, a cigarette was a delight to a soldier.

On the fifteenth, 180 volunteer replacements arrived and the following day joined the battalion in a seven-mile march to Colombieres. The battalion bivouacked and with the 5th Ranger Battalion became part of U.S. First Army reserve. Seventy more volunteer replacements came in, were interviewed, and assigned or rejected. Of the 250 total that arrived 90 men were sent back to the replacement depots. Throughout the battalion, each company was rebuilding its strength and training hard to pass on the knowledge and experience gained at such a high price.

Some of the replacements came in wearing the red, white, and black scroll of the 1st Ranger Battalion. They were not members of the 1st Battalion, but had been able to get the scroll in England. The Ranger scroll featured unit identification whereas the blue and gold diamond (the "Blue Sunoco") insignia was generic. The men of the battalion wanted the scroll insignia identifying them as the 2nd Ranger Battalion. The father of Lt. Frank Kennard owned a textile business, so Lieutenant Kennard sent an example insignia home to the United States and the insignia were forthcoming.

There were opportunities for trading and scrounging and men used their wiles. Medic Frank South and a jeep driver took three German pistols and went back to the beach area looking for alcohol. They found an LST unloading cases of ten-in-one rations. This was home cooking compared to the the assault rations the men had been eating. The Navy did not care where the rations went as long as they had an officer's signature. South reasoned that Capt. Duke Slater was missing in action and therefore would not mind, so he got two cases of rations by signing Slater's name.[4]

On the nineteenth, Slater, Lieutenant McBride, and nineteen other men who had been on Dog Company LCA 860 that sank on the way to Pointe du Hoc returned to duty. Slater became the battalion operations officer (S-3) and Lieutenant McBride, who was senior to Kerchner, took over command of Dog Company. In a surprising move, Col. Eugene Slappey, formerly commander of the 115th Infantry Regiment of the 29th Infantry Division, was given command of the two-battalion Ranger Group. The division commander, Maj. Gen. Charles Gerhardt, did not find Slappey sufficiently aggressive. Lieutenant Colonel Rudder reverted to command of the 2nd Battalion. It appeared that no thought had been given to the role of the Rangers after the invasion.

On June 20, the kitchens and hot food arrived. Awards came as well. On the twenty-first, Lt. Gen. Courtney Hodges, who had been appointed commander of U.S. First Army, awarded Distinguished Services Crosses. On the twenty-third, Maj. Gen. Charles Gerow of the 29th Division made a short speech of gratitude and awarded Silver Stars. In total the officers and men of the battalion were awarded eight Distinguished Service Crosses and fourteen Silver Stars for their performance during the invasion of Normandy.

Perhaps even more anticipated than medals was mail from home. The mail clerk stood on the hood of a jeep calling out the names and handing out letters and packages. Below him were faces showing hope, joy, or disappointment. Some fortunate men got letters every time. Bill Klaus was one of those as Olive wrote everyday. She told him of their child and the scrapbook she was keeping. Olive and the baby were living with her parents, and there was a Blue Star service flag in the window representing Bill. Olive was also doing her bit on the homefront, serving as an aircraft spotter on a New Jersey hilltop. Bill wrote at every opportunity. What the men wrote was censored by battalion officers, and the letter was later photographed and reduced in a process called V Mail.

On June 25 the battalion moved to Valognes, where, until July 2, they served as guards for German prisoners at Foucarville, Continental Enclosure 19. The camp was intended to hold twenty thousand prisoners but had twice that number, including 218 German generals and admirals. The men of the battalion hated guarding and escorting someone else's prisoners. They kept the Germans in a barbed-wire-enclosed open field with wooden platforms topped by .30-caliber machine guns at each corner. PFC Helmuth Strassburger of Headquarters Company had been born in Germany and spoke the language fluently, thus greatly assisting in the mission. During the time the Rangers performed prisoner escort, some 10,000 captured enemies were taken from prisoner cages of the 4th and 79th Infantry Divisions and escorted to the Utah Beach area for further processing, often to prison camps in the United States. There were many prisoners and few trucks so companies vied with each other to see how many Germans could be packed into a single vehicle. Charlie Company claimed the record, reporting eighty-three Germans stuffed onto one 2$\frac{1}{2}$-ton truck.

On July 3, 1944, the battalion moved to a former German military post in a chateau near Beaumont-Hague, complete with barracks, showers, and sports. All this was peripheral to the training however. Day and night training was conducted, progressing from dry to live-fire exercises and marches that increased to thirty miles plus hand-to-hand fighting, scouting and patrolling, and reduction of pillboxes.

Men wounded on D-Day began to return to the unit. Capt. Fred Wilkens went AWOL from an English hospital to come back to the battalion. Rudder and Block looked at the deep gash in his back and ordered Wilkens back into the hospital system until he was fit. Others that came back and were allowed to stay included 1st Sgt. Manning Rubenstein of Baker Company and Lt. Bob Edlin of Able Company.

On July 11, the 2nd Rangers relieved the 24th Cavalry Reconnaissance Squadron of the defense of the Beaumont-Hague Peninsula. There was little German activity, but the enemy held the Guernsey Islands, which were just off the coast.

Rudder decided he could best employ the battalion by organizing it into what would normally be two task forces of three companies each. Capt. Edgar Arnold would lead Task Force Arnold (Force A) consisting of Able, Baker, and Charlie Companies, and Dog, Easy, and Fox Companies under Capt. Duke Slater would form Task Force Slater (Force S). The arrangement improved Rudder's control and coordination between the various companies.

Their youth and the release of tension after combat resulted in a series of pranks and excitements. Capt. Duke Slater, Lt. Gerald Heaney, and the men in the S-3 (operations) section sought to use some German flares that made a screaming sound to frighten those walking outside their office. Instead, they succeeded in terrifying the men inside the building. The flare sounded like an incoming "Screaming Meemie." It was said that "half the Commo Section tried to dig fox holes in the floor."[5] A few nights later, Lt. Elmer Vermeer set off some mines he had laid in the road. A movie was in session, and the entire audience tried to get through the single door simultaneously, creating a near riot. There were passes to the naval bastion of Cherbourg, where houses of ill repute were located. The pleasure was soon banned and the houses placed off limit to American soldiers with stalwart military police standing guard to ward off customers. A Ranger in need rented the uniform off the back of a French sailor, passed the guard, and enjoyed himself greatly. Though he could not speak French, the Ranger could not resist mumbling words he thought sounded like the language while he asked the military policeman for a light for his cigarette. Fortunately the MP could not speak French either.[6]

Dr. Walter Block used his spare time to open a private practice treating French civilians, including a two-week-old baby and an eighteen-year-old paralyzed boy. Block's payment usually came in fresh eggs with an occasional lobster from a nearby fishing village, *avec vin rouge.*

On July 19 the 15th Cavalry Reconnaissance Group relieved the Rangers, and battalion training was resumed. Lt. Robert Page, leader of the 2nd Platoon of Charlie Company, gave instruction in the use of captured German weapons. This knowledge had proven valuable at Pointe du Hoc. Page was demonstrating how to load and fire a German shoulder-fired recoilless rocket launcher called a *Panzerfaust,* when the weapon exploded in Page's hands, killing him instantly and wounding six other men.

While recruiting and training, Colonel Rudder had the additional task of selecting men to fill gaps in leadership positions. Any good officer keeps the mission, health, and welfare of his men as his goal, but the troops also need one of their own as representative. The battalion sergeant major serves as the enlisted man's representative and is not required to go through a chain of command to have the ear of the battalion commander. Rudder chose the senior enlisted man in the battalion, 1st Sgt. Leonard Lomell of Dog Company.

The training continued. Lt. Elmer Vermeer led twelve expert marksmen to sniper school from July 26 to 31 with the 2nd Infantry Division near Fort de Cerisy. The training consisted of hunting Germans. The sniper needed to be more than a crack shot. As in real estate, location, location, location is critical to the sniper. An elevated spot was often selected, one that would give an overview of the battlefield. German snipers were often found in church steeples. There was a paucity of such steeples after the army had passed as American artillery delighted in the challenge of blowing the German marksman from his perch.

On August 6, the battalion left Baumont Hague and arrived in Canissy the following day. Both the 2nd and the 5th Ranger Battalions became part of a combat team that had a mix of infantry, artillery, and armor. Four days were spent training in hedgerow fighting with the 759th Light Tank Battalion to prepare for a mission that was subsequently canceled. The battalion was then trucked to high-ground positions near Buais, arriving on the eleventh. Here they were responsible for securing the right flank of the First Army at Mortain and pinning the enemy in position on that flank. Along with the 188th Field Artillery Battalion, the Rangers were attached to the 4th Infantry Division of VIII Corps. After twenty-four hours of working to prepare positions the battalion was suddenly relieved from that mission and trucked to Mayenne, where they were attached to the 9th Infantry Division and placed on outpost duty on the bridges across the Le Mayenne and on the approaches east and northeast. Patrolling resumed.

The patrol is the testing ground of infantrymen's skills as they are often conducted forward of friendly lines. Aggressive patrolling was stressed in training and, as demonstrated on Pointe du Hoc, assiduously practiced in combat. Reconnaissance patrols would normally be small in number as the fewer the men the easier it is to escape detection by the enemy.

Lt. Bob Edlin of Able Company was among those Rangers of the battalion who excelled as a patrol leader. Edlin believed in accomplishing missions with a small number of select individuals. Four was his magic number and it began with a patrol initiated by Edlin and his men. Able Company had men on outpost and as Lieutenant Edlin and Sgt. Bill White checked the positions they came to one occupied by Bill Courtney and Bill Dreher. As they talked, someone said, "Hell, there ain't any Germans out there." With that remark, Courtney got up and started walking into enemy territory. Caught up in Courtney's unspoken dare, the other three men followed. Edlin estimated they walked for six or seven miles through territory that had been believed occupied by the Germans and saw no one. It was worthy information to pass on to senior commanders.

With that patrol the saga of "The Fabulous Four" began. They comprised perhaps the most highly decorated four-man patrol in the history of the United States Army. For their courage in various actions, Edlin, Courtney, Dreher, and White would each be awarded the Distinguished Service Cross, and White would win a battlefield commission. Day after day, the four men left their foxholes in search of the enemy. Going after German pillboxes was a frequent mission, with the four men trying to get in close and destroy the enemy position or force the surrender of the occupants. If they got pinned down by enemy fire, Bill Klaus would use a 60mm mortar firing smoke shells to blind the German observers while the four men backed off and called air, artillery, tanks, or tank destroyers to work over the enemy position.[7]

When using radio or telephone, security required that unit designations not be given. Radio call signs changed frequently so that a unit might be "Old Rose" one day and "Thunder" the next. Telephone designators changed less frequently, and a battalion had been "Veteran" for months until it became "Marauder Blue" on August 13.

The men of the battalion continued to live as nomadic creatures. Sometimes they moved by truck and sometimes they marched. Mile by mile, step by step, they were coming ever closer to the port and the great German forts of Brest.

At a number of towns, the Rangers were the first Americans to arrive. They were frequently greeted with cognac and flowers, and one town even turned out a brass band. There was a good amount of foraging and impromptu cooking. A large metal chamber pot was found in a French house. The pot was taken to the river and cleansed, then placed over a fire to boil away. While the boiling was underway, the men imbibed from liberated bottles of cognac and felt cheery. A loose goose wandering nearby was executed and dismembered. Potatoes, carrots, and onions were found. All the ingredients were dumped into the pot and a tasty, flavorful stew was the result.[8]

It was no wonder Doc Block was always seeking ways to improve the medical care of the battalion. A combat unit frequently ignores "authorization" and, by whatever means necessary, gets the equipment or weapons it needs. Block wanted and got an ambulance and PFC Virgil Hillis was assigned as driver. An enterprising man, Hillis stocked the ambulance with needed supplies and in the course of his efforts came across a bottle of the potent drink called Calvados. Hillis told Sgt. Frank South of his find, and the two men found a cozy place behind the battalion headquarters building and began to drink. After several drinks Hillis and South began to sing, growing louder with each drink. Sergeant South was emoting at full volume when a window on the second floor flew open and Colonel Rudder's head appeared at the opening.

"Private South," bellowed Rudder, "shut up and get to bed. Report to me in the morning!"[9] It was a sobering prospect that led to a restless night. It was the kind of night when the hands fly to the arms to see if the stripes are still in place.

The next morning, the sergeant reported as ordered. As far as his condition would permit, he was determined to meet his fate valiantly. With aching head and upset stomach South did his best to stand tall and render a snappy salute.

Rudder was not deceived. "Not feeling too good this morning are we, sergeant?" he growled. South waited for the axe to fall on a budding career. "Don't let this happen again! Dismissed."

Frank South described the incident as "an example of the toler-ance and patience [Rudder] had with his young, rambunctious Rangers, and one of the reasons he commanded our respect and affection. His major requirements were that all of us preformed every-thing expected of us with competence and dependability."[10]

From August 13 to 17, the Rangers occupied defensive positions guarding bridges across the Mayenne River and all the assault compa-nies were active in patrolling. Able Company's Fabulous Four, contin-ued to roam the front picking up prisoners and information.

Colonel Rudder did not think it wise to have Edlin, Able Com-pany executive officer, and 1st Sgt. John White on the same patrol. Unhappy with the decision but following direction, White stayed back. The other three men looked for someone to fill the final corner of their diamond-shaped patrol formation.

The three men selected Warren D. Burmaster. A Louisiana native, he could speak French and did not drink alcohol. Edlin, Courtney, and Dreher knew that Burmaster's linguistic abilities would be useful on patrol and reasoned that as he did not drink there would be more for the other three whenever they liberated some cognac or cham-pagne. In his early days as a soldier, Burmaster had been tossing around what he thought was an inert training round when he dropped it. The explosion and his miraculous escape from harm earned him the nickname "Half-Cracked." In time it softened to "Half-Track."

Men at war delight in nicknames. Courtney was called "No-Neck," Dreher was "Big Stoop," and Edlin was called "Fire Eater," or "Crazy," depending upon the mood of his companions. Burmaster said of Edlin, "No one, but no one ever got in front of Bob Edlin." Capt. Ralph Goranson of Charlie Company, no stranger to danger himself, told the author, "Edlin took a lot of chances, but he pulled it off."[11]

On the seventeenth, the 2nd Rangers were attached to VIII Corps and alerted for movement. On the nineteenth, a long column of olive-drab trucks arrived and the men and their equipment were trucked 200 miles in one day to the Brittany Peninsula. There was a problem at a port called Brest.

CHAPTER EIGHT

Brest, France
August 17–September 18, 1944

*As a general rule, the maxim of marching
to the sound of the guns is a wise one.*

—*Antoine Henri Jomini*

B rest was the second largest port in France at some 80,000 people. The deep-water port had excellent rail connections inland and was a principal submarine base for the German Navy. The city had been bypassed in earlier attacks, leaving the German defenders isolated. But Brest was a fortress city, heavily defended against attack by land or sea.

The German position was a series of lines with strongpoints containing self-propelled guns and automatic weapons, protected by mines, wire, and antitank ditches. Intelligence thought there were 20,000 Germans in Brest; the actual number was close to 50,000. The German units included crack troops of the 2nd Parachute (*Fallshirmjäger*) Division, the 266th and 343rd Infantry Divisions, marines, sailors without ships, and several *Ostbattalions* of Russians and East Europeans.

The German command structure was fragmented. Around August 5, command of the German forward forces was given to the arrogant, opportunistic, but nonetheless talented and courageous Gen. Herman Ramcke of the 2nd Parachute Division while General Rauch, commander of the 343rd Infantry Division, controlled the forts. Well experienced in combat, Ramcke had fought at Crete and led the 1st Parachute Division with determination in the fighting for Monte Casino in Italy. On August 13, Ramcke was promoted by Hitler and took command of all the fortified areas of Brest. Hitler's orders were "unconditional holding to the last of even the smallest fortifications."[1]

In time, the besieged German defenders could have been starved out, but in the opinion of senior logistical planners, there was no time to wait. The supply men said the port facilities of Brest were urgently needed to process the logistical flood of men and material that was pouring into Europe. Gen. Omar Bradley did not agree that the port was needed. Bradley was concerned about the aggressive Ramcke leaving his defenses to raid the American supply lines and wrote "I went ahead with the costly siege at Brest, with Eisenhower's approval, not because we wanted that port, but because Ramcke left us no other solution."[2]

Gen. Troy Middleton's VIII Corps was commissioned to capture Brest. To accomplish this mission, Middleton's Corps was given forces that included the 6th Armored Division; the 2nd, 8th, and 29th Infantry Divisions; and the 2nd and 5th Ranger Battalions, comprising in total some 80,000 troops, a number that while formidable was far less than the desired three-to-one ratio of attacking troops to defenders.

Ramcke paratroopers were tough and dedicated. One of their songs drove home the point: "When Germany is in danger there is only one thing for us; to fight, to conquer, to assume we shall die, from our aircraft my friend there is no return."[3]

Lt. Robert Meltzer, recently assigned as 1st Platoon leader of Able Company, hated Hitler and Stalin with equal vigor. As a youth, he had attempted to join the Abraham Lincoln Brigade in the Spanish Civil War. Meltzer was eager for action and delighted when ordered to take a patrol to make contact with the 8th Infantry Division who supposedly had a group of captured Germans.

Meltzer led his men through an opening in a hedgerow into a field where the Germans were supposed to be waiting. The Germans were there, but they were crouched behind MG42 machine guns that opened fire on the advancing Americans. Bob Meltzer's zeal died with him in his first action. Ramcke's paratroopers also killed Cpl. Seymour Goldman, PFC Peter Bolema, and PFC Constantine Anagnos. The appearance of surrender was often an ambush when fighting Ramcke's men, a number of whom would kill even while under the white flag. This subterfuge cost some German prisoners a rifle butt in the face or worse.

The battalion was attached to the 29th Infantry Division and during the campaign would be given three missions: the first to secure the right flank of the 29th Infantry Division; the second to capture the Lochrist (*Graf Spee*) battery of 280-millimeter guns; and the third to mop up of Le Conquet Penisula. The missions required the companies to scatter. Able, Baker, and Charlie provided security for VIII Corps Headquarters, and Dog Company and elements of the 86th Mechanized Cavalry Reconnaissance Squadron went patrolling together while Easy and Fox Companies took outpost duty near St. Renan. Rudder believed in keeping the men informed. As often as possible, men were called together to be briefed on the overall situation, to get the big picture, and to understand their place in that picture. War is a cocktail of confusion and uncertainty and many times men were attacking or defending hamlets and hills without having any idea of how their location fit into geography.

In Able Company, the Fabulous Four ran seventeen patrols behind German lines in fifteen days. On one patrol, a German lieutenant with an MG42 and several men saw the four Americans and threw a potato-masher grenade over a hedgerow at them. Edlin picked up the grenade and threw it full force through an opening to the German side. He then jumped through the hedgerow and landed on the back of a German sergeant lying prone. Edlin hit the German over the head with the butt of his Tommy gun and knocked him out. The German officer was stretched out nearby, out cold, when the grenade, which turned out to be a dud, hit him in the forehead.[4]

Not all patrols were as successful as those conducted by the Fabulous Four. Medic Frank South was on a daylight patrol that was working its way through a German mine field. South described what followed: "Most of the unit had cautiously worked their way through . . . but one of those ahead of me did set off the trip wire of a 'bouncing betty.' The mine did precisely what it was designed to do: with a 'humph' it jumped out of the ground, rose about one meter and exploded throwing ball-bearings in all directions. The man who tripped it collapsed without a sound. He was still conscious when we got to him, he had two nasty wounds in his back and did not respond when I pinched his legs nor could he move them. His spinal cord had been severed. We got him off the field with as little damage to him as we could manage by using field jackets suspended between two rifles as a litter. His bleeding from a larger wound in the side became more severe, and while I was still trying to control it with additional bandages, he mumbled something like 'Thanks, Doc,' took a few more breaths, turned grayer and simply died. By then I had tended many wounded and dying men and knew I would continue in the future, but I don't recall another time when I couldn't hold back tears. It was so damned frustrating—and we hadn't even been under fire."[5]

On August 22, 1944, Dog, Easy, and Fox Companies were attached to the 29th Infantry Division for rations and supply in the St. Renan area. The Germans in this area were prone to operate patrols with as many as fifty men. These could be rifle companies that had seen prolonged action or sailors-turned-infantry who lacked sufficient infantry-experienced leaders. Tipped off by the French Forces of the Interior (FFI, of the civilian resistance) that a German patrol was coming, the Rangers set an ambush. Three Germans were killed and the remainder dispersed. Soon thereafter, the Germans attacked the positions of Fox Company, and were repulsed. Because of experience and alert thinking, the Rangers remained unscathed. Knowing their positions had been revealed, the Rangers withdrew several hundred yards to a new location. No sooner had they done so when intense German fire from 88mm guns fell on the position they had just left.

On the twenty-third, the entire battalion was attached to the 29th Infantry Division for the impending attack on Brest. Attached to the battalion were four tank destroyers from the 644th Tank Destroyer Battalion, seven light tanks from the 741st Tank Battalion, four medium tanks from the 709th Tank Battalion, and five scout cars and two reconnaissance platoons from the 86th Reconnaissance Squadron.

At 0800 on the twenty-fifth, in order to better understand the German defenses, the battalion intelligence officer, Capt. Harvey J. Cook, and select men of his section began to infiltrate German lines to establish an intelligence gathering point where French resistance fighters could bring them information.

The VIII Corps attack on Brest began at 1300 hours on August 25. Awed by the intense artillery barrage that preceded the attack, Doc

Block wrote in his diary, "Boy-oh Boy, What a show!"[6] The 29th Infantry Division attacked with the 115th and 116th Infantry Regiments and met heavy resistance.

Capt. Duke Slater, battalion operations officer, led Force S, which consisted of Baker, Dog, Easy, and Fox Companies, scout cars, and light tanks, in an aggressive screening of the right flank of the 175th Infantry Regiment, 29th Division reserve force. On the twenty-sixth, the 175th Infantry was committed, and the Rangers roamed south and west, killing fifteen Germans. The terrain was open, and when nighttime positions were dug, the orders were "Stay in your hole. Anything moving gets shot."[7]

On the twenty-sixth, 81mm mortars used by Charlie Company supported a French attack on a German fort. The situation was fluid creating an especially hazardous situation for the men of Headquarters Company who were messengers, laying wire, or bringing supplies forward. A mistake in map reading, the absence of a road sign, or some other misdirection could result in capture or death. Motor messenger PFC Wallace Young was one such casualty when he did not return from a trip carrying maps and messages.

Able and Charlie moved on the twenty-seventh to join Force Slater which was at Kervaourn. Slater's group was attached to Task Force Sugar of the 29th Infantry Division. Task Force Sugar included a battalion of the 116th Infantry, the 2nd and 5th Ranger Battalions, the 224th Field Artillery Battalion and elements of reconnaissance, engineer, 4.2-inch mortar, and antiaircraft artillery units. Moving from a position near St. Renan on August 27, Task Force Sugar sent elements south and west. On the south shore of the Le Conquet Peninsula, near a town called Lochrist, was a German battery of powerful 280mm (11-inch) guns. The battery was called by varying names the Le Conquet or Lochrist Battery for geographical description or the Graf Spee Battery in honor of a famed German admiral.

The huge naval guns of the Graf Spee Battery were part of the defenses of the submarine pens at Brest, home to the German U-boats that prowled the North Atlantic. These shells could tear through hedgerows like paper. When shells passed through the air overhead they sounded like freight trains complete with double-headed engines and caboose. The Rangers felt that a fuse delay was being used as the shell would land and tear through fields and hedges before it exploded. The men called these guns "Chattanooga Choo Choos" after the popular song by Johnny Mercer. A 600-pound shell would roar overhead and some quaking soul would sing out from his foxhole, "Pardon me boy, is that the Chattanooga Choo Choo?" For a while it brought a brittle laugh and broke the tension.

Able and Charlie under Capt. Edgar L. Arnold had the mission of clearing the enemy from the east coast south of Tresien. There were thousands of Frenchmen who, after years of occupation, had a score to settle with the Germans. Some 700 of these French came along with the Rangers and battalion officers tried to blend them in to the effort. Many of the German weapons that were captured were given over to the French, and though in civilian clothes they wore armbands identifying themselves as FFI (French Forces of the Interior). These French civilian fighters were useful in providing intelligence about enemy positions and movements and it was a hard passage for any German they captured. They also provided additional strength to the Rangers, but had a tendency to depart for home when the German artillery fire got heavy.

The pressure from high command to eliminate General Ramcke and his forts and capture the port of Brest was intense. Major General Middleton and his VIII Corps fought furiously against the superb German defense. The forts of Brest were pounded by bombardment from air by the Ninth Air Force medium and fighter-bombers, and the British battleship *Warspite* unloaded her 15-inch guns on the forts. The role played by Task Force S was becoming increasingly important to the 29th Infantry Division. As of August 28, the task force came under the command of Col. Edward McDaniel, 29th Division chief of staff. The Americans cut the Brest–Le Conquet highway and the fort at Pointe du Corsen. German communications among the forts greatly depended on underground cables, the location of which were known to the French. The Rangers found and cut the the Brest–Le Conquet cable isolating the batteries on the Le Conquet Peninsula. In other battalion action that day, Able and Charlie Companies and attached tank destroyers of the 644th Tank Destroyer Battalion came through morning fog to attack a German strongpoint. The Rangers pounded the Germans, killed nine, captured ninety-four, and eliminated the enemy position.

Also on the morning of the twenty-eighth, Force Slater began conducting aggressive reconnaissance to the west. Ranger observers located German positions and ordered artillery strikes on them. The Germans responded in kind and five Rangers were wounded. At 1115, Easy and Fox, accompanied by light tanks, moved west on reconnaissance. Three Germans were killed and two captured. Reconnaissance continued, with Dog and Easy Companies working as a team and Baker and Fox doing the same.

The Dog Company advance was being delayed by Germans holed up in a fortified building. Ranger Dominick Sparaco was skilled in the use of firing rifle grenades. "I'll get the bastards out of there!" yelled Sparaco, and fired a grenade through an opening.[8] In the excitement of the moment, Speraco had forgotten to remove the safety pin from the grenade, but the effort was not in vain. The sight of the unexploded fragmentation grenade bouncing around the interior of their building resulted in the surrender of over thirty Germans.

The battalion was becoming increasingly international in scope. In addition to the over 700 men of the FFI, they had picked up 162 Russian prisoners that the Germans had been using as slave labor or impressed as soldiers. The Russians had their own leadership and quickly armed and organized into a fighting force under Rudder's command. Ike Eikner came to know the captain who commanded the Russians well and later asked him if he would return to Russia after the war. The captain replied, "Hell no. They would" (then raked his finger across his throat) "do me in."[9] Unfortunately for Russian prisoners, the United States would cooperate with Josef Stalin and send them back under Communist control, where they were shot or sent to labor camps.

In the afternoon of the twenty-eighth, Arnold's men attacked another strongpoint on Pointe de Corzen. This was a tough fight, and supporting artillery was requested but not received. With the tank destroyers giving covering fire, the Rangers advanced under a hail of enemy artillery, mortar, automatic-weapons, and small-arms fire. By nightfall, it appeared the Germans might be ready to surrender, but they hung on grimly. The Russian contingent ambushed an eight-man German patrol and killed them all. The Russian commander apologized to Captain Arnold for not saving a German for interrogation.

Task Force Slater's Dog and Easy Company team, with elements of the 86th Cavalry Reconnaissance Squadron, continued west against light resistance to Kersturet while Baker and Fox Companies followed Dog and Easy Companies, then moved to Kervegnon, where Force Slater went into defensive positions for the night.

At 0730 on the twenty-ninth, Arnold's Force A began pounding the Germans with tank-destroyer fire. The Rangers closed on the German position, holding their fire and sending a German prisoner forward to encourage his comrades to surrender. The tank destroyers had killed eight, and the remaining seventy-two Germans surrendered. Force A then continued south to the coast. As darkness fell on a rainy night, the Rangers were brought under German 20-millimeter fire. Unable to locate the position of the guns, Arnold put his men into night bivouac and awaited the dawn.

On the morning of August 30, Dog and Easy Company continued west to Hill 63. One Ranger was wounded, but fifteen of the enemy were killed and fourteen were wounded. Baker and Fox Companies also moved to Hill 63, and a perimeter defense was established. The Germans had accurately surveyed the area, and soon artillery and mortars began to beat on the Ranger position. A deep foxhole was necessary to survive, as Ranger casualties climbed. Despite wounds, men were reluctant to leave their comrades, and it took a serious injury to be evacuated. It wasn't just officers who stayed after being hit; privates and PFCs would call for a medic or treat their own wounds and keep fighting. They considered it shameful for a man who was still capable of fighting to leave his brothers in arms.

On the morning of the thirtieth, Arnold's men found that the German 20mm defended a German strong point. The Germans occupied a hill flanked by two other hills. Without being detected by the enemy, Company A and several tank destroyers climbed to the top of a hill that overlooked the German position, and took out the 20mm gun. But, heavy supporting fire from other German positions held up the Rangers, who dug in for the night.

On August 31, the fight intensified. The 20mm gun was back in action, and mortar fire added to its punch. With Able Company, 60mm and 81mm mortars, tank destroyers, and 105mm artillery in support, Charlie Company managed to close by infiltration, but the Germans brought down a rain of fire on the attackers, forcing them to withdraw under the cover of smoke. The Ranger cannon platoon moved to a hill-protected location close to the enemy and began firing 75mm artillery, knocking out the 20mm gun. The night closed a stalemate, but it was the Germans who had most to dread from the dawn.

Meanwhile, Force Slater was dug in patrolling from Hill 63. German artillery and mortars continued to work over the hill. One Ranger was killed and ten wounded on the thirty-first.

On September 1, Captain Arnold called on the 240mm howitzers to blast the Germans out of their holes. The big tubes could not find the mark, but the artillery officer directing the 105mm batteries was skilled and efficient. Using ammunition designed to penetrate concrete, he directed the 105mm howitzers in accurate and deadly fire. Meanwhile, Able and Charlie Companies moved closer to the German positions. Two P-38 fighters were requested to bomb the Germans, but their bombs splashed harmlessly into the sea. Both sides continued to pour fire on each other. To the disgust of the Rangers, the Germans put the pesky 20mm gun back in action.

Lieutenant Colonel Rudder had other priorities to attend to. As darkness fell, he sent Captain Arnold with Able Company and the tank destroyers on another mission.

Captain Slater's force was still holding Hill 63. Ranger reconnaissance patrols reached the coast, while combat patrols rooted out German defensive positions. On September 1 two Germans were killed and over 100 captured. German artillery continued to be the nemesis, wounding eleven Rangers.

The battalion found itself facing a courageous German defense at the strongpoint in front of Force A. The German mortars poured a rain of fire on the Rangers, who dug foxholes with tunnels that ran back under the hedgerows. The Americans could hear the *thunk* as a mortar fired and with mortars it is possible to put a number of rounds in the air before the first one lands. Among the men hit was Sgt. Ed O'Connor, who was struck in the leg by shrapnel. Rudder decided to attack elsewhere. On September 2, twenty men of Charlie Company were left in position while the remainder of the force moved to a road junction. Able Company was ordered to take Trebabu to the west, while the remaining men of Charlie had the mission of seizing Tremail in the south.

Supported by tanks and accompanied by French of the FFI, Able Company occupied Trebabu and killed three Germans manning a machine gun beyond the town. Ranger patrols, leading the advance, destroyed two German machine guns, killing four and capturing one German. The Charlie Company Rangers, with some FFI men, encountered a force of some 150 Germans, but the FFI broke and ran under fire. Under artillery fire and enemy counterattack, the Rangers withdrew from Tremeal and set up a defense for the night.

On September 3, the last German submarine to go into action from the twelve-foot-thick concrete pens of Brest set sail. The U-boats had sunk 2,840 ships in their day, but the lair of the hunter was no longer safe.

Charlie Company, now reinforced with the two 75mm guns on half-tracks of the cannon platoon and two tank destroyers, moved on Tremeal. The Germans had departed, so Charlie Company continued on until they engaged a thirty-man German patrol. The Ranger trigger fingers were faster, and five of the enemy were killed, six captured, and the rest scattered. Only three Rangers were wounded, two lightly enough that they stayed in the battle.

A Baker Company patrol set out to find the German positions. While they were still in the assembly area, S/Sgt. Paul Shave was seriously wounded by a German sniper firing from the direction the patrol had to take. PFC Wilbur Eason, who had recently learned he was a father, was lead scout. Eason successfully led the patrol past a booby trap but, while crossing a hedgerow, was shot in the leg and fell on the German side of the earthen barrier. Eason called for help and the other members of the patrol set out to rescue him. As they tried to cross the hedgerow, PFC John Toluka was shot in the head and seriously wounded. Each time the Rangers moved, they were pinned to the earth by German fire. The German riflemen amused themselves by firing into the wounded Eason and soon his calls for assistance ceased. Knowing more men would be sacrificed in trying to bring back Eason's body, Lt. Bill Sharp, who was leading the patrol discontinued the effort. Wilbur Eason was a good man and a good soldier, and his death plunged his comrades into gloom. They knew that back home the telegram of sorrow would soon be arriving, a piece of yellow paper with a few terse words that would forever change the life of a young mother and child.[10]

Later in the morning, heavy resistance was encountered. P-38 fighter aircraft were available for ground-support missions, and the Rangers took off their soiled white undershirts and spread them on the ground to mark their position. The fighters strafed the Germans while 105mm artillery fire hit them hard.

On the third, Able Company continued its advance against light resistance, killing eleven Germans. As darkness fell, Able and Charlie companies made contact with each other. September 3, however, was not a good day for Force Slater. Still holding on to Hill 63, Slater's men came under fire from German 88mm guns and the big 280mm guns of the Graf Spee Battery at Lochrist. Two Rangers were killed and twenty-one wounded.

Rudder and Slater decided that something had to be done to reduce the Hill 63 casualty list. Dog and Fox Companies were moved off the hill to a rest area some 500 yards away. The men of Baker and Easy Companies spread out and maintained a thinned-out defense. The German shelling continued, but with fewer Rangers to serve as a target, only three men were wounded for the day.

On the fourth, Captain Arnold held his positions, with Able and Charlie Companies contenting themselves with directing artillery on the Germans. This accurate fire silenced an enemy battery and broke up an enemy force moving as though it intended to attack Charlie Company.

The following day, Dog and Fox Companies moved back onto Hill 63, while Baker and Easy Companies went to the rest area. German positions to the front were identified in an area close to the French. American 4.2-inch mortars brought the Germans under the horror of white phosphorus. The terrified and burning Germans ran and, in doing so, came under the sights of French snipers who took a heavy toll. In their turn, the Germans fired their mighty 280mm guns at Hill 63.

Ranger Vince Hagg said, "We'd see this big flash from the guns when they fired. There was always plenty of time to get in your hole. Then the damn train would come in and RAAP! She'd hit. And oh my God, the damage those big shell could do! I've seen whole hedgerows just disappear before my eyes."[11]

Rangers were buried alive by the heaving of the earth. An entire squad was covered by one such avalanche. Amid the bursting of shells other Rangers left their holes and trenches and dug with their hands and entrenching tools to rescue their friends. One by one they pulled them free. It was an experience beyond the routine horror of war and though rescued, the men who had been buried were in a state of shock. The German shelling caused the FFI to flee their positions again, and battalion headquarters personnel had to fill the gap.

On the fifth, Arnold's Force A continued to work over German positions with supporting fire. One P-38 mistakenly dropped a bomb on Able Company positions: No one was injured, but the bomb did wonders for the chaplain's collection plate. The battalion was preparing for the attack and all available men were needed, even though the tough German position at Kergolleau was still holding out. Fourteen more Rangers of Able Company were taken from Kergolleau to strengthen Force A, leaving only one officer and five men to hold the Germans in their Kergolleau dugouts. To give the appearance of strength, the Rangers dressed fourteen Russians in American uniforms and added them to the dugout watch force.

At 0830 on the morning of September 6, the battalion moved against the Germans at Hill 63. Behind heavy preparatory fire, Baker, Dog, and Easy Companies attacked abreast with Fox Company in reserve. Arnold with Able and Charlie Companies launched a diversionary attack. This was a day of heavy fighting, under fire from German self-propelled 75mm and 88mm guns. By late afternoon Force Slater had gained 1,000 yards. Germans fleeing shelter ran under the guns of Able and Charlie, the latter killing five Germans. The two companies captured twenty-two more of the garrison. At the close of day, the attack had killed sixty enemy and captured another forty. One Ranger was killed and nineteen wounded.

At 0730 on the seventh, Force Slater resumed the attack. By the close of day, the Rangers had reached their objective and were astride the Brest–Le Conquet road. The withdrawing Germans left eleven dead and twenty as prisoners. By mid-afternoon, the task forces of the battalion had merged. Patrols continued, and 144 more of the enemy were captured and 30 killed without the loss of a Ranger. The night of the seventh, the 2nd Rangers were in position, with the 3rd Battalion of the 116th Infantry on their left. The Germans continued to pound the men of Task Force S with artillery including the massive 280mm guns. Charlie Company was dug in near Berbougius and the line was spread thin.

New men who had only been with the battalion a brief period found themselves alone in foxholes facing the night and German attack. This circumstance of isolation is a defining time in the loneliness of the battlefield. The muscles and the senses strain as every sound and every fear is magnified in darkness. The German attack came in and the tracers from machine guns, the bark of rifles, and the explosions of grenades were heard. When the attack was repulsed, the men called to each other, and some did not answer. With the coming of daylight they could move without being shot by their comrades. It was then they found the body of PFC Walter Lukovsky. Lukovsky was one of the new men, not well known until his death, but he would be remembered. To the front of Ranger Lukovsky's foxhole were six dead Germans.

In Dog Company area, Sgts. Joe Stevens and Ed Secor were on a two-man reconnaissance patrol when they encountered fifteen Germans hiding in the bushes eager to surrender. While being led back into American lines, one of the Germans told Stevens that he knew where there were other men who might also surrender. Stevens was a leader both by nature with his stalwart six-foot frame, a piercing look, and a drillmaster's voice, and by habit that came from the many patrols he took out with a cigar clamped firmly between his teeth. Sensing opportunity, Stevens went to Colonel Rudder and told him what the German captive had reported.

"I think we can get those Germans," said Stevens.

"There's no assurance they are ready to surrender," said Rudder. "They may have changed their minds and ambush you."

"Secor and I would like to try." replied Stevens.

"OK," said Rudder.[12]

Stevens, Secor, and the German passed through the line of foxholes. The German led them down from the hill and along a winding road. There was little sound. In the far distance, an occasional rifle shot or short burst of an automatic weapon pierced the silence. Stevens chomped the cigar as they moved an anxious 500 yards. At a bend in the road the German paused and signaled the two Rangers to halt.

Keeping his voice in a conversational tone the German began to speak in his language while the two Americans scanned the roadside bushes. A German soldier stepped out, without helmet or weapon, then another and another until 103 Germans stood lined up on the road before the two Rangers. It was a cautious re-entry into Ranger lines. As an added benefit, Dog Company was able to move forward and occupy the foxholes the Germans had dug.[13]

At 0700 hours on Saturday, September 9, Task Force Sugar launched a coordinated attack to overwhelm the German defenses on the Le Conquet Peninsula. The battalion attack on Objective "F," which was the Graf Spee Battery at Lochrist and its supporting installations, would be made by Able, Baker, and Charlie Companies. Dog, Easy, and Fox Companies were in blocking position to prevent German escape. American artillery, tanks and tank destroyers, and airpower had been used unsparingly in beating down the German defenses. The Rangers had come close enough to the fort to be within reach of the 280mm guns, but the Germans had plenty of other weapons. The plan of attack called for the companies to be widely spaced, but converging on the battalion objective. Rudder's orders were to move rapidly and hit hard, catching the enemy off balance and keeping him that way. It was the tactic Gen. Nathan Bedford Forrest called "bulge." The 3rd Battalion of the 116th Infantry was attacking on the left of the 2nd Rangers to seize Plougonvelin, while the 5th Rangers were on the right, going after the town of Le Conquet. The attacks would be supported by preliminary medium bomber, fighter-bomber, and artillery strikes.

Rudder ordered patrols sent forward to establish the location of German minefields. Edlin was told to take the 1st Platoon of Able Company forward, check the route, grab a prisoner if possible, and see if the Germans had been beaten down enough to surrender. Edlin took the platoon and a mortar forward, but opted to reduce the number of lives he had at risk by calling for his three patrolling comrades. If they had to get out fast, the plan was to obscure the German vision with smoke.

The Fabulous Four moved out in well-spaced, diamond formation with Edlin at the lead, Dreher to the right, Courtney to the left, and Burmaster as rear security and the man to get back for help if needed. "*Achtung Minen*" signs were to their front. They closed in on a huge concrete and steel bunker, one of several that guarded the giant fort that was home to several hundred Germans. Above the fort pointing like fingers on the hand of death, the great guns of the Graf Spee Battery loomed over them.

Suddenly Bill Courtney yelled, "I see a way through the damn minefield," and began to run forward toward the large bunker to their front. The horrendous bombing of the German positions had exploded the German mines and created a safe path. Edlin followed with Dreher and Burmaster close behind.

They ran onward, weapons at the ready. Ahead lay the large pillbox, its firing apertures yawning black and ominous. The German death-dealing machine guns, the MG42s, could not be seen, but the four Americans knew the guns would be there. They always were. Thirty yards, then twenty, then ten, and still no fire. Each yard, each step forward was filled with tension.

They slowed as they neared the bunker, flanking it to find the entrance. Warily they circled the bunker, and there it was, an open doorway. Edlin signaled his men. Burmaster covered the rear as Edlin dove through the doorway. Courtney followed to the right and Dreher to the left.

The machine guns were there waiting, pointing outward from the firing slits, and so were the Germans. Some twenty of Ramcke's *Fallschirmjägers* stood in the harsh glare of the bunker lighting, but these Germans wanted to survive the war. They stood silently, their weapons lying on the floor or stacked in corners.

"*Hände hoch!* (Hands up!)" yelled Edlin.

Courtney knew high-school German, and Edlin told him to identify the man in charge. A German lieutenant stepped forward to face Edlin. "Sir, I speak fluent English. I went to college in America."

"How do we get into the fort from here and to your commander?" Edlin asked.

"I can take you to the fort commander," said the German officer.

Edlin explained his intent to the rest of the patrol to enter the vast fort, and they agreed. Courtney would go with Edlin. They would throw the German weapons outside the bunker and Dreher would keep the prisoners inside while standing guard. Burmaster would make his way back to the platoon and have the radio operator send a message to Colonel Rudder to lift all supporting artillery fire on the fort. Burmaster also knew the route and could bring the rest of the Able Company 1st Platoon forward on order. The German lieutenant briefed his men that for them the war was over.

The sun was shining as the two Americans and their German guide walked across the open ground toward the fort. Edlin and Courtney knew they were under the eyes of a great many German defenders. They carried their Thompson submachine guns slung over their shoulders and made casual conversation with the German officer, each talking about where they were from and the experience of the German while a student in America. As they entered the fort and began to climb stairs, they encountered armed guards. At each stop the lieutenant would say a few words to the guards. Courtney told Edlin the German officer was telling his troops the three men were going to see Oberstleutnant Furst and the guards should lower their weapons.

The vast fortress was a masterpiece of defensive art towering above the surface of the earth. It was a battleship on land, but its magazines and hospital were buried safely beneath the surface. There were even comfortable dormitories and recreation rooms. The fort had taken an enormous pounding, but was still capable of resistance.

The German lieutenant stopped at a door and raised his hand to knock. Taking his weapon from his shoulder, Edlin said, "Don't knock, don't touch the door. Just step back." The German complied, and Edlin opened the door and charged into the office. Oberstleutnant Martin Furst sat in full dress uniform in a swivel chair behind a large mahogany desk. The comfortable office was decorated with the memorabilia of long service and the pageantry of his cause. Yelling "*Hände hoch!*" Edlin charged across the room and shoved his Tommy gun at the German officer's throat.

Courtney followed Edlin and closed the door behind him, leaving the two Americans and the German commandant alone in the room. Oberstleutnant Furst put his hands up but showed no sign of fear.

Edlin said, "Courtney, tell him who we are," and Courtney began the translation.

Furst rose from his desk, strolled to a sideboard, and poured himself a drink. "What do you want?" he asked in English.

Courtney began to speak in German, but Furst waved a hand. "You don't need your interpreter, lieutenant. I'm fluent in English."

"Fine," said Edlin. "Why don't you just surrender the whole fort and all your prisoners and get this whole thing over with."

The expression of Furst hardened at the mention of surrender. "Well, why should I do that? You can't capture this fort, and you can't take the Brest Peninsula."

Edlin felt that Furst was bluffing and countered with a bluff of his own. "You're completely surrounded. There's Rangers all around you and the air force is going to bomb you. You're going to loose every man you've got. Why don't you do the right thing and save not only your lives but American lives as well?"

"I'm not going to surrender!" barked Furst as he moved to pick up a telephone. "I'm going to use my telephone to call my outpost."

Courtney told Furst to talk slowly so that he could translate Furst's remarks to his men.

Furst talked for a few moments, then hung up. "They'll call back in a few minutes," he said calmly and began a casual conversation. "Would you care for a drink?"[14]

Edlin and Courtney declined the offer. Either there was going to be a surrender or there would be death—and Oberstleutnant Furst would be the first to die. The continued resistance of the great Graf Spee Battery was now a matter of will on the part of Furst and the salesmanship of Lieutenant Edlin. Edlin thought that Furst wanted to surrender but his pride would not allow him to do so. Furst needed to believe that all that was possible had been done to save his honor and that of the German army. If he didn't, he might choose to reach for a gun.

Long moments passed and the phone rang with startling authority. Furst picked up the phone, asked quick questions, and received short answers. Courtney looked at Edlin and shook his head in the negative. Furst replaced the handset and gave Edlin a cold look.

"There are only four of you," he said grimly. "You here and two in my outpost, you are my prisoners."

"No, sir!" snapped Edlin. "We will never be your prisoners." The two men stood eyeball to eyeball. Edlin held out his hand to Courtney. "Give me a grenade." Courtney complied.

The American World War II fragmentation grenade was made of cast iron and about the size of a large lemon. The outside surface was deeply serrated both horizontally and vertically so that fragments would burst outward equally. A lever at its top enabled the grenade to be held though the safety pin was removed. If the safety lever was released it would detach and the grenade would explode in four seconds, killing or maiming for a radius of thirty yards although fragments had been known to fly as far as two hundred yards.[15]

Edlin had reached the point where determination replaces the instinct of self-preservation. He pulled the safety pin on the grenade

stepped forward and rammed the grenade against the German officers testicles. All that was necessary was to release the safety lever and
the act was irreversible. "Either surrender or you are going to die
right now!" snarled Edlin.

Furst grimaced and struggled to keep his composure. "Well, so
are you," he replied.

Edlin rammed the grenade harder into the German's crotch. "I'm
going to count to three . . . One . . . TWO . . ."

Oberstleutnant Furst could read the look of determination in
Edlin's eyes. Furst said, "Okay!"

Edlin had held on to the safety pin which he now reinserted into
the grenade.

"Tell your men that this fort is surrendered to the Americans. Tell
them to fall out with their arms and line up in the courtyard."

"I would prefer to surrender to a more senior officer."

"I don't give a rat's ass who you surrender to," said Edlin. "I'll take
you to my battalion commander."

Oberstleutnant Furst had a public address system in his office that
he used to announce the surrender requirements to his men. Edlin
and Courtney watched from a window as hundreds of German troops
moved into formation. Furst also called his superior, General Ramcke,
who was being pounded by American artillery and airpower. Ramcke
knew that the days of his resistance were numbered.

Outside the fort, Burmaster had brought the rest of the 1st Platoon of Able Company forward to the bunker. When Edlin, Courtney,
and Furst went down, the courtyard around the captured Germans
filled up with Americans.

Lewis Gannett, a reporter for the *Herald Tribune*, filed a story that
a forward artillery observer had called Lt. Bob Arman, Able Company
commander, and said, "That fool lieutenant of yours is up there
already; you might as well go in." The nickname "The Fool Lieutenant" stuck with Bob Edlin and became the title of his memoirs, but
Bob Edlin was not silly or simple as the word denotes. Edlin and those
Rangers who went with him were brave men.[16]

Edlin contacted Colonel Rudder by radio and Rudder, accompanied by Battalion sergeant major Len Lomell soon arrived at the fort
in a German staff car. Rudder wanted all credit for the surrender to
go to the men who had made the capture and told Edlin to be stand-

ing by with his three men. A formal surrender was arranged that occurred in the small town of St. Mathieu near to the great fort. At 1330 hours on September 9, 1944, several armed companies of Rangers stood in ranks behind Rudder and his staff while Colonel Furst and his entourage stood to the front of the German soldiers whose arms were stacked. White flags were hanging from various German buildings and the count showed 814 prisoners taken. There was a great deal of heel clicking and half-bows on the German side, followed by an exchange of salutes. Furst reached for his pistol to present it to Rudder then remembered that Edlin had disarmed him. Edlin returned the German colonel's pistol. Furst put it in his holster then took it out and presented it to Rudder.[17]

Furst had a beautiful German Shepherd named Asgaard as a pet. He asked that one of the Rangers take care of the dog. Capt. Duke Slater accepted the pet and the two became companions. In time Slater's frequent need to go in harm's way resulted in the dog being given to a jeep driver.

Oberstleutnant Furst was put in a jeep and driven off as his men were marched away. As there were more prisoners than men in the battalion, Rudder's Rangers established their own barbed-wire prisoner holding point until other soldiers could move the Germans to ships. The irony was that the German prisoners were going to the United States while the victorious Rangers were heading for Germany.

The Rangers roamed the towering fortress, awed by its immensity and scope. They found they could put their heads in the muzzles of the 280mm guns while still wearing a steel helmet. It was a careful search as many of the doors had been pre-wired with Tellermines. The Rangers searched the hospital, sleeping quarters, and recreation areas and found their foes had lived well. There were well-stocked storerooms with cases of beer and wine and a case of cognac for every man. Cigars and chocolate were found. PFC Frank Lewis of Dog Company filled a burlap bag with cigars and would not be parted from it. Some Germans had tried to render their weapons inoperable, but many had merely tossed them on piles, including prized German pistols like the superb Luger 9mm Parabellum and the Walther PPK. There were trophies enough for any man who wanted one.

Groups of Germans surrendered at various points. Ranger Charles Hoff Jr. told Bill Klaus that a group of about fifty German sol-

diers accompanied by about twenty-five French women had surrendered to him, and he put the women in charge of guarding them.
Soon a Ranger approached and left with one of the women, then
another Ranger came and left with another woman. Soon all the
women had gone away with Rangers. It was some time before the
women began to drift back.[18]

Bill Klaus had found a leather-covered folding alarm clock in the
German officer's quarters and put it in his shirt pocket for future use.
Later Klaus found parts of a German pistol he liked. He could see that
the surrendering German soldier had thrown the other parts of the
pistol just over a barbed-wire fence. Not seeing any signs of a mine
where the remainder of the pistol lay, Klaus jumped the fence. As he
hit the ground the alarm clock in his pocket sounded. Terrified, Klaus
instinctively bounded back over the fence. It was some time before he
could recover his composure. Klaus rated the experience as one of the
worst scares of his life.[19]

There was still mopping up to do. A final strongpoint remained. The
battalion kept pressing forward, and the German fortifications tumbled while the prisoner-of-war count continued to swell. Baker Company saw Germans running into a house. The mortars were brought
forward and accurate fire placed on the building which soon began
to burn. Thirty Germans came out with their hands in the air.

Easy and Fox Company were on the verge of attacking a town
when Baker Company came through the streets from another direction. Company commander Sid Salomon had his men hold their fire
until they were close to the unsuspecting enemy. When Salomon
opened fire, his men followed suit, and the Germans promptly surrendered.

The final objective was Kergolleau where a tough and determined
German garrison had been softened up for several days by American
artillery and P-47 fighter-bombers. At 1100 hours on September 10,
Able and Charlie Companies under Captain Arnold moved to attack
behind the marching thunder of American 105mm howitzer and
155mm self-propelled guns. The Germans were well protected behind
the thick concrete walls of a hilltop bunker. To get to the German posi-

tion the Rangers had to charge down the open face of a hill, pass through a mine field, and wade in a waist-deep stream that ran parallel to the German position. They moved quickly, resulting in the German mortar fire falling behind them. When close in, Arnold prepared to give the order to assault, but the final effort was not necessary. A white cloth appeared over the German positions, and at 1515 hours the Germans surrendered. Seventy-four prisoners were taken.

On the eleventh, the Le Conquet Peninsula was turned over to the members of the French Forces of the Interior. Rudder had made a practice of allowing these FFI to take the lead in marching into liberated towns. It was good for their national pride. The battalion became VIII Corps reserve and the men had the opportunity to shower and eat hot food.

On September 14, a motor convoy arrived to take the battalion for refit and rejuvenation. There were passes to the towns of Landerneau and Lesneven, where romance overcame language. There were rumors that they would be making another amphibious landing. That was not good news to those who had come ashore at Normandy, but the rumors were ill founded. New orders came on September 17, when the battalion was attached to the 8th Infantry Division. The 2nd Rangers relieved the 8th Division Task Force Alpha, a grouping of cavalry and infantry, and assumed the mission of clearing the Le Fret Peninsula. The mission was quickly accomplished. Le Fret was a German hospital town that had been declared an open city. There was no resistance and some 1,600 prisoners were taken, 1,000 of whom were wounded. Whenever and wherever German prisoners were taken, German officers and noncommissioned officers sought to convey their notion of superiority. There was much heel clicking, with left thumb hooked over the waist belt and right arm thrust upward and out with a "*Seig Heil!*" The Rangers were not pleased by these displays and anger increased when orders from on high reached the battalion that they must bivouac in an open field while the Germans had freedom of the town. The anger remained while the German captives were sent on their way. One pleasure was the release of 400 American and Allied soldiers from German captivity. One of the happy Americans rescued was PFC Wallace Young of Headquarters Company, the messenger who had been captured on August 27.

On September 18, the German garrison of Brest surrendered to Brig. Gen. Charles Canham, 8th Infantry Division's assistant commander. On D-Day, June 6, it was then-Colonel Canham's 116th Infantry Regiment that the Rangers had been attached to. Thanks in large part to having the 5th Ranger Battalion and the remnants of Able, Baker, and Charlie Companies at hand when he did not have control of his battalions, Canham had accomplished his mission.

Ramcke met Canham wearing full-dress uniform with decorations and carrying a swagger stick. The German's attitude was one of disdain. When the surrender terms were read out, Ramcke demanded of Canham, "Let me see your credentials." Angered, General Canham pointed to his infantrymen and said, "These are my credentials."[20]

Some men of Capt. Edgar Arnold's Baker Company elected to get Mohawk haircuts before they left the marshaling area to move to Weymouth and board the LCAs. Here, T/5 Charles J. Bramkamp cuts the hair of T/5 Elmer P. Olander. *From left to right are* Sgt. Joseph W. Shedaker, PFC Robert D. Herlihy, PFC James L. Roush, PFC William E. Gower, PFC Charles J. Davis, and S/Sgt. Paul L. Shave. Shedaker, Davis, Bramkamp, and Olander would be killed on Omaha Beach on D-Day. NATIONAL ARCHIVES

The 2nd Ranger Battalion at Fort Dix, New Jersey, October 1943. The officers—some of whom did not remain with the battalion—stand in the front row. *From left to right:* **Headquarters Company:** Capt. George Williams, Lt. James Eikner, Lt. A. A. Likens, and unidentified. **Company A:** Capt. Cleveland Lytle, Lt. Joseph Rafferty, Lt. Gilbert Baugh, and Lt. Stanley White. **Company B:** Lt. James McCullers, Lt. Robert Brice, and Lt. James McDonough. **Company C:** Capt. Ralph Goranson, Lt. Sidney Salomon,

Training at Bude, Sandown, and other points on the Isle of Wight, spring 1944. The 2nd Ranger Battalion used amphibious trucks called DUKWs. Rockets loaded with rope and grapnel were fired from landing craft toward the cliffs.

LOU LISKO COLLECTION / USAMHI

Lt. Paul J. Candleana, and Lt. William Moody. **Company D:** Capt. Harold Slater, Lt. Walter S. McCracken, Lt. John J. McDonald, and Lt. Morton McBride. **Company E:** Lt. Richard Merrill, Lt. Wilfred C. Majane, and Lt. Ted Lapres. **Company F:** Capt. Otto Masny, Lt. Jacob Hill, and Lt. Robert F. Arman. **Medical Headquarters:** Capt. Walter Block. **Seated on bench:** Capt. Fred Wilkens, Capt. Peter Staples, Lt. Col. James Rudder, unidentified, and Lt. Joseph Smudin. RICHARD MERRILL COLLECTION

These are the 100-foot-high cliffs of Pointe du Hoc climbed under fire by Dog, Easy, and Fox Companies, 2nd Ranger Battalion, on D-Day. The point is in the distance.

FRANCK MAUROUARD COLLECTION

Training for the attack on Pointe du Hoc, spring 1944. The DUKWs were equipped with ladders from the London Fire Department. In theory a DUKW could land beneath a cliff and run a 100-foot ladder to the top while a machine gunner provided cover for the men scaling the ladder. Rough surf and shell holes combined to spoil that plan on D-Day.

The initial German effort to fortify the Normandy coast was minimal until early 1944. This photograph shows the beach that would later be code-named Omaha before intensive fortifications began. FRANCK MAUROUARD COLLECTION

German WN 73. The fortified house above Charlie Beach on Omaha was taken by Charlie Company, 2nd Ranger Battalion, on June 6, 1944. FRANCK MAUROUARD COLLECTION

The French-made 155mm guns captured by the Germans were originally intended for open positions with a 360-degree firing radius, but Allied air superiority forced the Germans into a major construction effort to protect their guns at Pointe du Hoc, which were rated as the primary threat to the American invasion since they could fire on both Omaha and Utah beaches and reach well out to sea. FRANCK MAUROUARD COLLECTION

This 75mm gun located on the slope below the fortified house was part of WN 73. Coordinated with an 88mm gun in WN 72 at a lower elevation, this gun could fire across the entire length of Omaha Beach. FRANCK MAUROUARD COLLECTION

Pointe du Hoc gun position called #5 by Allied planners. Nearby were reinforced underground quarters for gun crews and concrete machine-gun and mortar emplacements to protect the guns. FRANCK MAUROUARD COLLECTION

Located well forward on Pointe du Hoc, this observation post was the position from which the Germans coordinated their guns. FRANCK MAUROUARD COLLECTION

Men of the 2nd Ranger Battalion enjoy coffee and doughnuts courtesy of the Red Cross prior to boarding their LCAs at Weymouth, June 1, 1944.

Forty-two A-20 bombers of the 409th and 416th Bomb Groups, 97th Bomb Wing, strike Pointe du Hoc on June 4, 1944. Forty-two aircraft participated, dropping 204 500-pound bombs while encountering heavy anti-aircraft fire. Afterwards, sixty new craters were reported on Pointe du Hoc.

Led by Able Company, the 2nd Ranger Battalion marches to Weymouth, June 1, 1944. At the left is the intelligence officer, Capt. Harvey Cook. To his right is Able Company commander, Capt. Joseph Rafferty. Lt. Col. James Rudder is at the extreme right. At the left, behind Cook and Rafferty, is Lt. Stanley White, and to his left is Company A 1st Sgt. Edward Sowa. Behind White is Sgt. (later Lt.) John White. Marching to the rear of Rudder is Lt. Robert Edlin. NATIONAL ARCHIVE

Able Company sets sail for their mother ship, HMS *Prince Charles,*
June 1, 1944. NATIONAL ARCHIVES

The 2nd Ranger Battalion marches to their embarkation area at
Weymouth on June 1, 1944. NATIONAL ARCHIVES

The mother ship *Ben My Chree* was a steamer for the Isle of Man in the Irish Sea before becoming a troop ship. She carried Fox Company, a platoon of Easy Company, and part of Headquarters Company to war. In the Gaelic "Manx" language, the name means "Girl of My Heart."

Lt. Bob Edlin was acclaimed as the first man to board an LCA for the cross-channel invasion of Normandy.

Aboard their LCA, Charlie Company prepares to move to the HMS *Prince Charles*. The third man from the left is Sgt. Walter B. Geldon, who would be killed on his third wedding anniversary, June 6, 1944. At his right is Sgt. Harry Wilder. One third of Charlie Company would be killed, and another third wounded, on Omaha Beach. NATIONAL ARCHIVES

"Thank God for the U.S. Navy." Naval gunfire was critical to the success of the Normandy invasion. While battleships and cruisers pounded the German defenses, destroyers—such as the USS *Satterlee*, seen here—sailed so close to shore that they scraped their hulls and exchanged point-blank fire with German shore batteries. NATIONAL ARCHIVES

Lieutenant Colonel Rudder at his command post near the eastern-most German anti-aircraft emplacement on Pointe du Hoc on D-Day. Behind Rudder is signal lamp EE-84, which was critical for communicating with the ships providing gunfire support. NATIONAL ARCHIVES

The sixth gun and its ammunition dump were found and destroyed by John Burnett and other members of the Easy Company patrol on D-Day. This gun was intended to be a replacement for one of the Pointe du Hoc guns damaged by American bombing. JOHN BURNETT COLLECTION

The incessant aerial bombing and the 14-inch guns of the USS *Texas* created fighting positions on the flat plateau of Pointe du Hoc. The non-commissioned officer at top right is firing a light machine gun. To his rear is an officer, as signified by the vertical white strip on his helmet. NATIONAL ARCHIVES

Italian workers and German soldiers captured by Rangers on
Pointe du Hoc, prior to being loaded for evacuation to England.
It is likely these guards are LCA crewmen since the Rangers
could not spare men to watch over prisoners on the beach.
NATIONAL ARCHIVES

Rudder's command post on D-Day. At right, with an M-1 across
his knee, is Lt. Elmer H. "Dutch" Vermeer, the battalion's
engineer officer. Lying on his back is radioman Cpl. Louis F.
Lisko. At front, beside the 284 radio antenna is T/4 Steven A.
Liscinsky. U.S. ARMY SIGNAL CORPS

Another look at Rudder's Pointe du Hoc command post, June 6, 1944.
At lower right, with his head bandaged, is British commando Lieutenant
Colonel Trevor. To his left is intelligence officer Capt. Harvey Cook.
Behind Cook is Sgt. Lenny Goodgall (506th Parachute Infantry Regi-
ment). Drinking from canteen is communications officer Lt. James "Ike"
Eikner. Behind Eikner is medic Frank South. To Eikner's left, wearing a
helmet with a net and loading a carbine magazine, is Dutch Vermeer.
Rudder is descending the hill at far left. LOU LISKO COLLECTION / USAMHI

Capt. Harvey Cook is in the center, with his arms raised, searching a German prisoner. To Cook's right, with a Thompson submachine gun, is
T/5 Gerald Eberle of Headquarters Company. Lieutenant Colonel Rudder is to the rear of Cook. At the left front, bareheaded and carrying a
submachine gun, is Sgt. Jack Kuhn of Dog Company. To his right is Sgt.
Murrell F. Stinnette of Fox Company. June 7, 1944. NATIONAL ARCHIVES

Wounded Rangers and German and Italian prisoners of war are taken by LCVP to the USS *Texas*, June 7, 1944. NATIONAL ARCHIVES

German prisoners (top of photo) are brought in for evacuation. The individual observing the prisoners at top right is believed to be Lieutenant Colonel Rudder. Cpl. Lou Lisko is at lower left with his back against bunker rubble. The American flag was displayed when American P-47s appeared ready to strafe the cliff top.

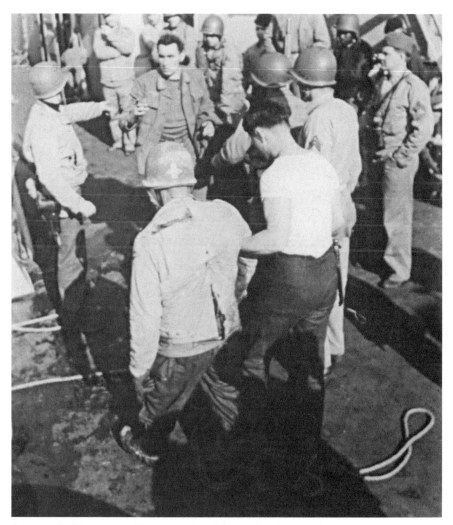

A wounded Ranger officer is assisted by a member of the USS *Texas* crew. In the background, a German prisoner receives instruction. NATIONAL ARCHIVES

Another look at the collapsed cliff, June 7, 1944. Directly above this point was Rudder's command post. Cliff climbing equipment is shown: toggle rope, free ropes, and tubular ladder. U.S. ARMY SIGNAL CORPS

Lt. Col. James Rudder commanded the 2nd Ranger Battalion from June 30, 1943, until December 6, 1944, when he was ordered to take command of the 109th Infantry Regiment, 28th Infantry Division.

FRANCK MAUROUARD COLLECTION

A group of Rangers from the 2nd Battalion's cannon section and the 5th Battalion's F Company arrives on the beach below Pointe du Hoc, June 7, 1944. This is where part of the cliff collapsed from naval gunfire.

NATIONAL ARCHIVES

Lt. Col. James Rudder and Maj. Jack Street at Pointe du Hoc, June 7, 1944. Street had served with Darby's Rangers in the Mediterranean and, during the Normandy invasion, served on Admiral Hall's staff. He secured a landing craft and personally brought ammunition and food to the Rangers at Pointe du Hoc.

STREET FAMILY COLLECTION

Men from Headquarters Company's communication section relax, June 12, 1944. Cpl. Lou Lisko, at left, feeds a small puppy named "Ranger." To Lisko's right is T/4 Stephen A. Liscinsky. In center, wearing steel helmet, is T/Sgt. James B. Parker, battalion communications chief. At right Lt. Ike Eikner holds a bottle of St. Emilion wine. An EE8 telephone and SCR 300 radio are visible. NATIONAL ARCHIVES

Men of the 2nd Ranger Battalion on the move, June 13, 1944.

FRANCK MAUROUARD COLLECTION

French citizens of the town of Grandcamp celebrate the liberation of their community. FRANCK MAUROUARD COLLECTION

Rear view of Lt. Leonard Lomell's steel helmet. Lomell served as Dog Company 1st sergeant and battalion sergeant major. He later received a battlefield commission. LEN LOMELL COLLECTION

In this photograph captured from the enemy, German artillerymen prepare a gun at the Brest batteries in France. The huge 280mm guns were protected and supported by a strong concentration of 20mm, 40mm, and 88mm guns.
FRANCK MAUROUARD COLLECTION

The Fabulous Four: the four Rangers who captured the Graf Spee Battery in September 1944. *Standing, left to right:* Lt. Robert Edlin and S/Sgt. William Dreher. Kneeling, left to right: Sgt. Warren "Halftrack" Burmaster and S/Sgt. William Courtney. A reporter called Edlin the "fool lieutenant" for leading his patrol into the heart of a German installation, the surrender of which yielded more than 800 German prisoners. JULIE FULMER COLLECTION

The Brest campaign, September 9, 1944. The 280mm (14-inch) guns of the German battery were called by the various names of "Graf Spee," "Lochrist," or, as seen here, "Keringar." The fortress included underground living quarters, hospital, and wine cellar. The German commander surrendered to a four-man Able Company patrol led by Lt. Robert Edlin.

Men of Charlie Company, 2nd Ranger Battalion, preparing for a mission near Rhurburg, Germany, on March 3, 1945. The Ranger at right has an entrenching tool with a shortened handle. To his left, wearing a wool cap under his helmet liner, is PFC Michael Gargas, and to his left is PFC Stanley A. Zarka. Loading his M-1 rifle is S/Sgt. Elijah Dycus, Jr. NATIONAL ARCHIVES

Steep hills, rain, mud, mines, cold, and forests reduced to sticks by shrapnel: the Rangers found the Hurtgen Forest to be hell. November–December 1944. FRANCK MAUROUARD COLLECTION

The Church at Bergstein, Germany, after wartime damage had been repaired. Hill 400/Castle Hill overlooked the town and the church, whose basement served as headquarters of the 2nd Ranger Battalion.

Sixty years later, trees and undergrowth surround a German bunker at Hill 400/Castle Hill, where on December 7–8, 1944, the 2nd Ranger Battalion captured and held their ground against all odds.

Lt. Col. George Williams, commander of the 2nd Ranger Battalion, leads
staff members in General Patton's parade in Prague, Czechoslovakia. *From
left to right:* Capt. Edgar Arnold, executive officer; Capt. Harold "Duke"
Slater, S-3; Lt. Gerald Heaney, assistant S-3; Capt. Harvey Cook, S-2; and
Lt. Frank Kennard, S-1. FRANCK MAUROUARD COLLECTION

The 2nd Ranger Battalion's Able Company, under Capt. Robert Arman,
passes in review during Patton's Prague parade. JOHN SHOBEY COLLECTION

Able Company Rangers with captured Nazi flag. *From left to right:* Sgt. Elmer "Red" Davidson, T/Sgt. Ronald "Swanie" Swanson, PFC Francis "Webb" Kohl, PFC Richard "Beans" Campbell, S/Sgt. Fred Culbreath, PFC Charles Dassaro, S/Sgt. John Bodnar, PFC Bob King, 1st Sgt. John W. "Whitie" White, and S/Sgt. Charles McCann. Lying in front is Sgt. Delbert Ferguson.

JULIE FULMER COLLECTION

Another form of relaxation was crap games on payday. A pair of dice, an Army blanket, a surface for rolling the dice, and a few bucks were all it took to play. Summer 1945.

JULIE FULMER COLLECTION

Rangers dancing with Czechoslovakian girls at the close of the war, summer 1945. JOHN SHOBEY COLLECTION

From May to
October 1945,
training continued
as the battalion
awaited orders that
would take them to
the Pacific. Here
they are practicing
with 81mm mortars
in Czechoslovakia.

JOHN SHOBEY COLLECTION

Going home via first-
class rail passenger
service from
Czechoslovakia to
France, October 1945.
From left to right: Sgt.
Robert Page Gary, PFC
Eugene Pycz, and Capt.
Robert Arman, all of
Able Company.

JULIE FULMER COLLECTION

Capt. Sidney Salomon,
who led a Charlie Com-
pany platoon on Omaha
Beach on D-Day and later
commanded Baker Com-
pany. He is shown here
receiving an oak leaf
cluster to his Silver Star.
One of the most popular
men in the battalion, he
would live ninety years
and win rowing medals
into his seventies.

SID SALOMON COLLECTION

"The end of the fight is a tombstone white" (Kipling). The graves of fallen Rangers at the American cemetery at Colleville-sur-Mer near Omaha Beach are decorated by Franck Maurouard, who is retired from the French Navy, and his family. FRANCK MAUROUARD COLLECTION

Shoulder insignia worn by the 2nd Ranger Battalion. The blue diamond was worn for the invasion of Normandy. As the battalion continued into Belgium, it adopted the scroll insignia worn by Darby's Rangers and the 1st, 3rd, and 4th Ranger Battalions. By the end of the war, all six Ranger battalions were wearing the unauthorized scroll.

AUTHOR COLLECTION

CHAPTER NINE

To the Hürtgen Forest
September 19–November 3, 1944

"Whom shall I send and who will go for us?"
"Here am I, send me!"
—Isaiah 6:8

The front had moved toward Germany at a much faster rate than Allied planners envisioned. The expansion of the invasion had also been followed by the St. Lô breakout in late July and August. Exploitation became pursuit. The port of Antwerp, Belgium, was captured on September 4, and though it would not be fully opened until late November 1944, its capture—in conjunction with Cherbourg, Le Havre, and other French ports—cancelled any Allied need for the port of Brest.

To the east, the German commander, Field Marshal Von Rundstedt, was fighting a desperate battle to establish a defensive line and stem the Allied advance. The once-famed German West Wall that ran from the vicinity of Arnhem in the north to Karlsruhe in the south was in a bad state of repair, and the Germans worked feverishly to repair it. The Americans and British saw the Rhine River draw ever closer and continued their logistical miracles as men and material poured into Europe.

On September 20, the 2nd Rangers were released from attachment to the 8th Infantry Division and moved to Kirbilben, France. It was time for rest an recuperation. Men wrote letters home and sent packages of war trophies and loot from the German captives. A number of German motorcycles had been captured and Rangers who had ridden captured German horses after D-Day now roared up and down the roads on mechanical steeds. The men played sports to keep up their physical conditioning. The weather was cold, wet, and miserable, and men looked forward to going home.

They took a step closer to victory on September 26, when along with the 5th Ranger Battalion, they entrained at Landerneau. They would share the World War I experience of their fathers by traveling on the notorious French boxcars known as "*40 hommes ou 8 chevaux*" for the number of men or horses the car was capable of carrying.

The soldiers said that if forty men fit in the cars they must have been midgets. For the thirty-six American Rangers jammed into each car with packs, weapons, and rations, the five-day ride to Esch, Luxembourg, was an experience in misery. The cars were littered with filth. The sides and roof were no obstacle to the rain and cold. Sleeping was done by "You've had your feet in my pocket for 20 minutes now it's my turn."[1]

Fortunately, there was liquid refreshment, chocolate, and cigars from the captured German forts. During the day the men rode with the boxcar doors open, the fortunate ones sitting on the edge of the door frame with their feet dangling. Others became so disgusted that when weather permitted they would climb to the roof and accept the challenge of sleeping without rolling off. The slight addition of space allowed for the inevitable crap games to begin. In some cars the men of the companies were intermixed. An Able Company man brought a guitar on a Baker Company boxcar. When night came and men tried to lie down, an argument arose over the space the guitar occupied and it was pitched out the door. During one portion of the trip they could see the Eiffel Tower. There were many comments about the good life in Paris that others were enjoying. For 750 miles they endured the swaying, jerking motion that threw angry men against each other. Their ears were assaulted by the constant clack and clatter. Their bodies collected the filth of the boxcars and the ash thrown from the engine and they smelled of sweat and urine and German cigarettes.

At length the train ground to a halt at Longuyon, France. The boxcar doors were thrown open and men leaped to the ground dragging their equipment behind them. There was a railroad station and men pitched tents around it or rolled up in their sleeping bags. A few, seeing that there was now space, slept on the boxcars.

The next morning, after eating cold rations, they were moved by truck across the Belgian border to Arlon, at a point near King Leopold's hunting preserves. PFC Alfred Baer of Dog Company was a man with an eye for nature's beauty and the skill to describe it. Baer wrote of the forest at Arlon, "The dim light filtering through the tall interlocked fir trees, the greys and greens of the lichens embroidering their gnarled trunks, the hushed cathedral atmosphere; even forty men made no sound as they walked across the deep carpet of moss."[2]

Of course, the battalion wasn't located in the romantic world of the King's hunting preserve. The 2nd Rangers were across the road where the moss was worn off the ground and only mud remained from intermittent rains. They pitched their pup tents with a careful eye to the slope of the ground. Many a soldier has gone to sleep on dry ground and awoke to find a stream of chill water flowing through his blankets.

Light German resistance would occasionally arise as they trained at Arlon. They speed marched five to ten miles at a time. There was weapons practice, map and compass problems. Many were wounded in the Brest campaign, but fortunately few men were killed. Any wounded Rangers who could come back did so. Four new officers and twenty-two enlisted men had come in on the first of October, and another four officers and twenty-seven men arrived on the seventeenth.

The soldiers had time to organize football games. During one of these, a German sniper concealed in a tree opened fire with his Mauser. The ball was in the air as Rangers on the sidelines fired a wall of bullets at the German. The sniper fell from the tree and the ball was shot out of the air.[3]

After training there were passes to the city of Arlon. They were the first Americans in the town and the benefits of that were enormous. The women were excited, and the bars were open and inexpensive. They went to the theater and saw old movies in French. The dialogue didn't matter, it was a movie. There were restaurants and shops filled with good things to eat. They found a shop that sold something the owners called "ice cream." It didn't taste like the ice cream back home, but in the memories of the men, it ranked as high as the women and the bars.

At one of the bars a mature woman would arrive each evening with a beautiful teenage girl. The woman would survey the Rangers until she saw one she liked, then invite him to her table. She was looking for a husband for her daughter.

As a sign that they were civilized, the battalion staged a dance. There were about a dozen Rangers for every woman and few of the women knew American dancing. The dance was a flop, but all things considered, Arlon was rather nice.

PFC Bill Anderson, the extraordinary scout of Fox Company, loved the forest and hunted in it often; coming back to camp with the carcass of a deer slung over his shoulder was a memorable sight to his comrades. Anderson was always ready to go on patrol and seemed fearless, but carried a packet of coins in his left breast pocket over his heart.

Dr. Block was fascinated with the thought of being near a hunting preserve. He had seen the 1935 movie *Lives of a Bengal Lancer* starring Gary Cooper, and a few had read the book. Block decided to organize a boar hunt. None of the medics had a firm idea of what a boar looked like, but they thought it might be a great hunt. Armed with M1s, two Tommy guns, and a liberated Damascus wire-wound shotgun, the hunting party set out for King Leopold's private hunting preserve in a jeep and the ambulance.

They scoured the woods for hours without result. A woodsman showed them a grove of trees where a boar had rubbed off some bark. They searched that area in vain. The idea of a boar hunt was beginning to give way to the need for a beer and a bit to eat. At length, the weary hunters debouched from the forest and traveled to a wayside inn. While at the inn they told the owner of their intent; he laughed and showed them the head of a huge and ferocious-looking boar with dagger-like tusks above the bar. The hunters went back to camp not so disappointed they didn't find one.

Some Rangers, including Frank South and Ike Eikner had the experience of visiting the recently liberated concentration camp at Buchenwald. Starting in 1933 at Dachau, the Germans had established a network of some twenty-six major camps and hundreds of subsidiary camps that increasingly grew in volume. Millions of political prisoners, Social Democrats, Communists, Freemasons, Protestant and Catholic clergy, homosexuals, Gypsies, Russian soldiers, even members of the deposed brown-shirt S.A., and most of all Jews were funneled into the camps. The weak were exterminated while the strong were worked to death on starvation rations. Frank South passed through the deceptively peaceful entrance with its terrazzo fountain. It was always that way: the Germans sought to give their victims hope before they killed them. It made the slaughter easier. Various entrance signs were seen: "*Arbeit macht frei*" ("Work makes one free") and "*Jedem das Seine*" ("To each his due"). Inside the camp, the Rangers met walking skeletons who staggered about in what appeared to be thin striped cotton pajamas. Corpses were piled high and there was a pile of ashes near the crematorium. Near the ashes were small terra cotta jars. From the pile of ashes, the efficient Germans could fill a jar and sell it to any relative of the deceased, passing it off as the ashes of their loved one. As with other Americans who visited the camps the urge to help overcame reason. The Rangers left a case of rations, a dangerous gift for those who are starving. Witnessing Nazi inhumanity built a rage in the Rangers. Frank South started asking to go on combat patrols.[4]

Men seriously wounded at Omaha or Pointe du Hoc began to return. Duncan Daugherty reported to Easy Company and he and Hub Hubbard had stories to tell each other. They resumed the buddy system in combat they had practiced before D-Day.

On October 6, Lt. Gen. Homer Simpson, commanding general of the U.S. Ninth Army, visited to award Silver and Bronze Star medals. The battalion sergeant major Leonard Lomell was discharged from the United States Army. His separation was brief. The next day, Len Lomell was appointed a 2nd lieutenant in his beloved Company D. His company history would record, "There was not a man who did not feel proud to serve under him."[5] Len Lomell would be replaced as battalion sergeant major by Manning Rubenstein of Baker Company who would himself soon become an officer. Four men would be commissioned from the ranks in the 2nd Ranger Battalion: Lomell, Rubenstein, Joseph Stephens of Dog Company, and John White of Able.

As some went up in rank others went down. The irrepressible medic, Sgt. Willie Clark, went a remark too far. Seeing Willie without his equipment Dr. Block said, "Where is your aid kit? Get it!"

"What do you want me to do, sleep with the f—ing thing?" replied Clark.

"From now on, Private Clark, you will report to Sergeant Bayer," was Doc Block's response.[6] The incident resulted in a razor blade being taken to the thread that held Clark's sergeant stripes on his sleeves. Willie Clark was dismissed from the battalion headquarters and sent to Baker Company as their medic. That was okay with Clark as he got along well with Sid Salomon who was in command of Baker. Block was furious and sent a letter that Clark was to give to Salomon. Clark opened the letter and found that Block was asking Salomon to give him the most hazardous duty. The request was meaningless as it was hard to find more hazardous duty than a medical aid man in a Ranger company. It is probable that Block knew enough about Willie Clark that he felt the letter would be opened en route and Block wanted to twist the scalpel. Clark gave the letter to Salomon, who read it without comment or action.

On October 20, the men of the battalion moved by truck for the two-and-a-half-hour drive to Esch, Luxembourg. The following day Sid Salomon, the dynamic commander of Baker Company, was promoted to captain.

At Esch the battalion was relieved of attachment to Simpson's U.S. Ninth Army and attached to VIII Corps of U.S. First Army. The sadness at leaving Arlon was replaced by the joy of being in little Luxembourg's second largest town. The good life got even better as men were housed in a German youth camp in the heart of Esch that had brick dormitories. There were flush toilets and showers with hot water. They had cots and mattresses and wall lockers and a mess hall that allowed the cooks to perform what seemed culinary wonders. There were some problems on the streets with rear echelon officers whose favorite admonishment was "Act like a soldier!" but the Rangers were the only combat unit in the town and Esch opened its arms to them. Young women who spoke English were particularly popular but enterprising men had learned enough in France to say important things to the women there. In Luxembourg, men were finding they would need to know basic German phrases. To keep his men available, Rudder instituted a nightly bed check. The chief complaint in Luxembourg was that cigarettes were in short supply. Six men might get a puff from the same cigarette. The cigarette habit was so strong that some men tried to smoke pipe tobacco in rolled up newspaper.

Those who had joined the battalion after the invasion were now trained to an acceptable level or dismissed. Training while at Esch consisted of staying in good physical condition. Football games in the square and streets of Esch had the locals scratching their heads in wonder or holding their stomachs in laughter.

At 1200 hours on October 27, a zealous staffer at First Army got approval to make the town of Esch "off limits" to the battalion. Colonel Rudder was furious and voiced his complaint up the chain of command. At 1500 hours on the twenty-eighth, the town of Esch was back "on limits," and passes were issued.

Something besides fog and rain was in the air on November 1. Colonel Rudder and the intelligence officer, Captain Cook, were called to General Middleton's VIII Corps Headquarters. The next day Rudder called the operations officer, Captain Slater, and told him to have the battalion ready to move. V Corps had been given the mission of attacking across the Roer River and on to the Rhine. The 28th Infantry Division whose red keystone shoulder insignia led to the nickname "The Bloody Bucket," would lead the attack against the Germans on the high ground in the vicinity of Schmidt.

On November 3, a chilly winter day, the battalion boarded trucks to their next assignment. Despite the weather, the townspeople turned out to line the streets. Women and even men waved and cried openly as the trucks drove by and the Rangers responded in kind. Many men felt the separation was like leaving home in the United States. Bude in England and Esch in Luxembourg were special, memories and friendships that would live long.

After several hours on trucks, the battalion arrived in the vicinity of Neudorf, Belgium, where they returned to living in pup tents. The battalion was attached to V Corps and further attached to Combat Command A of the 5th Armored Division. The battalion telephone identifier was once again "Veteran."

Snow and rain alternated and the mud in the bivouac area grew knee deep. Capt. Sid Salomon moved Baker Company into a barn. As many men as possible slept in the hay loft but the entire barn was crowded with Rangers and cows. A farm girl named Hedy took care of the cows and was the object of admiration from all the occupants of the barn. The Rangers marveled at how much feed and manure Hedy could fork and shovel. Having some sixty-five men ogling her was bewildering to Hedy but she made the manure fly. There was not much else for the men to do but play cards, watch Hedy shovel manure, and wade through an acre of mud to get to the mess tent.[7]

The 28th Infantry Division had part of its force advancing south and west to capture Steckenborn while other units were moving south along the Hurtgen-Rollesbroich road to clean up resistance north to Rollesbroich. The 4th Cavalry Group was attacking and covering the 28th Division north flank in coordination with Combat Command A of the 5th Armored Division.

The 2nd Ranger Battalion had the mission of mopping up in its sector. Company F of the 85th Reconaissance Battalion (light tanks) and the 1st Platoon from Company A of the 893rd Tank Destroyers were attached to the battalion. Circumstances had changed since Camp Forrest and it was good to have the men and the big guns of the TDs at hand. On November 4, the 2nd Rangers were given an attack mission, and commanders and staff spent the day in reconnaissance and planning, but the attack was postponed.

Back at the barn, one of Hedy's cows was about to calve and a lottery started to pick the date of birth. The men could see German buzz bombs (V1 and V2 rockets) flying low overhead toward England. One malfunctioned and blew up so the men were told to dig foxholes. They quickly filled with water.

On November 8, the battalion was placed on two-hour alert as a counterattack force for the Vossenach area, and planning began for the mission. The following day, new orders were received and planning began again. In war a huge amount of effort goes into making plans that are not carried out. Day and night staff members study reports seeking to penetrate the fog of war. Warning orders come down, preparations begin, missions are received, subordinate leaders are briefed, and reconnaissance made—and then the situation changes. The old mission is rescinded and a new one begins. At the foxhole level the feeling is akin to being turned on and off like a light switch. Men in foxholes are not concerned with long-range planning.

On November 14, the battalion was alerted to move to the 28th Infantry Division, which had been hit hard by the Germans in the vicinity of Schmidt. Colonel Rudder was ordered to corps headquarters for briefing. He learned that the Germans were counterattacking and the 28th had been driven from Schmidt. At 1040 Rudder called to say that the battalion was to move to the vicinity of Vossenack as quickly as possible. The battalion would be attached to the battle-weary 28th Division and relieve the 2nd Battalion of the 112th Infantry. The battalion left their positions at noon, traveling part way by truck then dismounting outside the range of German artillery and moving forward by foot to Germeter and Vossenack. Germeter lay just a few miles from the Belgian-German border, Vossenack was a short distance to the east. Both towns were located on a high open ridge that bordered the Hürtgen Forest.

While German guns searched the area, the Rangers moved to position on fire cuts and trails through heavy forest. The cuts and trails were heavily traveled and the glue-like mud would mire a jeep to its bumper. There were shell holes and shattered and splintered trees that conspired with the deep mud to slow the battalion. Projecting from the sea of mud were rifles, helmets, packs, boots, and lumps that appeared to once have been men. Dead animals lay about and Alfred Baer, the penman of Dog Company noted, "If living things must die, it is only proper it should be the humans who brought the war into being. But not their horses, nor these dogs, nor these cattle . . . it isn't their fault."[8] Baer described a dead American who had been driving a jeep. "The jeep was hit head on by an 88 shell. Now the driver is reared back away from the steering wheel as though in surprise at such violence. His hands still grasping the wheel, have turned black, despite the snow and bitter cold. His face too, has that bluish-black metallic cast. His steel helmet is cocked at quite a rakish angle, and his lips are stretched tight in an awful grin. The teeth seem very white."[9]

The grueling march was considered by many to be the worst the battalion had experienced. Snow was falling at 1700 hours when they arrived at the 112th Infantry's positions. Within half an hour the relief of the 28th Division was complete. The gaunt, battered men of the 28th looked pathetically grateful as they stumbled from their holes. On the way out German shells fell among them. Nine men were left dead on the road including their colonel. The Rangers brought in nineteen wounded. Dr. Block and the battalion medics did all they could to save lives, but three more men of the 112th Infantry Regiment died. Block wrote that Rudder had ordered him to stop going forward with the litter jeep to evacuate wounded. "You might get hit," said Rudder, deeply concerned about losing the battalion surgeon.

The area occupied by the Rangers in and around the towns of Germeter and Vossenack had once been picturesque. Now the trees that
lined the roads into town had been rigged for demolition by the Germans. Between the trees and across the road were numerous German
and American telephone wires that could decapitate a man speeding
in an open jeep with windshield down in case of ambush. Iron hooks
were welded on front bumpers to protect those in the vehicles.

In the towns, houses were shot up, walls were blown in, and por-
tions of roofs were missing. Those Rangers who lived in town could
frequently find houses whose basements were sturdy. Medic Frank
South and another medic, Cpl. Charles Korb, used the litter-equipped
jeep to bring in wounded who had initially been treated in their
assault companies. They had to keep the engine warm to prevent
stalling in the bitter cold. Their run was through a gauntlet of German
artillery fire, mortars, and small arms. Weaving among shell and pot
holes, the two men traveled as fast as they could. When a wounded
man was brought to the battalion aid station he was treated and sent
back to his company or sent on to a field hospital by ambulance.[10]

Rudder's crowded CP was in the basement of a factory that had
been ravaged by fire and shell. The Germans kept random artillery
fire on the towns with 88s, 120-millimeter mortars, and French 75s.
Maintaining wire communication with the companies meant constantly running a gauntlet of enemy shells, which frequently cut communications. Radio was unreliable, and when wire and radio failed,
foot messengers were used. PFC Frank Remington of Baker Company
was hit by shrapnel while carrying a message and was evacuated.

German artillery shelled crossroads frequently. A road junction at
the southeast of Germeter had been frequently shelled by the Germans. A military policeman was stationed at the junction to direct
traffic. The MP scurried in terror for cover in a deep hole at each
screech of incoming fire. Going though this junction was called "running the gauntlet at Purple Heart Corner."[11]

Charlie and Dog Companies were stationed in Vossenack. The
town was in a small valley and the Germans held high ground on
three sides. German artillery had practically destroyed a battalion of
the 28th Infantry Division and now the Rangers were being offered
up. Major Williams said the battalion "acted as moving targets for German artillery."[12] Cpl. Lou Lisko, a runner from Headquarters Com-

pany, arrived at the Dog and Charlie CP after dark and stumbled over something in the doorway. The next morning Lisko saw he had fallen over the headless body of a German soldier. A cat was eating its way into the body and only its twitching rear end was visible. Lisko booted the cat and said, "Go eat a dead horse you sonofabitch."[13]

The CP of Len Lomell's 1st Platoon of Dog Company was in the basement of a destroyed hotel. Lomell ran shifts with half the platoon in the basement and half outside in the wet and cold foxholes. The work of a leader in combat is never finished. Lieutenant Lomell went through artillery fire to bring his men Jerry cans of coffee and water. He prowled the foxholes to make certain his men had what they needed and stayed alert. When it was time to change shifts, Lomell would have coffee heated and bedrolls laid out for the men coming in. They were often so cold that they could not remove their boots, so Lieutenant Lomell would help them, then rub their feet until circulation was restored. PFC Leonard Rubin said, "He treats us just like a mother."[14]

On the fifteenth, Rudder participated in a coordination meeting with commanders of flank and support units. Company K of the 121st Infantry Regiment of the 8th Infantry Division was in a forward and exposed position. Able and Baker Companies had the mission of running four patrols each twenty-four hours and were the only contact Company K had with friendly infantry. Shivering with cold, Rangers moved through rubble-strewn streets among the bones of what had once been a prosperous town.

The Germans frequently ran "infiltration patrols." These movements were designed to spot command posts, artillery positions, and troop movements. The enemy observers also presented a constant sniper threat: As Company K's headquarters was in a house designated by the Germans as a prime target, the incessant fire chipped away at it little by little.[15]

Day and night soliers had to go into the open splice the wire. The snow was heavy and men dug deep foxholes through the mud. The foxhole was often sufficient to hold four men. Soldiers made log roofs for their foxholes which was then covered by the two sections of a pup tent called shelter halves to help keep out the precipitation. The tops were cut out of oil cans discarded by armor units and makeshift stoves were constructed.

Ranger and German patrols were active in the darkness. Tripped flares would hiss, ignite, and pop, then oscillate to earth through the purple darkness. Men in foxholes leaned forward, straining their eyes to identify movement while other men froze in position to escape detection.

German signal personnel found the frequency used by the battalion SCR (Signal Corps Radio) 300 radios and jammed it. The Signal Operating Instructions (SOI) anticipated such problems and messengers were sent from battalion to tell the companies that at 0155 hours on the sixteenth the radios were to be switched to a new channel. The change sent the Germans signalers back to the routine of turning dials and listening for the English language.

When daylight came on the sixteenth, the game of cat and mouse continued. At 0800 a Baker Company patrol led by Lt. Bill Sharp passed through the lines with Sgt. John Muhl on point. Moving warily through the snow-covered forest, Muhl saw a German outpost and crept close, surprising a German soldier in his foxhole and capturing him. The patrol then moved forward and was able to flank a machine-gun position. The Rangers were on them before the Germans could fire and three more Germans threw their hands in the air. Sharp's patrol came back with four prisoners.

To help soften up the German positions, the air force planned a major raid. On November 11, the Battalion S-2/S/3 Journal noted: "Possibility of our being bombed by mistake is very good as this bombing may be done by instrument."[16] On November 16, large numbers of American fighters and bombers swept overhead. Tension mounted as the Rangers watched from rubble and foxhole, but none of the bombs fell short. The planes left and German artillery resumed firing on the town and American artillery responded. As darkness fell the Germans unsuccessfully attempted to infiltrate through Able Company. Flares were tripped in front of the Fox Company positions, and artillery and mortar fire was received on a random basis.

November 17 and 18 were routine days on the line. A German tank dug in about seventy yards from Easy Company and fired a shell that wounded Sgt. Richard Hubbard. Fox Company suffered a shell hit to Captain Masney's CP, but there were no casualties. Battle reports read, "Situation unchanged." That meant living filthy in a cold, wet hole in the earth, scratching numerous itches, and searching the worn clothing for vermin. Dinner was cold rations and yearning for a hot cup of coffee or a can of peaches. Some equally filthy man across the way would throw a mortar round down the tube and temporarily scare the living bejesus out of a man. Just for spite, the Kraut might get an eight-round clip emptied in his direction from an M1 rifle. Happiness became a pair of dry socks.

On November 19 at 1430 hours, the 2nd Ranger Battalion became attached to the 8th Infantry Division and were alerted for relief. Charlie, Delta, Easy, and Fox Companies sent guides to the rear to bring the relieving troops of the 28th Infantry Division forward. The four Ranger companies moved out with one section of each platoon leaving at a time thus ensuring the line was manned.

The four companies moved to an assembly area about 2,000 yards west of Vossenack. German artillery continued to strike the area, but no casualties were sustained and the relief was completed by 2200 hours. Able and Baker Companies remained in position on line running contact patrols to Company I, 112th Infantry of the 28th Division.

On the twenty-first, Baker Company was ordered to move forward in the Hurtgen Forest to protect the flank of the 121st Infantry Regiment of the 8th Infantry Division. The 121st was preparing to launch an attack on the twenty-third to clear a road block leading to the German town of Hurtgen. As darkness fell, a guide from the 121st met Captain Salomon at a destroyed house occupied by men of Company K. The guide was to lead the Rangers forward to their new positions. Movement began around 2200 hours while American artillery and mortars pounded German positions to keep the enemy occupied. The Hürtgen was the forest of hell, replete with torn earth and shattered trees. There were minefields that were not recorded and forgotten booby traps rigged by German and American soldiers who were dead, wounded, or had gone elsewhere. Holding on to the belt of the man in front and daisy-chaining through the darkness, Baker reached the dispersal point where the two platoons were to move into their separate positions. The 1st Platoon moved off without mishap, but as the 2nd Platoon proceeded to its objective, PFC Paul Bryant was killed by a mine.

The ever-present tension was heightened by the explosion and magnified by the darkness. Men could not see the trip wires or spines of the mines. Each step into the blackness could end or impair a life forever and each cautious step was accompanied by a prayer. Another explosion and Sgt. John Zuravel fell with part of a foot blown off. Still another mine was activated and PFC Thomas Moore fell wounded. The mines sprayed their lethal content, and Sgt. Paul Donlin was hit. The men were in the open and exposed to enemy fire, but now the darkness concealed them and German artillery was quiet. Captain Salomon yelled, "2nd Platoon stay where you are. Don't try and move through till dawn!" Salomon told the 1st Platoon to dig additional foxholes so that the men of the 2nd would have cover with the coming of dawn.[17]

The hours were endless as the men of the 2nd Platoon waited on the mangled floor of the Hürtgen Forest. Cold, exhausted from tension, and at war with their imaginations, they knelt or stood in the minefield throughout the night. Meanwhile their comrades of the 1st Platoon attacked the frozen earth with entrenching tools.

The hilly terrain limited the range of the line-of-sight radios. Baker Company relayed its messages to battalion through Able Company who then relayed the response back to Baker Company.

Rudder scheduled Able Company to relieve Baker and a patrol was dispatched to coordinate with Baker and bring back some of the wounded. A jeep and litters would be taken as close as possible to the Baker Company position to facilitate the evacuation. Lieutenant Edlin of Able led a patrol of Courtney, Dreher, Burmaster, medic William Geitz from Headquarters Company, and a jeep driver. The ride forward meant running a gauntlet of artillery fire through a blinding snowstorm. Dismounting, Edlin and his five companions worked their way up the icy slopes amid shell holes and shattered trees. Artillery and mortar fire continued to fall and the rapid belch of a German machine-gun fire was heard. A trail of luminous engineer tape was laid behind them to identify the route back to the jeep.

On the forested winter hillside, within the minefield shrouded in darkness, wounded men tried to stifle sounds of their agony. The German positions were close at hand and much of Baker Company was without the protection of foxholes. Medic Willie Clark had been moving with the 1st Platoon and was clear of the mines. Hearing the moans of wounded men, Clark walked into the minefield to help them. With each cautious step Willie Clark rose above fear, put his life in other hands and went to his duty. The wounded were close together, trapped on the cold ground in pain and loneliness. Without light, Clark found and treated the wounds. His presence calmed the men. There would be no retracing of steps as Clark stayed in the minefield with the wounded until dawn. Sid Salomon wrote of Clark's performance, "In the black of night, [Clark] did his best to attend the wounded and performed admirably."[18]

With the first light came the German artillery. Working their way free of the minefield, the men of the 2nd Platoon sought the closest shelter at hand. At times these were German positions and, despite the artillery, men were cautious about mines and booby traps. The enemy observers could see that movement had taken place during the night. They pounded the Baker Company position with 88-, 105-, and 150-millimeter guns. The Baker Company mortars had come forward and one of their men, PFC Gilbert Mitchell, was hit in the head by shrapnel and killed, and T/5 Keith Bragg was wounded. Bragg and the wounded from the minefield were carried back to Germeter on litters. Bragg would die of his wounds on November 27.

Salomon and Edlin discussed the relief, and Edlin prepared to take two of the wounded out. Courtney and the Jeep driver started back with one litter. Edlin and Medic Geitz picked up another litter and a mine concealed beneath Geitz's foot exploded, blowing off a foot. The explosion threw Edlin against a tree, tore his hand and face with shrapnel, knocked him out, and temporarily blinded him with mud. Lt. Bob Fitzsimmons fell with shrapnel in his face.[19]

At 0817 Able Company relayed a message to battalion that Edlin's patrol was coming back. Men from Able and Baker Company worked together to get the wounded off the hill. The men who carried the litters back to Germeter faced an arduous and dangerous journey on mud- and snow-covered slopes amid shell holes and fallen trees. The wounded bit their lips to cover the pain of the jostling and tried to control the groans. On the treacherous surface a litter bearer would lose his footing and fall, jostling or even spilling the wounded man. The wounded would frequently apologize to the bearers. "Damn, I'm sorry to be such a bother," or "When I get back, I'll make it up to you."[20]

In the meantime, Captain Salomon had established his CP in a German-built, log-covered dugout. While a coordination meeting was taking place, the position took a direct hit from German artillery, wounding 1st Sgt. Edward Andrusz, Platoon Sgt. Walter Fyda, Platoon Sgt. Kenneth Young, and PFC David Brady.

The artillery was unceasing. The terror of the night was followed by the horror of the day. Three men were unable to continue and were evacuated. Sgt. Ray Alm and Sgt. James Kerr made the rounds checking on the condition of the men in foxholes. The conversation always included updates of those who had been wounded or killed.

The survivors tried to keep their minds off the fear of imminent death. PFC Herb Appel carried the book *An Outline of College Chemistry* in his pack. He was also becoming an expert on incoming German artillery. Appell noted, "When they were close, there was very little warning. When they burst within a few feet there was no warning whatsoever, just a tremendous 'crack' so sharp that it defied description. Then the sickening sweet odor of cordite would drift down into my hole."[21] Appel came to feel that if sudden death had an odor it would of the burnt smokeless high explosive, cordite.

It is leadership that holds men together in such trial. Capt. Sid Salomon and Lt. Tom Victor seemed to disregard the crash of German artillery fire as they carried rations and water from hole to hole. They talked with the men, encouraging them, lifting their spirits and giving them hope. When night came, the artillery ceased and thankful men took turns curling up in the bottom of their holes and sleeping.

Rudder called division headquarters for engineers to clear the German minefields, and messages went back and forth between battalion and higher headquarters, but when the engineers arrived, they went to the 121st Infantry area. There were many mines there as well. With the dawn of the twenty-third, the German artillery resumed, and four more men were wounded.

There was happiness in Baker Company when the word passed down the foxholes that an 8th Infantry Division combat team was trying to fight its way through to relieve the Rangers, but the relief did not come. The usual activity throughout the day heated up at night when a firefight erupted in a nearby area. The Germans opened up all along the line with artillery and began to shell Baker Company. Amid the whistling death was the shriek of the German six-barreled rocket launchers called *Nebelwerfers* (literally, "mist-throwers"). American artillery and mortars responded. An adjacent American unit called for artillery to hit a draw between them and the Rangers. The American gunners made an incorrect plot, and Sid Salomon's Rangers were soon being pounded by both German and American artillery. The Rangers had dug deep and worked hard to cut trees and build roofs over the holes. Sweat and luck combined and no one was injured in the terrible ordeal. Captain Salomon managed to notify battalion and Rudder had the American gunnery support firing on German lines.

With darkness German artillery stopped. Salomon passed the word that Able Company was on the way to take over the position. The men climbed out of their holes and gathered their equipment and weapons. They started at the smallest sound and felt out of place, uneasy at standing up above ground. The litter bearers started to move off with men taking turns carrying the litters that held the bodies of the dead. Lieutenant Victor said, "Handle them gently boys, they're not garbage, but a comrade who wasn't as lucky as you were."[22]

Baker Company moved down from the forest into the rubble of Germeter. To be in the basement of a destroyed house was a feeling of total security. There were few guards posted and little German artillery, and they were able to sleep.

The next day, Friday, November 24, Baker moved to the battalion assembly area. Men from other companies came by to ask about friends. All too often the news was not good. Faces would harden and men would curse. It was Thanksgiving and the cooks had prepared hot food including turkey. Sid Salomon's men were no longer thinking about themselves. They knew what they had been through and were thinking about Bob Arman's Able Company and hoping they would not have the same experience.

Back on the line, it rained, and the chill water collected at the bottom of the holes. Men had one blanket and a shelter half and the night was misery. The Germans did not shell much at night as they wanted to use ammunition on observed fire. Instead they contented themselves with enough night fire to keep nerves on edge and disrupt sleep.

Morning brought a horrendous bombardment of German artillery and mortars. Sgt. Julius "Tex" Remmers Jr. and PFC Fred Anderson were killed. Remmers's body was torn apart by the shrapnel and a German prisoner was made to bag up the various parts. One of the positions caved in, burying its occupants alive. Their comrades risked their lives to dig them out. One man was badly concussed and had to be evacuated. The remainder stayed on duty. Anything outside of the holes—blankets, rations, equipment—was torn by shrapnel. The U.S. 4.2-inch mortars fired white phosphorous in close support, the flowery rounds bursting just 200 yards from the Ranger position were unnervingly beautiful. Able Company spent Thanksgiving dining on K-rations with a D-bar dessert and jumping up and down in the holes to fight off frostbite in the chill light rain. The heavy shelling continued, and several more men had to be sent to the rear.

Another night of misery followed, a night of cold, wet, frostbite, and trenchfoot. The shelling was lighter the next morning. Other American units were attacking and drawing German fire. American artillery seemed to be gaining an advantage over the Germans. Soon the front was moving past the Ranger positions. Another night was spent in the foxholes. The next day there were no German patrols or direct fire and the soldiers experienced only light shelling. Suddenly, as though in farewell, the Germans fired one more heavy barrage with one Ranger wounded as the result.

At 1557 hours on Monday, November 27, Rudder sent a message to Able Company: "Duke is on his way to see you with good news."[23] Less than an hour later Capt. Duke Slater, Lt. Gerald Heaney, and Dr. Walter Block arrived in the Company A position. Food, water, ammunition, more blankets, and dry socks were brought forward. The fifty-seven enlisted men and three officers of Able Company came down from the forest among the wreckage of Germeter. There was uninterrupted sleep, and hot food and coffee and fires in makeshift stoves warmed the body. They were finally off the line.

CHAPTER TEN

Castle Hill (Hill 400)
December 1–10, 1944

Then out spoke brave Horatius,
The Captain of the gate:
"To every man upon this earth
Death cometh soon or late.
And how can man die better
than facing fearful odds
for the ashes of his fathers
And the temples of his gods"

—Thomas Babington Macaulay, *"Horatius at the Bridge"*

December 1944 found the Allied forces primarily along the western German border. The 21st Army Group comprising of the British Second Army and the Canadian First Army were on the left (north). In the center was the U.S. 12th Army Group consisting of the U.S. Ninth, First, and Third Armies, and on the right flank (south) was the U.S. 6th Army Group which was made up of the U.S. Seventh Army and the French First Army. The U.S. 12th Army Group was continuing the attack to seize a crossing site over the Rhine River. The Rhine represented more than just a body of water to both the Allies and the Germans. The Rhine was steeped in legend and was psychologically, geographically, and militarily important. Crossing the Rhine was penetrating the German heartland.

The mission of Gen. Courtney Hodges's 250,000-man U.S. First Army continued to cross the Rhine in the vicinity of Bonn and Cologne. If the crossing was not feasible, the 1st Army was to occupy itself clearing German resistance from the western shore of the river. They quickly found themselves mired in the Hürtgen Forest.

The Hürtgen Forest was so thick that in many places vision could not penetrate more than twenty-five or thirty feet ahead. The fir-covered hills rose steeply and within the ravines and draws white water thundered relentlessly while they fathered rivers. These woods formed part of the West Wall, the much publicized Siegfried Line of Nazi Germany. Aptly named for the famed knight of the fifth-century legend of the *Nibelungenlied* ("Song of the Nibelungen"), the line of fortifications was deadly and in the Hurtgen Forest doubly so. Large numbers of the vaunted MG42 machine gun lay in cleverly concealed bunkers and pillboxes. The positions were protected by minefields and barbed wire and artillery and mortar fire was registered on all approaches.

Within the forest were many towns and cities that were on or near dominant terrain. To the west was Hürtgen, Germeter, and Vosse-nack, and to the east lay Brandenberg, the road junctions of Schmidt, and the high ground adjoining Bergstein that overlooked the Roer River and its critical dams. Beyond the eastern towns and the Roer River lay the fabled Rhine.

The First Army consisted of V, VII, and VIII Corps. Lt. Gen. Leonard Gerow's V Corps was in the center of the First Army attack and was comprised of the 4th, 9th, and 28th Infantry Divisions and the 5th Armored Division. Maj. Gen. Norman "Dutch" Cota's 28th (Key-stone) Division had been attacking since early November. The 28th had taken Schmidt, but were driven out by a ferocious German coun-terattack. Unable to regain the high ground, the 28th Division was in bad shape and desperately in need of rest and refit. The 4th Infantry Division was the next to be thrown into the meat grinder and fared lit-tle better than the 28th. The 8th Infantry (Golden Arrow) Division was borrowed from VIII Corps as of November 19 and was instructed to resume the attack. Col. Glen Anderson's Combat Command R of the 5th Armored Division and the 2nd Ranger Battalion were attached to the 8th Infantry Division. The 2nd Ranger Battalion was considerably understrength, with companies closer to the size of rifle platoons. V Corps designated the Rangers as a rapid-reaction, counterattack force and kept them under corps control. The 8th Division began attacking on November 21 and seized the town of Hurtgen on November 28.

Also on the twenty-eighth, the 2nd Rangers received a mission to serve as a counterattack force. Planning and reconnaissance by offi-cers began. Meanwhile, the men prepared covered foxholes and log shelters, and while they waited for the call to action, there was hot food for nourishment and dice games for relaxation.

Missions were repeatedly changed. On November 30, the 8th Infantry Division ordered the Rangers to reconnoiter the Hurtgen-Kleinhau area while the commander of the 28th Infantry Regiment was ordering them to move on another mission. It was hurry up, wait, then just as the men were moving, all the missions were canceled. The end result was the 2nd Ranger Battalion remained at Germeter.

On December 2, battalion operations had a call from higher headquarters that trucks were standing by to move the battalion. No one had told Rudder that the battalion was going anywhere so Rudder called 8th Division and found that the trucks were transporting the battalion in the event it was needed to counterattack. That afternoon twenty $2^{1}/_{2}$-ton trucks and twenty-eight men of the 445th Antiaircraft Artillery Battalion arrived and were placed in a nearby area.

Sunday, December 3, in the Hürtgen Forest, Dr. Block recorded as a day and night of heavy shelling by the Germans. A Christmas package arrived that included a wool scarf and socks; unfortunately no mail came with the package. He was anxious to have someone send flowers to Alice for her birthday.

Despite some companies being at less than 50 percent of authorized strength, training for the survivors continued. On the afternoon of the third, the battalion did a practice road march. The practice run became the real thing when German fighter aircraft saw the marching men and hurriedly strafed them. The aircraft were part of a body of fifty German Me-109 fighter planes assembled to attack the American lines. Allied fighters far outnumbered the Germans and there were numerous antiaircraft units eager for a target. It was a chancy run for the pilots, and their aim was poor. The Rangers scattered from the road just before the machine guns ripped up its surface, and no one was injured.

Training continued and December 4 saw the men clambering through the woods in tactical exercises. The following day another road march was conducted. Interspersed with the foot marches were practice alerts for truck movement. Rudder gave the companies thirty minutes from notification to pack all gear and board the trucks. The night alerts had men searching frantically for their gear in the darkness.

Men constantly strived to improve their living conditions, some-times at the expense of their lives. About 1700 hours on December 5, a truck carrying engineers drove along a road near the Ranger area. The driver and his companion saw a man wearing Ranger insignia bending over objects stacked by the road. PFC Stanley Sachnowski from Easy Company was foraging when he saw four boxlike objects about three feet long and four inches wide. Likely thinking these might be useful in the camp area Sachnowski reached for one of the objects. What Sachnowski picked up was one of four German "Riegel 43" antitank mines, each equipped with a sensitive fuse and the four mines constituting eighty pounds of explosive. The horrific blast that followed killed Sachnowski and eight engineers on the passing truck.

Capt. Richard Merrill, commander of Easy Company, and battal-ion executive officer Edgar Arnold went to the scene the next morn-ing and searched outward in all directions for a distance of seventy-five yards from the center of the blast. They found a piece of steel helmet showing the Ranger insignia on the outside and part of Sachnowski's name painted in yellow on the inside.[1]

Word came down that some men would be going home to the states for a month leave. In order to qualify a man had to have six months' combat service, two Purple Hearts, two hospitalizations, two awards, and prolonged service overseas.

In the V Corps sector, a mission was assigned to the 8th Division to seize several towns. Among the division objectives was the town of Bergstein and the adjoining high ground which rose 400.5 meters and was variously described as an inverted ice cream cone, or a big wart. The Germans called this high ground Burgberg, the Rangers would remember it as "Hill 400," and American Army historians called it Castle Hill. Civilians said a castle had stood there in the twelfth century. Although that fortification was gone, a victim of time and Napoleon's artillery, the hill itself was a castle, a defensive work of nature. From its summit the Roer River dams could be seen, and the surrounding towns and countryside lay before an artillery observer's eyes. American generals did not realize the importance of Berg-stein—and in particular Castle Hill—to the enemy.

The Germans were concluding three months of preparations for a major counter stroke in the Ardennes Forest, one the Americans would call the Battle of the bulge. To achieve their aim, the Germans assembled twelve armored and twenty-nine infantry divisions that were well supported by artillery. The attack, to be launched on December 16, was designed to reach the port of Antwerp and in the process split the American and British forces, isolating the British 21st Army Group. To achieve success, the high ground on the northern flank had to be held. Gen. Rudolph Freiherr Von Gersdorf, Chief of Staff of the German Seventh Army, later wrote, "The commanding heights in the forest clearings at Huertgen, Vossenack, Bergstein, and Schmidt should remain in our hands in view of the planned Ardennes offensive. The possession of this elevated terrain was of decisive importance."[2]

Though it is questionable if it was the original American intent of the Hürtgen Forest campaign, possession of the seven dams on the Roer River was so vital that General Bradley described the position after the war as "a powerful weapon."[3] If the Germans controlled the dams, they could destroy them after American forces crossed the river. Bridges would be carried away and forward American units would be trapped. Two of the dams were of particular importance. The Urft Dam was made of concrete and held a reservoir of some 42,000 acre-feet of water, while the larger Schwammenauel dam was earth with a concrete core, and held approximately 81,000 acre-feet of water.[4]

Engineers told General Bradley that if the 180-foot-high Schwammenauel Dam was destroyed the water level in the Roer River would rise twenty-five feet and create a flood one and a half miles wide.[5] German commander Gen. Walter Model was determined that if the dams were to be destroyed it must be done at German convenience. Whoever held them could interfere with offensive operations by the other side. Therefore, possession of Bergstein and Castle Hill was critical.

The approach to Bergstein was suitable for an armored attack, and Combat Command R of the 5th Armored Division was given the mission of seizing the town. With men of the 47th Armored Infantry Regiment riding tanks, the Americans attacked on December 5. They found the Germans waiting with tanks, antitank guns, and a storm of artillery. Supported by air and artillery, the 5th Armored succeeded in capturing the town after a bloody fight, but exhausted men knew the inevitable counterattacks would come.

General der Panzertruppen (General of Armored Troops) Erich Brandenburger, commander of the German Seventh Army, had committed the last elements of the 47th Volks Grenadier Division. Now frustrated by the conflicting needs to hold Bergstein and Castle Hill and prepare for the Ardennes campaign, Brandenburger reluctantly took part of the force assembling for the latter to throw at Bergstein.

The 272nd Volks Grenadier Division under Oberst Georg Kosmala was a battle-hardened unit with men that had traveled to Bordeaux in France as well as to the gates of Moscow. The 980th, 981st, and 982nd Grenadier Regiments were well supported by the 272nd Artillery Regiment. Hoping he could shut down the American attack, General Brandenburger decided to use much of the 272nd to counterattack and hold Bergstein and Castle Hill. After the situation stabilized, he would return the 272nd to the Ardennes attack force.

On the morning of December 6, the Germans pushed home three counterattacks supported by tanks and self-propelled guns under a withering hail of artillery. In heavy fighting, the men of the 272nd gained a small portion of the east edge of town, but the Americans grimly held the rest. Combat Command R was beaten and in need of relief.

At 0700 hours on the sixth Colonel Rudder received a message to report to V Corps Headquarters and departed the battalion area. The afternoon wore on and Colonel Rudder did not return. Men began to worry. At 1705 hours an urgent message came alerting the battalion to move to Bergstein. Captain Williams ordered the company commanders to prepare to move. Immediate attempts were made to reach corps headquarters by radio and phone to learn the whereabouts of the battalion commander. Word finally came back that Colonel Rudder had departed corps at 1530 hours. The experienced staff was working with speed, and less then three hours later, the companies had been provided with maps and overlays of friendly force positions in the destination area. Passwords were established for the following three days.

The battalion would move to Bergstein to establish a defense perimeter around the town. Able, Baker, and Charlie were to establish blocking positions on the Brandenburg-Bergstein ridge south, southeast, and southwest of Bergstein. One platoon of Charlie Company would be in battalion reserve prepared to use 81-millimeter mortars in support of the rest of the battalion. Two platoons of Company C, 893rd Tank Destroyer Battalion, would be attached to the battalion. Four tank destroyers were to be with Able Company and two each would be positioned with Baker and Charlie. Under the command of Captain Slater, Dog, Easy, and Fox Companies were to move to attack an objective called "Sugar Loaf." The name of the towering rock at Rio de Janeiro was an apt code designation for the 400.5-meter Castle Hill.

The battalion's attack on Castle Hill was scheduled to begin at approximately 0800 on the Seventh. Eleven minutes after the issuance of the order, Rudder returned to the headquarters. Smiles of welcome turned to concern as Rudder announced he was being taken from the battalion. Gen. Norman Cota of the 28th Infantry Division wanted a replacement regimental commander for the 109th Infantry Regiment, and General Gerow, V Corps commander, agreed to send Rudder. Against his wishes, Colonel Rudder was ordered to report to the 28th Infantry Division.

Six minutes after Rudder returned to the headquarters, he promoted Capt. George Williams to major and announced that Williams would be taking command of the battalion. Staff officers looked at Major Williams with a feeling of sympathy. George Williams was a charter member of the battalion. He had proven his worth throughout training and in combat. But so far, he had been primarily concerned with the logistical needs of the battalion, not its operations. He had not fought, planned, or controlled battles as a company commander. There was no time to become settled into his new assignment. The battalion was moving to contact, and no one could envision how serious this next fight would be.

Rudder could have left immediately to his new assignment, but to the relief of Major Williams and the staff, he stayed as long as possible. At 2255 hours an advance party consisting of Colonel Rudder, Major Williams, Captain Slater, Captain Cook, Doc Block, and several key enlisted men departed the battalion area en route to Brandenburg, where they would meet with the commanding officer of the 47th Armored Infantry Battalion, who knew the dispositions at Bergstein. Lt. Howard K. Kettlehut, a forward observer of the 56th Armored Field Artillery, 5th Armored Division, would accompany the attacking companies. Captain Slater continued forward with an advance party and established a CP in a basement on the western edge of Bergstein. Slater then took a small number of men and went into the town for his planning reconnaissance. The weather was miserable, cold, and rainy. The Germans had gone underground, but could be heard talking in the basements of the houses. Slater and his men went through the town, and he determined how his three companies would attack. Slater's patrol then came back to the rear CP, and Slater waited for the battalion commander to approve his plan and to issue orders to the company commanders.

The vehicles of the 445th AAA had been well dispersed in the muddy fields and some had difficulty reaching the road. A fire started on a kitchen truck of the battalion and men hurried to extinguish the flame before German artillery found the spot. At 2330 hours on December 6, Captain Arnold ordered engines started, and trucks bearing the 2nd Ranger Battalion began a trip under blackout lights traveling northeast through Hurtgen to Kleinhau. The U.S. V Corps front looked like a clenched fist with the left knuckle swollen and distended shoved up against the German line. Kleinhau sat at the base of the swollen knuckle and to the right of it was Brandenburg and then Bergstein.

Five minutes after midnight on December 7, Maj. George Williams assumed command of the 2nd Ranger Battalion. Capt. Edgar Arnold remained the battalion executive officer. The night was chill and rain contributed to the gloom, and as they drew closer to Kleinhau the small blackout lights of the trucks were extinguished. The lead truck lost the road and got stuck. German artillery began to fall nearby, so at 0130 hours the battalion was dismounted at Kleinhau. Marching in the order of Able, Baker, Charlie, Dog, Easy, and Fox, they began to move through Brandenburg toward Bergstein. They moved with a minimum of five yards between men. They had learned there was truth to the frequent enjoinder of the sergeants: "Spread out, one mortar round will get you all!" The men and their equipment were wet, overcoats and bedrolls soaked through by cold rain. The muddy road was flanked by water-filled ditches and was slippery with ice and burned-out tanks, shot-up trucks, and bodies that lined the way. Overhead, German buzz bombs sputtered or roared on the way to targets in England. Artillery fell near the road, but the men had to chance it as the German penchant for mining roadside ditches was well known.

When the column was moving the men felt purposeful, but there were frequent pauses while those in the lead sought to check what lay to their front. The Rangers stood hunched over at the edge of the road with rain and misery as their companions. Then with a sudden jerk, the column began moving again. Some of the men were friends of long standing, so the long, cold marches weren't as lonely for them. But for the replacements, such as nineteen-year-old PFC Lee Taylor Jr. of Middletown, Ohio the battlefield was a lonely place.

As the men passed along the road, Rudder said farewell. Rudder thanked them and told them to "Dig in fast and deep." Rudder was their rock, the soul of the battalion, and as he passed down the line, the men felt a mix of love and loss like that of the passing of a beloved father. After the initial shock some men felt anger and betrayal. They were going into battle, and they knew they needed experienced leadership. They did not give a damn about the problems of some other outfit. Why was he being taken from them? Some felt Rudder wanted promotion, others that he had his orders and must obey them. There was no satisfactory answer for the cold, weary men.

The Ranger companies arrived at Bergstein at 0200. Captain Arnold and the forward observer Lt. Howard Kettlehut went to Company C of the 10th Tank Battalion to coordinate supporting fires. Combat Command R had plotted Able, Baker, and Charlie companies' move through the northwest edge of Bergstein, then deployed west and south up the ridges that were their objectives to take up defensive positions. Some German artillery and mortar fire was received during this movement, but there were no encounters with enemy soldiers. Bob Arman's Able Company occupied abandoned German positions and was in position by 0530, but Sid Salomon's Baker Company had to dig positions in an open field. Incoming artillery inspired the men to dig quickly. Ralph Goranson reported at 0622 that Charlie Company was in position and could hear German activity to the south. A forward CP was established in a church and Dr. Block set up his aid station here as well. Casualties would be brought in by litter or litter jeep, then taken by half-track to Brandenburg, and from there by ambulance to the rear area hospitals.

Meanwhile, Dog, Easy, and Fox Companies were moving to take up positions that would enable them to pass through the remnants of the blended companies of the 10th Tank and 47th Armored Infantry

Battalions. Easy Company was ordered to clear the eastern section of Bergstein, seize the road to Castle Hill and set up flank security. Dog and Fox, using a line of departure at the east edge of Bergstein, would then pass through Easy and attack Castle Hill.

The Hürtgen Forest was a meatgrinder for American combat units. Ernest Hemingway in his novel *Across the River and Into the Trees* compared the Hürtgen to "Passchendaele," a terrible battle in World War I where British soldiers were slaughtered, "with tree bursts." He described the usage of men in the Hürtgen: "We got a certain amount of replacements, but I can remember thinking that it would be simpler, and more effective to shoot them in the area where they detrucked, then to have to bring them back from where they would be killed and bury them. It takes men to bring them back, and gasoline and men to bury them. These men might just as well be fighting and get killed too."[6]

Using the high ground at Castle Hill as their observation post, German artillery forward observers had decimated Combat Command R of the 5th Armored Division, knocking out American tanks whose crew died in flames and exploding ammunition. American infantry was butchered. Lt. Richard Lewis, commander of Company B, 47th Armored Infantry Battalion, and his men had experienced heavy fighting in Bergstein. Lieutenant Lewis's company had some thirty-seven men left. Reinforced with the wounded of other units of the 47th and some men from the 85th Reconnaissance Squadron they continued to fight, but were so badly fatigued and shot up that some men were out of their minds. Twenty more wounded men were sent from the hospital armed with whatever they could find and put in foxholes.

Lieutenant Lewis told historian Forrest Pogue about the arrival of the Rangers: "We sat down for the counterattack, which we expected would come in the morning. We had a faint promise from Corps of the 2nd Rangers but we weren't too hopeful. About midnight a guy came down the road, then two others, each one five yards behind the other. They were three Ranger Lieutenants. They asked for enemy positions and the road to take; said they were ready to go. We talked the situation over with the officers. They stepped out and said 'Let's go men.' We heard the tommy guns click and without saying a word, the Rangers moved out. Our morale went up in a hurry."[7]

Bergstein and Castle Hill were now defended by Germans of *Hauptmann* (Captain) Adolf Thomae's 2nd Battalion, 980th Grenadier Regiment of the 272nd Volks Grenadier Division. Captain Thomae had thirty-six artillery pieces in direct support and could call on many more. Thomae's aggressive defense of Bergstein had already won him the Knight's Cross (*Ritterkreuz*).

Both sides were using interdiction, harassing fire with artillery and mortars. The *crump* and *crush* of high explosives were muffled in the whiplash of a driving rain. Despite the rain, some houses were burning in Bergstein. Reaching the town at 0335, exhausted men, miserable with wet and cold, took what shelter they could find. Though the charred bodies of the crewmen lay nearby, some men found shelter under the burned-out hulks of shot-up American armor, while other Rangers crawled into basements. Those concealed could light a small canned heat and warm a ration or try to dry their gloves. At 0540, Easy, Dog, and Fox were roused and began to move forward.

Reconnaissance is done at all levels. McBride of Dog and Masny of Fox Companies decided to send reconnaissance patrols of five men each to check the approaches to Castle Hill. Dog Company's patrol was led by the experienced Lt. Len Lomell to reconnoiter the right side of Castle Hill. Lt Ken McClure a new officer, had volunteered to lead the Fox Company patrol, but he would be guided by the superb scout PFC Bill Anderson. The getaway man of the Fox Company patrol was PFC Milton Moss, a new and highly regarded replacement. The patrols moved together through Bergstein hugging the walls of shattered buildings as they moved along rubble-strewn streets. As they passed through an outpost of the 47th Armored Infantry, McClure questioned a soldier there. The soldier did not know much about what lay ahead.

Fox Company Rangers continued to move forward until they came to the squat, stone Catholic Church of Moorish Martyrdom and cemetery at the eastern edge of Bergstein. A low voice from the roadside said what sounded like "Halt!" but the Rangers ignored it and kept moving. Passing up the street by the church, they worked their way beyond the line of departure for the attack. Behind the church the sunken road ran off to the right. McClure said, "You could just *smell* death up that way."[8] They could hear German voices first to the north and then the northeast. While the patrols lay in prone position, Bill Anderson went ahead alone. After a time he came back and reported more Germans on the hill. The men could hear the sounds of equipment being moved and heavy weapons being cleaned. Since it is not the purpose of a reconnaissance patrol to fight, they laid low, listening for about fifteen minutes, then came back past the church. The low "Halt!" sounded again, and again they ignored it and kept moving. Suddenly, someone yelled in German and bullets began whizzing about them.

"That was no American outpost," said Lieutenant McClure. "It was purely German! They started hollering then, and you should have seen us flying down that street. Like striped ass gazelles, boy in full flight! When we got back to the C.P. we were so damn' scared Captain Slater stuck cigarettes in our mouths and had to light them for us. We were shaking too bad to do it for ourselves."[9]

Not all of McClure's men fled. PFC Milt Moss remained behind at the edge of the church courtyard. Disgusted that his comrades had taken flight, Moss felt Anderson would not run and he called the lead scout's name. A burst of German fire was his answer. Moss crawled backward to get clear of the fire and heard Anderson quietly say, "Over here, Moss." Anderson was near a line of tombstones. After orienting Moss on their location, Anderson said softly, "Let's go," and the two Rangers made their way to the battalion CP.

Lomell did not remember any outposts or contacts, or being with McClure once they reached the hill. Lomell believed his patrol went through the town and up the hill scouting all the way to the top. Lomell remembered no difficulty on return. Slater and Assistant S-3 Heaney must have felt the the patrols did not locate the Germans since the battalion S-2 and S-3 journal entry reads, "Rcn Patrols of D & F returned—rptd no enemy contacted."

Capt. Duke Slater formed Dog, Easy, and Fox Companies among the rubble of Bergstein. Crouching along shattered walls, the Rangers listened to Slater calling words of encouragement. At 0540, Easy Company led off in the attack, moving rapidly and hugging the burned out buildings. Random surviving chimneys pointed accusingly at the sky. Covering each other as they moved and gambling on surprise, Easy Company pressed on. The gamble paid off—the Germans had relaxed and Easy captured thirteen of the enemy while they were having breakfast. Hands over their heads, the Germans were hustled to the rear as other German soldiers fled. Easy occupied the eastern edge of Bergstein and took defensive positions.

The weather was so cold that Sid Salomon figured, "The warmest thing around was the barrel of a BAR."[10] Under intense artillery fire, Dog and Fox Companies passed through Easy. Men hit by fire lay in the open calling for medics. Lt. Lawrence Schelper of Dog Company was severely concussed by an artillery round as they passed through Bergstein. Alfred Baer of Dog Company saw the bodies of three dead German soldiers sprawled on the steps of the church. They moved onward toward Castle Hill. Behind them, Captain Slater, Lieutenant Kettlehut and some communications men and medics established a forward CP in the basement of the church, Slater; and Kettlehut took position in the church bell tower which resembled a witch's hat. With the church bell hanging just above their heads they studied the hill to their front. Radios were on hand for communication and soon field telephone wire would be strung.

As Dog and Fox moved forward, Able, Baker and Charlie Companies observed what looked like self-propelled German artillery vehicles at a distance of several hundred yards. The Rangers and a 5th Armored Division tank drove the Germans to cover.

About 100 yards beyond the church was a road which would serve as the line of departure for the attacking Rangers. Castle Hill lay to the right front of the church and to the right of the sunken road. One side of the road was terraced, providing the Rangers with a protective embankment from frontal small-arms fire. This embankment was some 200 yards long and approximately two-and-one-half feet high.

By 0700 Dog and Fox Companies were in position along the sunken road and facing Castle Hill. Capt. Otto Masny's Fox Company was on the left, and Dog Company commanded by Capt. Mort McBride was on the right. Though the embankment provided some protection from direct-fire weapons to the front, there was no protection from the rear and flanks, and the position was vulnerable to attack by mortars and artillery. The hill was forested, but in front of the Rangers' position was an open field about seventy-five yards wide sloping up toward high wooded ground. This openness made some veteran Rangers edgy. The old timers knew it was a bad spot and were uneasy about crossing the field.

The attack of Dog and Fox Companies was to be preceded by a rolling barrage of artillery. Moving closely behind these fires, the Rangers would keep the Germans pinned in position until they were upon them. As the Rangers bent low behind the embankment, a German soldier at the edge of the wood line leaped into the open and fired a red signal flare. The German then ran toward his right in the direction of the unreported fortification that had observed the Ranger movement. Soon after the flare was fired, German artillery and mortar rounds began to explode among the Easy Company positions and behind the Dog and Fox Company Rangers. A few moments later, the forward observer Lieutenant Kettlehut called in American artillery which fell on the German guns.

The distance between the exploding American artillery rounds and the crash of the German high explosive was some 200 yards and the German fire was rapidly shrinking that distance. Caught between the two barrages, the Rangers were keenly aware that the German fire was closing on them and their position offered no protection from it. Tension built to anxiety—men knew it was only a matter of minutes before the shrapnel ripped them.

Lieutenant Kettlehut marched the American supporting fire up Castle Hill. Along the line of departure, men dug in. Lt. Thomas Rowland, a replacement officer and new to battle, squatted beside Sgt. L-Rod Petty, platoon sergeant of the 2nd Platoon of F Company. Rowland knew the ground had to be crossed and did not want to risk the platoon without having some idea of German dispositions

"Send out a scout," Rowland ordered Petty.

Petty did not know how they would take the hill from the Germans, but he believed that sending a scout was knowingly sacrificing a man. Petty's explosive temper flared. "Fuck you, no way!" he told the lieutenant.[11]

Angrily, Rowland then turned to Sgt. William McHugh, 2nd Platoon section sergeant, and repeated his order. Rowland was an officer, but he was a new man while McHugh had seen much combat beside Petty and trusted him.

"No, sir!" replied McHugh

Rowland turned to PFC Gerald Bouchard and said, "Get out there and check it out!"

Bouchard obeyed the order, went over the embankment, and had moved only a few feet when he was shot. Petty and others crawled forward to drag the wounded Bouchard to safety. The German mortar shells were bursting closer behind them now, and the pent-up tension in the men was itself explosive. All that was needed was a spark—and that spark was Sergeant McHugh. Leaping to his feet, the young Ranger brandished his submachine gun over his head and yelled, "Let's go get the bastards!" All the coiled tension in the men suddenly released, and they leaped to their feet and swarmed over the embankment, snarling, cursing, yelling in blood lust. Firing from the hip and shoulder, the line of Fox Company Rangers swept up the hill.

Sergeant Petty's efforts to save Bouchard had left him a few paces behind. Seeing the assaulting line of Rangers going forward with fixed bayonets was a memory he would never forget. "I know that I will never see a more brave and glorious sight," Petty recalled. "It was for me indeed a moment of being proud to be a Ranger."[12]

The German defense included several machine guns sited behind the tree line. A well-concealed German bunker fired at them from their left as they crossed the field.

Dog Company had moved on Captain McBride's "GO!" signal and went into action, shouting and firing as they went. While turning sideways to give the order Captain McBride was shot through the buttocks. Bleeding, cursing, and complaining that he considered it a disgrace to be shot in the ass, McBride limped down from the hill.

At the sight of the oncoming Dog and Fox Company Rangers, the German soldiers left their positions. Some fled up the hill, some surrendered, and others died. Temporarily pinned down by German fire, PFC Milton Moss followed after the initial Ranger assault. Moss saw a German gunner and his assistant slumped over their weapon. The remainder of the German machine-gun section had died trying to dig in or lay sprawled in a fruitless run for safety. American artillery was still falling on the position, and the earth heaved under the force of explosives.

Dog Company, led by Lt. Len Lomell, attacked up the slope of Castle Hill, losing Pvt. Alfred Kmitt, who fell and would die from a stomach wound. Some Germans fired until the Rangers were upon them, at which point they threw down their weapons and sought to surrender.

Lomell met Captain Masny, who was senior American officer on the hill near the German troop bunker. Masny instructed Lomell to clear the back slope of the hill. Some of the men were close to the

Roer River when they were recalled by Lomell and given orders to dig in. A German counterattack would surely come and a perimeter defense was needed on the forward crest of Castle Hill.

The few moments of euphoria over the successful attack was replaced by the certainty that the Germans would quickly respond. The men tried to dig in, but the frozen earth was a cover for shale interlaced with tree roots. Though they were hurriedly digging, most of the Rangers did not have foxholes and were above ground among trees when the German artillery opened fire on them.

Leaving nothing to chance, Hauptmann Thomae had planned fire on his own positions on Castle Hill and was now calling on all weaponry within range. German mortars, 88-millimeter and 120-millimeter guns, and self-propelled artillery pounded the hill with murderous precision. The air was rent by the shriek of incoming shells and thunder of explosions. The ground heaved and shuddered. Trees were shattered, limbs went flying, and splinters transformed into deadly missiles. Men desperately sought to find shelter in depressions and beneath fallen tree trunks. There was little or no protection. For three hours the German artillery fell so rapidly that men compared it to a belt-fed machine gun. Courage and skill did not help a man under this kind of fire—"It was a matter of luck," Lomell said.[13]

In the Fox Company area, Silver Star winner PFC Carl D. Winch Jr., who had survived climbing the cliffs of Pointe du Hoc, and replacement PFC Lee Taylor, died beneath the rain of shrapnel. They were comrades, brother Rangers at the last.

Platoon integrity had broken down. Men moved as individuals and small groups. Sgt. Bill McHugh, whose action kicked off the Fox Company portion of the attack, was wounded. PFC Bill Anderson, PFC Cloise Manning, and Sergeant Petty reached the top on the F Company side of the hill. Manning, who had become a close companion of Anderson, led the charge. The surviving Germans who could flee did. Captain Masny, Petty, and Bill Anderson saw a large bunker and went after it. Made of thick walls of reinforced concrete, it seemed impervious to shells. There was no return fire as Masny kicked open the main entrance and threw a grenade inside. On the left was a hallway about eight feet long ending at a steel door. The door had a small opening in it to pass messages through. The Rangers could hear the excited Germans inside the room. Petty pushed the muzzle of his Browning automatic rifle under the metal flap over the opening and fired a twenty-round magazine. He then held the flap open while Anderson shoved two grenades through.

Waiting to get clear of the exploding grenades, both men raced back into the open, with Anderson in the lead. A German shell exploded in front of Anderson and blew his body back into Petty's arms. A large fragment had struck Anderson in the heart. Petty put his arms around his friend to support him, but the force of the geysering blood drove his hand from Anderson's body. Petty felt something strike his hands. It was coins that Anderson kept in his breast pocket.

For a few moments, Petty was alone with his dead friend near the bunker. Dog and Fox Company Rangers soon arrived and set about eliminating any other Germans that remained in the bunker. Twelve Germans were still alive and were taken prisoner. With the bunker cleared, the frustrating task of trying to dig in the frozen, rocky soil began anew. Captain Masny, Lieutenant Rowland, Sergeant Petty, and another Ranger were discussing the situation when four German artillery rounds hit the bunker. Though the explosive knocked them over and terrified them, they were not wounded, but one man became hysterical. Petty slapped him across the face, but the man was out of control and had to be placed inside the bunker.

When the Rangers charged the slopes of Castle Hill they had entered a forest. Now trees were blown down and men torn by shrapnel were trapped under the boles and branches. The bunker offered the only protection. Used to shelter the wounded, it was also a magnet for men who wanted to escape the German fire. It took considerable fortitude to remain outside in the face of the shrapnel, as unprotected men were hit repeatedly. Ranger wounded came down under their own power or were carried by litter to the church where they were transferred to a battalion jeep that would take them to the aid station at the rear CP. The jeep ride through Bergstein was a dangerous one; three of the Ranger litter vehicles were destroyed during the evacuations.

The capture of the hill was reported at 0830, but the Rangers were angry. Men were suffering and felt they were not getting assistance from battalion. Captain Masny knew the handful of Rangers on top of Castle Hill needed help so he decided to go back to battalion and personally get the assistance. Masny and Petty disagreed on the route Masny would have to take. Petty had heard German voices and knew the enemy was about. Masny took a different route from the one Petty had recommended and disappeared from Petty's view. Within moments Petty heard Masny cry out "*Kamerad!*" and he knew the company commander had been trapped by the Germans. In a mix of sorrow, petulance, and apprehension, Petty cried out, "Goddammit, Otto, I told you not to go that way!"[14]

Although Dog and Fox Companies had Castle Hill, they were in bad shape. The men had been shot up, the company commander of Dog Company was wounded and evacuated from the hill, and the company commander of Fox Company had been captured.

On the way up the hill, Sgt. Herm Stein, section sergeant of the 1st Platoon, Fox Company, led his men to the left in a half circle around the hill. On the forward slope, Stein decided to dig in and hold. The ground was frozen, rocky, and difficult to dig, and the men were under fire from the Germans. As Stein and his Rangers dug, the Germans used variable-time fuses on their artillery and air bursts began to take their toll. PFC John Greenke and PFC John Biaze were wounded, Biaze badly.

Ranger Carl Bombardier, nicknamed "Bomber," went up to check the top of the hill. Stein and Milt Moss were alone on the forward slope. Lt. Len Lomell of Dog Company came over to Fox Company to tie together the fires of the two companies. Lomell was the only officer left in the company. His hand was a bloody mess, with one finger hanging by a thread of flesh. Stein briefed Lomell, who suggested the two Fox Company men link with Dog Company just over the next plateau. Lomell then continued on his rounds.

On the way down the wooded hillside, Stein and Moss met a Dog Company Ranger looking for his unit. The three men went down the hill a considerable distance, but they were going in the wrong direction and did not find Dog Company. Though exhausted, they breathed more easily in the absence of incoming artillery. They were near a gorge through which flowed the Roer River. Near a foot bridge, they could see several Germans. They could hear water rippling over a dam and saw what appeared to be a power station. German Volkswagen command cars were going to and from the power station, indicating that it was a CP.

Another car was visible, this one a four-door convertible Mercedes-Benz sedan used by senior officers. Germans were gathered around this car, and the group seemed to be in good spirits, laughing and gesturing. Just then, a ten-man German patrol in grey-green uniform spread out and, moving like veterans, came along the trail where the Rangers were, but the three Rangers let them pass. After a brief rest, the three men decided to go back to the crest of the hill. The climb was difficult, but a German artillery observer spotted them and gave them reason to move rapidly. Unable to locate Dog Company, Stein and his men dug in about forty yards from the top of the hill. The location was forward of the rest of the Fox Company positions, but it offered the best field of fire. As Stein and Moss struggled to dig their hole, Sgt. Carl Bombardier came down the hill and began to dig beside them.

The Germans wanted Castle Hill with a desperation that caused them to spend their men and materiel extravagantly. The Rangers would endure five counterattacks over a two-day period as German artillery and mortars subjected the hilltop to a constant and terrible pounding. A battalion of the 6th *Fallschirmjäger* (Parachute) Regiment located to the north of Bergstein was committed to the counterattack. Around 0930, a German attack of 100 to 150 men swept in like the tide on the Dog Company positions. German troops of several units attacked from the north and southeast. Until artillery fire destroyed the trees, their attacks were initiated in woods that offered concealment until they were close to the Rangers. In the 0930 fight, Ranger S/Sgt. Edwin Secor of Dog Company, who was normally a mild-mannered man, led a Ranger counterattack. They broke the attack and chased the Germans back down the hill.

Many men exhibited valor while defending the hill. PFC Fred Dix, whose foot was mangled, hobbled to Platoon Sergeant Petty's location to tell him that PFC Garness Colden was in desperate need of attention. Petty ran to the position and found Sgt. Murrell Stinnette had already arrived and was attempting to help Colden. Petty could see that Stinnette was himself seriously wounded, pale from loss of blood and bleeding from the mouth. Petty decided that he would take Stinnette to the bunker and return for Colden. Sergeant Stinnette insisted Colden should be the first to be treated. When Petty hesitated, Stinnette said with force that he had his hand on Colden's stomach. It was ripped by shrapnel, and Petty would take Colden first. Murrell Stinnette had served a hitch in the Navy and service on land

and sea had given him a rich and aggressive vocabulary. Stinnette lashed Petty with curses, startling the platoon sergeant. Petty followed Stinnette's order, picking up Colden and carrying him to the bunker. Petty then made another run through shell fire to get back to Stinnette. The effort was in vain: Stinnette was dead, his body contorted from the agony of his final moments. Petty's grief was overwhelming, and he took solace that Stinnette had sacrificed himself to save Colden. Petty did not know that Garness Colden was dying, too.

Across the hill, the few leaders were called from one location to another, responding to cries for assistance while the bunker filled with wounded. At such times the belief grows that help should be coming but is not. A rage was building inside some of the men, generated by the feeling that some officers and senior noncommissioned officers were not on the hill. One of the badly wounded that Sergeant Petty carried to the bunker was Jack Anderson, the brother of Bill Anderson. Petty could see Jack Anderson would also succumb to his wounds. Castle Hill would claim both the Anderson brothers.

Determination, fear, and frustration boiled in the men of Dog and Fox Company. Wounded men lay on the hill repeatedly hit by the German guns, but there was nothing that could be done for them. Seeing men bleeding to death and helpless to stop it, Lieutenant Lomell gathered his senior sergeants and, with tears of frustration pouring down his face, proposed they pull off the hill. The sergeants dissuaded him and they fought on. In both Dog and Fox Company area the Germans rushed the Americans, supporting their attacks with machine guns and using bayonet-fixed rifles, machine pistols, and potato-masher concussion and fragmentation grenades. At times the fighting was hand to hand, but the Rangers held.

Two German probes came from Fox Company's left rear, each of which was repulsed without Ranger casualty. Sergeant Petty and PFC Paul "Whitey" Barscenski did a reconnaissance to pinpoint where the Germans were coming from, and found the Germans organizing for an attack. Hurrying back up the hill, Petty went to the bunker and began to get wounded soldiers who could still handle a weapon out on the hill into a defensive posture. Lt. Thomas Rowland was seen among the men, encouraging them.

By now the Germans were up the left side of the hill. This attack was faced by eight Fox Company Rangers. The Germans were prone or kneeling, but the Rangers were seeking to close with them and most were standing, firing, and moving toward the Germans. Lieutenant Rowland yelled, "If you gotta go you gotta go!" and charged forward only to fall shot in the chest. As Rowland dropped, there was a brief lull. Barscenski went to Rowland, hoisted the officer on his shoulder, and began moving up the hill. Another bullet hit Rowland, killing him.

Captain Masny was a prisoner; Lieutenant Rowland was dead; Lieutenant McClure was wounded and evacuated. In command of Fox Company, Platoon Sergeant Petty had scarcely more than a squad of men fit to fight. Glancing to his left, Petty saw German soldiers moving to their left to flank the Rangers. Petty and another man moved toward the Germans and higher ground to spoil the enemy plan, but some of the Germans had already gotten above the Rangers. As Petty was running, he saw an enemy soldier in prone position taking aim at him. Petty fired a burst, emptying his BAR. The German fired simultaneously. A bullet from the German soldier passed through Petty's shoulder. Petty's shots killed the German, but Petty found he could not raise the weapon to reload.

Assisted by the other Ranger, Petty retreated toward the bunker. Some men from Dog Company fired on the Germans and they withdrew.

Sgt. Herm Stein saw Petty coming up the hill. Petty had four men left in his platoon and had carried the burden of leadership for most of the Fox Company fight. Caught up in the intense emotion of battle, he was raging at the losses of his platoon, crying and worrying about his Browning automatic rifle. PFC Milton Moss heard Petty screaming, "Where is God, why did they die and not me? There is no God!" Petty kept repeating, "Who's going to take my BAR?" Seeing Petty's emotional state, Sergeant Stein said, "I'll take it, L-Rod," and accepted the weapon. Stein would compare this to "passing on the baton in a mad relay race to nowhere."[15] Stein and the surviving Rangers pulled back, while the Germans did the same. For a brief period, while their men got clear, the Germans lifted their artillery fire. The Rangers felt like drowning men getting a last, clear, clean breath of air. Then the German artillery began to fall again.

After getting first aid in the bunker, Petty moved down the hill to battalion headquarters to get some help sent up to the men on the hilltop. As he entered the basement, Petty saw the Fox Company first sergeant relaxing against a wall smoking. The sight infuriated Petty, who believed the man should have been on the hill, and he began kicking and cursing him. The highly strung Petty was screaming with grief and rage, and when battalion officers intervened, Petty turned his ire on them. It is commonplace for men in grave danger to feel they have been deserted. Petty felt those officers and men in the battalion CP were shirking their duties. Petty was wrong. The thick walls of the church had taken eighty-two hits by German artillery.

Battalion was having problems keeping communications going with the companies. Wire lines were laid and immediately torn up by artillery. Radio was the primary means of communication, but it was not functioning well. Able Company moved into Bergstein to position itself as a reserve or counterattack force. Baker and Charlie Companies adjusted to fill the gap left by Able Company. Efforts were being made to get reinforcements for the men on Castle Hill from the 8th Infantry Division, but the hours of hell dragged on without relief.

At 1242, Captain Slater came back from the hill, reporting to Major Williams that only seventeen men of Fox and fifteen men of Dog Company were still in fighting condition. The evacuation of the wounded continued using practically every jeep in the battalion. Cpl. Charles Korb of the medical detachment risked his life repeatedly to drive litter jeeps through shell fire to get men to medical assistance. Three jeeps were shot up in the process. Korb and medics PFC Joe Guerra, Cpl. Frederick O'Neal, and T/5 Michael McDonough were wounded.

At 1450 another German attack came from the northeast, but it was repelled with the aid of artillery. Because of weather, terrain, and the enemy, communication with 8th Division headquarters was scant. While the Rangers were beating back German attacks, a message arrived for Major Williams that read, "Hold all your positions, do not withdraw. Dig in deep and provide overhead cover." Williams would not insult his men by passing on a message that even implied they might withdraw.

At 1606 Lieutenant Lomell sent the following message to Battalion, "Counterattacks on hill, all afternoon; very heavy artillery; only 25 able bodied men left: help needed badly; are surrounded."[16]

Sgt. Herm Stein was now senior man in the Fox Company sector. Stein organized his defense with Rangers Bombardier and PFC Joseph Piche on his right and PFC Alvin White on his left. There were six other men, but they were much farther down the line, and there was a wide and threatening gap.

As darkness fell on a miserable night of cold and rain, Stein took the watch. Stein's men were exhausted, and he had to stay awake to maintain security. Alvin White was snoring while Herm Stein fidgeted. Stein had an urgent need to make a call of nature, but to leave the position meant the likelihood of being killed by foe or friend. Stein solved the problem by going in a K-ration box, then heaving it down the hill. White, waking with a start, blazed away with his rifle, and it took some time for Stein to convince White of the nature of the target.

At 1913 hours, six tank destroyers arrived in Bergstein. Two each were attached to Able and Charlie and one each to Baker and Easy Companies.

The faint rattle of equipment and weapons heralded the arrival of help. Lt. Richard Wintz, executive officer and with the loss of Captain Masny now commander of Fox Company, came up with a platoon from Easy Company and moved the men into positions on the hill. The men from Easy Company were part of Lt. Maurice Jackson's 2nd Platoon. Jackson had taken the platoon from Lt. Ted Lapres, who had lost a foot after stepping on a mine. Lieutenant Wintz brought up much-needed ammunition and rations, then took position at the bunker with Lieutenant Kettlehut, the artillery forward observer.

Around 2100, more wounded men were evacuated from the hill, including Lt. Len Lomell, who had been struck again. Dog Company was now led by the capable Sgt. Joe Stevens. At 2345, rations, water, ammunition, and additional weapons were brought in. Some resupply reached the hill while German artillery continued to pound. The sound of explosions was continuous and horrifying.

At 0333, Company C of the 121st Infantry arrived in Bergstein. A heavy-machine-gun team from this company was sent to assist Dog Company elements on the hill, but a German attack killed them all. Combat Command R of the 5th Armored was being withdrawn. 2nd Ranger headquarters was sending up machine guns and 81-millimeter mortars, expecting a last-ditch stand near the forward command post in the church.

About 0600, Herm Stein and Ranger Moss were talking at the entrance to the bunker when German artillery hit with a fury. For nearly half an hour, an eternity to an infantryman, the German shells fell like rain. When it ended, Stein could hear the cries of PFC Joseph Piche and PFC Alvin White. The crackle of small-arms fire spread across the hill. As the Germans tried to attack again, Herm Stein assisted his men. When Stein got back to his position, he found his raincoat and canteen were riddled with shrapnel. Being away from his foxhole had saved him from serious harm.

At 0700 another German attack began. Battalion estimated each attack at about company strength. This one was supported by fire from armored cars and directed at Baker and Charlie Companies. German artillery beat on the town with such ferocity that its repetition seemed like a drumbeat. The shells landing on the hill came one on top of the other without pause. German self-propelled guns tried to shoot their way into town, but the Rangers, tank destroyers, and artillery beat the Germans back. At 0850 on December 8, the 2nd Ranger Battalion received a report from Dog Company. There were only ten men left.

In Fox Company zone, Herm Stein was occupied for some time caring for wounded and seeing to the evacuation of those more seriously hurt. When the work was done, PFC Milt Moss joined him and the two of them began to snipe at the Germans in the valley. It was long-range shooting, but they caught two unwary Germans walking along a railroad track and shot them down. At 1036, artillery was used to break up a German attack from the south.

In the afternoon, a flight of P-47 fighter-bombers worked over the German positions southeast of Bergstein. The Germans tried to attack Charlie Company, which was now in Bergstein, but were driven off.

At 1330, officers of the 1st Battalion, 13th Infantry, arrived to relieve the Rangers. At the church that was the forward CP, German artillery, mortars, and shells from self-propelled artillery had been falling heavily. One shell went through one window cleanly and out a second window on the other side, tearing away part of the frame. Doc Block left the CP to supervise medical evacuation and was killed by shrapnel from an artillery round. As they learned of the death of their beloved doctor, grief, gloom, and bitterness filled the hearts of the men. Block was a superb physician, a respected leader, a warm and caring human being. Another good man would fill his position, but no one could replace Doc Block.

There were few men left to occupy the positions on the hill. For the Americans it became a battle led by sergeants. Dog Company had less than twelve men, Fox Company had about five, and Easy Company was down to a dozen. Herm Stein's foxhole resembled an arsenal. Spread out before him were two Browning automatic rifles, an M1 rifle, and a .45-caliber pistol, plus fragmentation grenades. Stein was cleaning his weapons when the German artillery began another pounding. Bending low in the foxhole, he waited until the shelling eased then looked over the edge of his hole. Two Germans had risen and were standing about twenty yards distant, talking with each other. Stein took aim, but the bolt of the automatic rifle slid forward with a dull thud. There is no more empty and lonely feeling in life than to be on a battlefield with a jammed weapon. Stein yanked back the bolt and squeezed the trigger again. This time the weapon fired true, and the two Germans died.

The Germans counterattacked. As they came up the hill, they made whistling sounds and cried *baa, baa*, like sheep. The Rangers felt the Germans were making the sounds as a control device and were grateful as the noise pinpointed the German location. Targets were plentiful, and the handful of Rangers fought furiously. Sergeant Stein, Moss, Bombardier, Hanahan, and "The Mad Russian" Uhorczuk were wounded. The Germans kept coming into the Ranger crossfire, and for three hours, the fight continued. Amid the clash of weapons, the crash of artillery, mortars, and grenades, and the moans and screams of wounded, the whistles and sheep sounds of the German leaders sounded bizarre. The Germans obviously were using the bunker at the top of the hill as their objective. As the enemy pressed closer to the top of the hill, Lt. Richard Wintz told Lieutenant Kettlehut where he wanted artillery fired. Kettlehut called in a hail of shrapnel that ringed the American positions. The surviving Rangers had scratched out shallow holes in the earth and pressed themselves down, but even for them, the experience was a thing of terror. The Germans were fully exposed to the fires and the *baas* and whistles turned to screams of agony.

Meanwhile, the Germans had also attacked Baker, Charlie, and Easy Companies. The artillery battle was terrifying, but the German artillery was losing its observers. The remarkable Lieutenant Kettlehut was calling in the combined fire of eighteen American artillery battalions. American ammunition bearers later told Rangers they had been worked to exhaustion carrying rounds to the hot barrels of the artillery. There were 105mm, 155mm, and 8-inch howitzer battalions and 240mm guns pounding the Germans. Kettlehut would never be forgotten by the men of the battalion. The eighteen battalions of American artillery responded to him as a symphony orchestra responds to its conductor. Kettlehut put artillery on top of the Germans and on their flanks. He terrorized the soldiers of the 6th German Parachute and the 980th Volks Grenadier Regiments. Kettlehut even used artillery as a broom, sweeping Germans into the vengeful mortar and small arms fires of the few remaining Rangers who were doggedly clinging to Castle Hill.

PFC Moss of Fox Company was angry at some Easy Company Rangers. Early in the fight someone had taken refuge in a shell hole near the bunker and dug the hole deeper for protection from shrapnel. Moss could see that the position did not have a good field of fire. It covered little because a large fallen tree was near enough to block the occupant's range of vision. While answering the call of nature, Moss heard furious firing from the other side of the bunker. Moss picked up his rifle and proceeded cautiously toward his foxhole. As he passed the bunker, he saw two dead German soldiers near the bunker, one more in the open and a line of German dead near the fallen tree. The dead men were German paratroopers in camouflage battle jackets. The enemy had been able to infiltrate up the hill close to the bunker, but were on the wrong side of the fallen tree and the Easy Company Rangers killed them. Moss jumped into the Easy Company hole and heard two of them quarreling over which man had killed a particular German.

Moss began crawling back to position near Herm Stein. Moss could see puffs of smoke in the air that signified German fire preparing for an assault, so he jumped into another foxhole. He had no sooner reached this position when the Germans came up a draw to his front. The few Fox Company men with Herm Stein laid down a withering fire on the enemy.

The Germans were still coming, moving in assault fire. Moss heard Sergeant Lare of Easy Company call to the Fox Company men that American artillery would be coming in. Lieutenant Wintz yelled to Lieutenant Kettlehut to bring the fire within 100 yards of the bunker. Moss knew that would put the artillery directly in front of his foxhole. Hearing the air split with the incoming rounds, Moss ducked low in his foxhole as shrapnel rattled on his helmet.

The German attack was stopped and the survivors went to ground. Moss saw a German who thought he was unobserved give hand signals to men to move right and left. Moss took aim at the German leader. To the right of the man Moss saw a white cloth fluttering from near a tree stump. The Germans were setting a trap. Remaining in his foxhole, Moss called out in German, "*Hände hoch, kommen sie hier!*" A German burp gun opened fire, and Moss shot the German paratroop leader and the soldier with the white cloth.

Whistles sounded and the Germans went down the hill again. The German paratroopers began to reorganize and the Americans could hear the roll being called. They could also hear that the same voices were making many answers in an effort to conceal their numbers. Once more the Germans tried to come up the hill, but the attack lacked desire and momentum. The Rangers from Dog, Easy, and Fox Companies beat back the attack with small-arms fire. Herm Stein had only a couple of rounds of ammunition left for his BAR and Moss had two eight-round clips remaining for his M1 rifle.

Capt. Duke Slater had been up and down Castle Hill coordinating artillery and mortar fires, relief, and evacuation. Checking positions, Slater saw T/5 Bill Roberson of Dog Company, who was manning a light machine gun covering the south slope of the hill. A line of German dead lay to the front of Roberson's position. Some were just a few yards from the muzzle of his gun. American dead lay strewn about the hill. Some of the dead would be hard to find. It would be a year before the remains of PFC Lee Taylor would be recovered and identified. His time with the battalion had been brief and in later years only Private First Class Moss could remember him.

On the night of December 8, relief finally arrived. As the men of the 1st Battalion, 13th Infantry, 8th Division, came up the hill, Sgt. Herm Stein of Fox Company; Sgt. Harvey Koenig, Sgt. Edwin Secor, and Sgt. Morris Webb of Dog Company; and Sgt. Lawrence Lare of Easy Company stayed behind to guide the newcomers into position.

From Dog and Fox Companies and the platoon from Easy Company, only twenty-two Rangers remained to come down from Castle Hill. Moving as though in a trance, they came down with gaunt faces and hollowed eyes fixed upon some distant spot on the horizon. PFC Moss got on the Fox Company truck and saw that three quarters of the truck was empty.

Castle Hill was one of those thousands of bloody small-unit fights that historians pass over. History would well record the climbing of the cliffs at Pointe du Hoc by the 2nd Ranger Battalion though more of its men died on Omaha Beach. There is scant mention in the histories of the terrible battle the Rangers would remember as "Hill 400."

The German high command knew the importance of Castle Hill. Generalfeldmarshall Walter Model, chief of the German general staff, promised the Iron Cross and a seven-day furlough to each member of the unit who succeeded in retaking the hill. The German grenadiers and paratroopers fought with skill and courage, but they did not succeed. The American Rangers bought Castle Hill with their blood, and though no marker stands on that hill in Germany, it is forever Ranger.

As the men of the battalion came down from the bloodied slopes of Hill 400, a thick snowfall began to lay a peaceful mantle of white over the torn and ruptured earth. The Rangers had captured the difficult objective and held it for fifty-six hours despite five German counterattacks, each of which were preceded by intense shelling. Approximately 450 Germans were found dead in the immediate area and 64 German prisoners were taken. The price was high—twenty-three Rangers dead, eighty-six wounded, twenty injured, and four missing in action. At 0615, December 9, the remnants of the 2nd Ranger Battalion closed into an assembly area and were attached to the 28th Infantry Regiment, 8th Infantry Division.

CHAPTER ELEVEN

Winter War
December 11, 1944–
February 4, 1945

I have eaten your bread and salt,
I have drunk your water and wine,
The deaths ye died I have watched beside
And the lives that ye led were mine.

—*Rudyard Kipling*

Away from the hell of battle in the Hürtgen Forest, the survivors were given hot coffee and food. The ground was covered with a blanket of snow, but the men could wrap themselves in a blanket and shelter half and seek the luxury of sleep.

Returning to a semblance of humanity after such horror is not immediate. Men shake from more than the cold. Body parts may move independent of thought. An arm or leg may fly up or out without warning. It is not only the battle that is terrifying, the aftermath may be as well.

At a quartermaster shower point the men were able to shower and scrub away the grime of living like burrowing animals. They shaved and put on clean clothes and dry socks. There was plenty of clothing as the pile of duffle bags included those of men who would never need them again. There were not many men left for duty. The battalion strength was approximately the size of a single line infantry company. The assault companies could not muster the authorized strength of one of their platoons.

Of the 120 men given leave, sixty went for two days to the V Corps rest center at Eupen, and sixty plus three officers were given two days' leave in Paris. The city of light became a celebration of life for survivors. Women, wine, and song helped men cope with the reality of war. The brief rest ended as the battalion attached to the 8th Infantry Division as a counterattack reserve.

L-Rod Petty was determined that his men would receive recognition for their efforts on Castle Hill. He chose to nominate a man of Fox Company who was very deserving for the Distinguished Service Cross. Although the accomplishments of this Ranger alone would have earned him the decoration, Petty chose to prove instead that the awards system was bullshit and used the story of Roger Young for the recommendation. Earlier in the war in the Pacific a young infantry sergeant named Roger Young had found himself losing his sight and hearing. Young took a voluntary reduction to private. When his platoon was trapped under the fire of a Japanese machine gun, Young voluntarily crawled forward, ignored the calls of his lieutenant and despite being wounded, knocked out the Japanese gun and crew, though he died in the attempt. Roger Young was posthumously awarded the medal of honor and a song "The Ballad of Roger Young," was written in tribute.

Petty proved his point and the award came through. The brave and worthy soldier who received the decoration said, "I never did what that citation says." Petty replied, "That's OK, you deserved it anyway."[1]

Major Arnold and battalion officers were already visiting the 11th Replacement Depot recruiting volunteers to begin building the battalion strength. Arnold had competition. The replacement system of the U.S. Army was in a shambles—so many infantrymen were being lost to trenchfoot that they could not be replaced. Rifle companies all along the line were short of men. The few days rest passed quickly. They did not know that events beyond their control were in motion.

Mid-December 1944 was an optimistic time for the allies. Progress on the front was going well, the logistical system to support combat operations was in place and operating effectively, and General Eisenhower planned a major offensive in the beginning of 1945 that would finish the German Army.

But the German cause was not hopeless. German scientists had some impressive developments in the works. There were improved, long-range rockets that could punish England, and the Me-262, a jet-propelled fighter plane, had the capability of sweeping Allied aircraft from the sky. If a bold attack was successful, the Allies could be forced to the negotiating table.

Throughout his political career, Adolf Hitler showed himself to be a gambler. Against the advice of his generals, Hitler decided to launch a winter attack through the Ardennes Forest. The American VIII Corps was in the Ardennes in a thin, defensive posture, and few intelligence officers thought the Germans could mount an armored attack through these forests in the cold and snow. The Germans, however, had learned much about fighting winter war in Russia, and they knew what was possible. Hitler believed the audacity of the attack could bring it success. He hoped to attack over a direction of Bastogne, Brussels, and Antwerp—if successful, every Allied force to the north of that line would be cut off and destroyed.

At 0530 hours on December 16, 1944, the Germans attacked. The U.S. 28th and 106th Divisions were chewed up, and confusion reigned in the Allied ranks. At 0940 hours on the sixteenth, the 2nd Ranger Battalion was alerted that it would be released from its attachment to the 8th Infantry Division to join the 78th Infantry Division. Soon orders were received to move to defensive positions in the vicinity of Simmerath.

The battalion had died in the fires of Bergstein and Castle Hill, but like the legendary phoenix it rose from its own ashes. Men were hastily recalled from their brief pass to Paris while every man that could carry a weapon turned out for movement. By 2300 hours, under heavy artillery fire, the battalion was closing into position near Simmerath on the northern flank of the German attack. The battalion headquarters was in the basement of the ruins of a maternity hospital and under frequent attack. The remnants of Able, Baker, and Charlie Companies, each of which were of platoon strength or less, were on line with Easy in reserve. The nineteen men left in Dog Company had been designated to serve as 81-millimeter mortar crews, and the small number of Fox Company men were operating light machine guns in support. Company C of the 310th Infantry and Company K of the 309th Infantry were attached to the battalion.

Digging in the frozen earth was exhausting and in some areas water was encountered when the frost line was penetrated. Those positions in open fields had no overhead cover. Wet, cold, and miserable men endured the enemy rockets and artillery that probed the Ranger positions. German self-propelled artillery would move forward, fire rapidly then retreat to return in another location. High explosives with variable-time fuses showered jagged shrapnel upon the open foxholes beneath. The battalion wire lines were cut repeatedly and communication had to be maintained by radio and foot messengers running a gauntlet of fire. American artillery was responding in counterbattery fire and the sky was filled with rumbling harbingers of death and white phosphorous shells that exploded close to the Ranger position. At night German aircraft droned overhead accompanied by probing searchlights and the hammering of the antiaircraft guns. Small numbers of German paratroopers dropped to ambush and harass. They did not pose a major threat, but were sufficient to add to the constant state of tension.

Baker Company, 2nd Platoon sniper Pvt. Roy McKinney cautiously crawled into a position where he had good observation and an excellent field of fire. Within his range was a German troop shelter. The Germans were unaware that any American could see them and were walking in and out of the shelter at will. When daylight came, McKinny began picking off Germans as they left the doorway. As bodies piled up someone in the shelter realized what was happening and the Germans stayed concealed within.

Capt. Sid Salomon would never ask his men to do anything he was unwilling to do, so he led men forward of the Baker Company positions for two nights to install concertina wire in front of the Ranger positions. Salomon and Lt. Tom Victor frequently took combat patrols in search of enemy positions.

When in defensive positions, men dug deep to avoid the constant rain of German artillery and mortar fire. If next to a house, a tunnel could be made underneath it. When the shells were falling close men could crawl back under the house for protection. As soon as the shelling lifted they occupied the firing position.

On the seventeenth, the 81-millimeter mortars of Dog Company were engaged in a duel with German gunners. The Rangers would fire, then run for shelter before the inevitable response came in. The main German attack was not falling on the sector held by the Rangers, though there were frequent alarms and messages from higher and adjacent headquarters warning of impending German attacks. Work on defenses was feverish. On the eighteenth, fifty-three replacements were received. There was no time for training and these unfortunate men were thrust into line with the companies.

Work on the defenses continued as concertina wire, mines, and booby traps were positioned. Incoming artillery began to lessen as the German gunners were called elsewhere. Though the rain of shrapnel and high explosive was not as extensive, it did not cease, and no one felt safe. As the replacements were added, men from Dog Company joined the other companies in the line of foxholes. There were no attacks by either side but movement brought artillery and mortar fire. Patrolling was constant, and Baker Company had a six-man German patrol pinned down. American 4.2-inch mortars fired a smoke mission which unfortunately covered the German escape. A German soldier who had penetrated Able Company wire was killed. On the night of the twenty-first, PFC Walter Kacala of Charlie Company left his foxhole and decided to check out the area to his front. The Germans were alert and took him prisoner.

The foxholes were spaced forty to one hundred yards apart in snow-covered fields. The frontage was so great that many holes were occupied by a single man and in many of those lonely positions were men who had no combat experience. They waited, shivering in a cold so intense no future warmth could erase it from their souls. Now and then incoming artillery or mortars would strike, the blast of high explosive heaving the earth about them with a violence that shook every bone in the body. Men cringed low, helpless before such power. The feeling of trying to get the entire body under the scant protection of a steel helmet was normal though futile. Body armor did not exist. If the firing continued long enough, inevitably someone would be hit. An incoming round would be fused to explode above the earth sending a rain of death earthward. There would be screams of agony and desperate calls for a medic. No matter the danger, the medic always came, though the run through hell might be in vain. Sometimes by the chance of war an incoming round landed in the foxhole, granting the mercy of a quick death to the occupant, but leaving a scene of horror for his comrades who found him. The mindless beast that was the incoming shell had no regard for the time or season.

At Simmerath, Christmas Eve of 1944 was a clear and cold night, the moonlight reflecting on the snow-white battlefield. In the Able Company area, PFC Neil Shira, a replacement fresh from basic training, was huddled alone in a foxhole. Though his head and feet were wrapped, the cold penetrated and Shira hunched his body and shivered. He wanted to be a surgeon not a soldier, but war had changed his life. Now he was far from his dreams and alone with his foes. There are many foes in such a circumstance. In addition to the armed enemy, a man must fight his fear, his weariness, and his imagination. When Neil Shira saw the German, the man was some twenty-five yards away moving in slow caution upward along the snow-blanketed hedgerow that concealed Shira's position.

Had he been a veteran Shira would have shot the German and put a quick end to it. But Shira was a youth, poorly trained and thrust into action. He decided to put down his rifle wait until the German was close then pull the pin on a grenade, place it outside the foxhole and duck down while it rolled down and exploded on the German soldier. Shira forgot that when the pin is pulled and the safety lever released there is a popping sound clearly audible on a still night. When the pop of the grenade sounded, the experienced German turned and made a run and dive for cover. The grenade did not roll downhill. Confused, Shira reached outside the hole to pick up the grenade and throw it after the German. As his fingers closed around the grenade the 4.5-second fuse expired and the grenade exploded, blowing off his right hand. Though in shock Shira grabbed his rifle with his left hand and fired two futile shots after the retreating German. He then managed to fashion a tourniquet out of a handkerchief and a bayonet. For a time he stayed in the foxhole, aware of his duty to protect that portion of the line then pain took its toll and he clambered out, searching until he found assistance and evacuation. Behind him at the blood-stained foxhole he left his steel-rimmed glasses and the remnants of a hand that could have saved lives.

Replacements arrived in Able Company and set about digging their foxholes. One of these did not have a chance to meet other members of his platoon—German Nebelwerfer rockets landed on his position and killed him. In Able Company men in basements opened food packages that had been sent from the United States—food packages of men who had been killed.

Christmas day dawned clear and shimmering white contrails of Allied fighters spilled across the bright blue sky. The thunder of their engines heralded of doom for the German offensive. Soon the incoming artillery ceased; there were no gunshots, no nighttime raids by German planes. Coffee and turkey sandwiches were brought forward. The men of the battalion still stood watch from muddy foxholes over the snow-covered earth, but it was a peaceful watch. The Ardennes offensive of the Germans was smashed and the Battle of the Bulge passed into history.

December became January. More replacements arrived to relieve men in the cold foxholes. Incoming artillery still fell, but when not on watch, men could withdraw to a basement. It was reasonably dry in these shelters where makeshift stoves provided warmth and food and rest fortified the body. Many basements had been used for coal storage and the black dust covered their bodies.

Patrols went out each night. Easy and Fox Company patrols welcomed in the new year. Artillery shells the Germans sent over and tripped flares in front of Charlie Company lit up the sky.

The battalion was attached to the 311th Infantry of the 78th Infantry Division. At 0815 on the morning of January 2, a messenger arrived from the regimental commander of the 311th. The message read, "We must have a prisoner by 2400 hours." Able Company was alerted to the mission and planning began. The day was relatively quiet. There was some incoming German mortar fire, and a German self-propelled gun fired twenty-five rounds without causing injury. Seven enemy planes flew overhead but they did not strafe. As evening came on heavy vehicular movement could be heard from the German lines but it was soon quiet.

Lt. Sylvestor "Pop" Porubsky would lead the Able Company patrol consisting of Sgt. Joe Drake, Sgt. Garland "Gabby" Hart, T/5 Richard Rankin, T/5 Gerald Shroeder, and PFC Eugene Pycz. All patrol members were briefed on the mission, routes out and back, and specific assignments. Weapons were cleaned and tested and ammunition checked for serviceability. The men would carry only the essentials.

White capes would help them blend with the snow-covered terrain. When all was ready, each man tried to rest.

As the winter night closed in, the patrol readied itself and conducted final checks. At 1935 hours Pop Porubsky led them out from battalion lines to search for a lightly manned German outpost, a forward position. They followed the trace of a road that the Germans would likely have covered by fire. Blending among the shadows of the battlefield they moved carefully, measuring each step. The German positions were not that far away so the men had to be patient. They hoped to catch the enemy offguard.

The Germans and the Americans saw each other simultaneously and at close range. The Able Company Rangers dove to the snow-covered earth and opened fire. A German MG42 fired a stream of bullets and men on both sides threw grenades. Fifty-nine minutes had passed since Porubsky's patrol had crossed into this no-mans-land. Now the quiet night was rent by the rattle and rip of gunfire, men yelling in German and English, and the crash of exploding grenades. Another German outpost opened fire and that fire was returned. Dick Rankin was crawling forward to close on the enemy when a potato-masher grenade exploded beside his head seriously wounding him. Porubsky and another Ranger followed their grenades and found two of the Germans sprawled dead or dying beside the machine gun. A third German was dazed and cringing from the explosions. He was seized and hurried from the gun position. Pop Porubsky and Joe Drake then turned their attention to Dick Rankin, whose head wounds were pumping blood.

With the man's lifeblood streaming from him, caution was not a factor. Porubsky and Drake hastily bandaged Rankin's wounds and carried him back to friendly lines. Medic Joe Guerra administered plasma, and Rankin was evacuated. For Dick Rankin the war was over. He would be treated in hospitals in Belgium, France, England, and the United States, where he met a Red Cross volunteer named Lucy Lolli. In time they married.

Captain Cook, the intelligence officer, interrogated the German prisoner who revealed he had been in an antiaircraft unit until he had been reassigned to a replacement depot. He was then sent to the 7th Company, 981st Regiment, 272nd Infantry Division, consisting of one officer and thirty-five enlisted men. They were armed with rifles and two machine guns. For protection from artillery and from the cold, all men remained in a fortified bunker except for two outposts consisting of three men each whose mission was to give warning and allow fighting positions to be occupied. He pinpointed on a map the locations of the bunker and outposts and revealed that the Germans kept the guns in a bunker by day. At night they moved them to the two observation posts. They had good reason to be wary of the Dog Company mortars. The prisoner related that two rounds had killed or wounded nine Germans.

The Germans responded to the patrol action by firing nearly 100 mortar rounds on the battalion, but no one was hit. American artillery struck back and Fox Company continued patrolling at 0250 hours. There was excitement in the CP that soon spread to the basements and foxholes. The battalion would be relieved that day for rest, refit, and to begin training of the replacements. These volunteers arrived in small groups of three to five men per company. Some of these men became casualties before they could receive proper training, but others adapted well.

Representatives of the 1st Battalion, 311th Infantry, were attached to the battalion and were briefed on the situation. On January 2 the Rangers began moving by foot to Lammersdorf where a convoy of quartermaster trucks were waiting. The initial destination was the town of Rotgen.

There was always a mission. Now the battalion was released from attachment to the 311th Infantry and attached to the 102nd Cavalry Group. While regrouping and training, the Rangers would be part of the third line of defense for the 78th Infantry Division. Engineers had been constructing log-covered bunkers and stringing barbed wire. While in reserve, the Rangers would complete these emplacements. It was not hard duty, and a rotation system was established. The companies took turns working on the emplacements, training or replenishing their bodies and equipment. Officers were dispatched to replacement depots and rear area installations to recruit new men for the battalion.

After considerable sweat and toil to prepare the defensive positions it came to no one's surprise that the battalion was ordered away. Released from attachment to the 102nd Cavalry Group and the 78th Infantry Division on January 8, Major Williams and his men were ordered into XIX Corps reserve and sent to Schmidthof where they would finally have an opportunity to train the many replacement troops. The men of the battalion lived in buildings, patching broken windows with cardboard, scrounging furniture, and constructing field expedient stoves to ward off the cold.

The battalion was now allowed 15 percent over-strength and carried approximately 33 officers and 564 enlisted men. Despite the numbers it was not the unit that had come ashore at Normandy, stormed the guns of Brest, or endured the hell of Castle Hill. Many of the volunteers had no experience beyond basic training; some were men from supply or signal units with no infantry experience. They were good men, but untrained. Veteran officers and noncommissioned officers were selected as instructors. Work began on the construction of firing ranges and classrooms. The replacements were divided into twenty-man training platoons each headed by an experienced sergeant who introduced a strong physical training program. The course followed that of infantry basic training. A second level of training was for the more advanced students; even the old guys brushed up on their skills.

The training began at 0830 and often lasted until after midnight. The German forests and fields were covered with snow and ice and sudden thaws brought thick, glutinous mud. At night, the men learned to move as a unit hindered by the darkness. The lead man traveled by compass azimuth and those behind clung to the cartridge belt of the man in front or kept in sight the small white marking on the back of a helmet.

They learned to camouflage themselves and their equipment to blend with snow and woodland and how to freeze in position at the popping sound of a flare. Patrolling often required infiltration and the Germans were skilled in mine warfare. The men learned to move carefully and slowly when seeking to close on a German position at night. They learned to explore the ground ahead of them with the soft touch of their hands. They learned how to silently kill a sentry. The companies practiced by infiltrating each other's defensive positions.

The intense training for the new men paid off and they soon adopted the confident, cocky air of Rangers. The old guys were allowed more time to relax, and they set up their own beer hall and now and then procured a movie projector. Able Company celebrated the commissioning of their 1st Sgt. John White to 2nd lieutenant on January 19, and he was reassigned to Fox Company. As leader of 1st Platoon, Bill Klaus filled the vacancy left by White and had the opportunity to write Olive that he was now First sergeant of Able Company. When they had time on their hands, the veterans went fishing. Rod and reel were not available, but hand grenades and dynamite could put a tasty meal in a mess kit.

On January 29, individual training was followed by training in small-unit firing problems and reconnaissance exercises. Though not as skilled as they had been before Castle Hill, they were needed for combat. On February 4, 1945, the battalion was attached to the 9th Infantry Division of U.S. First Army and alerted for operations.

CHAPTER TWELVE

The Roer and the Rhine
February 5–March 26, 1945

Forty miles a day on beans and hay.
—Old cavalry song

From Supreme Command through Army, Corps, and Division, the orders flowed to establish a bridgehead across the Roer River. In the early morning of February 5, thirty olive drab trucks arrived. Carrying weapons and equipment, the men scrambled aboard. The destination was Wollseifen on the western bank of the Roer River. The winter wind bit into the huddled men and the trucks moved slowly on congested roads. Pressing close against the cold, they traveled in rut and mire through the ruins of Rotgen and Monschau to Hofen, where 9th Division guides met the convoy to guide them to the dismount point near the river. Staying clear of enemy observation they climbed to high ground and occupied drab, unfinished stone German barracks. From the windows the men could see beneath them the rushing waters swollen by early thaws as the river thundered through a narrow gorge. Fog rose and swirled in the breeze. The water looked cold and forbidding. Outposts were put into position as the enemy line of defense was 500 yards away on the opposite side of the Roer River.

On February 7, American infantry entered Schmidt, the German strongpoint that had resisted throughout the winter. Success at Schmidt allowed the 9th Infantry Division to contemplate a variety of efforts to cross the Roer. One option called for the Rangers to establish a bridgehead at the Urft Dam and seize the pumping station there. In mid-afternoon staff officers and company commanders made a daylight reconnaissance to determine how best to accomplish the projected mission. The battalion plan was for Able Company to cross at the dam while Baker forded the river 500 yards downstream. Fox Company would be in position on high ground overlooking the river and provide covering fire with the battalion machine guns. When the crossing was made, the remainder of the battalion would follow at the best location and a perimeter defense would be established for the bridgehead. Engineers would come forward and lay a pontoon bridge and a combat team of the 47th Infantry, 9th Infantry Division, would cross and expand the bridgehead with the vast Schwammenauel Dam as the final objective.

Able and Baker Companies sent patrols for a closer look at their possible crossing sites. Able reported that water flow was increasing over the dam and fissures were appearing on the north face. Baker Company observed that a German artillery piece was putting interdiction fire on the dam at a rate of about one round every five minutes. Planning proceeded with alacrity. Capt. Edgar Arnold, the battalion executive officer, made a daring one-man reconnaissance north of the dam to search for a better crossing site. Forward observers from the 84th Field Artillery Battalion and the 82nd Chemical (4.2-inch) Mortar Battalion began to plot supporting fires. An engineer major arrived to study the condition of the dam, and the German civilian who was the supervisor of the dam system was brought in and interrogated by the officer with a German-speaking Ranger along to translate. The engineer, the German, and a patrol then went forward for a closer look at the dam.

The area was quiet until the battalion kitchen was set up and a chow line formed. A canny German forward observer had been waiting for such an opportunity and fired his 120-millimeter. Food was forgotten for the moment but the observer missed with his first shots. The only casualties were some German refugees that had been allowed to stay in the same area.

On the eighth, the battalion moved to the west of Wollseifen to the mountain area of Kalterherberg. Steel helmets of both armies lay about torn by bullet and shrapnel. The ripped jackets and trousers of bloody uniforms showed the desperate attempts by medics to save the lives of comrades. The sickly sweet aroma of rotting flesh rode the breeze as the area was littered with the bloated bodies of dead sheep, horses, and cattle strewn among barbed wire, burned-out buildings, and shell holes.

On February 10, Major Williams received the order to conduct the bridgehead attack on the following day. Plans were now turned to action. Officers and men departed to establish an observation post above the dam and a forward command post. Weapons and equipment were checked and checked again. The men ate a hot meal, trucks arrived, and loading commenced. Then at 1430 the message arrived, "Hold up on move until further orders from Corps."

Hurry up and wait. The words so familiar to the soldier rang true as men of the battalion stood about for two hours chain smoking cigarettes and anxious to get on with the mission. Two hours later, without explanation the message came from corps headquarters that the operation was canceled. A motor messenger was dispatched to recall the advance party and men began to unpack their equipment. Another unit had not taken its objective, thereby jeopardizing the crossing. The angry veterans knew an opportunity was lost as it was perfect weather for an attack. A blinding snowstorm was driving west to east into the face of the Germans.

Training promptly resumed with night patrolling and exercises. Able, Baker, and Charlie Companies trained for river crossing while Dog, Easy, and Fox held small-unit training. The battalion had recovered from its severe losses and was once again ready for battle. On February 22, Major Williams received orders that promised high adventure. The Rangers were to attach to the 102nd Cavalry Group. By 1435 hours on the twenty-third, the battalion was at its new station and eager to roll. The idea of riding into battle rather than being footsore and carrying heavy loads was appealing.

Commanded by a tank officer, Col. Cyrus A. Dolph III, the 102nd Cavalry Group was a former New Jersey National Guard horse cavalry outfit with the heritage of the "Essex Troop" from the French and Indian War. Federalized and brought to active service in January of 1941, the 102nd rode horses until April 1942 when the men converted to a mechanized outfit. The 102nd arrived in England in October 1942 where it was equipped with M8 armored cars (six-wheeled vehicles each armed with a 37mm gun and a coaxial .30-caliber and .50-caliber machine gun) and M5A1 light tanks each carrying a 37mm gun and three .30-caliber machine guns. The cavalrymen came ashore in a later wave on D-Day at Normandy and had fought well. Nine months later, the 102nd was an experienced combat unit organized into the 38th and 102nd Cavalry Reconnaissance Squadrons. These two squadrons totaled six reconnaissance troops. As there were six Ranger companies, the blend was ideal.

Dolph's command also included the 62nd Armored Field Artillery Battalion (105mm howitzers), engineers, and tank destroyers. At the time of the union, the 38th Squadron had recently received seventeen new M24 light tanks with 75 mm guns.[1]

For four days the Rangers and Cavalry practiced teamwork. Rapid loading and unloading and firing exercises were rehearsed. The concept emerged of having one platoon of a Ranger company distributed among the lead vehicles of the cavalry while the 2nd Platoon would be held intact at the rear as a cohesive fighting unit.

The cavalry vehicles could use tank main guns and .50- and .30-caliber machine guns to lay down a heavy base of fire. The Rangers provided infantry protection against enemy soldiers close to the vehicles. Supported by the firepower of the cavalry, the Rangers could flank and assault enemy positions. On February 28, Major Williams was called to a meeting at the 102nd Cavalry Group headquarters. Shortly thereafter Williams called the battalion and ordered Dog and Easy Company to prepare for movement. The 38th Cavalry Squadron had been given the mission of relieving Company I of the 309th Infantry, 78th Division, along the west and north banks of the Roer River near the Schwammanuel Dam. Dog and Easy Companies would accompany the 38th Cavalry. Williams looked after his men and left nothing to chance. Capt. Duke Slater was assigned as Dog and Easy Task Force commander as well as Headquarters Company commander, and Capt. Ike Eikner headed up the rear elements. Major Williams, Captain Slater, and the Dog and Easy Company commanders left on the morning of March 1 to make a reconnaissance of the sites the companies were to occupy and meet with the commander of the unit being relieved. Major Williams passed the word that Dog and Easy Companies should be ready to move out in the morning.

At 1045 a dispatch rider delivered a message from Colonel Dolph to Major Williams: "Be prepared to cross the stream [Roer River] tonight."[2] Dolph and Williams considered their options. The Rangers were given the mission of clearing the enemy side of the Roer River. The Germans had not blown up the dams, instead being content to destroy the control machinery causing a constant flow of water designed to slow the American advance. The water level of the river had since fallen leaving behind flats and steep banks that were blanketed with mud. A German soldier of the 1st Battalion, 980th Regiment, 272nd Volks Grenadier Division, had crossed the river to surrender and revealed that only fifty to seventy-five men remained in his unit.

Williams decided to have Dog and Easy send combat patrols across the river to check out the far shore and high ground beyond it. 2nd Lt. Kendall B. McClure would lead the Dog Company patrol, and 1st Lt. Fred W. Trenkle headed the men from Easy Company. Moving by separate routes the patrols would meet at a prearranged point. If the way was clear, Lt. Richard Wintz, Fox Company commander, would use the information to make a night crossing and take the best route to high ground. Fox Company would establish a perimeter defense and the patrols of Dog and Easy would be attached to Fox Company until their parent units arrived.

If resistance was light the remainder of the battalion would cross in daylight. If the resistance was heavy the battalion would make the crossing on the night of the second. Moving out at 2100 hours the patrols made their way across slopes covered with slick mud and crossed the river at two different locations. They found the water cold and swift but only one-and-a-half to three feet deep at the crossing sites. Under cover of darkness two scouts from each patrol waded the river and made a thorough reconnaissance of the far bank, then the remainder of the patrol crossed single file. Before midnight all the men had crossed and were proceeding on their patrol routes and reporting they had no enemy contact.

By 0200 on the second, Williams had the remainder of the battalion alerted for movement and Fox Company began to cross at 0345.

The patrols found that roads were blocked by felled trees. Booby traps and mines lined the pad. The fear of mines greater than that of meeting the enemy. Sgt. Colin Lowe, lead scout of the Dog Company patrol, heard voices in a cluster of houses. A German-speaking patrol member called for surrender and some fifteen terrified civilians came out with their hands in the air. They were eager to cooperate and pointed out minefields. By 0625 the patrols traveling by different routes met on the high ground, two German soldiers fled at their approach. Knowing the area ahead was clear, Fox Company could now move with speed and reached the high ground at 0720.

Williams took the remainder of the battalion across at 1215. Dog and Easy Companies crossed the river and were soon followed by Able, Baker, and Charlie. The men went down to the riverbank in a column of twos. Knowing that the opposite bank was clear, the men of some companies then stripped from the waist down. The day and the water was cold, but wet clothing, boots, and socks would be a problem on the other side.

By afternoon, sunshine had given way to snow. Charlie Company had the lead, followed by Williams and the command group, then Able, Baker, Dog, Easy, and Fox moving in double column to high ground. Dismounted cavalry and engineers were among them and all were wary, studying the ground for signs of minefields. Lt. Edward Kucinski and Sgt. Julius Belcher of Charlie Company led the eight-man point. Belcher tripped a "Bouncing Betty" that jumped into the air, but failed to explode. It was difficult to find the mines under the snow. They passed Riegel antitank, shoe-type antipersonnel, and concrete mines successfully by moving in single file and being careful to stay in the tracks of the point men. They passed wide of five roadblocks consisting of felled trees and mines. The obstructions averaged 200 feet in length. One of these roadblocks was later found to contain fifty mines. They were dangerous, but such a position must be covered by fire to achieve full effect and the Germans had retreated. Engineers who were following the battalion had the training to perform the dangerous work of removing the mines and clearing the roadblocks.

Charlie Company sent Lieutenant Kucinski, Sergeant Belcher, and six other men on ahead to attempt to make contact with the 310th

Infantry of the 78th Infantry Division. Near the place they hoped to make contact, they encountered thirty or forty Germans who pinned down the Rangers with machine guns and 120mm mortar fire. Cpl. Peter T. Bubanovich, who was decorated with the Silver and Bronze Stars, was killed instantly. The remainder of the patrol took cover and opened fire. Lieutenant Kucinski, Sergeant Belcher, and PFC Isaac Brilley were wounded by the German mortars. American artillery was called, and a 60mm mortar were set up and began to fire. The Germans were firing a machine gun from a deep standing trench, but a Charlie Company mortar crew put a round into the trench killing the gunners. As American artillery began to fall on their positions, both the Germans and Kucinski's patrol withdrew. Darkness was setting in as the men tried to dig defensive positions in the frozen earth. Snow was falling and the men wrapped themselves in their single blankets and shivered through the night.

The remainder of the battalion came up and with high ground attained, Williams put the battalion into a defensive position with Charlie on the left, Able on the right, and Baker coming up behind Charlie in reserve. Dog, Easy, and Fox were on a line to the southwest, their territory including high ground overlooking the Urft Dam. Lt. Joe Stevens was seriously wounded when he stepped on a mine. When the companies began to dig in, three men in Baker Company—Pvt. Johnnie Cox, Pvt. Zorack Organski, and PFC Lawrence Jackson— chose not to dig but to occupy a prepared German position. Their action resulted in the explosion of a booby trap, causing all three to be casualties and additional work and danger for other men. All wounded had to be carried by litter for 2,500 yards to where vehicles could to evacuate them. Rations and water had to be brought forward over the same distance. Ranger luck prevailed, but a stray horse using the same route was blown apart by a mine.

The Rangers' efforts continued to link up with the 78th Infantry Division and to keep a wary eye out for the 2nd Infantry Division which was attacking from Heimbach south on Gemund. Patrolling continued throughout the night and both Charlie and Dog took prisoners. The Dog Company captive revealed the location of the last three men of his unit. When captured the next morning the three Germans were found to be starving and lacking the will to fight.

Contact was made with a surprised patrol from the 78th Infantry Division who had no knowledge that the Rangers were in the area. Williams received a message from Colonel Dolph to move the battalion to a highground position to protect the flank of the 2nd Infantry Division. Despite having to skirt numerous minefields, the battalion traveled quickly. Before daylight failed on March 3, the Rangers had made contact with 2nd Infantry Division troops and were in position guarding the flank.

The 2nd Division, which was identified in Ranger message traffic as "Big Neighbor," was moving rapidly and crossed the front of Rangers. It was soon evident that the flank protection for Big Neighbor was not needed and the two days and nights of misery in snow, cold, and minefields was for naught. The Rangers were still known as "Veteran," and the 102nd was "Vertical." A message came from Colonel Dolph that read, "Assemble Battalion and move to Vertical area." For the men of the battalion, the order amounted to retracing their route. They had made the crossing with little more than basic needs for combat and raincoats were all they had to shelter them from the cold. Wet and exhausted and with no contact with the enemy they had taken shelter in some cabins. They had scarcely laid down to rest when the order came to prepare to move in thirty minutes. The battalion staff was hard at work as a rapid shift of the battalion's front and rear contingents, supply, and mess was necessary. Carrying parties were bringing up food for the assault companies. With a wide frontage, the battalion did not have enough food containers to feed all troops. The headquarters personnel went without food so the assault companies could eat.

Beginning at 0210 on March 4, the men endured an extremely cold march. Each step on the frozen ground beneath the snow was like a hammer blow to the soles of the feet. At length the soldiers linked up with guides from the 102nd Cavalry Group who led them to trucks, and at 0445 the battalion reached the 102nd Cavalry Group assembly area. It was snowing but there was no shelter, so the men wrapped themselves and lay down on the ground to sleep. By dawn many of them were covered with snow.

After their first hot meal in sixty hours, the merger of cavalry and Rangers began. Able, Baker, and Charlie would be under the command of Capt. Edgar Arnold, and Dog, Easy, and Fox would be led by

Capt. Duke Slater. Task Force Arnold and Task Force Slater would be blended with the cavalry as follows:

38th Cavalry Squadron	**102nd Cavalry Squadron**
Able Company & Troop A	Dog Company & Troop A
Baker Company & Troop C	Easy Company & Troop B
Charlie Company & Troop B	Fox Company & Troop C

Major Williams and some staff were with Colonel Dolph. Captain Arnold and Captain Slater and all company commanders and platoon leaders had jeeps, and each company had two halftracks and two 6x6 trucks. Vehicle mounted radios provided communication reliability that the backpack radios of the Rangers could not match. The best part for the Rangers was that the cavalry always had a kitchen truck at hand. It was infantry heaven for the Rangers and the cavalry loved it. After the war cavalrymen said, "this turned out to be the finest small combined-arms teams you ever saw."[3]

Cavalry tactics of speed and firepower were used until the column was halted by German emplacements, then the cavalry would mass their fire, including those of the attached artillery, on the objective. The Rangers would dismount and follow in the supporting fire, flanking the position or attacking head on to close with the enemy and kill or rout him. It was lightly held, road-bound country between the Roer and the Rhine and the German defenders were no match for the artillery/cavalry/Ranger team that was screening to the front of V Corps.

The system worked from its first usage on the fourth when Charlie Company of the Rangers and Troop B of the 38th Cavalry went through the town of Hertgarten. Five prisoners were taken in town and on the opposite side a firefight erupted against German small arms, mortars, and machine guns. Charlie Company's lead platoon followed their supporting fires in with marching fire, while the reserve platoon and some of the cavalry came in from the flank. Two German machine guns were knocked out with three Germans killed and five prisoners taken. The rest of the Germans fled.

The cavalry and the Rangers fought as one, and all along the V Corps front, the army was advancing. The 2nd and 78th Infantry

Divisions moved fast and in close proximity. Prior to darkness each day, a combined Ranger-cavalry team cleared an area where the soldiers could halt. During the evening, Command Group leaders held meetings where they decided which towns would be taken the next day and who would lead the assault teams. Men cared for their equipment and each other, supplies were ordered and received, and vehicles were maintained during these stops. This combined-arms team functioned as a moving, fighting town as far as fifty miles in front of the American advance.

During the night, Ranger reconnaissance patrols ranged outward to nearby towns. Sgt. Warren "Half-Track" Burmaster led PFC Henry Ware, PFC Leo Virgin, and PFC Charles Korb to the town of Berg. Baker Company had also sent a patrol into Berg, which consisted of Lt. William Sharp, T/Sgt. Carl Craft, and Sgt. John Muhl's BAR team. Both small patrols were credited with the capture of the town. Ten prisoners were taken by the Baker Company patrol, but the rest of the Germans seemed to be eager to get on the east side of the Rhine River.

Injuries came primarily from mines or mortars and in the rush forward confusion could occur. On the afternoon of March 4, Dog Company was sent on foot to occupy the town of Duttling. Unknown to the Rangers the 2nd Infantry Division Reconnaissance Troop had the same mission. As the Rangers came into the town from the north, the 2nd Infantry troopers entered from the south and opened fire. Dog Company flanked the recon men, but the Rangers wisely held their fire until they made positive identification, and as a result neither side suffered casualties.

Working with waves of cavalry light tanks, Easy Company and Troop B of the 102nd overran the high ground controlling Vtatten. The German towns fell like bowling pins: Hertgarten, Berg, Floisdorf, Sehwerfen, Ober Gartzem, Lessenich, Antweiler, Satzvey, Rissdorf, Firmenich, and Gehn. While en route to Gehn, Charlie Company of the Rangers and Charlie Troop of the 38th Cavalry surprised 100 Germans laying a minefield. The fires of the combined-arms team cut down the Germans and sixty surrendered.

Able Company took Rissdorf and Baker Company found a magnificent castle filled with hunting trophies and custom made weapons.

Williams had a hard time getting the men to leave. At Kommern they were close behind the retreating enemy. A German soldier was seen running into a house. An M8 armored car fired three rounds of 37mm fire into the house and the Rangers followed in. Fox Company searched the houses, the 1st Platoon taking one side of a street and the 2nd Platoon the other. Two scouts led the way. Fox took four prisoners and Captain Slater took two more. One fortunate German escaped in a hail of gunfire. Slater established his command post at a building that appeared to have been a Gestapo headquarters—fires were blazing, chicken stewed on the stove, and German packs were lying about.

Baker Company was searching the houses of Hertgarten when a German self-propelled artillery piece fired a shell into the town. The shell hit in the street, failed to explode, and tore through the wall of a building, hit another wall, then skipped around a room containing a Ranger search party. The shell came to rest at the feet of PFC James Roush. The room was cleared in an instant and, expecting another shell to follow, the men ran to the basement. Fortunately, the German gunner did not fire again.[4]

Easy Company rolled and fought for five days with only cat naps and no change of clothes. Near Wachendorf they captured two vast German ammunition dumps. The advance was swift and they captured many prisoners. They pressed on through Kreuzweingarten, Arloff, and Kircheim. The 62nd Field Artillery had to displace forward frequently to be able to provide support. Time and again American units would enter a town thinking they were the first to arrive only to be greeted by a cavalryman and a Ranger who were leaving for the next town east.

By March 6, the combined-arms team adopted the tactic of leap-frogging. Able, Baker, Charlie, and the 38th Cavalry Squadron would rest one day while Dog, Easy, Fox, and the 102nd Cavalry Squadron would attack. The following day they would switch. In each task force the Ranger companies and cavalry troops did not limit themselves to a single road, but spread outward over the existing road network often acting independently and communicating by radio.

The tactics employed brought the men in contact with outlying German farmers and vintners. Men quickly mastered key words and phrases of what Mark Twain called "that awful German Language."

Capt. Ike Eikner had the unfortunate duty of attempting to keep men from being men. Fraternization was forbidden, and there was a $65 fine for any American caught engaging in sexual activity with German women.

In a defeated country, a pack of cigarettes, a chocolate bar, or packet of coffee are better than money. It takes very few words of a foreign language to make a soldiers basic needs known. The men learned in German how to search for cognac, wine, beer, schnapps, milk, bread, and meat, and they could sign that they wanted to eat. When a rugged-looking Ranger with a submachine gun under his arms made the request, the German *hausfrau* sprang to her stove.

At Vischel, a platoon of Able Company caught up with a rear column of the retreating 272nd Volks Grenadier Division and surprised them, killing eight Germans and taking nine prisoner. Baker Company observed a German column of six to eight horse-drawn wagons. As the range was long a tank destroyer in the column was ordered to fire. The horses ran away, the wagons tipped over and began to burn, and the Germans ran for hills. As they closed on Altenahr, Baker Company caught another German column of about 100 men and 15 to 20 vehicles, all but two of which were being drawn by horses. Again the tank destroyer fired, and the Germans deserted the vehicles and fled into wooded high ground.

The Ranger officers wanted to use infantry tactics and clear the high ground that overlooked and controlled the town. The cavalry were accustomed to relying on speed in the attack so the column raced forward toward the town. Meanwhile the Germans took up defensive positions above the town and opened fire with small arms, mortars, and machine guns. The American advance was stopped on terrain that was too rugged for the cavalry to leave the road. The lead Ranger unit, Lt. Thomas M. Victor's 2nd Platoon of Baker Company, dismounted from trucks and rode cavalry jeeps forward close to the town. They then dismounted and sent the jeeps to the rear. Lieutenant Victor moved his platoon forward to the attack, but had to do so with the Germans above them and without the benefit of the cavalry's massed fires.

A railroad track into Altenahr led to a station that overlooked the Ahr River bridge. Victor separated the two sections of his platoon to each side of the railroad track. The Rangers ran forward firing and shouting and the sound of their voices seemed to panic many of the Germans who ran about in the town. PFC Henry Kowalowski shot a German officer who was setting up a machine gun. The Baker Company mortar section was moving close behind Victor's men using their 60-millimeter mortars. The skilled Ranger gunners fired from one side of a building at Germans on the other side. To do so, the mortar tubes had to be in an almost vertical position. On higher ground Germans who were dug in began to deliver accurate fire on the Rangers. PFCs William Cook, James Lorenze, Rocco Scione, Joseph Brenner, and Warren Wilson were hit. There were German soldiers in and around the railroad station and nearby buildings who were firing small arms, machine guns, *Panzerfaust* rocket launchers, and mortars. The Baker Company Rangers reached the houses on the outskirts of the town and in house-to-house fighting began killing the German infantry inside. Fifteen German soldiers were captured. From upper floors they got above a German self-propelled gun, which they captured along with its five-man crew. Soon Lieutenant Victor's platoon routed the surviving Germans from the railroad station.

Capt. Sid Salomon came forward and on learning the situation committed his first platoon to join in the attack. Salomon also brought forward 81mm mortars and called for artillery and tank support, but the tankers were reluctant to enter the narrow streets and the artillery had interests elsewhere.

The stone bridge over the Ahr River was about fifty feet long and was flanked on the opposite side by two- or three-story buildings. To continue the attack the bridge had to be crossed. Lt. Tom Victor led the way. As he ran forward, he was shot in the stomach. Victor was close to the German side of the bridge and managed to crawl onward and take cover. Without regard to his own safety, PFC Paul H. Hickling raced across the bridge to assist the wounded officer. Hickling dragged Lieutenant Victor to the side of a building shielding him from the German machine-gun fire that sprayed the street. Hickling treated Victor's wound and stayed with him until nightfall.

Heavy house-to-house fighting continued and eight men were wounded. Sgt. William J. Thomas had a critical stomach wound. Thomas was a replacement, the tent-mate of PFC Herb Appel at the replacement depot. Appel grieved for his friend, whose words "I don't think I'm going to make it" were prophetic. As night fell, Sergeant Thomas died. By the close of day the Rangers had cleared the Germans from the western side of the river. After dark Capt. Sid Salomon made his way across the bridge and Salomon and Hickling brought Lieutenant Victor back to friendly positions as cavalry light tanks began to move into the town.

Charlie Company was ordered to clear the high ground above Altenahr and had the mission accomplished by 0300. At 0600 Baker Company attacked across the bridge and killed twelve and took fifty Germans prisoner without friendly casualties. Altenahr was secured, but at a high price. The Ranger officers were bitter that their experience was ignored and Rangers were killed or wounded as a result. Knowing the high ground overlooking the town should have been taken first, Major Williams said, "The way to take a town is to stay out of it."[5]

While the civilian inhabitants stood shaking in fear, Baker Company Rangers explored and collected souvenirs. There was a good hotel in town with a superb wine cellar. Some of the men carried bottles, others carried cases and most of the men had the experience of sleeping in a good bed. The Baker Company history noted, "Everyone was satisfied there."[6]

It took experience for the Rangers and the cavalry to improve their tactics. If the town was on flat land, a jeep, a half-track, and an armored car were sent in. If there was no resistance, the column moved on without leaving an occupying force. With rare exception civilians knew that resistance was futile. Flag staffs where once the swastika flew now carried a white sheet. It appeared that every house was so adorned. Civilians waved and cooperated when asked for information. Most civilians tried to go about their daily chores as though it were a normal day. The wayside was often strewn with the gray-green uniforms of the German Army and men of army age in civilian clothes would be seen wearing army boots. If the Germans were not carrying weapons, the Rangers had orders to leave them for follow-on units to deal with.

Charlie Company moved to Binzenbach, where they surprised an armed German contingent. They killed three Germans and captured a captain and twenty-three enlisted men. They pressed onward after dark and again caught a group of unwary Germans, this time taking thirty prisoners.

Able Company had moved to the high ground west of Mayschoss, where they seized thirty-nine Germans and twenty-one impressed Frenchmen in German uniform. During the pursuit the Rangers had captured large ammunition dumps and a wide variety of equipment. On high ground near Mayschoss, Able Company patrols located two vast tunnels that were part of the German system to protect its war production from Allied bombers. One tunnel contained a huge power plant that powered an equipment repair facility and housed a number of German vehicles being put into service. In the stygian darkness of the second tunnel the Rangers found the workforce the Germans had used for their repair facility. Pressed together in fear and suffering were 3,500 slave laborers, men and women of varied nations, forced from their homes and families into a life of misery and despair. Their joy was overwhelming and gratitude unchecked as they emerged blinking into the sunlight.

Hurried radio transmissions were sent as the battalion sought help from civil affairs units. For their own safety, the 3,500 slave laborers could not be turned loose on the countryside so the liberated were kept under guard and assisted as best as the Rangers could manage. For the former slaves, hope was reborn and the path to home lay ahead.

For every combat soldier there are images of war that remain throughout his life. PFC Morris Prince of Able Company described such an incident on March 6: "The 2nd Platoon was in possession of the town of Lessinich. They had dismounted some distance from the objective and had proceeded to take the town on foot. A burning house on the outskirts of town illuminated their entrance, and sky-lined them against the crest of the hill which gave egress to the town. It was a ghostly and eerie scene as the men passed one by one, in front of this blazing pyre which so distinctly outlined them momentarily, only to have them vanish into the darkness again."[7]

As they moved toward Anteiler in the dark, Able Company Rangers held on to the cartridge belt of the men to their front. In Able Company, Sgt. Warren Burmaster gripping the belt of his best friend, Cpl. John Lazar, when German artillery hit the column, seriously wounding Burmaster. Corporal Lazar's remains could not be found. Four other Rangers were wounded.

There are times when the action of small units in one area can effect the action of large units in another. The widespread activity of the cavalry/Ranger teams near the juncture of the Ahr and Rhine Rivers was disruptive to German efforts to withdraw behind the Rhine in that area. The American Army tried again and again to seize a bridge over Germany's most historic river only to see an explosion and tangled steel as the bridge fell to the waters beneath. On March 7, a tank/infantry team from Combat Command B of the 9th Armored Division neared the junction of the Ahr and Rhine. They passed through woods near the town of Remagen and came out on high ground overlooking the Rhine River gorge. To their amazement the Americans saw beneath them a two-track railroad bridge. A disorganized mass of German soldiers were delayed in making the crossing. Supported by tank guns, American infantry stormed across the bridge. Despite last-minute efforts by the Germans to destroy it with demolitions, the damaged bridge held up. Within twenty-four hours, thousands of American infantry with engineers and armor were across and the guts of Germany were exposed.

The battalion staff was now concerned with time to rest, refit, and reorganize the men. The down time was useful to the Rangers. New winter clothing was issued. The men were examined for trenchfoot and several mild cases were found. Resupply of dry socks was a high priority and sitting on an upturned steel helmet putting on a pair of dry socks was the height of pleasure to the men of the battalion.

On March 7 at the village of Dietz, the 1st Platoon of Able Company became embroiled in a firefight with Germans and killed four and captured five without Ranger loss. The next day at the wine-growing center of Mayschoss, Able Company sent one platoon in from the front while the other platoon hit the town from the rear. There were sixty German soldiers in the town but they were not fighting. They were sitting at the cafes and the town hotel having a last beer before being taken captive. Able Company accommodated their desires and marched them off as prisoners. Then the Rangers took over the town hotels, used flush toilets, slept between sheets, and dined on German food washed down with German wine.

On March 10, while the other companies maintained defense and patrolling, Dog Company was attached to the 9th Infantry Regiment and sent to make contact with elements of George Patton's U.S. third Army operating to the south. Around 1130 the Rangers met units of the 11th Armored Division near Neiderzissen. At Franken, Dog Company Rangers killed six and captured sixteen fleeing German soldiers without a Ranger being hurt.

The German Army was in rapid retreat to get eastward of the Rhine River in the desperate hope that the legendary waters would serve as a barrier to the German heartland. At Allied headquarters, commanders and staff officers studied the terrain and road networks, the weather, the availability and condition of their forces, fuel and ammunition supply, and a multitude of other factors. Then based on the information they drew the lines on maps that would translate into action on the ground. On March 9, as they approached the Rhine River, the boundaries of the Rangers and cavalry came to an arrowhead and were pinched out as the U.S. first and third Armies converged.

During the period of March 2–9, three enlisted men were killed in action, and another died of his wounds. Two officers and twenty-seven enlisted men were wounded in action. Officers and men came and went, wounded were sent to hospitals, and replacements arrived. Of the platoon leaders, only two had landed with the battalion in the invasion of Normandy, and those two men, Lt. Joe Stevens of Baker Company and Lt. John White of Fox Company, had come ashore as enlisted men. Only one of the company commanders, Ralph Goranson of Charlie Company, had occupied that position at the time the battalion had landed at Omaha and Pointe du Hoc.

Captain Arnold's three companies were detached from the 38th Cavalry Squadron on the eleventh, and Baker and Charlie Companies joined Able at Mayschoss. On the same day Captain Slater's task force of Dog, Easy, and Fox Company was detached from the 102nd Cavalry Squadron and assembled near Ahrweiler. In mid-month the battalion was unified at Mayschoss and troops from an artillery battalion took over the mission of guarding the tunnels and liberated German prisoners. Colonel Dolph's 102nd Cavalry Group Headquarters and the 38th Cavalry Squadron were sent on a mission to third Army. The

102nd Cavalry Squadron commanded by Lt. Col. George S. Saunders remained in same area as the Rangers.

Mayschoss was located in wine country. Gingerbread houses and terraced hills with ordered ranks of vines gave a fairytale appearance to the area. The men were billeted throughout the community and slept in luxury. Major Williams's headquarters, and all of Headquarters Company, were billeted at a prewar resort hotel. The amenities included a well-stocked wine cellar.

Rest and recuperation for the Rangers meant preparation for the next mission. The Rhine River still had to be crossed and fierce fighting was expected. The battalion promptly began physical training: speed marches in mountainous terrain, weapons firing, and combined-arms training with the 102nd Cavalry Squadron, who were breaking in their new 75mm M24 tanks. Intelligence briefings were held. Some briefings made listeners doubt the intelligence of those who passed the information down. The men were told that among the German secret weapons they might have to contend with was a sleeping bomb that when exploded put all those within range into a deep sleep.[8] Many men felt they would welcome that bomb.

There was opportunity for showers and worn clothing was replaced by new. Equipment beaten up by months of combat was refurbished or replaced. All vehicles were repainted and communication equipment was tested. Working with the cavalry had shown the value of long-range, vehicle-mounted radios. By March 1944, American assembly lines had produced a wealth of war material other combatants could only marvel at. Major Arnold asked for and was quickly granted SCR-506 radios. Two of these were mounted in $^3/_4$-ton trucks, which would serve as mobile command posts for task force commanders Slater and Arnold. Another SCR-506 radio was mounted in an American command halftrack that had been recaptured from the Germans. This would serve Major Williams. The new mobile command post communication arrangement worked well. Now communication could be maintained over a forty-mile range.

There was time for relaxation. The strict non-fraternization policy imposed on American soldiers left some men engaging in athletics or going to the movies. Film projectors required power so a generator was set up outside the building in which the film would be shown. As the men watched the film, carbon monoxide from the generator began to seep through the window, and rows of men began to drift into unconsciousness. Those who were not affected corrected the situation, but the event was more exciting than the film.

A pile of mortar shells left behind by the Germans proved useful for river fishing, and fish fries and liberated German beer were in abundance. While detonating the water some soldiers noticed that the Germans had thrown a number of pistols into the river and the souvenir hunters became avid divers.[9] On March 25, the old guys who had been granted a month of home leave returned. Just in time to carry the new guys across the Rhine.

On March 26, the battalion moved toward the Rhine. Task Force Slater, consisting of Dog, Easy, and Fox Companies, was joined to Troops A, B, and C of the 102nd Cavalry Squadron and much to their joy found the crossing was easy. The 9th Armored Division was out front leading the V Corps attack. The German Army was in disarray and Slater's task force made the crossing on the longest combat pontoon bridge ever built, the remainder of the battalion following behind them. For the battalion, crossing the Rhine, the Nazis' last line of defense, was scarcely more than an administrative road march. The battalion moved to Neuweid, where the combined-arms team received the mission of relieving the 27th Armored Infantry Battalion of the 9th Armored Division. The roads were jammed with long lines of American vehicles moving troops and supplies into the heart of Germany. Tanks and artillery rolled in what seemed like endless lines and fleets of American fighter-bombers prowled the skies overhead.

CHAPTER THIRTEEN

Götterdämmerung
March 27 to Home

In war there can be no substitute for victory.

—Gen. Douglas MacArthur

The European war was now a pursuit, a race among armies bent on forcing their enemy to unconditional surrender. The 102nd Cavalry Squadron and Capt. Duke Slater's task force were ordered to screen the U.S. first Army (V Corps) boundary with Patton's U.S. third Army which was also driving east. The combined arms-team would also contact with Patton's troops. With the remainder of the battalion following to the rear, the team moved at 0555 on March 27. The fast moving cavalry/Ranger team spread out and struck quickly. Fox Company and Troop C captured ninety-seven Germans and destroyed six of the vaunted 88mm guns; Easy Company and Troop B captured thirty-five Germans; and Dog Company with Troop A captured another sixty-two of the enemy. All captures were made without the loss of a single American. Fox Company settled in for the night at Welshneudorf, while Easy Company occupied Holzappel. Company Headquarters and a platoon of Dog Company settled in for the night at Horbach. Throughout the night outposts and patrols were maintained by all companies.

Lt. John William "Wild Bill" Henderson's platoon of Dog Company with some cavalry swept into Langdonscheid on the west bank of the

Lahn River. The Germans soldiers had fled across the river and the townspeople surrendered. Across the river stood the sister town of Bollingsteidt and above that was a high hill. The steep slopes of the hill were barren, open terrain well-suited to defense. Atop the hill stood the massive Shaumberg Castle, a gigantic hexagon of gray stone built around 1785 with five vast cylindrical towers, one at each of its principal angles. The main tower was over 100 feet high. The castle dominated the towns, fields, forest, and river and appeared a throwback to a time when armored knights ruled the land. The castle was in third Army territory, but it was a tempting objective.

Lieutenant Henderson maintained a sentry studying the castle through field glasses and the Ranger soon reported that he had counted twenty-five to thirty Germans. Henderson decided to drive the Germans from their perch. To make the attack, he choose six Rangers and a cavalry driver named Frank Maruk.

The bridge across the river had been destroyed. Its steel girders lay in the water, making a difficult, but accessible means of crossing. Some of the men observed that a ferry was at hand that could have taken them across, but Wild Bill had his blood up and was not there as a tourist. Henderson led the patrol in clambering across the twisted girders, then began the climb of the hill. The eight men had no covering fire and no armor; they were moving up a steep hill that offered no concealment, and a force at least three times there number was above them. There is a fine line between audacity, luck and damn foolishness. Henderson and his men were soldiers with the taste of victory in their mouths. The Germans were beaten men who wanted only to survive. Not a shot was fired as Henderson and his men swept through the entrance to the castle.

After months of living in the earth or coal-dust-encrusted basements, it was disconcerting to walk on carpeted floors and stand in a fully furnished room. They spread out and began searching the castle, dragging four Germans from their hiding places. With the help of the Germans they learned that the castle was honey-combed with secret passages. On each floor concealed sliding panels and hidden doors led down narrow passageways to tunnels beneath the castle. Most of the Germans, some of whom were naval personnel had fled through these exits. Shaumberg Castle had been used both as the headquarters of a German artillery unit and as the repository of the history of the German Navy. A vast collection of books was shelved or boxed in corners. Estimates of the number of volumes ran to 300,000 These had been moved from German Naval Headquarters at Wilhelmshaven to prevent their destruction. Few men could read German but the books were beautifully bound and photographs told the story. They contained pictures of the *Bismark* and the *Graf Spee*. There were also photographs of submarines and uniformed men. Many photographs were of ships and men who would not be coming home.

The library contained books that shocked the Americans. "Know what those bastards had?" asked Cpl. Sheldon Bare. "They had a book full of information about every decent sized town in the United States. I'm from Altoona [Pennsylvania], you know, and they had a book over an inch thick on that city alone. I learned more about Altoona from that book in a half hour than I'd learned from living there for over twenty years!"[1]

Germany is a land rich in history and the men frequently encountered castles and palaces. Some castles were little more than piles of stone, their walls broken by the artillery of Napoleon Bonaparte or the Typhoons and Thunderbolts of the Allied air forces. Some of the centuries-old structures were works of art. In a fifty-room palace, the aged, titled owners huddled together in two rooms without electricity or running water. They had one bucket for a toilet and one to carry water. They wore layers of clothes and burned ornate wood paneling for warmth. In Germany in the spring of 1945, a title and ancient lineage meant little.

At 0235 on March 28, Major Williams received orders to immediately send a company to the 102nd Cavalry Squadron at Holzappel. The mission was to link up with U.S. third Army and relieve elements of the 3rd Armored Division at Diez. Major Williams, his command group, and Baker and Charlie Companies would follow. Able Company was turned out of their bedrolls and went hungry as they hurried off to their mission. The remainder of the battalion breakfasted then moved to follow Able Company across the Lahn River. They were conquerors and the move through the city of Lahn took on the air of a parade. They continued south, took up defensive positions and sent out patrols. T/Sgt. Joe Craft of Baker Company led a patrol that captured thirteen Germans.

In the early afternoon, battalion communications men stringing telephone wire between the companies reported movement to the south. Able Company dispatched a patrol and made contact with vehicle-mounted members of the 346th Infantry Regiment 87th Infantry Division of the U.S. third Army. Meanwhile Dog Company and Troop A of the 102nd Cavalry were in hot pursuit of Germans trying to escape. Searching north of Holzappel, they captured eighty-two prisoners and thirty abandoned vehicles.

Rapid movement forward continued on the twenty-ninth as more German towns surrendered. Guckingham, Laubusech, Bach, Munster, Eisenbach, and Hasselback hung out their white bed sheets and peered out from behind shutters at the advancing Americans. The town representatives understood that in this war the alternative to cooperation was destruction.

If more transport and shipping home had been available, truckloads of what soldiers call souvenirs (and civilians call loot) could have been sent home. As it was, many custom-made shotguns would grace American gun cabinets. There were cameras, watches, and other souvenirs that were sent back to the U.S. Throughout the war rear echelon troops had benefitted by their position, now the combat men had first pick—Rangers were making money selling souvenirs to those in the rear. Germany was a prosperous country that had looted Europe, and the practice came home with a vengeance as Americans, British, Canadians, French, Poles and Russians helped themselves. It took a major score to bring the heat of the law to bear. In 1945 only the Germans cared what happened to the Germans.

"Loyalty is my Honor" was the motto of the highly indoctrinated soldiers of Hitler's SS, and they attempted to ambush the advancing Americans. On the night of the twenty-ninth, logistical vehicles of Troop A, 102nd Cavalry, were ambushed about a mile northeast of Winden. The convoy leader had stopped to check his directions. Elements of the 6th SS Mountain Division *Nord* ("North") opened fire on the kitchen truck which mired itself in the mud while seeking to turn around on the earthen road. The cooks escaped, but the truck and a maintenance half-track were captured by the Germans. The vehicle that provided food was important to the Americans and the Germans considered this kitchen truck a prize.

Shortly after midnight on the thirtieth, Lieutenant Henderson led a fifteen-man combat patrol from Dog Company and two armored cars to provide covering fire in an attack to recover the vehicle. The Germans were still in the area, dug in with five machine guns and *Panzerfaust* rocket launchers. They were an experienced foe. The 6th SS Mountain Division had its beginnings as a combat group in Norway in 1941. They endured over three years of combat in the northern sector of the Russian front and had fought in Finland and against the Americans in the Ardennes offensive. These veterans of Arctic Circle warfare were proud of their designation as the "North" Division.

Henderson had only a small patrol on this mission as it seemed likely there would not be serious opposition. High hills flanked their route of approach. Henderson had been briefed that this road would dead-end into a "T" and beyond that dead end was the high ground from which the Germans had fired. The wind was blowing toward the Rangers, and Henderson stopped the armored cars to listen as they approached the scene of the ambush—he and other men thought they heard the engine of the kitchen truck.

Expecting to disperse the Germans, the lead armored car raced forward firing its machine guns. The response was immediate and furious as the Germans fired on the Americans from the direct front, left, and right.

Lieutenant Henderson leaped to the ground yelling at his men to take cover, then yelled to PFC George Schneller to follow him. Robert Wells and Edgar Whipple followed as Henderson and Schneller climbed the hill to the right, then turned along the ridge to get above the road junction. As they reached the dominant position, Henderson sent Wells and Whipple back to bring up the remainder of the Rangers. A German with a *Panzerfaust* began firing rockets near Henderson—one round landied close enough to roll the lieutenant over.

As Henderson's men came up, he placed them into position along the ridge line. A furious battle erupted, with Rangers firing from the ridge line, one armored car continuing to move slowly toward the road junction, and the Germans responding with everything they had. Henderson was disgusted that the crew of the second armored car was doing nothing. He went back down the hill and got them to move up in support and open fire. Henderson then ran forward and tried to get closer to the road junction to determine where the kitchen truck was. Forward of the armored cars he found a rope stretched across the road. Investigating he found that six rocket launchers were rigged to fire into any vehicle that ran over the rope.

Henderson used his knife to cut the cords and disable the trap. While doing so he was caught in a vicious crossfire and barely escaped with his life. Returning to the rear of the armored cars, Henderson learned that Tippett had been hit in the leg and Wells was seriously wounded and pinned under German fire. Sigurd Sundby and Charles Homan crawled under fire to drag Wells to safety, but Wells had lost a considerable amount of blood. Henderson could tell from the reduced amount of tracers that three of the five machine guns had been silenced. He also knew he did not have the force to accomplish the mission. Signaling the armored cars and bringing his men down from the hill, Henderson broke contact. Ranger Wells died in the hospital the next day.

At first light on March 30, Fox Company, a platoon of tanks from F Troop, and a platoon of assault guns from Troop E, 102nd Cavalry Squadron, moved to attack the German position. They found the enemy had withdrawn, taking the kitchen truck with them. They pressed on and three towns were cleared with only one prisoner taken. From high ground, Duke Slater saw approximately 200 German soldiers moving in the zone of the 87th Infantry Division. Slater established radio contact with the 87th and requested permission to bring artillery fire on the enemy. Likely concerned that the identification might be faulty, the 87th denied permission. It would be a costly refusal.

Near Heimgenberg, a tank/Ranger team moved to attack a German outpost. As the eighteen-ton tanks with 75-millimeter guns began to fire, the Germans fled eastward into the woods. Some Rangers dismounted and followed the enemy. The tanks stayed on the road attempting to sweep around the woods and trap the Germans. The Germans, who were later identified as three companies of the 6th SS Mountain Division *Nord*, had skillfully set an ambush. A *Panzerfaust* destroyed the lead tank and killed three Rangers who were riding on it. The remainder of the American tanks—many carrying Rangers—spread wide and attempted to flank the position. The Germans were waiting for this and let the tanks get into the open before firing on the tanks. The Americans bravely risked a storm of antitank fire to cover the withdrawal of the Rangers. T/5 Charles J. Villa, and PFC Julius Hanahan, PFC Irvin B. Hill, PFC Jack LaMero, and PFC James B. Taft were killed, and PFC J. F. Tillis would die of his wounds. PFC George Mackey of Easy Company had been the big winner at cards in the marshaling area prior to the invasion of Normandy. Mackey's premonition of death during the invasion had been accurate. Now Charles Vella who had won $1,200 at craps and lost it when his secondary pack was thrown overboard was dead. Luck at cards and dice does not bring luck in war.

The Germans had won this fight, but a ring of steel was closing. All along the American front divisions of the first and third Armies were racing to encircle the Germans in the Ruhr Pocket. Total air supremacy gave freedom of movement. As far as the eye could see, all roads were jammed with American tanks, armored cars, half-tracks, jeeps, and trucks with infantry marching among them. For the combined-arms team of cavalry and Rangers the missions became that of engaging by-passed German units, clearing German towns, and providing flank security for V Corps. A wide frontage and frequent displacements were the norm with Ranger companies and cavalry troops scattered.

April 1, 1945, was both April Fool's Day and Easter. Two momentous years had passed since the day the battalion was activated at Camp Forrest, Tennessee. If a battalion formation had been held, few of the faces would have been the same. Many were dead, wounded, injured or had served their time and been rotated home. Some wounds were even self-inflicted. T/Sgt. Carl Craft was injured by a bullet he fired trying to shoot a lock off a door. PFC James Matyger put a bullet in his leg while attempting to clean his .45-caliber pistol, and several others were wounded by Luger pistols they had collected.

When Baker Company found themselves anxious for news of the world, PFC Herb Appel, who could speak German, would take a radio from a German family. Appel had no intention of carrying a civilian radio so he would tell the owners they could look for it after the Rangers left. While Appel was searching he saw Baker Company 1st Sgt. Manning Rubenstein with a Nazi official. Rubenstein had the terrified Nazi standing at attention and was walking around the German shouting and shooting into the ground near the man's feet. Appel knocked at the door of a well-furnished house and told the weary middle-aged couple who responded that he wanted a radio. They responded that they had lost their only son to the war and wanted to be left alone. Appel told them that he did not want to be in Germany and they could blame Adolf Hitler. He took the radio.

When the situation allowed, the Rangers would move into German houses for the night. During the pursuit beyond the Rhine River the houses of the smaller towns were often in good condition. The German civilians found what accommodations they could for the night while the Rangers attempted to sleep in feather beds. The transformation was difficult as the men of the battalion were accustomed to sleeping on the ground. There were times when the relationship between German civilian and Ranger was that of a gracious host to a traveler and common interest prevailed. When an elderly German farmer and his wife were awake throughout the night attending to the birth of a calf they were assisted by PFC William Gower, who had been a farmer before the war.[2]

Major Williams and his command group merged with Colonel Dolph's 102nd Cavalry Group Headquarters. They left Laudorf at 1150 and set off on a ninety-nine-mile movement, part of which took them driving in black-out conditions on the famed German Autobahn divided highway. It was close to midnight when they arrived at Riede.

Task Force Arnold (Able, Baker and Charlie) remained connected to the three troops of the 38th Cavalry Squadron. Task Force Slater (Dog, Easy and Fox) was with the 102nd Cavalry Squadron. The 102nd and Task Force Slater were assigned the mission of clearing the city of Fritzlar and its nearby airfield. The Nazi mayor of the city had made an impassioned speech to the Hitler Youth and Volksturm of the city to "die rather than fail the Vaterland," then left town. The *Gauleiter*'s speech was effective, however, and as the combined-arms team entered the city, they were met with heavy sniper fire. The desire to die for the Fatherland was fulfilled. The battalion narrative reported, "The German women reappeared from their cellars to find the streets littered with their men."[3] Sixty-six prisoners were also taken. The Americans suffered no casualties.

Dog, Easy, and Fox Companies and their cavalry companions raced to the airfield where they scattered light resistance and captured seventeen aircraft. Eleven Junkers 88 night fighter-bombers, four Messerschmitt 110 night fighters, a Messerschmitt 109, and a Storch observation plane were taken. Most of the aircraft were operational but without fuel. On April 2, Task Force Slater took forty-three prisoners.

Captain Arnold was dispatched to attend an air indoctrination school. In Arnold's absence Major Williams did double duty as battalion commander and commander of Task Force Arnold. Moving with the 38th Cavalry Squadron this force followed and relieved the 102nd Cavalry Squadron and Task Force Slater at Fritzlar. To secure the flank of V Corps, Able Company and Troop A secured Merxhausen, Charlie Company and B Troop took Hadamar, and Baker Company and Troop C cleared Ober Mahlich. The 38th Squadron headquarters and Williams' CP were at Lohne. Baker Company controlled the roads of Fritzlar and the airfield. Baker Company men found German civilians trying to loot the airfield buildings and booted them out. Loot was the province of the victors.

Relieved by the 38th Cavalry/Task Force Arnold, Task Force Slater and the 102nd Cavalry Squadron pursued two German artillery battalions who were seeking to evade capture. Slater's men found four abandoned German artillery pieces. Captain Arnold returned on April 5 and resumed command of his task force. German towns continued to fall before the onrushing Americans on the ninth. While Task Force Slater provided security for V Corps forward headquarters, Task Force Arnold took Sichelnstein, Nienhagen, Escherode, Oberode, Steinberg, Klein, Amerode, and Rossbach.

Though rapidly running out of space between the American/British and Canadiens in the west and the Russians in the east, the Germans were using a variety of methods to evade capture in the Ruhr Pocket. V Corps warned that the Germans were using captured American trucks to carry their soldiers. Drivers and faux guards were dressed in American uniforms. To combat these tactics, roadblocks, checkpoints, outposts, and foot and motorized patrols were used. The uniform did not matter. If a stranger or unknown unit approached, suspicion ruled the mind. One hundred and sixty-four prisoners were taken.

Charlie Company spent two days at Gatterstadt sending out patrols and capturing eighteen prisoners. Part of the 2nd Platoon made their abode in a castle owned by a German baron. The wine cellar was magnificent and occupied much of the platoon's attention. The 1st Platoon of Charlie was less fortunate. They relied on a former slave laborer of Polish descent to find them some alcoholic refreshment. The man knew the town and returned that evening with several bottles. He explained that the liquid had been distilled at 4:00 and that as it was now after 7:00 P.M., it had been properly aged and was ready to drink.[4]

As darkness came on the April 30, a German car came from the west to an Able Company checkpoint at a crossroads. Other cars had been stopping, but when the occupants of this car where challenged the car containing four occupants sped up and attempted to pass through and make a turn to the south. A Ranger BAR man opened fire and as the car made the righthand turn, other Rangers began to shoot with Thompson submachine guns, Browning automatic rifles, and M1 rifles.

Pierced by a rain of bullets the car veered off the road into a ditch and crashed. All four of the occupants were dead. Taking no chances, the Rangers made a sieve of the car. One of the dead Germans was *Generalmajor* Gustav Feller, commanding general of Panzer Corps-Wehrkreis IX. The three other dead men were members of the General's staff including his youthful aide Count Von Girsewald. General Feller was carrying maps and documents which were turned over to intelligence. The pistols, wrist watches, insignia, and other useful items became Ranger souvenirs.

The general's body was sent off for a formal funeral. Two German soldiers who had passed themselves as civilians dug a common grave for the other three men. These two men thought they were digging their own graves and their sweat was more fear than exertion. Their relief was joyous when they were spared.

The roads were frequently clogged with displaced persons—commonly called "DPs"—refugees from throughout Europe who had been taken from their homeland to provide labor for the German war machine. On occasion a DP would come across his former master and justice would be quickly served unless the Americans were nearby to take the German into custody. There was also a restless tide of German civilians who had lost their homes. Among them were German soldiers who had changed to civilian clothes. Desperate for food, some of these were attempting to raid American supply lines. No matter if in uniform or civilian clothes, those Germans who did not surrender were summarily shot. Two German soldiers surrendered. One was found to be wearing a number of American watches on his arm. That cost the German his life. The Headquarters Company history noted, "It was a common sight to see apparently innocent civilians lying riddled along the roadside or piled up in the nearest village square as a warning for any stragglers to come out of hiding. Anyone in civilian clothes and carrying a weapon was shot out of hand. Bitter, quick justice."[5]

In a last-ditch stand the Germans had assembled hundreds of antiaircraft guns that had once been used against Allied bombers. These guns were now employed against the U.S. 2nd Infantry Division that was attempting to cross the Saale River. Task Force Arnold and their cavalry comrades were relieving elements of the 2nd Infantry Division. Under artillery fire the American team reached the Saale on the fifteenth, and the following day a combat patrol from Able Company successfully crossed the river. On the seventeenth, a Charlie Company patrol clashed with Germans armed with 20-millimeter antiaircraft guns, machine guns, and small arms. The Rangers responsed within several well-aimed bazooka rounds which landed on the enemy position. Task Force Arnold cleared the towns of the area and in six days captured 597 prisoners.

On April 18, a patrol from Easy Company moved into Mockern where they found a hospital where wounded American and British prisoners of war were kept. The liberation was both joyful and heartrending. The Germans had little for themselves and many of the wounded or sick were in poor health. Despite their condition the first request of most of the prisoners was for an American cigarette. Radio messages for help were sent and Ranger medics did all they could to help the patients.

PFC Donald Lindheim of Easy Company was Jewish and spoke fluent German, a combination that made German prisoners quake in their hob-nailed boots. Lindheim was well on the way to being a horticulturist when the war interrupted his plans. A man with a personal mission to bring Germany down, Donald Lindheim took unnecessary chances. The destruction of captured German weapons was a necessary part of capturing enemy soldiers and towns. Small arms and machine guns would be placed in piles and tracked vehicles were run back and forth over them. On occasion, Rangers would swing rifles and shotguns against stone walls or buildings to shatter the stocks. Lindheim swung a German shotgun to destroy it but had failed to check if the weapon was loaded. The shotgun pellets tore open Lindheim's stomach killing him and nearly hitting Richard Hubbard who was nearby. Lindheim would be the last man of the battalion to be killed in World War II.

In defeat an army is alone, survival of the individual and his comrades is the prime concern. Hungry German soldiers sought help from patriotic civilians, but when that failed they coerced German farmers or officials at gunpoint to get the food and supplies they needed. Many of the SS felt a loyalty to Hitler unto death. For the *Heer*, the German Army, the loyalty that remained was to each other. Thus, German farmers were beset by hungry roving bands of their own soldiers and frequently turned to the Americans for help.

Some Germans were eager to be of assistance. Informed by a civilian that a Hitler Youth school had been located at Schulpforte, Easy Company raided the facility and arrested twenty-two men who were identified as former instructors at the school. Many of the men taken prisoner were not German, but adherents to the Nazi philosophy from other nation.

Except for isolated pockets of those willing to die, German resistance crumbled. Some German units surrendered en masse, others disbanded and some disintegrated when their men deserted. Soldiers tried to disguise themselves as civilians and Nazi party officials tried to conceal themselves or sought escape routes to neutral countries. As April 1945 drew to a close, the war resembled a police action. On April 21 and 22, Task Force Arnold was clearing Forst Burgwenden and Forst Allsted, woods south and north of Sonderhausen. Outside the woods, cavalry vehicles waited to engage any Germans who came into the open. The action was similar to a drive by hunters with both Germans and large numbers of deer fleeing before the Rangers. Captain Arnold's men killed eighteen Germans and captured sixty-eight. Baker Company encountered fourteen Germans and killed them all as they were flushed from hiding. In the action one Ranger was seriously wounded, becoming the last casualty the battalion would suffer in the war. The following day two enemy were killed and twenty-seven taken prisoner.

Sonderhausen, a bastion of fascism, lay supine beneath the worn boots of the Rangers. As the cavalry cordoned off the town on the outskirts, Able Company moved into the heart of the town and assembled the quaking inhabitants. The battalion interpreter explained the screening process. While the townspeople were processed by some Rangers, others searched the houses, rousting out those in hiding. Germans who attempted to flee were killed. Fifteen of the top Nazi officials of Sonderhausen were arrested and delivered to V Corps.

April 30 found Easy Company leading near the battalion Grafenwohr, a German training area close to the Czech border. At Grafenwohr, German soldiers had learned "blitzkrieg," or lightning war. It was here that fast moving armor/infantry teams practiced the gunnery and tactics they would use to terrorize Europe. German Panzer forces were taught to break the enemy lines on a narrow front and race along lines of least resistance into the enemy rear.

There is a tower at Grafenwohr. Tradition has it that a division commander who believed in Blitzkrieg stood in this tower to observe the 7th Panzer (Ghost) Division that he would lead successfully through France. The structure is known as "Rommel's Tower." At the close of April 1945, Rommel's Tower belonged to the U.S. 2nd Ranger Battalion.

V Corps Headquarters followed and established itself at Grafenwohr, beginning an American presence there that would last throughout the Cold War.

Task Force Slater, consisting of Dog, Easy, and Fox Companies, provided the security for V Corps Headquarters. In cold, driving rain they controlled the roads with checkpoints and motorized patrols and established a perimeter defense of the headquarters. Fourteen prisoners were taken during these operations. German civilians would come with complaints of being raided by groups of German soldiers seeking to avoid capture. Ambushes were set and two German soldiers were killed and nine captured. Dog Company sent a platoon to Zettlitz at the request of German civilians. A group of some twenty SS men had told the civilians to have guns and vehicles for them the night of May 1 or they would burn down the town. The Americans prepared an ambush, but the SS did not come into town. Fox Company later captured three of the Germans in an adjoining forest.

The Nazi leadership envisioned a guerilla campaign conducted from bases concealed in German forests by raider groups called "Werewolves." Many of these bands were led by SS officers or non-commissioned officers, but the guerrillas were often boys of twelve to sixteen from the Hitler Youth. Militaristic societies and religions have long practiced indoctrination of the young and most people find it difficult to change beliefs instilled in childhood. A boy of twelve can pull a trigger, throw a grenade, or ignite a demolition charge. The Werewolves cut telephone wires, mined and blocked roads, and stretched wire from trees across roads to decapitate men in vehicles. They served as snipers and employed any tactic they could to slow the advancing armies. These young Nazis were dangerous and soldiers quickly learned to treat them as enemies. Many did not go home to mother. They were shot in battle, executed by firing squads, and some who murdered were beheaded.

A band of Werewolves was known to be operating from Steinwald. Captain Arnold with Able, Baker, and Charlie Companies moved into the area and in two days destroyed the raider base, killed two, captured two, and wounded one of the enemy without cost. Charlie Company captured thirteen Germans at Bischosgrun.

With the drive through Germany completed, the U.S. 1st Infantry Division was ordered to move to Pilsen, Czechoslovakia. The 102nd Cavalry Group with attached Rangers was ordered to move to an assembly area at Asch, then link up with and screen the north (left) flank of the 1st Division and V Corps as they moved forward. Capt. Duke Slater's Ranger Task Force had become the palace guard for Corps Headquarters. On the seventh, Dog Company moved to Pilsen and captured eight prisoners while securing an area for the corps command and staff. Easy and Fox remained on guard at Grafenwohr. Major Arnold's command group was crossing the Czech border when the mission was cancelled. Rumors began to circulate and hopes began to rise that the long ordeal was over. Nothing could be confirmed and Task Force Arnold settled into billets at Asch to wait.

V Corps Headquarters moved on to Pilsen on the eighth with Fox Company providing security en route and Easy following the next day.

Before Easy Company left Grafenwohr, four German Storch observation aircraft landed and six officers and two women surrendered to the Rangers. Shortly thereafter another German aircraft was observed flying overhead and a nearby antiaircraft unit damaged it. The plane landed and it was found that the pilot was a Polish captive who had stolen the plane in Berlin.

The news was official on May 8, 1945. The Germans had surrendered. It was VE Day, Victory in Europe. Men shouted and whooped, sharing the joy of survival. Most of them had calculated the number of points they had accrued to go home. The battalion personnel section was hard at work confirming the status of each man. For many replacements there was the consideration that the war with Japan continued and the invasion of the Japanese home islands would include a need for Rangers.

Despite the pleas of the British, General Eisenhower made the decision not to strike for Berlin. Eisenhower made that decision based on purely military grounds. The boundaries of an occupied Germany had already been drawn and approved by Russian dictator Joseph Stalin and terminally ill President Roosevelt. Germany was to be divided into four parts with Berlin occupied by the four powers. It was predetermined that to get to Berlin after the war, the Americans would need to have access through 110 miles of Russian-controlled territory. Eisenhower felt that the defense of Berlin would cost many Allied lives and he would then have to pull back as a result of the political agreements. Roosevelt was now dead, and President Truman and other American political leaders were responsible for the future, but Americans had been fed the nonsense that Josef Stalin was friendly "Uncle Joe." Czechoslovakia had also been included in the Soviet zone, so the American Army could only advance to Pilsen near the German border. The Russians took Berlin, and even when divided the city became an island in a Communist sea.

On May 11, after weeks of separation, the battalion said farewell to their cavalry comrades and came together to bivouac at Dolni Lukavice, Czechoslovakia, about ten miles from Pilsen. This was a liberated country. The lilacs were in bloom. The Czech people stood on the sidewalks and waved flags, threw lilac blossoms, and cheered as the Rangers came through. There were no fines for fraternization in Czechoslovakia, but those looking for feminine companionship were largely disappointed. The females were described as "a handful of gimmie and mouthful of thank you."[6] There were those among the civilians who did not cheer. It had been part of the Nazi policy to settle Germans on conquered land. Many of these people would never see Germany again.

The battalion's headquarters occupied the palace of a vast baronial near Pilsen. The intensity of the European war vanished quickly and it was difficult for the mind and body to adjust. The soldiers were glad the war was over and yet the experience had drawn them together, and many found themselves more tied to the past than the future. They had found a bond such as they would never again experience.

Slowly, they began to return to normal. The battalion had a superb softball team. Fox Company won a battalion track meet. Some of the best track and field men were selected to participate in a theater-level track meet. The speedy Sgt. Ed O'Connor was running the hundred-yard dash and took the lead. It appeared that O'Connor would win the event, but unfortunately, he was not wearing a jock strap. Trying to hold his shorts outward while running, O'Connor veered out of his lane and was passed by other contestants who were better attired.

A light-hearted battalion newspaper was published called, *Characters* after Major Lytle's remark at the party prior to D-Day, June 6, 1944. There was time for statistics, and it was learned that Johnstown, Pennsylvania, had provided more men to the battalion than any other city. One lieutenant told Ike Eikner that he had a Czech girl who seemed willing but every time he attempted to communicate that he wanted to be intimate with her the girl said, "Oh no!" Eikner said he taken the time to learn a little of the Czech language, and the word for yes was "*Ano.*"[7]

The legendary scrounger Pvt. Henry Sobal of Dog Company was reported to have sent home everything but the 280-millimeter guns the Germans had at Brest. Lt. Len Lomell recovered from his Castle Hill wound at Valley Forge General Hospital in Pennsylvania. T/5 Bill Roberson was with Lomell. They had made contact with other men of the battalion who had returned to the United States including Capt. Otto Masny of Fox and a number of Easy Company men who had been prisoners of war. Lt. Maurice Jackson wrote that he missed the men of the battalion more than he missed his amputated leg.

In May, Maj. George Arnold began to wear the silver oak leaves of a lieutenant colonel. Arnold had been promoted earlier but he would not wear his new rank until he felt he earned it. MSgt. Manning Rubenstein was commissioned a 2nd lieutenant, the fourth man of the battalion to be so recognized. It was reported that Bill Petty slept with his Browning automatic rifle, and Petty replied, "So what, it's my baby." Behind the pitching of Lt. Bob Edlin, Able Company had an undefeated softball team, including a no-hitter against Charlie Company.

Victory in Europe did not bring peace. Now the vast military might of the United States had to be shifted from the European theater to the Pacific. Planners predicted that the numbers of casualties that would be suffered in the invasion of the home islands of Japan would dwarf the experience at Normandy. An estimated 100,000 American soldiers would likely be killed or wounded. It would be inevitable that Rangers, Marines, and airborne forces would be deployed as assault troops for the invasion of Japan. Men of the 1st and 3rd Ranger Battalions who had fought valiantly at Dieppe, North Africa, Sicily, and in Italy had been killed or captured on a deep raid at Cisterna in Italy. Many of the 4th Battalion had fought these battles and gone home, and those that remained were transferred to the 1st Special Service Force. The 6th Ranger battalion had been formed in the Pacific and performed superbly in raids and in rescuing 511 prisoners from the Japanese prison camp at Cabanatuan. Now the 2nd and 5th Ranger Battalions began training in preparation for transfer to the Pacific theater.

While some men in the battalion prepared for the move to the Pacific, others were doing their math. Sixty-eight out of every one hundred men in the army had served overseas. Thirty-five percent of the Army had seen combat. Nineteen percent of the Army were fathers (of acknowledged children).

On September 6, 1944, the War Department had put into effect a worldwide demobilization plan. This plan was based on interviews with thousands of soldiers. The first priority was the needs of the service. For those individuals who were not essential to victory in the Pacific, the demobilization plan would favor those who had served the longest, seen the most combat, and had young dependent children. Servicemen and women would be assigned points based on the following criteria:

1. The Service Credit was based on the total number of Army Service since September 16, 1940. One point would be given for each month.
2. The Overseas Credit was based on the number of months served overseas since September 16, 1940. One point would be given for each month served overseas.
3. The Combat Credit was based on the first and each additional award to the individual of the Medal of Honor, Distinguished Service Cross, Legion of Merit, Silver Star, Distinguished Flying Cross, Soldier's Medal, Bronze Star Medal, Air Medal, Purple Heart, and Bronze Service Stars (battle participation stars). Five points would be awarded for first and each additional award.
4. The Parenthood Credit gave credit for each dependent child under eighteen years up to a limit of three children. Twelve points would be awarded for each child.

The example the army used was a soldier who had been in the army for thirty-six months, had served overseas for eighteen months, had won the Silver Star and the Purple Heart, participated in three major campaigns, and was the father of a child under age eighteen. That soldier would receive thirty-six points in service credit, eighteen points in overseas credit, twenty-five points in combat credit, and twelve points in parenthood credit. His total score would be ninety-one points. Initially, eighty-five was the magic number. For the battalion they went in seven-man increments starting with the highest number of points. With eighty-five points a man could begin to pack his duffle bag with his uniforms, gifts, and whatever other loot and souvenirs he had taken. The points required soon dropped to eighty, then seventy, but many men elected to go to the Pacific with the battalion.

Victory over Japan (V-J Day) was announced on August 15, 1945. The men of the battalion took the news with satisfaction, a feeling that justice was served. There was mild celebration, but not the exuberance displayed on the home front. It took time to make the transition from civilian to soldier and it would take time to again think like a civilian. For many, what they had lived through in the battalion was the biggest event of their lives.

The news that the battalion was going home was first announced over Armed Forces Radio. For some, it was hard to leave Dolni Lukavice. Friendships had been made, many of them with the Czech children who received candy and jeep rides. For some Rangers a bond developed. In later years PFC John Shobey of Able Company returned to Dolni Lukavice and was buried there, honored by the people of the community. On October 5, the battalion was ordered from Czechoslovakia to the vicinity of Reims, France. Three days were spent traveling by rail on the "*40 hommes et 8 cheveaux*" French boxcars.

The staging area camps at Le Havre were called "Cigarette Camps" as they were named after American cigarettes; the assembly camps near the city of Reims were named after American cities. The battalion arrived near Reims and spent four days at Brooklyn Camp.

In the battalion, there was a mix of high-point men who could have gone home in early shipments and low-point men with relatively little time with the unit. In recognition of their service, Gen. Omar Bradley ordered that the 2nd Ranger Battalion could go home as a unit. There was objection to Bradley's decision by units who were not so favored, and a team from the Inspector General's office arrived to review all service records. At the close of the war, General Bradley commanded forty-three divisions. His decision was obeyed. After four days, $2\frac{1}{2}$-ton trucks arrived, and the battalion was taken to Camp Lucky Strike near the port of Le Havre east of where the soldiers had landed sixteen months before. Souvenirs had to be registered here and only one pistol could be taken home. This resulted in barrels filled with Lugers and Walther P-38 pistols—a gold mine for the rear echelon soldier. The bulletin boards showed the units in camp, the name of the ship that would take them home, and when it would arrive. The men stood in chow lines—a hated aspect of military service—and watched the huge rats that infested the camp. They were well accustomed to the rain and mud. Now they just wanted to go home. On October 15, 1945, they were trucked to Le Havre.

On October 16, the battalion sailed for home on the 35,000-ton USS *West Point*. The ship was the former SS *America*, built in 1940. She had been a superb luxury liner and as a troop carrier took more than 450,000 servicemen and women to and from the war zones. There were many stowaways—not people but dogs. Unwilling to part with their canine buddies, the men hid them in barracks bags and brought them aboard. Medic Frank South became an expert at giving the dogs a pentobarbital sodium sedative, so not a bark was heard until the ship had sailed. Sympathetic, the captain of the *West Point* turned the afterdeck of the ship into a kennel.

On the way to war, soldiers had eaten English food. Now it was all American, and all those who were not seasick could eat their fill. The trip was a rough crossing of four days in gale-force winds and high seas. Arriving at the port of Newport News, Virginia, the men of the battalion joined thousands of other troops in boarding shipside shuttle trains that took them to nearby Camp Patrick Henry, a 1,700-acre processing point for troops coming from going to the European theater. Camp Patrick Henry could only hold 35,000 troops and was little more than a way station.

Some units came home to tickertape parades. For many units, especially the smaller battalions and separate companies, leaving the army was little more than "Here's your ticket to your local discharge station." There was no formal closing ceremony, no speeches by dignitaries, no crying as the colors were folded. The men were told the battalion had been deactivated on October 23, 1945.

Their colors and guidons would be shipped to an Army storage depot. Officially, their unit no longer existed, but for each of the men, it could not leave their hearts. As they caught their various trains and buses spreading out toward home, the parting came so fast that it was brutal. It was so difficult to say farewell to men who had been more than brothers. Herm Stein said, "I was so thankful and glad to get home, but part of me was decimated."[8] Stein and many other men wept at the parting.

Epilogue

The battalion played their role in winning World War II, coming home to a grateful nation before going their separate ways. They went home to wives or girlfriends, and most married and raised families. Many went to college under the GI Bill. James Earl Rudder went back to Texas and stayed in the Army Reserves rising to the rank of major general. Rudder went back to education and is credited with the rise of Texas A&M to prominence. Ike Eikner went back to Texas to the same office he had occupied at Southwest Bell Telephone four years before. Ike rose to be senior engineer in Special Services design and after retirement was a real estate broker. Bill Klaus went home to Sussex, New Jersey. Bill's beloved Olive, a.k.a. "Smitty," had the Plymouth convertible with wooden spoked wheels and a rumble seat waiting for him. Bill Klaus became a master carpenter.

Len Lomell practiced law in New Jersey, and Jack Kuhn became chief of police in Altoona, Pennsylvania. Bill Stivison, who had ridden the swaying ladder at Pointe du Hoc, became the postmaster of Homer City, Pennsylvania, and Richard Hubbard became an Ohio Insurance man. Bill "L-Rod" Petty ran a camp in New York state for disadvantaged inner-city youth. For many mistreated children he became the loving father that he and they had never known. Herm Stein made his skill in climbing a profession as a roofer in Fort Pierce, Florida. Duke Slater remained in the army. In the early stages of the Korean War, he was captured by the North Koreans. Both Duke Slater

and Ed Arnold rose to colonel. Lt. Sylvestor V. "Pop" Porubsky, who
was now the father of four young children, earned a Distinguished
Service Cross and was killed in Korea while serving with the 27th
(Wolfhounds) Infantry Regiment of the 25th Infantry Division. Dun-
can Daugherty was killed in Korea with the 1st Cavalry Division. Bob
Edlin lived in Texas and became a skilled auctioneer of antiques.

Sid Salomon worked in sales for the American Can Company and
remained an outstanding athlete, winning competitions for rowing in
his eighties. Lt. Gerald Heaney became a federal judge. Willie Clark
joined the Washington, D.C., police force as a detective sergeant.
Frank South earned a Ph.D. in physiology and biophysics, working as
a researcher and teacher in medical school at the University of
Delaware. Along the way he married an English major/writer and
took up sailing. Ed O'Connor became a county sheriff.

The ephemeral bond that they had known in battle diminished to
friendship as they returned to a society where self-interest was dominant. They formed an association of the six Ranger battalions, but as
in all such organizations, squabbling was inevitable. In the early years
the arguments ran, "My company was better than your company, my
battalion was better than your battalion. We fought against the Germans, and you only fought against the Japanese." As actions were discussed and histories written or presented by the media, some felt that
certain individuals or units were trying to take too much credit for
themselves. At every reunion there is a presentation of stories and
some have grown as acorns become oaks. Memories and friendships
have been formed between men of different companies and battalions, but there is an undercurrent to be found, usually expressed as
"That sonofabitch wasn't even with us when we went up Pointe du
Hoc," or "We were on Hill 400 before they were." Those who were not
there wonder why this conflict happens among men who were
bonded in battle, but it is in the nature of warriors. The undercurrent
still flows, but at this writing the survivors are men in their mid-eight-
ies and nineties, and they are more tolerant and inclined to the philosophy of "I'll listen to your story if you'll listen to mine."

Many of them are now gone from earthly life. The last taps
sounds, and perhaps another adventure begins. There is something
precious about what they did, something eternal, something vividly

expressed by PFC Alfred E. Baer Jr., when in August 1945, he closed
the war and his book *D for Dog* with these words:

> The crashing loom is silent now and the unfinished fabric still
> in it. It is a somber weave of black blood and fire and hidden
> tears, and the golden threads that wander through it are with-
> out pattern. They have no pattern, but they gleam brightly,
> and they will never tarnish.

APPENDIX A

Roster of the 2nd Ranger Infantry Battalion in World War II

NOTES:

Bold last names indicate Ranger participated in D-Day, June 6, 1944

    (1) = Ranger died on Omaha Beach

    (2) = Ranger died at Hill 400/Castle Hill

    PH = Purple Heart

    BSM = Bronze Star

    SSM = Silver Star

    DSC = Distinguished Service Cross

LAST NAME	FIRST	MI	CO	KNOWN RANK	ASN	KIA	PLACE OF DEATH	DECORATIONS
Adams	Herbert	H	B	Pfc.	38425004			
Adams	Leroy	G	D	Sgt.	31188572	12/7/44	Bergstein, Germany (2)	PH-2
Adams	Clark		HQ	Pfc.	20905866			PH
Adams	Clark		HQ	Pfc.	20905866			PH
Adams, Jr.	Bernie	W	E	Pfc.	37745313			
Adkins	Sammie		C	Pfc.	38322691	6/6/44	Point de la Percee, France	PH
Aguzzi	Victor	J	E	Cpl.	34625138			BSM, PH
Ahart	John	R	HQ	Pfc.	32595831			
Akridge	Walter	O	HQ	Pfc.	35496679			
Alexander	James	R	F	Sgt.	36237524			SSM
Alm	Raymond	F	B	S/Sgt.	36378896			
Anagnos	Constantine	S	A	Pfc.	16028666	8/21/44	Le Folgoet, France	PH
Anderson	Fred	L	B	Pfc.	42005871	11/24/44	Germeter, Germany	PH
Anderson	Christopher	M	E	S/Sgt.	38127535			PH

LAST NAME	FIRST	MI	CO	KNOWN RANK	ASN	KIA	PLACE OF DEATH	DECORATIONS
Anderson	William	E	F	Pfc.	20918415	12/7/44	Bergstein, Germany (2)	SSM,PH
Anderson	Jack	D	F	T/5	20918408	12/7/44	Bergstein, Germany (2)	PH
Anderson	Richard	W	HQ,D	Pfc.	36579588			PH
Andrews	Frederick		A	Pvt.	42145337			
Andrusz	Edward	A	B	1st Sgt.	32130112			BSM,PH-2
Angyal	Joseph		C	S/Sgt.	36511177			PH-2
Antal	Paul	J	B	Pfc.	33941299			
Antio	Richard	E	E	Pfc.	36984344			
Anton	Elwood	J	A	Pfc.	33595279			PH
Appel	Herbert	R	B	Pfc.	16081987			PH
Arman	Robert	C	A,F	Capt.	01297475			SSM,PH
Armbruster	Thomas	J	HQ	Pfc.	37563373			
Arnold	Edgar	L	B,HQ	Maj.	01286417			DSC-6/6/44
Arthur	Lester	G	D	T/Sgt.	20311607	3/9/45	Konigsfeld, Germany	SSM,PH-2
Ashline	Donald	L	A	Pfc.	31198215			PH
Austin	Robert	L	D	Sgt.	34311205			PH
Baber	Grover	N	D	Pfc.	36989199			
Bachleda	Anton		E	Cpl.	32808036			PH
Bachman, Jr.	Clarence	E	E	Pvt.	13135738			SSM,PH-2
Bacho	John		F	Pfc.	33395327			PH-2
Baer, Jr.	Alfred	E	D	Pfc.	34148078			
Bailey	Donald	W	HQ	Pfc.	13083369			
Bakalar	John		A	Pfc.	31329313			PH-2
Baker	Eugene	B	B	Sgt.	20305131			PH
Bare	Sheldon		D	Cpl.	33569909			PH-2
Bargman	Kenneth	H	E	Pfc.	33562066			PH
Barker	Kenneth		A	Pfc.				
Barnard	James	A	A	Pfc.	37511510			PH
Barrett	Donald	G	C	Pfc.	39621814			
Barscenski	Paul	P	F	Pfc.	36673072			PH
Bass	William		HQ	Pfc.	32106708			
Baugh	Gilbert	C	A,E	1st Lt.	01296636			PH
Bayer	Otto	C	HQ	S/Sgt.	33355053			SSM,BSM,PH
Beech	Cecil	E	E	Pfc.	36687206			PH
Beedle	Frederick	A	C	S/Sgt.	20530778			PH
Beekler	Volney	E	C	Pfc.	32483491	6/6/44	Point de la Percee, France	PH
Behrent	Oscar	E	F	Pfc.	39607566			
Belcher	Julius	W	C	Sgt.	33213927			DSC-6/6/44, PH-3

LAST NAME	FIRST	MI	CO	KNOWN RANK	ASN	KIA	PLACE OF DEATH	DECORATIONS
Bell	William	D	E	Cpl.	35604873			SSM,BSM,PH
Bellows, Jr.	Charles	H	E	Pfc.	31299814	6/6/44	Pointe du Hoc, France	SSM,PH
Belmont	Gail	H	A	S/Sgt.	36895257			DSC,BSM, PH-2
Belt	William	B	F	Pfc.	37745729	3/28/45	Kirschberg, Germany	PH
Berg	Charles	T	A	Sgt.	35359231			
Berge	Archie	K	D	Pfc.	37594742			
Berke	Neal	B	HQ	T/5	36740254			
Bialkowski	Walter	T	F	Pfc.	32367175			PH
Biaze	John		F	Pfc.	39712353			PH
Biddle	John	C	A	S/Sgt.	33323260	6/6/44	Vierville-sur-Mer, France (1)	PH
Biesterfelt	Herbert	D	E	Pfc.	37676620			
Bisek	Louis	J	D	S/Sgt.	37178180			PH
Black	Halvor	B	HQ	Pvt.	39922368	12/7/44	Bergstein, Germany (2)	PH
Bladorn	Kenneth	K	A	T/5	36811180			PH
Block	Walter	E	HQ	Capt.	00483158	12/8/44	Bergstein, Germany (2)	SSM,BSM,PH
Blue	Joseph	P	A	Pfc.	34891225			
Blum	James	L	D	Pfc.	33185991	6/7/44	Pointe du Hoc, France	PH
Bock	George	R	C	Pfc.	32836096			PH-2
Bodnar	John	A	A	S/Sgt.	33294555			PH
Bogetto	Dominick	B	E	Sgt.	36330165			PH
Bolema	Peter	H	A	Pfc.	36412215	8/21/44	Le Folgoet, France	PH
Bolin	Brownie	L	C	S/Sgt.	37512357			SSM,PH-3
Bollia	Charles	E	A	T/5	35602958	6/6/44	Vierville-sur-Mer, France (1)	SSM,PH
Bombardier	Walter	T	F	S/Sgt.	32367175			PH
Bomgardner	William	C	B	Cpl.	37705631			
Borer	Robert	B	D	Pfc.	35842937			PH
Borowski	Walter	J	F	Sgt.	31066368			SSM,PH
Bouchard	Gerald	A	F	Pfc.	31252460			PH-2
Bowens	Howard		E	Pfc.	32772897	6/6/44	Pointe du Hoc, France	PH
Brady	David	F	B	Cpl.	12107617			PH
Bragg	Keith		B	T/5	36614970	11/27/44	Germeter, Germany	PH-2
Bramkamp	Charles	J	B	T/5	36583187	6/6/44	Vierville-sur-Mer, France (1)	PH

LAST NAME	FIRST	MI	CO	KNOWN RANK	ASN	KIA	PLACE OF DEATH	DECORATIONS
Branley	Michael	J	D	S/Sgt.	12086140	12/7/44	Bergstein, Germany (2)	SSM,PH-3
Brennan	William	P	A	Pfc.	33708057			
Brenner	Joseph	G	B	Pfc.	33821507			PH
Brewster	Harry	E	A	T/5	11048477			PH-2
Brice	Robert	M	B	1st Lt.	00495659	6/6/44	Vierville-sur-Mer, France (1)	PH
Brilley	Isaac		C	Pfc.	39229539			PH
Brindis	Anthony	A	HQ,D	Pfc.	32664486			
Brown	James	R	D	Pfc.	35733327			PH
Brown	Owen	L	HQ	Pfc.	15096870			
Browning	Maurice	R	D	Cpl.	35796724			
Bruce	Homer	F	A	Pfc.	36850022			
Bruce	Guy	A	E	Pfc.	37066601			PH
Bruce	William	M	HQ	Pfc.	35727584			
Bruno	Joseph	P	F	Pfc.	33703070			PH-2
Bryant	Paul	J	B	Pfc.	35796724	11/21/44	Germeter, Germany	PH
Bryson	William	C	B	Pfc.	34996583			
Bubanovich	Peter	T	C	Cpl.	13188945	3/2/45	Heimbach, Germany	SSM,BSM,PH
Bucher	Alexander	A	B	Pfc.	38493082			
Bucsek, Jr.	Nicholas	L	HQ	Pfc.	36544140			
Buehre	Richard	P	HQ	Pfc.	37562924			PH-2
Bullard	Gerald	D	E	Pfc.	17009919			
Bungard	Henry		HQ	T/5	32417439			
Bunker	George	A	D	Pvt.	42143548			
Burby	Edward	P	A	Pfc.	33685914			PH-2
Burgess	William	V	F	Pfc.	34813062			
Burmaster	Warren	D	A	Sgt.	18151771			SSM,PH-2
Burnett	John	S	E	T/5	20457332			PH-2
Burns	Howard	L	B	Pfc.	37680691			
Burns	Lloyd	C	B,HQ	Pfc.	31253507			
Butzke	Elmer	W	HQ	T/4	36511421			
Byzon	Paul	B	C	S/Sgt.	33159279			PH-2
Cady	Ivan	W	HQ	Pfc.	37560747			
Cain	Richard	E	D	Pfc.	35725714			
Caldwell	John	D	HQ	Pfc.	32939630			PH
Caler	Francis	M	E	Pvt.	39407151			
Campbell	Richard	J	A	Pfc.	11020025			PH
Caperton	Willis	C	C	T/5	36610503	6/6/44	Point de la Percee, France	PH
Caringola	Ernest	J	E	Pfc.	35174206			PH

LAST NAME	FIRST	MI	CO	KNOWN RANK	ASN	KIA	PLACE OF DEATH	DECORATIONS
Carman	William	O	A	Pfc.	35085906			
Carpenter	Ledford	L	HQ	Pfc.	33534711			
Carr	Elmer	C	A	Pfc.	13014087			
Carroll	Rea	V	A	Pfc.	33686272			
Carty	Robert	C	D	Pfc.	39277179	6/7/44	Pointe du Hoc, France	PH
Cascio	Belo		B	S/Sgt.	39140420			PH
Casino	John		HQ	T/5	36457220			
Catelani	Anthony	P	E	Sgt.	39011279			PH
Caudle, Jr.	Thomas	B	HQ	Pfc.	34607990			
Celis	Frank		C	Pfc.	39711332			PH-2
Center	Benjamin	F	B	Pfc.	15067610			PH
Cerwin	Carl	C	A	Pfc.	32234935			PH
Chalman	Robert	W	B	Pfc.	15323842			PH
Chapman	Daniel	W	C	Cpl.	39017920			
Chapman	Joseph	F	D	Pfc.	34201735			PH
Chapman	Wilbur	C	HQ	T/4	36511800			
Ciccarelli	Lawrence	B	C	Pfc.	35089242			
Clark	Rex	D	E	S/Sgt.	39378566			DSC,PH
Clark	George	M	HQ	T/4	15104777			
Clark, Jr.	William	C	HQ	T/5	33068952			SSM,PH-2
Cleaves	Joseph	J	E	S/Sgt.	36428501			PH
Clendenin	Harold	E	C	Pfc.	35407985	6/6/44	Point de la Percee, France	PH
Clifton	John	M	D	T/5	35159411	6/6/44	Pointe-du-Hoc, France	PH
Cobb	Madison	B	F	Pfc.	32547548			PH
Colden	Garness	L	F	Pfc.	36810684	12/8/44	Bergstein, Germany (2)	PH
Cole	Raymond	A	F	Pfc.	31265003	6/6/44	Pointe du Hoc, France	PH
Coley	Leonard	E	HQ	Pfc.	34178852			
Colvard, Jr.	E	G	E	T/5	34708304	6/7/44	Pointe du Hoc, France	PH
Conaboy	John	F	D	Pfc.	13127498			PH-2
Connolly	Francis	J	E	Pfc.	31300634	6/8/44	Pointe du Hoc, France	BSM,PH
Connolly	Warren	F	HQ	Pfc.	20515211			
Connor	Charles	E	A	Pfc.	33562892			PH
Constantinides	Luke		C	Pfc.	33543225			PH
Cook	William	I	B	Pfc.	35462999			PH
Cook	Harvey	J	HQ	Capt.	00393475			SSM,BSM-2, PH
Cooley	Robert	H	HQ	Pfc.	17051924			PH

LAST NAME	FIRST	MI	CO	KNOWN RANK	ASN	KIA	PLACE OF DEATH	DECORATIONS
Coonce	Billie	D	C	Pfc.	36984298			
Cooper	Oryee	V	A	Pfc.	35708593			
Cooper	Thorpe	T	C	Pfc.	19172059			
Cooper	William		F	Pvt.	35893821			PH
Cooper	Robert	F	HQ	T/5	35893821			
Corder	Frank	H	HQ	Capt.	00394557			SSM,PH
Cornwell	Vernon		C	Pvt.	36665927			
Corona	John	J	D	1st Sgt.	20250546			
Cory	Kenneth	C	A	Pfc.	3722244			
Cournoyer	Joseph	R	HQ	Sgt.	36145859			
Courtney	William	J	A	S/Sgt.	15104744			DSC-6/6/44, SSM
Cox	Johnny		B	Pfc.	35209466			PH
Craft	Carl	C	C	T/Sgt.	36941973			PH
Crane, Jr.	Kenneth	G	A	Pfc.	39140665			
Crego, Jr.	Floyd	H	C	Pfc.	12131820			PH
Cripps	John	I	F	T/Sgt.	35422303			SSM,PH
Crisp	Ketchell		B	S/Sgt.	35357132			PH
Crook	George	H	E	Pfc.	11131236			PH
Crull	Edison	W	E	Pfc.	36379412	9/3/44	Landiguinoc, France	PH
Cruz	William		D	Sgt.	39285076			PH
Culbreath	Fred		A	S/Sgt.	3433632			PH
Curley	James	M	C	Pfc.	31423507			PH
Dailey	Robert	L	A	Pfc.	15078906	6/6/44	Vierville-sur-Mer, France (1)	PH
D'Albert	James	G	B	Pfc.	35088777			
Daly	Lawrence	F	B	Pfc.	36990710			
D'Amato	Fiore	S	HQ	T/4	31377913			
Daniels	Joseph	V	A	Pfc.	37604291	6/6/44	Vierville-sur-Mer, France (1)	PH
Dassaro	Charles		A	Pfc.	32701933			PH
Daugherty	Duncan	N	E	Cpl.	36578082	2/15/51	South Korea	PH
David	Carl	E	F	Pfc.	34900769			
Davidson	Elmer		A	Sgt.	39201918			PH
Davidson	Fred	J	C	Pfc.	38444297			
Davis	Robert	G	A	S/Sgt.	13111833	6/6/44	Vierville-sur-Mer, France (1)	PH
Davis	Charles	J	B	Pfc.	39331299	6/6/44	Vierville-sur-Mer, France (1)	PH
Davis	Ralph	E	HQ,F	T/5	17124916			PH
Davis	Kenneth	W	HQ	Pfc.	33297577			PH-2
Davis	Ralph	E	HQ	T/5	17124916			
Day	Willie	H	A	Pfc.	35800812			PH

LAST NAME	FIRST	MI	CO	KNOWN RANK	ASN	KIA	PLACE OF DEATH	DECORATIONS
Day	Carl		C	Pfc.	36984342			PH
Days	James	H	A	Pfc.	36404723			
DeCapp	Donald	D	B	1st Sgt.	36435181			PH
Denbo	Charles	H	E	S/Sgt.	36025912			PH
Depottey	Walter	A	E	Pfc.	36833592			PH
Desiante	Frank		C	Pfc.	42163502			
Dettweiler	Billie	M	E	Pfc.	38516230			
DeVito	Bernard	A	A	Pfc.	31341309			
Devoli	Joseph	R	D	Sgt.	19066135			Soldier's Medal
Dexter	Charles	S	F	Pfc.	35218861			
Diamond	Isadore		HQ	T/4	31049014			
Dickerson	James	S	C	2nd Lt.	02017972			SSM
Disko	George		C	Pfc.	35173720			PH-2
Dix	Frederick	A	F	Pfc.	32253932			PH
Doinoff	William	K	B,HQ	T/5	35315529			PH
Dolinsky	John		B	Pfc.	20301727	6/6/44	Vierville-sur-Mer, France (1)	PH
Donahue	James	E	C	Pfc.	11104243	6/6/44	Point de la Percee, France	PH
Donlin	Paul	J	B	S/Sgt.	31223103			PH
Donovan	John	F	A	S/Sgt.	20304659			PH
Dorchak	Joseph	J	B	S/Sgt.	36511407			PH
Doster	Dennis	F	C	Pfc.	34845525			
Doughty	Eugene	C	HQ	Pfc.	35138413			PH
Drake	Joseph	J	A	Sgt.	33604644			
Dreher, Jr.	William		A	S/Sgt.	35051852			DSC-6/6/44, SSM
Dressel	Edward	E	C	Sgt.	36570793			PH
Drobick	Mike		A	T/Sgt.	36942403			
Duenkel, Jr.	Arthur	J	C	Sgt.	36266590			
Duffy	Joseph	J	B,HQ	Pfc.	20301762			PH
Dugas	William	F	B	T/5	33307262	12/7/44	Bergstein, Germany (2)	PH
Duncan	Delmas	O	C	Pfc.	36645411			PH
Dunlap	Charles	M	E	Pfc.	13053850			BSM,PH
Dupre	Floyd	J	HQ	Pfc.	34630868			
Durrer	Mack	L	D	Pvt.	33541107			PH
Dycus, Jr.	Elijah	D	C	S/Sgt.	15104990			PH-2
Earle	John	W	E	Pfc.	31423370			PH-2
Eason	Wilbur	L	B	Pfc.	20455339	9/3/44	Kersturet, France	PH-2
East	Archie	D	B	S/Sgt.	35132989			PH-2
Ebben	Roy	J	HQ	Pfc.	20616262			PH

LAST NAME	FIRST	MI	CO	KNOWN RANK	ASN	KIA	PLACE OF DEATH	DECORATIONS
Eberle	Gerald	A	HQ	T/5	13129169			BSM
Edlin	Robert	T	A	1st Lt.	01293387			DSC-9/9/44, PH-3
Edsall	Robert	L	A	Pfc.	35896593			
Edwards	Robert	B	D	Pfc.	35838590			
Eichelroth	Horst	A	C	Sgt.	11101687			PH
Eikner	James	W	HQ	Capt.	01301278			BSM
Elder	Eugene	E	F	T/Sgt.	37011822			BSM,PH
Elsie	Alfred	F	E	Pfc.	36581093			PH
Elzy	Clarence	L	HQ	Pfc.	35484619			PH
Encinas	Anthony	L	D	Pvt.	39711381			PH
Engle, Jr.	Albert	L	E	S/Sgt.	32929794			PH
Epperson	Conway	E	HQ	1st Lt.	01012207			SSM
Erdely	John		HQ	1st Sgt.	33088399			
Evans	William	M	HQ	T/5	34328886			
Ewaska	Anthony	P	A	Pfc.	35230227			
Fagan	Glenn	L	A	Pfc.	33574722			
Faris, Jr.	Charles	A	A	Pfc.	35820011			
Farrar	Henry	S	HQ	Pfc.	14029344	6/6/44	Vierville-sur-Mer, France (1)	BSM,PH
Farver	Richard	D	E	Pfc.	35608280			
Fate	Harry	J	D	T/Sgt.	36182049			SSM
Fattorusso	Joseph	A	B	Pfc.	42136469			
Faucher	L		D	B	Pfc.	37744971			
Fende	John	P	B	Pfc.	35522713			
Fendley	Donald	E	A	Sgt.	20530567			PH
Ferguson	Delbert		A	Sgt.	35653286			PH
Ferguson	Raymond	K	A	T/5	39464036	12/21/44	Simmerath, Germany	PH
Ferguson	Eugene	T	B	S/Sgt.	36370584			PH
Ferguson	Robert	W	HQ	Pfc.	36478546			
Ferguson	William	D	HQ	Cpl.	37579115			
Ferris	Wilford	E	E	Pfc.	39013624			PH
Ferry	Harry	J	F	S/Sgt.	13080410			PH-2
Fettig	Herman	J	D	Pfc.	35575643			PH
Fewell	Robert	L	D	Pfc.	33044425	11/17/44	Germeter, Germany	PH
Filzen	Paul	R	B	S/Sgt.	36582076			PH-2
Findish	Henry	J	HQ	Sgt.	33294572			
Fisk	Leon	W	C	Cpl.	13102716			PH-2
Fitch	Bernard		HQ	Sgt.	36411635			
Fitzsimmons	Robert	C	B	1st Lt.	01297863			PH-2
Flanagan	Charles	C	C	S/Sgt.	34132826			SSM,PH-2

LAST NAME	FIRST	MI	CO	KNOWN RANK	ASN	KIA	PLACE OF DEATH	DECORATIONS
Flanagan	Joseph	L	D	S/Sgt.	11048463	8/31/44	Ty Baul, France	SSM,PH
Forcelli	Frank	C	D	Pfc.	33891466			
Frank	Raymond	D	F	Pfc.	38469783			PH
Franklin	Earl	D	E	Pfc.	36885082			PH
Franklin	John	W	F	T/Sgt.	36994460			SSM,PH
Frazier	Otis		B	Pfc.	35434695			PH
Frechette	George	J	B	Pfc.	36807180			
Frederick	Charles	E	F	1st Sgt.	35159332			SSM,PH
Freeman	James	H	A	Pfc.	34845290			
French	Paul	W	HQ	Pvt.	31195274			
Fritchman, Jr.	Harry	G	E	Sgt.	13129178			
Fronczek	Louis	J	A	S/Sgt.	32587594			
Frost	Walter	R	C	Sgt.	36884770			
Fruhling	Robert	A	D	Pfc.	12085785			PH-2
Fulford	Charles	E	C	Pfc.	15112253			PH-2
Fulton	James	E	F	S/Sgt.	15090196			PH-2
Fyda	Walter	A	B	T/Sgt.	32212757			PH
Gallo	Dominick	F	B	T/5	32597937	6/6/44	Vierville-sur-Mer, France (1)	PH
Galloway	Paul		HQ	T/5	35330919			
Gamboa	Gilbert	N	C	Pfc.	39711455			
Gargas	Michael		C	Pfc.	32598808			PH-2
Garrett	Richard	G	C	S/Sgt.	15042062			PH-3
Gary	Robert	P	A	Sgt.	33561879			PH-2
Gavan	William	H	HQ	Pfc.	32063177			PH
Gaydos, Jr.	Joseph	P	E	T/5	33345744			PH
Geery	Edwin	O	D	Pfc.	37698009			
Geitz	William	A	HQ	T/5	32753649			SSM,BSM,PH
Geldon	Walter	B	C	Sgt.	33361391	6/6/44	Point de la Percee, France	PH
Gervais, Jr.	William	A	F	Pfc.	31140372	12/8/44	Bergstein, Germany (2)	BSM,PH
Getzfread	John	C	D	Pfc.	33947298			PH
Gilhooly	John	J	F	Pfc.	32825909			PH
Gillespie	Robert	E	HQ	Pfc.	15078946			PH
Gillhamer	Henry	J	HQ	Pfc.	39239466			
Gilmore	Richard	E	B	Pfc.	36744777			
Gleckl	Gilbert	N	HQ	T/5	33294620			
Goad	Wayne	D	C	Pfc.	38403468	6/6/44	Point de la Percee, France	PH
Golas	Henry	S	C	1st Sgt.	31061151	6/6/44	Point de la Percee, France	PH

LAST NAME	FIRST	MI	CO	KNOWN RANK	ASN	KIA	PLACE OF DEATH	DECORATIONS
Goldman	Seymour		A	Cpl.	36903253	8/21/44	Le Folgoet, France	PH
Goldsmith	William	H	F	Pfc.	33242165			PH
Goranson	Ralph	E	C	Capt.	01299035			DSC-6/6/44, PH
Gorman	John	W	D	Pfc.	17148760			
Gorsky	Stanley	T	F	Pfc.	32981101			PH
Gottel, Jr.	William	J	HQ	T/5	32207115			
Goudey	David	L	C	Pfc.	32597552	6/6/44	Point de la Percee, France	PH
Gould	Charles	E	B	Pfc.	15091468			PH
Gourley	John	S	C	Pfc.	31194348	6/6/44	Point de la Percee, France	PH
Gower	William	E	B	Pfc.	20301487			
Graham	Henry	N	D	Pfc.	20634815			
Graham	William	L	E	Pfc.	37653402			PH
Gray	Edmund	B	F	Pfc.	36593797			
Graziose	Eugene	H	E	Pfc.	31295481			PH-3
Groenke	John	H	F	Cpl.	15359686	12/8/44	Bergstein, Germany (2)	PH
Greenwood	Arthur	J	HQ	Pfc.	35408767			
Gregory	William	D	HQ	T/5	34133761			
Greguson	Harlan	J	HQ	Pfc.	37119889			
Gross	Charles	C	C	S/Sgt.	31249106			PH
Guerra	Joseph	A	A	Pfc.	38501223			PH
Gunther	Harold	W	E	T/Sgt.	20608263			SSM,PH
Gurney	Edward		HQ	T/Sgt.	36920405			BSM,PH
Gustavson	Richard	L	B	Pfc.	32772151			
Guthle	Bernard		E	Pvt.	PH			
Gutman	Francis	X	B	Pfc.	12189063			
Gutowski	George	L	A	Sgt.	36576861			BSM-2
Hadfield, Jr.	John	L	D	Pvt.	33947218			PH
Hagg	Vincent	R	D	Sgt.	33765500			
Hall	George	A	HQ	Pfc.	36212182			
Haluska	Alfred	R	A	Pvt.	35583459	8/1/44	St. Jean de Daye, France	PH
Hamilton	Richard	D	E	Pfc.	39043399			
Hanahan	Julius	B	F	Pfc.	14164300	3/30/45	Emmerhausen, Germany	SSM,PH
Hanlon	John	M	HQ	Pfc.	36029176			
Harding	Eddie	W	C	Pfc.	36430934	6/6/44	Point de la Percee, France	BSM,PH
Hareff	Norman	J	C	Pfc.	36578123			
Harris	Lester	W	D	Sgt.	12209683			PH

LAST NAME	FIRST	MI	CO	KNOWN RANK	ASN	KIA	PLACE OF DEATH	DECORATIONS
Harrison	Granville	P	A,F	Pfc.	36595166			PH
Harsch	Kenneth	R	D	Pfc.	37678332			
Hart	Garland	V	A	T/Sgt.	35342260			SSM,PH
Harte	William	J	A	Pfc.	12128984			
Hastings	Jack	W	C	Pfc.	20532694			SSM,PH
Hayden	Millard	W	E	S/Sgt.	33066939	6/6/44	Pointe du Hoc, France	PH
Hayes	Thomas	C	D	T/Sgt.	18005515			PH
Heaney	Gerald	W	HQ	1st Lt.	01309733			SSM,BSM
Hebbeler	Elmer	F	C	Pfc.	35156376			PH
Heffelbower	Melvin	C	D	Pfc.	36582978	6/6/44	Pointe du Hoc, France	PH
Hellers, Jr.	George	H	A	Sgt.	12190618			PH
Henderson, Jr.	John	W	D	1st Lt.	00536218			
Hendrickson	Kenneth	A	C	Sgt.	20529986	6/6/44	Point de la Percee, France	PH
Hensley	Clinton	M	D	S/Sgt.	34013341			
\Hentnick	Edward		B	Pfc.	31261187			
Henwood	John	R	B	Sgt.	32226720	6/6/44	Vierville-sur-Mer, France (1)	PH
Herlihy	Robert	D	B	Pfc.	31214517			PH
Herman	Louis		HQ	T/5	32642053			
Hickling	Paul	H	B,HQ	Cpl.	39460667			SSM
Hicks	James	O	B	S/Sgt.	36378274			PH-2
Hicks	Donald		HQ	T/4	35359014			
Hill	Jacob	J	F	1st Lt.	01291468	6/6/44	Pointe du Hoc, France	PH
Hill	Irvin	B	F	Pfc.	39053892	3/30/45	Emmerhausen, Germany	PH
Hillis	Virgil	A	HQ	T/5	36188516			BSM-2
Hinch	Milton	B	HQ	Pfc.	39330195			PH
Hines	Lloyd	L	C	Pfc.	35335349			PH
Hines	Mack		HQ	T/4	34243061			
Hinman, Jr.	Robert	P	E	Pfc.	16035747			
Hoff, Jr.	Charles	R	A	Pfc.	13021075			PH-2
Hoffman	Wilbur	K	D	Pfc.	12093414			PH
Hoffman	Robert	G	HQ	Pfc.	37277376			
Holland	Richard	L	HQ	T/5	33273590			
Holliday	James	H	HQ	Cpl.	15105088			
Holloway	Lawrence	W	C	Pvt.	36835649	12/8/44	Bergstein, Germany (2)	PH
Holmes	Arthur	R	D	Pfc.	32899213			
Homan	Charles	T	D	Pfc.	36739141			
Honhart	Robert	A	E	S/Sgt.	20311626			PH

LAST NAME	FIRST	MI	CO	KNOWN RANK	ASN	KIA	PLACE OF DEATH	DECORATIONS
Hooks	Tasker	L	HQ	T/4	33304909			
Hoover	Irving	J	D	Sgt.	33169373			PH
Horn	James	E	HQ	Pfc.	33556263			
Horvath	William	J	E,HQ	Pfc.	35255073			PH
Houchens	Barkley	C	HQ	Pvt.	35483073			
Howard	Carmel		B	Pfc.	36984301			
Hower, Jr.	Percy	C	A	T/5	33464851	6/7/44	Vierville-sur-Mer, France (1)	PH-2
Hoyt, Jr.	Ralph	W	A	S/Sgt.	11007228			PH-2
Hubbard	Richard		E	Sgt.	35791278			PH-2
Hubert	Raymond	N	HQ	Pfc.	31355543	9/2/44	Kervaouen, France	PH-2
Hudnell	James	H	D	Pfc.	34761449			PH
Huff	Harley	R	D	T/5	35342050			PH
Hurley	George	E	A	Pfc.	35027151			PH
Huth	James	L	E	Pfc.	33671754			PH
Inge	Samuel	W	B	Pfc.	33821567			
Innella, Jr.	Robert	C	C	Pfc.	32804080	12/8/44	Bergstein, Germany (2)	PH-3
Irvin	Leslie	M	C	Pfc.	36428350	6/6/44	Point de la Percee, France	PH
Isaacson	Sidney	L	B	Pfc.	32714447			PH
Jackson	Lawrence		A	Pfc.	35080473			PH
Jackson	Walter	M	HQ,E	1st Lt.	01287886			PH
Jackson	Orley	R	F	T/5	13130431			
Jacobus, Jr.	Jasper	D	A	Pfc.	13129920			
Jakubiak	Joseph	P	D,E	Pfc.	36570107	9/6/44	Kerouant, France	PH
James	Theodore	A	A	T/Sgt.	36938331			DSC,SSM, PH-2
Janostak	John		A	Pfc.	36873768			
Jarrett	Roy	J	C	Sgt.	35754136			
Jelsky	Robert		D	Pfc.	33568952			PH
Jimenez	Ernest	J	B	S/Sgt.	36968554			
Johnson	Lawrence	M	D	S/Sgt.	36709892	6/7/44	Pointe du Hoc, France	BSM,PH
Johnson	Edward	A	HQ	Cpl.	36505395			PH
Johnson, Jr.	Homer		C	Pfc.	39588547			PH
Johnston	Leroy	L	C	Pfc.	33798878			
Jones	James	E	B	T/5	34331394			PH
Jones	Dewey	B	B	Pfc.	37453524			
Jones	Emory	B	D	Sgt.	14004784			SSM,PH
Jones	Paul	M	E	Pfc.	36914651			
Jones	Ivor	R	HQ	T/5	33567457			PH

LAST NAME	FIRST	MI	CO	KNOWN RANK	ASN	KIA	PLACE OF DEATH	DECORATIONS
Kacala	Walter	F	C	Pfc.	33897257	12/21/44	Simmerath, Germany	PH-2
Kadoun	Kenneth	R	C	Pfc.	39466612			
Kahle	Adrian	L	C	1st Lt.	00442420			
Kane	James	A	C	S/Sgt.	13098407	6/6/44	Point de la Percee, France	PH
Kassmeier	Leonard	P	B	T/5	39388669			PH-2
Keating	John	V	HQ	T/4	31076213			
Keefer, Jr.	Mark	A	E	Pfc.	35548468			PH-2
Kennard	Frank	L	HQ	Capt.	00514714			BSM
Kennedy	Charles	E	C	1st Sgt.	20250355			PH
Kerchner	George	F	D	1st Lt.	01309569			DSC-6/6/44, PH
Kerepka	Francis	J	C	Pfc.	31430183			
Kerr	James	P	B	Sgt.	33434221			
Kettering	Charles	E	D	S/Sgt.	20312414	6/6/44	Pointe du Hoc, France	PH
Kiihnl	Herman	W	F	Pfc.	34497236			PH
Kilker	John	F	B	Pfc.	20248391			
Kimble	Dennis	F	F	Pfc.	13074023	6/6/44	Pointe du Hoc, France	PH
King	Robert	L	A	Pfc.	35759041			BSM
King	Herbert	A	HQ	Pfc.	31299588			
Kinmouth, Jr.	Stan	A	HQ	Pfc.	42007637			PH
Kirk	Marvin	D	C	S/Sgt.	35156956			PH-2
Kish	Elmer	S	HQ	Pfc.	31335665			
Klaus	William	V	A	1st Sgt.	12093650			SSM,PH-2
Klein	George	G	F	2nd Lt.	01167938			PH
Kleive	Manford	L	A	Pfc.	39619394			
Kmitt	Alfred	E	D	Pvt.	35523913	12/7/44	Bergstein, Germany (2)	PH-2
Knight, Jr.	Frank	J	A	Sgt.	14200503			PH
Knor	Paul	P	E	T/5	13089855			PH
Kobularcik, Jr.	Frank	J	B	Pfc.	33575719			PH
Kobylinski	Edward	J	B	S/Sgt.	20311440			
Koenig	Harvey	W	D	T/Sgt.	36917605			PH
Koepfer	John	V	HQ	T/Sgt.	33070778			
Kohl	Francis	W	A	Pfc.	36711117			
Kohl	James	E	F	Pfc.	36246030			PH
Kolodziejczak	Francis	J	HQ	T/5	33278370			BSM
Kopicko	Leonard	J	C	Pfc.	36587360			
Korb	Charles	W	HQ,A	Cpl.	33248275			DSC,SSM,PH-2
Korpalo, Jr.	Peter		D	S/Sgt.	32010019			PH

LAST NAME	FIRST	MI	CO	KNOWN RANK	ASN	KIA	PLACE OF DEATH	DECORATIONS
Kosina	Frank	J	HQ	Pfc.	36731473	6/6/44	Vierville-sur-Mer, France (1)	PH
Kowalowski	Henry	J	B	Pfc.	32787680			
Kucinski	Edward	S	C	1st Lt.	01318448			DSC-12/27/44, PH-3
Kudel	Carl	A	HQ	Pvt.	33947172	1/4/45	Roetgen, Germany	PH
Kuhn	Jack	E	D	1st Sgt.	33173086			SSM,PH
Kulp	Roy	G	A	Pfc.	37663911			
Kwasnicki	William	H	A	T/5	32771654			SSM,PH-3
Kyer	Charles	W	D	Pfc.	35758063			PH
Labrandt	Frank	J	E	T/5	32073436			PH
Lacy	Joseph	R	HQ	Capt.	00525094			DSC-6/6/44
Ladidess	Jack		E	Pfc.	37678027			PH
Lainson	Richard	C	HQ	Pfc.	36815929			
Lambert	Robert	C	HQ	T/5	35631065			BSM,PH-3
Lamero	Jack	W	F	Pfc.	39264129	3/30/45	Emmerhausen, Germany	PH-2
Landers	Jack		C	Pfc.	36678027			PH
Landin	Robert	G	F	Pfc.	12190655			PH
Lang	Robert	W	E	1st Sgt.	36362677			PH
Lapham	James	R	E	Pvt.	31431829			
Lapres, Jr.	Theodore	E	E	1st Lt.	01307833			SSM,PH
Lare	Lawrence		E	T/Sgt.	35408976			SSM,BSM, PH-2
Latham	Roy	L	A	Pfc.	34608049			PH-3
Lavandoski	Leonard	L	A	S/Sgt.	11101154			PH-2
Lawlor	Lawrence	J	E	Pfc.	31423344			PH
Lawrence	George	F	A	T/5	12067287			PH
Lawson	Ellis	L	D	Pfc.	38557543			
Lawson, Jr.	Jack		E	Pfc.	35435736			
Lazar	John		A	Cpl.	36449562	3/6/45	Anteiler, Germany	PH
Leagans	Joseph	E	E	1st Lt.	00462340	6/6/44	Pointe du Hoc, France	PH
LeBlanc	Wilfred	J	E	Pfc.	31263622			
Leboeuf	Henri	J	F	Pfc.	31303013			
Ledesma	Miguel	P	B	Pfc.	39266404			
Lefferts	Howard	J	HQ	T/5	33376376			
Leighton	Kenneth	H	HQ	Pfc.	31445560			
Lemay	Howard	A	B	Pfc.	37576860			
Lemin	Robert	N	HQ	M/Sgt.	35314388	6/6/44	Vierville-sur-Mer, France (1)	PH

LAST NAME	FIRST	MI	CO	KNOWN RANK	ASN	KIA	PLACE OF DEATH	DECORATIONS
Lengyel, Jr.	George		B	Pfc.	35230082			PH-2
Lesak	John		F	Pfc.	37471849			PH
Lester	Harold	E	D	Pfc.	35040951	6/6/44	Pointe du Hoc, France	PH
Levering	Charles	D	HQ	Pfc.	35757734			
Lewis	Stanford	M	B	Pfc.	37538105			PH
Lewis	Frank	F	D	Pfc.	31423260	12/7/44	Bergstein, Germany (2)	PH
Lick	Ira	E	HQ	Pvt.	38149713			
Lindheim	Donald	R	E	Pfc.	39054015	4/18/45	Bohlitz-Ehrenberg, Germany	PH
Lindsay, Jr.	William	R	B,C	2nd Lt.	02018027			PH
Liscinsky	Stephen	A	HQ	T/4	33282094			SSM
Lisko	Louis	F	HQ	Cpl.	33278363			SSM
Little	Charles	A	B,HQ	T/5	13088439			PH
Lock	Joseph	J	E	Pfc.	16141165			SSM,PH
Lomell	Leonard	G	D	2nd Lt.	00886900			DSC-6/6/44, PH-3
Long	Clarence	J	D	T/5	13154740	6/6/44	Pointe du Hoc, France	PH
Longest	Vergil	L	F	S/Sgt.	15042955			PH
Longwitz	John	W	F	Pfc.	36809435			
Lorbett	Harold	L	E	Pvt.	34825721			
Lore	Vincent	J	F	Pvt.	42091538			PH-2
Lorence	Richard	D	E	Pfc.	37722932			PH
Lorenze	James	F	B	Pfc.	42029903			PH
Lorett	James	A	HQ	Pfc.	11106763			
Lowe	Colin	J	HQ,D	S/Sgt.	15338723			PH
Lukovsky	Walter		C	Pfc.	37563376	9/3/44	Tremeal, France	PH
Luning	Gordon	C	D	S/Sgt.	12065767			SSM,PH
Lupin	Howard	F	A	Sgt.	42010225			
Lutz	Marvin	O	C	S/Sgt.	34008820			PH
Lynch, Jr.	William	W	C	T/5	34710686	6/6/44	Point de la Percee, France	PH
Lyons, Jr.	George	E	E	Cpl.	38034738			PH
Lytle	Cleveland		A	Capt.	00326170			
Mabbitt	James	W	A	Pfc.	35509552			
Macaluso	Joe	F	A	Pfc.	38197839			
Machan	James	A	HQ	T/5	19075237	6/6/44	Vierville-sur-Mer, France (1)	PH
Mackey	George	W	E	Pfc.	35604231	6/6/44	Pointe du Hoc, France	PH
MacKinnon	Edgar	J	B	Pvt.	31423851	8/26/44	St. Renan, France	PH

LAST NAME	FIRST	MI	CO	KNOWN RANK	ASN	KIA	PLACE OF DEATH	DECORATIONS
Magee	Carl	R	E	Pfc.	33892269			
Maher	James	H	C	Pfc.	36887342	12/6/44	Germeter, Germany	PH
Maimone	Salva	P	E	Pfc.	34188123			PH
Main	Harold	D	E	S/Sgt.	39183669			BSM,PH
Mains	Clifford	E	E	T/Sgt.	20606365			
Malaney	James	A	HQ	Capt.	01012197			
Malburg, Jr.	Theodore	A	HQ	Pfc.	13129045			
Malich	Albert	R	C	Pfc.	33697079			PH
Malisa	Vincent	W	HQ,B	T/5	33247561			BSM,PH
Manifold	Max	D	E	1st Lt.	01314161			SSM,PH
Manista	John	B	C	Pfc.	36835184			
Manning	Cloise	A	F	Pfc.	32576385			PH
Mannino	Peter	V	D	Pfc.	42134463			
Martin	Buckley	E	B	Pvt.	35874150			
Martin	Richard	J	D	Pfc.	12206307			PH
Masny	Otto		F	Capt.	01283639			DSC-6/6/44, PH
Mason	Ray	H	HQ	Pvt.	38691360	12/7/44	Bergstein, Germany (2)	PH
Massuto	Daniel	J	B	Sgt.	20301944			PH
Mathews	James	L	D	Pfc.	33459638			PH
Matty	William	C	B	Pfc.	33425264			
Max	Boyd	C	C	Pfc.	32985740			PH-2
Maxwell	Richard	H	C	Pfc.	13093316			
May	Robert	L	A	S/Sgt.	35797405			PH
McBride	Morton	L	D	Capt.	01309777			PH-3
McCaleb	Ralph		A	Pfc.	34900254			
McCalvin	Charles	G	E	T/5	15091484	6/6/44	Pointe du Hoc, France	PH
McCann	Charles	V	A	S/Sgt.	34581081			SSM,BSM,PH
McCloskey	Regis	F	F	Sgt.	33304963			SSM,PH
McClure	Kendall	B	D,F	2nd Lt.	01318738			PH
McCorkle	Andrew	P	D	Pfc.	34006331	6/8/44	Grandcamp-les-Bains, France	PH
McCreery	Donald	L	HQ	Pfc.	36457430	12/8/44	Bergstein, Germany (2)	PH
McCrone	Patrick	F	D	S/Sgt.	32309057	12/7/44	Bergstein, Germany (2)	PH
McCue	Harry	C	A	Pfc.	39249507			PH
McCullaugh	Robert	F	E	Pfc.	36583650	9/6/44	Kerouant, France	PH
McCullers	James	R	HQ,A	1st Lt.	01301851			SSM,PH
McDonough	Michael	J	HQ	T/5	12055479			PH
McFadden	Albert	A	HQ	T/4	36229663			BSM,PH-2

LAST NAME	FIRST	MI	CO	KNOWN RANK	ASN	KIA	PLACE OF DEATH	DECORATIONS
McHugh	William	M	F	Sgt.	36737391			PH
McKinney	Roy	E	B	Pvt.	35927089			
McKittrick	Robert	E	E	Pfc.	32599276			PH
McLaughlin	Richard	E	D	Sgt.	36428164			
McMullin	Raymond	G	F	Pfc.	13058496			PH
McNally	John	J	C	Pfc.	16145930			
McNerney	Jesse	C	A	Pfc.	36275971			
McNichols	Walter	R	HQ	Pfc.	39710737			
McWhirter	William	H	HQ	Pfc.	35284803	6/6/44	Vierville-sur-Mer, France (1)	BSM,PH
Mead, Jr.	Steven	M	HQ	T/5	16085554			PH-2
Meccia	Alban		E	S/Sgt.	32772980			PH
Medeiros	Paul	L	E	Cpl.	33320351			PH-2
Mellott	Herman	L	B	Cpl.	33685830			PH
Melo	Samuel		HQ	Pfc.	39707849			
Meltzer	Robert		A	2nd Lt.	01320956	8/21/44	Le Folgoet, France	PH
Mendenhall	Thomas	D	D	T/5	35405344	6/6/44	Pointe du Hoc, France	PH
Mentzer	Donald	F	HQ	S/Sgt.	13102004			BSM,PH
Merrill	Richard	P	E,HQ	Capt.	01295922			SSM,PH-3
Mickiewicz	Anthony	J	A	Pfc.	32797637			
Middleton	Raymond	L	C	Sgt.	35102318			PH
Miles	Roy	M	B,D	Cpl.	35359370			PH
Miljavac	John	J	D	Pfc.	37016766	6/6/44	Pointe du Hoc, France	PH
Milkovich, Jr.	Michael		E	T/5	33247595			PH
Miller	Vayle		C	T/5	20533813	6/6/44	Point de la Percee, France	PH
Miller	Norman	G	D	S/Sgt.	15011682	6/6/44	Pointe du Hoc, France	BSM,PH
Miller	James	R	E	Pvt.	33569910			
Miller	Paul	W	E	T/5	39340011			
Miller	Marcel		HQ	T/5	36318707			BSM
Miller, Jr.	John	R	C	Pfc.	35467574			
Milovich	William	J	B	Pfc.	42015444			
Miner, Jr.	William	P	B	Pfc.	33500215			
Minx	Frederick	R	B	Pfc.	36916173			
Mitchell	Gilbert	D	B	Pfc.	37679712	11/22/44	Germeter, Germany	PH
Mitchum	Dalphus	G	E	Pfc.	34998118			
Mlay	Andrew		B	S/Sgt.	33141370			SSM
Moak	Stanley	F	C	Pfc.	32853621			PH
Mohr	Christian	J	B	Pfc.	36810737			PH

LAST NAME	FIRST	MI	CO	KNOWN RANK	ASN	KIA	PLACE OF DEATH	DECORATIONS
Mollohan, Jr.	William	L	HQ	Sgt.	35437769	6/6/44	Pointe du Hoc, France	PH
Monacelli	Frank		D	Cpl.	36129881			
Monock	Robert	T	A	Pfc.	36884470			
Montgomery	Francis	E	E	Pfc.	15089560			
Moody	William	D	C	1st Lt.	01300357	6/6/44	Point de la Percee, France	DSC-6/6/44, PH
Mooe	George	E	HQ	Pfc.	32803471			
Mooney	Joseph	A	C	Pfc.	31398922			PH
Mooneyham	Bill	M	HQ	Pfc.	19099530			PH
Moore	Burl	C	E	Pfc.	35294738			
Moore	William	E	HQ	Pfc.	15115122			
Moore, Jr.	Thomas	F	B	Pfc.	31384633			PH
Morrison	Melvin	A	D	Pfc.	42026684			PH
Morrow	George	W	C	T/Sgt.	35176617			PH
Mosher	Alden	G	C	Pfc.	33908443			
Mosher	Paul	D	C	Pfc.	36956085			PH
Moss	Milton	N	F	Pfc.	39710772			
Moss	Shelton	V	HQ	1st Lt.	01307059			BSM
Muhl	John	A	B	S/Sgt.	37679236			
Murphy	Joseph		A	Pfc.	11062912			
Murphy	Ernest	B	A	Pfc.	35085898			
Myers	William	D	C	Pfc.	37039531	6/6/44	Point de la Percee, France	PH
Myers	John	L	HQ	Pfc.	33387067			
Nance	Alvin	H	D	Pfc.	34665795			PH
Nanista	John	B	C	Cpl.	36835184			PH
Nasset	Kenneth	G	A	Pfc.	37577105			PH
Nazarenus	Daryl	J	F	Pfc.	37546188			
Nelson	Roger	L	B	Pfc.	39194267			
Neugent	David	S	B,HQ	Pfc.	16157284			PH
Newsom	Sylvester		HQ,A	Pfc.	34493593			
Nezezon	Stephen	J	HQ	Pfc.	32583023			
Nier	Martin	L	C	Pfc.	37574810			
Niles	Roy	N	B	Cpl.	35359307			PH
Noble	Leroy	W	C	Pfc.	31286697			PH
Noland	James	W	A	Pfc.	35089203			
Nosal	Aloysius	S	E	Sgt.	33170436			PH
Noyes	Nelson	W	C	Pfc.	31254574			PH
O'Connor	Edward	J	A	S/Sgt.	16093864			PH
Oehlberg	John	D	D	Pfc.	16127068	6/6/44	Pointe du Hoc, France	BSM,PH

LAST NAME	FIRST	MI	CO	KNOWN RANK	ASN	KIA	PLACE OF DEATH	DECORATIONS
Ogle	Roy	H	HQ,B	Pfc.	20456115	12/23/44	Simmerath, Germany	PH
O'Keefe	William	F	F	Pfc.	32214605			PH
Olander	Elmer	P	B	T/5	36629444	6/6/44	Vierville-sur-Mer, France (1)	PH
O'Leary	James	W	F	T/5	36584489			
O'Neal	Samuel	J	C	S/Sgt.	33541562			PH
O'Neal	Frederick	A	HQ	Cpl.	34710774			SSM,PH-2
Opdenaker	Joseph	J	A	Pfc.	33778998			PH
Organski	Zorack		B	Pvt.	42134242			PH
Oropello	Frank	J	F	Pfc.	32825770			PH
Otto	Leon	H	F	Sgt.	39398058	6/7/44	Pointe du Hoc, France	PH
Oudibert	Bertrand	J	HQ	S/Sgt.	38185969			
Ouellette	Roy		HQ	Pvt.	31454204	12/7/44	Bergstein, Germany (2)	PH
Pacyga	Francis	J	D	S/Sgt.	35359196			PH
Page	Robert	K	C	1st Lt.	00414083	7/22/44	Beaumont-Hague, France	PH
Painkin	Martin	H	A	Pfc.	32790566			SSM,PH
Palmer	Roy	L	E	Pfc.	33128996			PH
Paniaha	George		B	Pfc.	13111808	6/6/44	Vierville-sur-Mer, France (1)	PH
Pannes	Hilgard		F	Pfc.	36696377	12/8/44	Bergstein, Germany (2)	PH
Paolucci	Dominick	J	C	Pfc.	12066364			PH
Paradis	Roland	J	HQ	T/5	35589999			
Parker	Charles	S	HQ	T/4	36576656			SSM
Parscenski	Paul		F	Pfc.	36673072			PH
Parsons	James	W	C	Pfc.	32897326			PH
Passetto	Geno	L	B	Sgt.	31214549			PH-2
Patrick, Jr.	James	K	HQ	S/Sgt.	13129473			SSM,PH
Pattison	Clyde	S	A	Pfc.	15078135			PH
Payne	Leverett	B	HQ	T/5	33126393			
Pechacek	Donald	C	F	Pfc.	36265454			PH
Peck	Austin	V	HQ	Pfc.	31194163			PH
Perkins	David	W	B	Pfc.	39126901			PH
Perrine	Everett	D	B	Pfc.	35382995			
Perugini	Alfred	E	B,D	Pvt.	31195956			PH-2
Peterson	Frank	H	E	Pfc.	11096301			SSM,PH-2
Petty	Willliam	L	F	T/Sgt.	34570205			SSM-2,BSM,PH
Pfeiffer	Clifford	F	E	Pfc.	34793134			PH
Piche	Joseph	R	F	Pfc.	31297689			PH

LAST NAME	FIRST	MI	CO	KNOWN RANK	ASN	KIA	PLACE OF DEATH	DECORATIONS
Pilalas	Theodore	M	E	S/Sgt.	31235920			PH
Plumlee	Fred	W	C	Pfc.	34764014	6/6/44	Point de la Percee, France	PH
Plyler	Walter	E	HQ	Sgt.	31232892			PH
Poche	Henry	P	B	Pfc.	39589254			
Porterfield	Eugene	F	HQ	Pfc.	33938176			
Porubsky	Sylvestor	V	A,D	1st Lt.	01313302	9/1/50	Chirwonhi, Korea	SSM,PH-2
Post	Francis	H	HQ	S/Sgt.	13011311			
Potratz	Melvin	G	D	Pfc.	36832478			PH
Poynter	Morris	D	C	Pfc.	15116155			PH
Prebenna	Virgilio	V	HQ	T/4	31144442			
Prentice	Wayne	E	D	Pfc.	37486138			PH
Prentiss	Hardy		C	Pfc.	34927759			
Priesman	Maynard	J	C	1st Sgt.	35040691			PH-2
Prince	Morris		A	Pfc.	33193094			
Pulaski	Andrew	A	A	Pfc.	31453735			
Putzek	George	J	E	T/5	35386446			PH-2
Pyles	Robert	S	E	S/Sgt.	36667602			PH
Pysz	Eugene	M	A	Pfc.	31466043			
Queen	Egbert	G	C	S/Sgt.	34724816			PH
Rachubinski	William	V	A	Pfc.	33731016			
Rafferty	Joseph	A	A	Capt.	01301879	6/6/44	Vierville-sur-Mer, France (1)	PH
Ramos	Vincent	G	A	Pfc.	31262433			
Rankin	Richard	E	A	Cpl.	33573253			BSM,PH-2
Ray	Garfield		A	Sgt.	34008623			SSM,PH-2
Ray	Joseph	C	E	Pfc.	35775288			PH
Raymond	Robert	J	C	Sgt.	32214705	6/6/44	Point de la Percee, France	PH
Reddin	Mordell	F	B	Pfc.	38512375			
Reed	Oliver	E	C	S/Sgt.	35176522			PH
Reed	Nathan	C	E	Pfc.	35643457			PH
Rembert	Raymond	D	F	T/5	34207505			PH-2
Remington	Frank	P	B	Pfc.	39140140			PH
Remmers, Jr.	Julius		A	T/5	38113573	11/24/44	Germeter, Germany	PH
Revels	Roland	F	HQ	Pfc.	36256101	6/6/44	Vierville-sur-Mer, France (1)	PH
Rice	Allan		F	Pfc.	37346325			
Rice, Jr.	Conrad	E	C	Pfc.	33766026			PH
Rich	Charles	E	A	Sgt.	31272144	6/6/44	Vierville-sur-Mer, France (1)	PH

LAST NAME	FIRST	MI	CO	KNOWN RANK	ASN	KIA	PLACE OF DEATH	DECORATIONS
Richards	Jacob	H	F	Sgt.	33395195	6/6/44	Pointe du Hoc, France	PH
Richardson	Ollie	D	B	Pfc.	34185579	6/6/44	Vierville-sur-Mer, France (1)	PH
Riching	James	W	D	Pfc.	36884717			
Riddle	Buford	L	HQ	T/5	18015009			
Riendeau	Raymond	J	D	T/5	31291216	6/6/44	Pointe du Hoc, France	PH
Riley	John	J	D	Pfc.	31303684			PH
Rinker	Randall	R	HQ	T/4	33382209			BSM,PH
Ritterscamp, Jr.	William		C	Pfc.	36884593			
Roach	Francis	J	HQ	T/Sgt.	35315684			BSM
Roberson	Bill	H	D	T/5	36882604			PH
Roberts	Jack	W	C	Pfc.	39727342			PH
Roberts	Harry	W	E	Pfc.	33422943			SSM,PH-2
Roberts	George	T	F	Pfc.	35730165			
Roberts	Richard	R	HQ	Pfc.	37369486			BSM,PH
Robertson	Innes	R	A	S/Sgt.	39392008			BSM-2,PH
Robertson	Harvey	E	B,HQ	T/4	38035419			
Robertson	Robert	L	E	1st Lt.	01313543			PH
Robey	Hayward	A	E	T/Sgt.	35386313			BSM,PH-2
Robida	Philip	G	HQ	T/5	31252505			PH
Robin	Nelson	J	D	Pfc.	36548432	9/7/44	Keruzou, France	PH
Robinson	Frank	B	E	S/Sgt.	20530005			PH
Robinson, Jr.	Claude	N	B	T/5	32759215			
Robison	James	K	B,C	Pfc.	37342359			
Roe	Robert	K	HQ	Pvt.	32588257			
Rogers	Kay	T	F	1st Lt.	01316672			
Rogers	Richard	A	B	Pfc.	35310970			PH
Rogers	Leroy		D	Pfc.	36697237	11/15/44	Germeter, Germany	PH
Roosa	Robert	G	F	Sgt.	35435119			PH-2
Roquemore, Jr.	Frank	U	A	1st Lt.	01295774			
Rose	Lee	G	C	Pfc.	36468528			
Rotthoff	Gerhard	C	HQ	T/5	33304767			PH
Roush	James	L	B	Pfc.	16109117			PH
Rowland, Jr.	Thomas	H	F	1st Lt.	01298764	12/7/44	Bergstein, Germany (2)	PH
Rubenstein	Manning	I	B,C	2nd Lt.	11047576			SSM,PH-3
Rubin	Leonard		D	Pfc.	36377365			
Rubio	Robert		E	Pvt.	39863024	7/12/44	Beaumont-Hague, France	PH
Rudder	James	E	HQ	LTC	00294916			DSC,BSM-2, PH-2

LAST NAME	FIRST	MI	CO	KNOWN RANK	ASN	KIA	PLACE OF DEATH	DECORATIONS
Ruggiero	Antonio	J	D	Sgt.	11130047			SSM,PH-2
Runyan	Jesse	J	C	T/5	38209213			SSM,PH
Rupinski	Frank	A	E	S/Sgt.	13097753			PH
Rustebakke	Alvin	S	HQ	T/5	39600002			PH-2
Ruta	Peter	A	HQ,A	Pfc.	36041928			
Ryan	Thomas	F	F	S/Sgt.	16069657			PH-2
Sachnowski	Stanley	P	E	Pfc.	20231950	12/5/44	Germeter, Germany	BSM,PH
Sackett	Irving	L	D	Pfc.	32705687			PH-2
Sakelos	Nicholas	A	B	Pfc.	10601949			
Salesky	Arthur	A	E	Pfc.	36587267			PH
Salomon	Sidney	A	B,C	Capt.	01302357			SSM-2,PH-2
Sampson	Harley	R	HQ	T/4	37120562			
Sanzone	Samuel	A	B	Pfc.	32898945	9/6/44	Kerouant, France	PH
Sargent	Oval	G	A	Cpl.	35546435			
Satterfield	Charles	C	F	Pfc.	33525299			
Saulters	Robert	W	B	Pfc.	36740078			PH-2
Scammon	John		C	Pfc.	31374436			
Schauer	Charles	F	B	Sgt.	12046903			
Schelper	Lawrence	J	D	2nd Lt.	01324364			PH
Schleusener	Dale	W	C	Pfc.	37482515			
Schmitt	Robert	G	HQ	Pfc.	36415368			PH
Schneller	George	O	D,E	Pfc.	11118060			PH
Schnurr	William	R	D	Pfc.	36985203			
Schouw	Alfred	C	A	Pfc.	36970537			
Schroeder	Gerald	H	A	Cpl.	35330199			PH-2
Schrufer	Joseph	M	HQ	Pfc.	13177155			
Schumacher	Lyle	L	B	Pfc.	36959582			
Schwarz	Elmer	S	B	Pfc.	38672752			
Scione	Rocco	A	B	Pfc.	31295521			PH
Scott	Billy	J	D	Pfc.	37745387			
Scribner	Donald	L	C	S/Sgt.	20533664			PH
Sczepanski	Stephen	J	D	Pfc.	33376640			PH
Seamans	Charles	F	B	T/5	32847055			
Secor	Edwin	J	D	S/Sgt.	36185883			SSM, Soldier's Medal, PH
Sehorn	Harold	W	E	T/5	20453922			PH
Sejba	Gerald	O	C	Pfc.	16024982			PH-2
Selepec	George	L	A	T/5	33306769			
Sellers	Carl	B	A	Pfc.	34949978			
Semchuck	Charles	J	C	S/Sgt.	35565704			
Serratte	Jesse	J	A	Pfc.	38565765			PH

LAST NAME	FIRST	MI	CO	KNOWN RANK	ASN	KIA	PLACE OF DEATH	DECORATIONS
Shalala	James	R	E	Pfc.	35912658			
Shanahan	John	C	A	Pfc.	36739612	6/6/44	Vierville-sur-Mer, France (1)	PH
Sharik	Michael		D	S/Sgt.	12009708			PH
Sharp	William	L	B	1st Lt.	01306191			
Shave	Paul	L	B	S/Sgt.	20636094			PH
Shedaker	Joseph	W	B	Sgt.	13097987	6/6/44	Vierville-sur-Mer, France (1)	PH
Sherertz	William	D	E	T/5	36651627			PH
Shermeyer	Edward	H	C	Pfc.	33510186			PH
Shira	Neil	H	D	Pfc.	33402460			PH
Shireman	Earl	W	A	Pfc.	35496642	6/6/44	Vierville-sur-Mer, France (1)	PH
Shirey	Robert	F	HQ	Pfc.	33254050			BSM
Shoaf	Guy	C	HQ	Pfc.	33271173			PH
Shobey	John		A	Pfc.	35837852			
Shock	Dorsey	L	HQ	T/5	35386902			
Sifferlen	Robert	F	D	Pfc.	35293456			PH
Sikes, Jr.	Henry	B	E	Pfc.	38431342			PH
Silagy	Victor	P	A	Pfc.	35829954			
Sillman	John	J	E	Pfc.	34607717			PH
Simich	Peter	P	C	Cpl.	36695041			PH
Simkins	Floyd	H	F	T/5	35631168			
Simko	Marvin	A	C	T/5	35345319	6/6/44	Point de la Percee, France	PH
Simmons	Curtis	A	E	S/Sgt.	32251141	6/8/44	Pointe du Hoc, France	PH
Simon	George	F	A	Pfc.	42143165			
Simons	William	H	F	S/Sgt.	33338618			PH-2
Sinbine	George	H	HQ,A	Pfc.	12050576			
Singleton	Alfonso		B	S/Sgt.	15061516			
Skokowski	Alex	P	C	Pfc.	36697815			PH
Slager	Fred		HQ	T/5	15078965			
Slagle	James	W	A	T/5	33253642			PH
Slater	Harold	K	D,HQ	Capt.	00412904			BSM-2,PH
Sluss	William	E	HQ	Pvt.	35587231	12/24/44	Simmerath, Germany	PH
Smiginsky	William		B	Pfc.	32019479			
Smith	Frederick	D	A	S/Sgt.	20127670	6/6/44	Vierville-sur-Mer, France (1)	SSM,PH
Smith	Simon		B	Pfc.	34311330			PH
Smith	Claude	A	B,HQ	Pfc.	33042710			PH
Smith	Winfred	P	C	Pfc.	34624164			PH
Smith	Arnold		C	Pfc.	36396478			

LAST NAME	FIRST	MI	CO	KNOWN RANK	ASN	KIA	PLACE OF DEATH	DECORATIONS
Smith	Lawrence	J	C	Pfc.	11073143			PH
Smith	Edward	P	E	T/5	31197729			
Smith	Clifford	T	E	Pfc.	13086330			PH
Smith	Raymond		F	Pfc.	39263726			PH
Smith	Ted	P	HQ	Pfc.	34013633			
Snedeker	James	B	B	Pfc.	33941482			
Snipes	Edward	W	E	Pfc.	34813161			
Snyder	James	W	E	Pfc.	33941482			
Sobal	Henry		D	Pvt.	35096283			PH-2
Sorger	Earl	W	HQ,A	T/5	36034090			PH
Sorvisto	Edwin	M	C	Pfc.	35314434			
South	Frank	E	HQ	T/4	36476980			PH-2
Sowa	Edward	L	A	1st Sgt.	32225998	6/6/44	Vierville-sur-Mer, France (1)	PH
Sparaco	Dominick	J	D	Pfc.	20248433			PH
Speechly	Charles		D	Pvt.	36368699	8/31/44	Ty Baul, France	PH
Spellman	Earl	W	E	Pfc.	35293222			PH-2
Spleen	Richard	J	D	T/Sgt.	32269677			
Springer	James	M	F	Pfc.	34836705			PH
Stader	Joseph	H	A	Pfc.	12027745			
Stanley	Coy	N	A	Pfc.	15055378			PH
Stanley	Robert	E	D	Pfc.	39574401			
Stecki	Henry	S	D	T/5	12203563			
Steele	Eugene	F	A	Pfc.	38685556			
Stefik	Rudolph		F	Pfc.	32683346			PH
Stein	Herman	E	F	S/Sgt.	32356794			DSC-12/8/44, PH
Stepancevich	Steve		C	T/5	35159579			PH
Stephens	Otto	K	C	Cpl.	20533605	12/6/44	Germeter, Germany	DSC-6/6/44, PH(2)
Stetz	Harry	J	B	Cpl.	33252903			
Stevens	Joseph	L	D	2nd Lt.	02000930			PH
Stinnette	Murrell	F	F	Sgt.	20362116	12/7/44	Bergstein, Germany (2)	PH
Stivison	William	J	F	S/Sgt.	20305701			SSM,PH-2
Stojkov	Alexander	M	HQ	Sgt.	35313000			
Stokes	Douglas		F	Pfc.	39119348			PH
Storm	James	C	HQ	Pfc.	33321236			
Strassburger	Helmuth	M	HQ	Pfc.	35697791			
Stumbaugh	Ralph	W	F	Pfc.	20725799			
Styles, Jr.	Mack	C	HQ	Sgt.	13128167			
Sundby	Sigurd		D	S/Sgt.	36268561			SSM,BSM,PH
Swafford	Glen	J	F	T/5	37211427			

LAST NAME	FIRST	MI	CO	KNOWN RANK	ASN	KIA	PLACE OF DEATH	DECORATIONS
Swanson	Ronald	E	A	T/Sgt.	33273045			
Sweany	Melvin	W	D	S/Sgt.	35359448			
Swedo, Jr.	Peter		HQ,A	S/Sgt.	33320939			BSM,PH
Sworsky	Edmond	A	HQ,A	T/4	17048438			
Szewczuk	Bernard		D	Sgt.	12085851	6/6/44	Pointe du Hoc, France	PH
Taft	James	M	F	Pfc.	34836857	3/30/45	Emmerhausen, Germany	PH
Talkington	Woodrow		E	Pfc.	35738831			PH
Taylor	Raymond	M	A	Pvt.	42145826			
Taylor	Bonnie	M	F	T/Sgt.	13014072			PH
Taylor	Lee	J	F	Pfc.	35801707	12/7/44	Bergstein, Germany (2)	PH
Theobold	Earl	A	E	S/Sgt.	36477655			SSM
Thomas	William	J	B	S/Sgt.	36662198	3/7/45	Altenahr, Germany	PH-2
Thomas	Jack	T	E	Pfc.	36834806			
Thompson	Leroy	J	E	T/5	36810273			PH-2
Thompson	Bill	L	F	S/Sgt.	36573030			BSM,PH
Tibbets	Billy		HQ	Pfc.	36463604			BSM
Tillis	J	F	F	Pfc.	33947188	3/30/45	Reiskirchen, Germany	PH
Tindell	John	W	HQ	Pfc.	36255707			PH
Tippett	Edward	L	D	Pfc.				
Tolias	Charles	S	HQ,A	Sgt.	31232892			PH
Tollefson	Raymond	R	HQ,A	Pfc.	36456734			PH
Tolson	Robert	E	A	Pvt.	35843072			
Toluka	John	E	B	Pfc.	33428964			
Tooley	Trenton		B	Pfc.	36653070			PH
Toth, Jr.	Albert	M	A	Pfc.	39128771			
Trainor	Joseph	R	A	Pfc.	36227819	6/7/44	Pointe du Hoc, France	SSM,PH
Trenkle	Fred	W	E	1st Lt.	01322820			BSM
Trombowicz	Edward	J	F	Pfc.	31256479			PH
Trout	Joseph	E	D	Pvt.	37576141	8/31/44	Ty Baul, France	PH
Troutt	Jack	D	D	Pfc.	39727332	12/7/44	Bergstein, Germany (2)	PH
Tucker	Wallace	W	F	Pfc.	34836838			PH
Turner	Ramsey	A	HQ	Pfc.	33203911			
Tutt	William	R	E	Sgt.	34702600			SSM,PH
Uhorczuk	William	J	F	S/Sgt.	33589624			PH-2
Upton	Frank	E	HQ	Pfc.	39567378			
Urban	Walter	R	E	Pfc.	37461985			
Uronis	Albert	J	E	T/5	35516559			PH-2

LAST NAME	FIRST	MI	CO	KNOWN RANK	ASN	KIA	PLACE OF DEATH	DECORATIONS
Vadasz	Andrew	J	HQ	Pfc.	33696622			
Valentour	Joseph	D	D	Pfc.	34950314			
Van Hassel	Joseph		B	Pfc.	16012974			
Vascocu	Francis	W	F	Pfc.	34070394			
Vaughn	William	D	D	T/5	36552326	6/6/44	Pointe du Hoc, France	PH
Vella	Charles	J	F	T/5	36579034	3/30/45	Emmerhausen, Germany	PH
Veraguth	Billie	B	D	Pfc.	37745359			
Vermeer	Elmer	H	HQ	1st Lt.	01103450			SSM
Verschave	Jean	N	F	Pfc.	36372151			PH-2
Vetovich	Michael		B	S/Sgt.	33307271	6/6/44	Vierville-sur-Mer, France (1)	PH
Victor	Thomas	M	B	1st Lt.	01324068			PH
Villa	James		D	Pfc.	33759753			PH
Virgin	Leo	F	A	Pfc.	31466122			
Voyles	James	W	HQ	Cpl.	39677247			
Wakerly	Robert	F	D	Pfc.	36108586			
Wade	William	D	A	Pvt.	33822612			
Wadsworth	Loring	L	E	Sgt.	31231880			SSM,PH
Wagner	George	U	E	Pfc.	37679689			PH-2
Walczak	Chester	S	HQ	Pfc.	15014549			
Walker	William	A	D	Sgt.	32598564			PH
Walker	Alfred	M	F	Pfc.	35916080			PH
Walker	John	S	HQ	T/Sgt.	33446631			
Walsh	William	D	F	Pfc.	33304756			PH
Ward	Charles	W	B	Pfc.	38467863			PH
Ward	Roy	I	F	Pvt.	36865244			
Wardell	John	M	E	Pfc.	32958716			PH
Ware	Harry		A	Pfc.	35653083			PH
Watkins	Elmer	P	C	Sgt.	20530853			PH
Watson	Perry	W	B	Pfc.	38519067			PH
Watson	Floyd	L	E	Pfc.	42016343			
Webb	Morris	N	D	T/Sgt.	07040361			PH
Weber	William	F	HQ	T/4	32597446			
Webster	Glenn	L	E	S/Sgt.	36455241			PH
Wedding	John	H	E	Pfc.	35616567			
Weilage	Charles	F	F	S/Sgt.	35475003			PH
Weimer	Martin	R	E	Pfc.	36378405	11/18/44	Germeter, Germany	PH
Wells	Robert	M	D	T/5	35585753			
Welsch	Paul	P	F	S/Sgt.	20301660			PH
Wetzel	Joseph	A	C	S/Sgt.	36332569			PH-4

LAST NAME	FIRST	MI	CO	KNOWN RANK	ASN	KIA	PLACE OF DEATH	DECORATIONS
Whaley	Clifton	F	HQ	Pfc.	31249821			PH
Wharff	Kenneth	L	HQ	Pfc.	36567766			PH
Whicker	Floyd	D	B	Pfc.	35726044			PH
White	Stanley	E	A	1st Lt.	01315454			PH
White	John	W	A,F	2nd Lt.	31135430			DSC-6/6/44, PH
White	Virgil		B	Pfc.	36958249			PH
White	Billy	J	D	Pfc.	37745339			
White	Alvin	E	F	Pfc.	11038426			PH-2
White	George	A	HQ	Pfc.	31217259			
Whitehead	Robert	R	B	Pfc.	33185998	6/6/44	Vierville-sur-Mer, France (1)	PH
Wieburg	George	A	F	Pfc.	36379512	6/6/44	Pointe du Hoc, France	PH
Wilde	Robert	E	B	Pfc.	31131047			PH
Wilder	Harry		C	S/Sgt.	20532839			PH
Wilds	Robert	L	HQ	Pfc.	35898151			
Wilkens	Frederick	G	HQ	Capt.	01013551			PH
Williams	Roger	T	B	Pfc.	31334524			
Williams	George	S	HQ	LTC	00351755			BSM-2
Williams	Arthur	H	HQ	M/Sgt.	33320417			
Williams, Jr.	Newton	R	D	Pfc.	34547211			PH
Williamson	Charles	W	B	S/Sgt.	35739595			PH
Williamson	Robert	O	B	S/Sgt.	34581770			PH
Willis, Jr.	Arcle	L	D	Pfc.	37745277			
Willis	James	W	HQ	Pfc.	33214154			PH
Wilp	Martin	J	C	Pfc.	36697578			PH
Wilson	Roy	M	A,C	1st Lt.	39201997			
Wilson	Warren	E	B	Pfc.	35843033			PH
Wilson	Clarence	A	C	Pfc.	35132702			PH
Wilson	Cosby	D	E	Pfc.	35709628			PH
Wilson	Thomas	P	E	1st Lt.	01319701			
Winsch, Jr.	Carl	D	F	Pfc.	32073153	12/7/44	Bergstein, Germany (2)	SSM,BSM,PH
Wintz	Richard	A	F	1st Lt.	00463883			SSM,PH
Wirtz	Benjamin	H	D	S/Sgt.	35434827	6/6/44	Pointe du Hoc, France	SSM,PH
Wisor	Harold	E	D	Pfc.	33258072			
Witt	Carl	W	E	Pfc.	15104036			PH-2
Wolfe, Jr.	Rolla	E	F	Pfc.	20737559			
Wood	George	R	A,C	Pfc.	20531215			
Wood	Henry	A	E	Pfc.	32772425	6/9/44	Grandcamp-les-Bains, France	PH
Worman	Russell	G	HQ	S/Sgt.	12204207			

LAST NAME	FIRST	MI	CO	KNOWN RANK	ASN	KIA	PLACE OF DEATH	DECORATIONS
Wright	Orville	E	A	T/5	35434764			PH
Wubbolt	Hans	W	D	Pfc.	42136799			
Wyder	Matthew	J	C	S/Sgt.	32233497			PH-2
Yadlosky	John		C	Pfc.	13167570			PH
Yager	James	R	D	Pfc.	42119124			
Yardley	Andrew	J	E	Sgt.	20927510			SSM,PH
Yater	James	C	HQ,D	Pfc.	35358733			
Yates	Leo	D	HQ	T/4	36076744			
Young	Kenneth	N	B	T/Sgt.	33012484			PH
Young	Wallace	W	HQ	Pfc.	33299917			PH
Youso	Robert	G	F	S/Sgt.	37324143			PH-2
Zacharias	Robert	T	B	Pfc.	36881396			
Zajas	Leonard	F	F	Sgt.	36583763			PH
Zarka	Stanley	A	C	Pfc.	36583903			
Ziekle	Eugene	J	HQ	Pfc.	36257423			PH
Zimkus	Joseph	J	HQ	T/Sgt.	32258500			
Zirkle	Dennis	B	HQ	T/5	35380054			PH
Zuravel	John		B	Sgt.	35592420			PH
Zyrkowski	Henry	A	D	Sgt.	36694928			PH

APPENDIX B

Table of Organization and Equipment, Ranger Infantry Battalion*

Section I
ORGANIZATION

A. Ranger Infantry Battalion
Designation: † _ _ _ _ _ _ Ranger Infantry Battalion

1	2	3	4	5	6	7	8
1 Unit	Headquarters and Headquarters Company (T/O & E 7-86)	6 Ranger Companies (each) (T/O & E 7-87)	Total	Attached Medical	Aggregate	Enlisted Cadre[a]	Remarks
2 Lieutenant colonel	1	——	1	——	1	——	† Insert number of
3 Major	1	——	1	——	1	——	battalion
4 Captain	3	1	9	——	9	——	
5 Captain or first lieutenant	——	——	——	[b]1	1	——	[a] Infantry only. See below for attached
6 First lieutenant	3	2	15	——	15	——	medical cadre
7 TOTAL COMMISSIONED	8	3	26	1	27	——	[b] To be furnished
8 Master sergeant	1	——	1	——	1	1	only as required and available within the
9 First sergeant	1	1	7	——	7	7	continental limits of the
10 Technical sergeant	6	2	18	——	18	18	United States. Will be

*Official War Department publication, T/O & E 7-85, 29 February 1944.

317

1 Unit	2 Headquarters and Headquarters Company (T/O & E 7-86)	3 6 Ranger Companies (each) (T/O & E 7-87)	4 Total	5 Attached Medical	6 Aggregate	7 Enlisted Cadre a	8 Remarks
11 Staff Sergeant	2	10	62	1	63	30	furnished prior to
12 Sergeant	3	6	39	——	39	——	departure for oversea
13 Corporal	4	1	10	1	11	7	duty.
14 Technician, grade 3	——	——	——	1	1	——	
15 Technician, grade 4	17	——	17	1	18	10	
16 Technician, grade 5	27	——	27	3	30	5	
17 Private, first class	27	45	297	4	301	——	
18 TOTAL ENLISTED	88	65	478	11	489	78	
19 AGGREGATE	96	68	504	12	516	78	
20 0 Gun, machine, cal. .30, light, flexible	——	4	24	——	24	——	
21 0 Gun, submachine, cal. .45	20	6	56	——	56	——	
22 0 Launcher, rocket, AT, 2.36-inch	2	2	14	——	14	——	
23 0 Mortar, 60-mm	6	2	18	——	18	——	
24 0 Mortar, 81-mm	6	——	6	——	6	——	
25 0 Motorcycle, solo	7	——	7	——	7	——	
26 0 Pistol, automatic, cal. .45	96	17	198	——	198	——	
27 0 Rifle, antitank, cal. .55	8	2	20	——	20	——	
28 0 Rifle, cal. .30, M1	50	46	326	——	326	——	
29 0 Rifle, cal. .30, M1903A4	——	2	12	——	12	——	
30 0 Truck, 1/4-ton	9	——	9	——	9	——	
31 0 Truck, 3/4-ton, command	1	——	1	——	1	——	
32 0 Truck, 3/4-ton, weapons carrier	4	——	4	1	5	——	

B. Medical Detachment, Ranger Infantry Battalion

Designation: Medical Detachment, † _ _ _ _ _ _ Ranger Infantry Battalion

1 Unit	2 Specification serial No.	3 Technician grade	4 Total	5 Enlisted Cadre	6 Remarks
2 Captain or first lieutenant, including	——	——	ᵃ1	——	† Insert number of battalion.
3 Medical officer, general duty	3100	——	(1)	——	
4 TOTAL COMMISSIONED	——	——	1	——	ᵃ To be furnished only as required and available within the continental limits of the United States. Will be
5 Staff sergeant, including	——	——	1	1	furnished prior to departure
6 Medical	673	——	(1)	(1)	for oversea duty.
7 Corporal, including	——	——	1	——	
8 Medical	673	——	(1)	——	
9 Technician, grade 3	——	——	1	1	ᵇ Also drives truck.
10 Technician, grade 4	——	——	1	——	
11 Technician, grade 5	——	——	3	——	ᶜIncludes 1 aid man per
12 Private, first class	——	——	4	——	company. For specification
13 Technician, medical	409	——	(ᵇ1)	——	serial numbers show in column
14 Technician, surgical	861	3	(1)	(1)	2, for enlisted men, see
15 Technician, surgical	861	4	(ᶜ1)	——	AR 615-26; and for officers
16 Technician, surgical	861	5	(ᶜ3)	——	see TM 12-406 and 12-407.
17 Technician, surgical	861	——	(ᶜ3)	——	
18 TOTAL ENLISTED	——	——	11	2	
19 AGGREGATE	——	——	12	2	
20 0 Truck, 3/4-ton, weapons carrier	——	——	1	——	

Section II
EQUIPMENT
MEDICAL DETACHMENT ONLY

For equipment of other components of this organization, see section II of the Tables of Organization and Equipment shown in column headings under section I of this table.

GENERAL

1. This table is in accordance with AR 310-60, and it will be the authority for requisition in accordance with AR 35-6540, and for the issue of all items of equipment listed herein unless otherwise indicated. This table rescinds all Tables of Basic Allowances and Tables of Equipment heretofore published except T/E 21, Clothing and Individual Equipment, so far as they pertain to the allowances of equipment for the organization and individuals covered by this table.

2. When there appears a discrepancy between the allowances shown in column 2, "Allowances," and column 3, "Basis of distribution and remarks," the amount shown in column 2 will govern.

3. Items of clothing and individual equipment, components of sets and kits, spare parts, accessories, special equipment, special tools, and allowances of expendable items are contained in the following publications:

Army Air Forces.
      Air Corps Stock List.
      Technical Orders of the 00-30-series.

Chemical Warfare Service.
      Standard Nomenclature and Price List.
      Chemical Warfare Series, Army Service Forces Catalogs.

Corps of Engineers.
      Engineer Series, Army Service Forces Catalogs.

Medical Department.
      Medical Department Supply Catalog.
      Army Service Forces Catalog, Medical 4.

Ordnance Department.
      Standard Nomenclature Lists SNL, index to which is the Ordnance Publications for Supply Index (OPSI).

T/A for Cleaning, Preserving and Lubricating Materials, Recoil Fluids, Special Oils and Similar Items of Issue

T/A 23, Targets and Target Equipment

Quartermaster Corps.

Table of Clothing and Individual Equipment, T/E 21.

Quartermaster Series, Army Service Forces Catalogs.

AR-30-3010, Items and Price Lists of Regular Supplies Controlled by Budget Credits and Price List of Other Miscellaneous Supplies.

Signal Corps.

Signal Corps Catalog (T/BA items).

Signal Corps Series, Army Service Forces Catalogs.

AR 310-200, Military Publications, Allowance and Distribution.

AR 775-10, Qualification in Arms and Ammunition Training Allowances.

ARMY AIR FORCES

1	2	3
Item	Allowances	Basis of distribution and remarks
Raft, pneumatic, life, A-2, complete with CO_2 cylinders and hand pump.	1	
Vest, life preserver, type B-4.	12	1 per indiv (10 percent overage included in and asgd to hq co).

CHEMICAL

Apparatus, decontaminating, 1.5-qt capacity, M2.	1	Per trk in T of Opns.
Mask, gas, service, lightweight, M3-10A1-6.	12	1 per indiv (mask, gas, sv will be issued as directed by the WD until exhausted).
Respirator, dust, M2.	2	1 per trk (respirator, dust, M1 will be issued in lieu thereof until exhausted).

ENGINEER

Net, camouflage, cotton, shrimp, 29 x 29-ft.	1	Per trk, 3/4-ton.

MEDICAL

Individual Equipment

1	2	3
Item	**Allowances**	**Basis of distribution and remarks**
Brassard, Geneva Convention	12	1 per indiv.
Kit, medical:		
Non-commissioned officers'	2	Per s sgt; cpl.
Officers'	1	Per med off.
Privates'	9	1 per techn med; techn surg.

Organizational Equipment

Autoclave, field, portable	1	
Basin:		
Pus	2	
Sponge	2	
Bedpan.	1	
Buckets, 3 in nest.	1	
Case, operating, small, improved, complete.	1	
Chest:		
Medical supplies, supplemental	2	
MD No. 2	1	
Cup, enamelware.	2	
Forceps:		
Bone, ronguer, 7-inch	1	
Hemostatic, Halstead, mosquito, straight	12	
Sponge	2	
Towel, 5.25-inch	12	
Headlight, metal band	1	
Inhaler, yankauer	1	
Kit, first-aid, motor vehicle, 12 unit	1	Per 2 trks or fraction thereof
Knife, amputating	1	
Litter, folding, wood	12	
Machine, imprinting	2	
Otoscope and Ophthalmoscope, combined.	1	
Retractor, tissue, 4 sharp prongs.	2	
Saw:		
Amputating	1	
Metacarpal	1	
Scissors, double blunt, 6.5-inch.	2	
Set, gas casualty, M2.	1	
Sphygmomanometer, aneroid.	1	
Sterilizer, instrument, 14-inch	1	

MEDICAL *continued*
Organizational Equipment

1	2	3
Item	**Allowances**	**Basis of distribution and remarks**
Towel, hand	15	
Tray, instrument, approximately 10-inch.	2	
Tube, breathing, large.	1	
Unit medical equipment pack:		
Case, empty	4	(97922).
No. 1	2	(97941).
No. 3	3	(97944).
No. 4	1	(97946).
Insert, empty	16	(97923).
Urinal, enamelware.	2	

ORDNANCE
Weapons and miscellaneous

Binocular, M13	2	1 per off; s sgt.
Watch, wrist:		
7 jewel	11	1 per EM.
15 jewel or more	1	Per off (in T of Opns outside continental limits of US).

Vehicles

Truck, 3/4-ton,		
4 x 4, weapons carrier.	1	(SNL G-502).

Motor transport equipment

Axe, handled, chopping,		
single-bit, standard grade, 4-lb.	1	Per trk.
Defroster and Deicer, electric,		
windshield.	1	Per trk. (when atzd by Army or T of Opns. cmdr).
Mattock, handled, pick, type II,		
class F, 5-lb.	1	Per trk.
Rope, tow, 20-ft long, 1-in diameter	1	Per trk.
Shovel, general purpose, D-handled,		
strap-back, round-point, No. 2	1	Per trk.

QUARTERMASTER
Individual Equipment

Bag, canvas, od, M1936.	1	Per off except in Alaska.
Belt, pistol or revolver, M1936.	12	1 per indiv.
Carrier, pack, M1928.	11	1 per EM except in Alaska.

QUARTERMASTER *continued*

Individual Equipment

1	2	3
Item	Allowances	Basis of distribution and remarks
Cover, canteen, dismounted, M1910.	12	1 per indiv.
Haversack, M1928.	11	1 per EM except in Alaska.
Strap, carrying, general purpose.	1	Per bag, canvas fld. (strap, carrying, od, bag, canvas, fld, will be issued in lieu thereof until exhausted).
Suspenders, belt, M1936	1	Per off.

Organizational equipment

Item	Allowances	Basis of distribution and remarks
Axe, intrenching, M1910, with handle.	1	Per 10 EM.
Bag, canvas, water sterilizing, complete, with cover and hanger.	1	
Bucket:		
Canvas, water, 18-qt	1	Per trk.
General purpose, galvanized, heavyweight, without lip, 14-qt.	2	
Burner, oil, stove, tent, M1941.	1	Per stove, tent, M1941 when atzd by WD.
Can, water, 5-gal	5	1 per 5 indiv or fraction thereof; 2 per det.
Carrier:		
Axe, intrenching, M1910	1	Per axe, intrenching, M1910.
Pickmattock, intrenching, M1910	2	1 per pickmattock, intrenching, M1910.
Shovel, intrenching, M1943.	9	1 per shovel, intrenching, M1943 (carr, shovel, intrenching, M1910, to be issued when shovel, intrenching, M1910, is issued).
Wire cutter, M1938	12	1 per cutter, wire, M1938.
Case, canvas, dispatch.	1	
Cutter, wire, M1938.	12	1 per indiv.
Desk, field, empty, fiber, company	1	
Drum, inflammable-liquid (gasoline), with carrying handle, 5-gal.	2	Per trk.
Flag:		
Geneva Convention, Red Cross, bunting, ambulance and marker.	1	
Guidon bunting	1	
Goggles, M1943 with:		
Clear lens	1	Per driver, trk. (goggles, M1938 or M1942, will be issued in lieu thereof until exhausted)
Green lens	11	1 per indiv not otherwise issued goggles, M1943 with clear lens when atzd by CG, SvC, or T of Opns.

QUARTERMASTER *continued*

Organizational equipment

1	2	3
Item	Allowances	Basis of distribution and remarks
Kit, sewing.	1	Per 12 indivs.
Lantern, Gasoline, 2-mantle, commercial.	2	
Packboard, plywood.	4	
Pickmattock, intrenching, M1910, with handle.	2	Per 10 EM.
Shovel, intrenching, M1943.	9	1 per off; 7 per 10 EM. (shovel, intrenching, M1910 will be issued in lieu thereof until exhausted).
Stove, tent, M1941, complete with grate.	1	Per tent, CP, when atzd by CG.
Strap, pack, release, packboard.	8	
Tent, command post, complete with pins and poles.	1	
Tube, flexible, nozzle.	1	Per trk.
Typewriter, portable, with carrying Case.	1	Per desk, fld.
Whistle, thunderer.	2	1 per off; s sgt

SIGNAL

Flashlight TL-122-( )	3	1 per off; s sgt; trk.
Lantern, electric, portable, hand.	2	

[A. G. 320.3 (11 Feb 44).]
BY ORDER OF THE SECRETARY OF WAR:

G. C. MARSHALL,
Chief of Staff.

OFFICIAL:

J. A. ULIO,
Major General,
The Adjutant General.

Notes

CHAPTER ONE

1. William Petty memoir.
2. Frank South, letter to Clark family, 25 May 1992.
3. Robert Selph Henry, *Forrest* (New York: Mallard Press, 1991), 424.
4. Second Army Ranger School Subject Schedules, 1943.
5. Stan White memoir, 9.
6. Richard Hubbard, interview with author.
7. Ike Eikner, e-mail to author, 17 December 2003.

CHAPTER TWO

1. Ralph Goranson, telephone conversation with author, 8 February 2004.
2. Ike Eikner, e-mail to author, 30 January 2004.
3. Ibid.
4. Sid Salomon, interview with author, September 1985.
5. Ike Eikner, e-mail to author, 5 February 2004.
6. Ibid.
7. Stan White memoir, 14.

CHAPTER THREE

1. Alfred E. Baer, Jr., *D-for-Dog: The Story of a Ranger Company* (Memphis: n.p., 1946), 11.
2. Bill Stivison, interview with author, December 2004.
3. Richard Hubbard, interview with author.

CHAPTER FOUR

1. Edwin M. Sovisto, *Roughing It With Charlie* (Privately published in Czechoslovakia by Novy Vsetisk, Pilsen, 1945).
2. Frank South, letter to Clark family, 25 May 1992.
3. 2nd Ranger Battalion narrative, 21 November to 1 December 1945.
4. Bill Stivison, interview with author, December 2004.

CHAPTER FIVE

1. George M. Clark et al., *2nd Ranger Battalion: The Narrative History of Headquarters Company, April 1943–May 1945* (Czechoslovakia: privately printed, 1945), 41.
2. Forrest C. Pogue, *Pogue's War: Diaries of a World War II Combat Historian* (Lexington, KY: The University of Kentucky Press, 2001), 16.
3. Military Analysis Division, *The Impact of the Allied Air Effort on German Logistics* (The United States Strategic Bombing Survey, 3 November 1945), 32.
4. Evans, Army Operational Research Report No. 292, 1945.
5. Samuel Eliot Morison, *The Two Ocean War* (Boston: Little, Brown and Company, 1963), 399.
6. Fritz Ziegelmann, *History of the 352nd Infantry Division* (Washington, DC: Historical Division, Headquarters, United States Army, 1946), 11.
7. The numerical designation of the battery is in question. Oberstleutnant Ziegelmann believed the 3rd Battery, 1260th Artillery, was at Pointe du Hoc. Recent research by German Army major Gunter Hiller has identified the unit as the 2nd Battery, 1260th Artillery.
8. Cornelius Ryan interview with Theodor Krancke.
9. Annex 2, U.S. First Army Report of Operations, 20 October 1943–2 August 1944.
10. Morison, *The Two Ocean War*, 399n.
11. Rear Adm. Alan G. Kirk, Action Report Naval Commander Western Task Force, 9 Nov 1943–3 July 1944, Annex 1 (Intelligence), 2–3.
12. Ziegelmann believed this was the 3rd Battery of the 1260th Artillery. German records show it to be the 2nd Battery.
13. Samuel Eliot Morison, *History of the United States Naval Operations in World War II*, vol. 11, *The Invasion of France and Germany* (Edison, N.J.: Castle Books, 2001), 126.
14. Bruce Condell and David T. Zabecki, ed. and trans., *On the German Art of War: Truppenführung* (Boulder, Colo.: L. Rienner, 2001), 17, 19.
15. Ziegelmann, *History of the 352nd Infantry Division*, 4.
16. Paul Carell, *Sie kommen!: die Invasion 1944* (Berlin: Ullstein, 1994), 84.

17. Bertil Stjernfelt, *Alarm I Atlantvallen* (Stockholm: Marinlitteratur-foreningen, 1953).

18. Ziegelmann, *History of the 352nd Infantry Division*, 33.

19. Cornelius Ryan interview with Paul Medeires.

20. Cornelius Ryan interview with Max Coleman, Co. C, 5th Ranger Battalion.

21. A Frenchman named Georges Mercader later claimed that he was a professional cyclist and the Germans allowed him to train in the Forbidden Zone. Mercader claimed that he notified Allied intelligence prior to D-Day that the guns of Pointe du Hoc had been moved. The story claims that Mercader was later inducted into the U.S. Army Ranger Hall of Fame. The Mercader story is recounted by Carlo D'Este in Jane Penrose, ed., *The D-Day Companion* (Oxford, England: Osprey, 2004), 263-65. In his extensive research, D'Este found no supporting evidence of this induction. In addition, as a member of the U.S. Army Ranger Hall of Fame, I know that Georges Mercader has never been inducted into that brotherhood.

22. Air Historical Branch, Air Ministry, RAF Narrative, *The Liberation of Northwest Europe*, vol. III, *The Landings in Normandy*, 120.

CHAPTER SIX

1. I. Evans, Army Operational Research Group Report No. 292, 1945, 9.

2. Cornelius Ryan collection, hospital interview with Reed and Noyes.

3. Walter Block diary, June 6, 1944.

4. Baer, *D-for-Dog*, 39.

5. Letter from Leonard Goodgall to Bill Frake.

6. ML 304 After Action Report, 19 July 1944.

7. *Small Unit Actions* (Washington, DC: Historical Division, U.S. Army, 1946), 30.

8. Navy Department Press and Radio Release, dated 12 July 1944.

9. Frank South, e-mail to author, March 2004.

10. USS *Satterlee* deck log, 6 June 1944.

11. Frank South, e-mail to author, 10 January 2004.

12. In later months, a replacement medic wore a red cross on his helmet, which no other Ranger medic of the 2nd Battalion did. In areas where German attacked them, the Ranger medics removed their red cross armbands, as they were armed and had to return fire.

13. Lambert would survive, though his voice was hoarse when he returned to the battalion.

14. Manning Rubenstein, letter to author, 27 May 2006.

15. Bob Edlin, interview with author, 2004.

16. Herm Stein, interview with author, January 2004.

17. Ibid.

18. *Small Unit Actions*, 30.

19. Cornelius Ryan interview with Avery Thornhill.

20. Maj. Gen. John Raaen, *Sir, the 5th Rangers Have Landed Intact: A Story of D-Day and of the 5th Rangers*, unpublished manuscript, 20.

21. Ibid., 21.

22. Cornelius Ryan interview with Wallace Young.

23. Cornelius Ryan interview with PFC Carl Weast.

24. Headquarters Company History, 62.

25. Cornelius Ryan interview with Avery Thornhill.

26. William Petty memoir.

27. Kerchner diary, approximately 13 June 1944.

28. Len Lomell, interview with author.

29. Ike Eikner, e-mail to author.

30. Zuckerman and Drury, Attacks on Batteries on the French Coast prior to H-Hour on D-Day, SHEAF Bombing Analysis Unit, 29 November 1944.

31. *Small Unit Actions*, 41.

32. William Petty memoir.

33. Cornelius Ryan interview with Carl Bombardier.

34. Herm Stein, interview with author, January 2004.

35. Ibid.

36. *Small Unit Actions*, 51.

37. Lt. James Weldon, *SIR Magazine* (February 1945).

38. Ziegelmann, *History of the 352nd Infantry Division*, 24.

39. Condell and Zabecki, ed. and trans., *On the German Art of War*, 17, 19.

40. Cornelius Ryan interview with Paul Medeiros.

41. Charles Taylor, *2nd and 5th Ranger Battalions, Normandy Landings, 6–8 June 1944.*

42. Ziegelmann, *History of the 352nd Infantry Division*, 5.

43. Raaen, *Sir, the 5th Rangers Have Landed Intact*, 35.

44. Ibid., 7.

45. Pogue, *Pogue's War*, 122.

46. Gen. Omar N. Bradley, *A Soldier's Story* (New York: Henry Holt and Company, 1951), 282.

47. Frank South memoir.

CHAPTER SEVEN

1. Baer, *D-for-Dog*, 47.
2. Ibid., 46.
3. B Company Combat History, 18.
4. Frank South memoir.
5. Lou Lisko, interview with author, September 1985.
6. Headquarters Company History, 65.
7. Bob Edlin, *The Fool Lieutenant: A Personal Account of D-Day and World War II* (Elk River, Minn.: Meadowlark, 2000), 129–32.
8. Sovisto, *Roughing It with Charlie*, 38–40.
9. Frank South memoir, 3.
10. Ibid.
11. Ralph Goranson, telephone conversation with author, 8 February 2004.

CHAPTER EIGHT

1. Oberst Kogard Rudoll, *The Battles in France, 1944,* Interviews with German Officers, USAMHI, 27–28.
2. Bradley, *A Soldier's Story*, 367.
3. Charles Whiting, *Hunters from the Sky* (London: Leo Cooper, 1974), 77.
4. Edlin, *The Fool Lieutenant*, 139–40.
5. Frank South memoir, 5.
6. Walter Block diary, 12.
7. Ed O'Connor, interview with author, 2004.
8. Baer, *D-for-Dog*, 54.
9. Ike Eikner, e-mail to author.
10. B Company Combat History, 31.
11. Baer, *D-for-Dog*, 56.
12. Ibid., 57.
13. Ibid.
14. Bob Edlin, interview with author, 2004.
15. War Department Army Field Manual, FM 23-30, Hand and Rifle Grenades, 14 February 1944.
16. Edlin, *The Fool Lieutenant*, 156–74.
17. Ibid., 170.
18. Ibid., 169.
19. Ibid., 168-69.
20. Whiting, *Hunters from the Sky*, 154–55.

CHAPTER NINE

1. B Company Combat History, 40.
2. Baer, *D-for-Dog*, 60.
3. Edlin, *The Fool Lieutenant*, 183.
4. Frank South memoir, 25–27.
5. Baer, *D-for-Dog*, 61.
6. Frank South, e-mail to author.
7. B Company History, 43.
8. Baer, *D-for-Dog*, 66–67.
9. Ibid.
10. Frank South memoir, 30.
11. Headquarters Company History, 73.
12. Forrest Pogue, Hürtgen Forest interview, 21 March 1945.
13. Baer, *D-for-Dog*, 66.
14. Sundby, letter to author, 22 December 2001.
15. B Company History, 46.
16. Ibid., 44.
17. Ibid., 49.
18. Edlin, *The Fool Lieutenant*, 218.
19. Ibid., 218–21.
20. B Company History, 50.
21. Herbert Appel memoir.
22. B Company History, 52.
23. 2nd Ranger Battalion S-2/S-3 Journal, 27 November 1944.

CHAPTER TEN

1. Maj. Richard P. Merrill report to the War Department, 25 September 1947.
2. USAMHI, Foreign Military Studies, A 877-A895, Box 3.
3. Bradley, *A Soldier's Story*, 442.
4. Charles B. MacDonald, *The Last Offensive: United States Army in World War II* (Washington, DC: Center of Military History, 1973), 70.
5. Bradley, *A Soldier's Story*, 442.
6. Ernest Hemingway, *Across the River and into the Trees* (New York: Simon & Schuster, 1950), 232–33.
7. Pogue, *Pogue's War*, 285–86; MacDonald, *The Last Offensive*, 461–62.
8. Baer, *D-for-Dog*, 78.
9. Ibid., 79.
10. Sid Salomon, *Hill 400*, 17.
11. William Petty memoir.

12. Ibid.

13. Len Lomell, interview with author, 2004.

14. William Petty memoir.

15. Herm Stein memoir, 4.

16. 2nd Ranger Battalion Narrative, 5.

CHAPTER ELEVEN

1. Cornelius Ryan interview with William Petty.

CHAPTER TWELVE

1. Col. Harold J. Samsel, Operational History of the 102nd Cavalry Regiment, Essex Troop, World War II. USAMHI 304 102 1983.

2. 2nd Ranger Battalion, After Action Report, March 1945.

3. Samsel, 9.

4. B Company History, 75.

5. Ibid., 83.

6. Ibid.

7. Morris Prince, *Overseas and Then over the Top: Co. "A" 2nd Ranger Bn* (Privately printed, 1945), 46.

8. Samsel, *History of the 102nd Cavalry Regiment*, 2.

9. Headquarters Company History, 88.

CHAPTER THIRTEEN

1. Baer, *D-for-Dog*, 111–12.

2. Herbert Appel memoir.

3. Ed O'Connor, interview with author, 2004.

4. Prince, *Overseas then over the Top*, 57.

5. *C-for-Charlie*, 67–68.

6. Headquarters Company History, 95.

7. *C-for-Charlie*, 69.

8. Ike Eikner, e-mail to author, 27 February 2005.

9. Herm Stein, interview with author, January 2004.

Glossary

ATS: Auxiliary Territorial Service: The British Women's Army Corps.

BAR: Browning Automatic Rifle.

Bazooka: The World War II nickname for the 2.36-inch rocket launcher. The name stemmed from a musical instrument played by comedian Bob Burns.

Bigot: Code name for those who had access to the plans for the Invasion of Normandy.

Blitzkrieg: German, translation "lightning war." A concept of mobile warfare using combined arms and air power.

CP: Command Post, the headquarters of a unit.

DUKW: A 2½-ton amphibious vehicle. DUKW was the manufacturers symbols. D was 1942, the first year of authorization; U was body style "utility truck amphibious"; K meant front wheel drive; and W meant two rear driving wheels.

Foxhole: A protective hole in the earth usually for one or two men. A well-prepared foxhole would allow a man to stand upright to fight, while exposing little of his body. Overhead cover of logs and earth was a luxury as were earthen shelves to hold grenades and spare ammunition. Some foxholes had a small hole at a lower elevation for drainage of rain. Infantry that moved frequently did the best digging they could fighting rocks, shale and roots.

GI: Government Issue; the common nickname for the World War II soldier.

Halftrack: A vehicle featuring two wheels in front and tracks at the rear. The American version was used to tow or mount artillery or to carry troops or mortars.

Heer: The German Army

Jeep: The quarter-ton, four-wheel-drive truck that was a marvel of American ingenuity in World War II.

Kitchen Police: Low ranking enlisted men on a roster were awakened usually at 0400 to assist the unit cooks. Men worked the sinks washing and stacking trays, silverware, and cups, or the oversized pots and pans. There were floors to be scrubbed and potatoes to be peeled. The duty often lasted well into the night. Many men considered this duty a punishment.

"Limey": American nickname for the British. The description probably stemmed from nautical usage when the British Navy used limes to prevent scurvy in its sailors.

Mine: An explosive device. On land these are often triggered by pressure from the victim's foot or a trip wire. Some mines explode upward such as the German "Bouncing Betty."

Mortar: A weapon with a high angle of fire. In World War II the American Infantry used 60 and 81 MM mortars and were supported by units firing 4.2-inch mortars.

Nebelwerfer: A German six-barreled rocket launcher

Panzer: A German armored vehicle

Panzerfaust: A German antiarmor rocket launcher. Similar to an American bazooka.

Police Call: A clean-up formation held one or more times a day when not in combat. The line of men pick up all paper, cigarette butts, and other trash. Corporals or sergeants supervise from the rear of the line.

Radar: A radio detection and ranging instrument.

SOP: "Standard Operating Procedure": Policies established by commanders to be a matter of routine.

SS: *Schutzstaffel.* The most ardent Nazi soldiers

Tommy Gun: Also Sub-Thompson. The .45-caliber Thompson submachine gun

USO: United Service Organizations: Entertainers and volunteers who improved soldier morale.

WAAC: Women's Army Auxiliary Corps—the forerunner of the WAC.

WAC: Women's Army Corps as of September 30, 1943.

WAAF: British, Women's Auxiliary Air Force.

WRNS: Women's Royal Naval Service. Pronounced and frequently written as "WREN."

Yank: From "Yankee." The nickname widely used by the British for the American soldier.

Bibliography

MEMOIRS, DIARIES, LETTERS, OR PERSONAL INTERVIEWS OF 2ND BATTALION RANGERS
Lou Lisko,Walter Block, Richard Merrill, Bill Petty, Ray Alm, Sid Salomon, Frank South, Ralph Goranson, Edgar Arnold, Manning Rubenstein, Len Lomell, Ike Eikner, Herm Stein, Bill Stivison, Stanley White, Bill Klaus, Bob Edlin, George Kirchner, Ivor Jones, Herm Stein, Frank Kennard, Moe Webb, Richard Hubbard, John Burnett, Kendall McClure., Sigurd Sundby, Milton Moss, Herbert Appel, Ed O'Connor, John Bakalar, Warren Burmaster, Rea Carroll, Conway Epperson, Frank Kennard, Maj. Gen. John Raaen (5th Ranger Battalion)

BOOKS AND MAGAZINE ARTICLES
Black, Robert W. *Rangers in World War II.* New York: Ballantine Books, 1992.
Blumenson, Martin. *Breakout and Pursuit.* Washington, D.C.: Office of the Chief of Military History, 1961.
Boatner, Maj. Mark M. *Military Customs and Traditions.* New York: David McKay Co., Inc., 1956.
Bradley, General Omar N. *A Soldier's Story.* New York: Henry Holt and Company, 1951.
Handbook of Artillery. Washington, D.C.: The Office of the Chief of Ordnance, Washington Government Printing Office, 1921.
Handbook of the 155mm Gun Material Model of 1918 (Filloux). Washington, D.C.: Washington Government Printing Office, 1918.
Heinz, W. C. "I Took My Son to Omaha Beach." *Colliers.* 11 June 1954.
Hemingway, Ernest. *Across the River and into the Trees.* New York: Simon & Schuster, 1950.

Hodenfield, Lt. G. K. "I Climbed the Cliffs with the Rangers." *The Saturday Evening Post.* 19 August 1944.

Ladd, James. *Commandoes and Rangers of World War II.* London: MacDonald and Jane's, 1978.

Pogue, Forrest C. *Pogue's War.* Lexington, KY: The University of Kentucky Press, 2001.

Stjernfelt, Bertil. *Alarm I Alantvallen.* Stockholm: Marinlitteraturforeningen, 1953.

Whiting, Charles. *TheBattle of the Hürtgen Forest.* New York: Orion Books, 1989.

Whiting, Charles. *Hunters from the Sky.* London: Leo Cooper, 1974.

ARMY ACCOUNTS / 2ND RANGER BATTALION

After Action Reports December 1944, 5th Armored Division. NARA 5th Armored Division Files

After Action Report: Landing of Combat Team 116 on Omaha Beach and Reduction of Enemy Defenses. NARA 29th Infantry Division Files.

After Battle Reports, 2nd Ranger Battalion, June 1944 through May 1945.

Army Operational Research Group Report no 292: Comparison of British and American Areas in Normandy in terms of Fire Support and its effects.

Baer, Alfred E., Jr. *D-for-Dog: The Story of a Ranger Company.* Privately printed in Czechoslovakia, 1945.

Balkoski, Joseph. *Omaha Beach: D-Day, June 6, 1944.* Mechanicsburg, Pa.: Stackpole Books, 2004.

Clark, George M., Gerhard Stalling, William Weber, and Ronald Paradis. *2nd Ranger Bn, The Narrative History of Headquarters Company, April 1943–May 1945.* Privately printed in Czechoslovakia, 1945.

Ewing, Joseph H. *29 Let's Go! A History of the 29th Infantry Division in World War II.* Washington D.C.: Infantry Journal Press, 1948.

First U.S. Army Report of Operations, 20 Oct 1943–1 August 1944.

Gunther, Harold W., and James R. Shalala. *2nd Ranger Battalion, Company E, 1943–1945.* Privately printed in Czechoslovakia by Novy Vsetisk, 1945.

Historical Division, U.S. War Department. "Pointe du Hoc (2nd Ranger Battalion, 6 June 1944)." *Small Unit Actions.* Washington, D.C.: Historical Division, U.S. War Department,1946.

The History of the 58th Armored Field Artillery Battalion. MHI.

Knickerbocker, H. R., et al. *Danger Forward: The Story of the First Division in World War II.* Washington, D.C.: The Society of the First Division, 1947.

MacDonald, Charles B. *The Last Offensive: United States Army in World War II.* Washington D.C.: Office of the Chief of Military History, 1973.

————. *The Siegfried Line Campaign: United States Army in World War II.* Washington D.C.: Office of the Chief of Military History, 1963.

McDonald, Joanna. *The 2nd U.S. Rangers at Normandy.* Redondo Beach, CA: Rank and File Publications, 2000.

Moen, Marcia, and Heinen Margo. *The Fool Lieutenant.* Elk River, MN: Meadowlark Publishing, 2000.

Morning Reports, 2nd and 5th Ranger Battalions.

Operational Narrative of the 2nd Ranger Battalion, 1943–1945.

Peddicord, Capt. Lloyd E. (Scouts and Raiders School Commander). Personal file MHI.

Prince, Morris. *Overseas and Then Over the Top: Co "A" 2nd Ranger Bn.* Privately printed in 1945.

Raaen, Maj. Gen. John. *Sir, the 5th Rangers Have Landed Intact: A Story of D-Day and of the 5th Rangers.* Unpublished manuscript.

Robinson, Wayne. *Move Out Verify: The Combat Story of the 743rd Tank Battalion*: MHI.

Ryan, Cornelius. Cornelius Ryan Interviews for *The Longest Day.* Courtesy of Ohio University, Athens, Ohio.

Salomon, Sidney A. *2nd U.S. Ranger Infantry Battalion 14 Nov–10 Dec 1944.* Doylestown, Pa.: self-published, 1991.

Samsel, Col. Harold J. *Operational History of the 102nd Cavalry Group.* Privately printed, 1983. MHI.

2nd Army Ranger School Subject Schedules, Headquarters, Second Army Ranger School, Office of the Commandant, Camp Forrest, Tennessee, 1943.

2nd Ranger Battalion Newspaper "Characters" April–September, 1945.

Sovisto, Edwin M. *Roughing It with Charlie.* Privately published in Czechoslovakia by Novy Vsetisk, Pilsen. 1945.

Taylor, Charles H. *Omaha Beachead.* Washington, D.C.: Office of the Chief of Military History, Department of the Army, 1946.

AIR FORCE ACCOUNTS

Attacks on Batteries on the French Coast Prior to H-Hour on D-Day. Bombing Analysis Unit. 29 November 1944.

Carter, Kit C., and Robert Mueller. *Combat Chronology: The Army Air Forces in World War II.* Albert F. Simpson Historical Research Center, Air University, and Office of Air Force History, Headquarters USAF, 1973.

Craven, Wesley Frank, and James Lea Cate. *The Army Air Forces in World War II, Vol Six: Men and Planes.* Chicago: The University of Chicago Press, 1958.

Military Analysis Division. *The Impact of the Allied Air Effort on German Logistics.* The United States Strategic Bombing Survey, 3 November 1945.

R.A.F. Narrative (first draft). *The Liberation of North West Europe, Vol III: The Landings in Normandy.*

NAVY ACCOUNTS
Operation Orders
Western Naval Task Force, Assault Group "O" Task Group 124.9, Gunfire Support Group 3, ComDesRon 18 No. 7-44 (2 June 1944).

Narratives
Amphibious Operations Invasion of Northern France. Western Task Force, June 1944, United States Fleet, Headquarters of the Commander in Chief.

Destroyers at Normandy: Naval Gunfire Support at Omaha Beach. Washington D.C.: Naval Historical Foundation Publication Series II, Number 30, Spring 1994.

Kirkland, William B. *Destroyers at Normandy.* Washington D.C.: Naval Historical Foundation, 1994.

Ladd, J. D. *Assault From the Sea 1939–45: The Craft, the Landings, the Men.* New York: Hippocrene Books, 1976.

Morison, Samuel Eliot. *History of United States Naval Operations in World War II.* Vol. 11: *The Invasion of France and Germany.* Edison, N.J.: Castle Books, 2001.

———. *The Two Ocean War.* Boston: Little, Brown and Company, 1963.

Neptune Monograph prepared by Commander Task Force 122, April 1944.

Action Reports
Assault Goup 0-4

Destroyer Division Thirty-Six

HMS *Glasgow*

HMS *Prince Baudouin*

HMS *Prince Charles*

HMS *Prince Leopold*

HMS *Talybont*

Naval Commander Western Task Force

Ship Deck Logs
6 June 1944: USS *Texas*, USS *Satterlee*, USS *Harding*, USS *Barton*, USS *Thompson*, USS *McCook*, USS *O'Brien*, USS *Thomas Jefferson*.

GERMAN ACCOUNTS

From U.S. Army Military History Institute

Richter, Generaleutenant Wilhelm. *History of the 716th Infantry Division.*

Triepel, Generalmajor Gerhard. *Cotentin Artillery, 6–18 June 1944.*

Ziegelman, Fritz Oberstleutnant. *The Fighting 15–17 June 1944.*

———. *History of the 352nd Infantry Division.*

From National Archives

Carell, Paul. *Sie Kommen!* Berlin: Ullstein, 1994.

Jenner, Martin: Die 216./272. Niedersachsische Infanterie Division
    1939–1945. Bad Nauheim: Podzum Verlag, 1964.

Telephone Log of the 352nd Infantry Division.

Acknowledgments

As a member of the combat-experienced Ranger brotherhood, I have been privileged to know many of the men who gave so much to keep us free. This work includes information gathered from friendships with men of the 2nd Ranger Battalion of World War II over a period of twenty-five years. A number of men I interviewed for *Rangers in World War II* (published in 1992) and this book are now dead: Lou Lisko, Bill Petty, Dom Speraco, Ray Alm, Sid Salomon, Ed O'Conner, Bob Edlin, Richard Merrill, and Tom Herring (5th Rangers) among them. Fortunately, others are still with us at this writing and many endured additional interviews or corresponded frequently. I thank the Rangers of the 2nd Battalion and Maj. Gen. John Raaen, who was commander of Headquarters Company, 5th Ranger Battalion, during the invasion of Normandy, and all other Rangers who provided much material.

The men of the 2nd Ranger Battalion were not only valiant fighters, but in individual memoirs and company histories, they complied a remarkable written record in or at the close of World War II. From these unpublished sources comes a wealth of detail not normally available to the historian. In 1983 I began a Ranger Research Collection at the U.S. Army Military History Institute (MHI) at Carlisle Barracks, Pennsylvania. MHI is a superb research facility that is the final repository of all my research on the history of the American Ranger and what Rangers have contributed. The Ranger Collection on the 2nd Battalion includes the Morning Reports, S-2, S-3 Journals, and unpublished or out-of-print references donated by Rangers. Lou Lisko had compiled much material on the 2nd Ranger Battalion, and that is also at Carlisle.

I thank my friends at the Military History Institute who allowed and supported the Ranger Collection at Carlisle. I have enjoyed the friendship of many of them for thirty years: Dr. Richard Sommers and Richard Baker, Dennis Vetok, Randy Hackenburg and Jay Graybeal.

The comradeship of the Rangers of World War II extends to their children who formed an organization of WWII Ranger sons and daughters. From the moment she learned of my beginning work on this history, major assistance was provided to me by Julie (Rankin) Fulmer of Lancaster, Pennsylvania. Julie is the daughter of Richard Rankin of Company A, 2nd Ranger Battalion. Julie Fulmer also keeps the data base for the Rangers of World War II and has expanded on my rosters in *Rangers in World War II* and done important research on those and other men who served in these battalions. Julie Fulmer's data base shows the names of more than a thousand men who at one time or another were a part of the 2nd Ranger Battalion. I do not feel it fair to those who completed training and fought with the battalion to list those who served a day, a week, a month in stateside training and were transferred out or who joined the unit at the end of the war. I chose to limit the roster in this book to those who served in combat with the unit. I also wanted it to show those who participated in the invasion of France, those killed and wounded, and as far as possible those decorated. Julie truly went above and beyond. Somewhere in Valhalla I think her Ranger father must be smiling and saying, "That's my girl." Julie Fulmer represents the continuation of the Ranger spirit generation to generation.

Thanks also to Ranger brat Lynn Towne who provided major assistance with information and useful photos on German units and the battlefields of Europe. It was a great pleasure working with the World War II Ranger Sons and Daughters. So efficient are these Ranger offspring that Marcia Moen and Margo Heinen have formed Meadowlark Publishing Company of Elk River, Minnesota and have produced a number of books on the men of the Ranger Battalions of World War II. These include Bob Edlin's *The Fool Lieutenant*, which Bob and Marcia graciously allowed usage of and is a work highly recommended.

Staff members at the National Archives II at College Park, Maryland, were of major assistance. Kenneth Schlessinger for land forces, Patrick Osborn for naval information and Holly Reed for still photos were all very helpful. I was treated with great kindness and given full support by the staff of the Air Force Historical Research Agency at Maxwell Air Force Base Montgomery, Alabama. Dr. Daniel L Haulman Historian, Joseph Carver, Archivist and Toni Petito, Archive Technician helped me find the answers I sought regarding Air Force strikes on Pointe du Hoc.

My fellow member of the 8th Airborne Rangers Calvin Wood became a professor at Texas A&M and provided information on James Earl Rudder as did Dean Tom Hatfield of the University of Texas, who is doing a biography of Rudder. Ranger Al Hennigan provided historical information on Tullahoma and Camp Forrest and James Barnes of St. Petersburg, Florida and the staff of the SEAL Museum at Fort Pierce, Florida provided information and photographs on the World War II Scouts and Raiders School at Fort Pierce. Dr. Craig Houston of Dickinson College, Carlisle, Pennsylvania, provided valuable translation assistance. Ranger historian and Hollywood film maker Bill Frake provided copies or allowed me to copy letters, documents, manuscripts, and photos.

Sigrid Hoffman was of great help in translations from the German language and sending letters of inquiry to Germany. My German friend Jorg Muth did research in Germany on units that opposed the Rangers. Maj. Gunter E. Hiller of the Bundeswehr Reserve provided information on the guns of Pointe du Hoc, and he and historian Stewart Bryant provided information on the German 352nd Infantry Division.

In England, Jimmy Green, Kevan Elsby and Norman Carter, friends of the Rangers, and Jane Macleod, Senior Librarian of the Wemouth Library, provided information and/or photos. Tony Chapman of the LST/LCA Association was of great assistance on landing craft and their crews. In the Czech Republic, Pavel Bartovsky and Jan Votypka and in Belgium Thierry DeBruyn were of help. A salute to my French friend Franck Maurouard of Normandy, whose knowledge of the Rangers' invasion sites is unsurpassed thanks to his decades of on-the-ground research and his great collection of photographs. We traveled more than six hundred miles together in Normandy, covering battle sites by land and water. He and his family care for the Ranger graves at the American cemetery. Franck and his family have never forgotten the sacrifice. His father in law, Jean-Claude Joussard, answered the question about the meaning of "Hoe" and "Hoc."

Joe Balkoski, author of the classic work *Omaha Beach*, provided information, including that on historians Lt. Col. Charles Holt Taylor and M/Sgt. Forrest Pogue, who conducted wartime interviews with the 2nd and 5th Battalion Rangers. Dave Hogan of the Center of Military History gave additional leads on Colonel Taylor and the Harvard University archives and University of Kentucky Press helped me to learn more of these two superb historians. Though both Taylor and Pogue are deceased, their World War II interviews and writings are a living monument. Like those they wrote about, they were very special men.

A very special woman was of great help to me. I am so fortunate to be married to my best friend, Carolyn (Kirchner) Black. My beloved Baltimore lass is a ruthless proofreader who overwhelms my tendency to get on with it

THE BATTALION

and let the semicolons fall where they will. A writer could not ask for a better editor than Chris Evans of Stackpole Books, and a man could not ask for a better friend.

All Rangers who participated in the invasion of Normandy on June 6, 1944, and I as a historian, pay homage to the other brave soldiers, sailors, and airmen of many nations who participated. The destroyers were magnificent, their ultimate fate heartrending. The USS *Satterlee* was decommissioned in 1945 and struck from the rolls in 1970. The USS *Harding* was struck by a Japanese suicide plane off Okinawa on April 16, 1945. Though fourteen of the crew were killed, the *Harding* survived. She was sold for scrap in 1947. The USS *O'Brien* was struck by two Japanese suicide bombers. The attack in March of 1945 left fifty of the valiant crew dead or wounded. The *O'Brien* survived to fight in both the Korean and Vietnam Wars and then was sunk as a target ship in 1972. No one who studies this battle could forget the valor of the English sailors who manned the landing craft and the HMS *Talybont*.

Nothing is certain in war including the actions of men. Some Rangers did not wish me to use the language of soldiers, name names and tell of the human failures that are a part of every great endeavor. As Achilles said to Odysseus, "I owe you a straight answer as to how I see this thing." I told this story as my evidence and my experiences indicate it happened. Not surprisingly, there were contradictions in remembrances of the men. Whatever errors there may be are mine and mine alone.

Index

French Forces of the Interior (FFI), 168, 170, 171, 174, 176, 185
furloughs, 36, 37
Furst, Martin, 180–83
Fyda, Walter, 114, 119, 202

gambling, 75
Geitz, William, 105, 200, 201
Geldon, Walter B., 87, 90
Gerhardt, Charles, 59, 145, 147, 157
Germeter Germany, 195, 196, 201, 203, 204, 206, 207
Goodgall, Leonard, 97, 98, 101
Goranson, Ralph, 19, 20, 23, 36, 39, 85–87, 91, 92, 100, 152, 155, 163, 213, 261
Graf Spee Battery, 169, 175, 178, 181, 183
Grafenwohr, Germany, 277–79
Guerra, Joe, 226, 240

Hall, John L., 58 63, 146
Hanahan, Julius, 229, 271
Harding, USS, 81, 145
Hart, Garland, 118, 239
Harwood, Jonathan H., 71, 134
Heaney Gerald W., 25, 50, 121, 159, 204, 216, 286
Henderson, John William, 265, 266, 269, 270
Hickling, Paul H., 257, 258
Hill, Jacob, 106, 107, 122, 123, 135, 271
Hill 400 (Castle Hill), 208, 232
Hill 63, 172, 173, 175
Hitler, Adolf, 54, 47, 235, 272
Hitler Youth and Labor Corps, 66, 276, 278
Hodges, Courtney, 157, 205
Holzappel, Germany, 265, 267, 268

Hubbard, Richard, 11, 12, 30, 33, 93, 95, 96, 102, 191, 198, 276, 285
Huebner, Clarence, 58, 59
Hürtgen, Germany 206, 209
Hurtgen Forest (Hürtgenwald), 2, 187, 195, 199, 200, 205, 206, 214, 233
Hürtgen-Rollesbroich Road, 194

Johnson, Lawrence, 75, 130, 144
Jones, Ivor, 42, 70
jujitsu, 29

Kennard, Frank L., 72, 146, 149, 150, 157
Kerchener George F., 75, 106, 112, 130, 140, 141, 155, 157
Kergolleau, France, 176, 184
Kettlehut Howard K., 211, 213, 217, 218, 227, 229–31
Kirk, Alan, 58, 61
Klaus, Bill, 15, 16, 31, 36, 117, 118, 121, 158, 161, 183, 184, 243, 285
Knudson, Dean H., 12, 13, 26
Korb, Charles, 113, 196, 226, 254
Kucinski, Edward, 250, 251
Kuhn, Jack, 5, 130, 132, 154, 285

Lacy, Father, 70, 78, 128, 156
Lambert, Robert, 91, 117, 118
Landerneau, France, 185, 188
Lang, Robert, 95, 130, 132
Lapres, Ted, 11, 30, 103, 111, 140, 227
Lare, Lawrence, 230, 231
Lazar, John, 259, 260
LCA (Landing Craft, Assault), xi, 77, 86, 87, 94

Stackpole Military History Series

Real battles. Real soldiers. Real stories.

Stackpole Military History Series

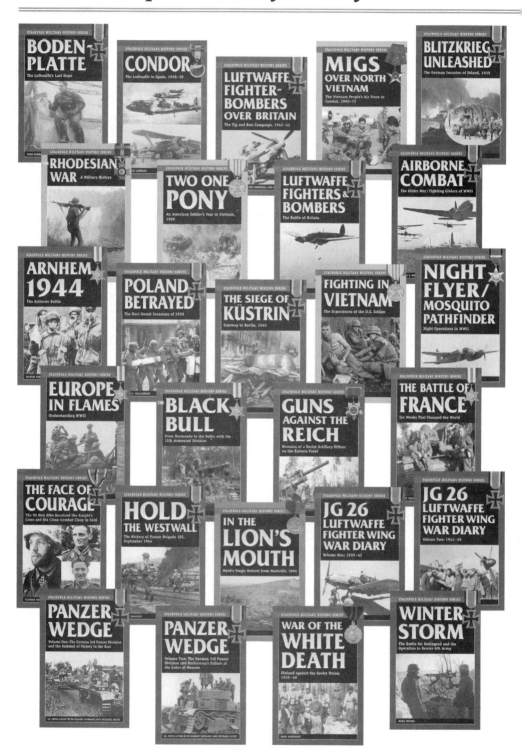

Real battles. Real soldiers. Real stories.

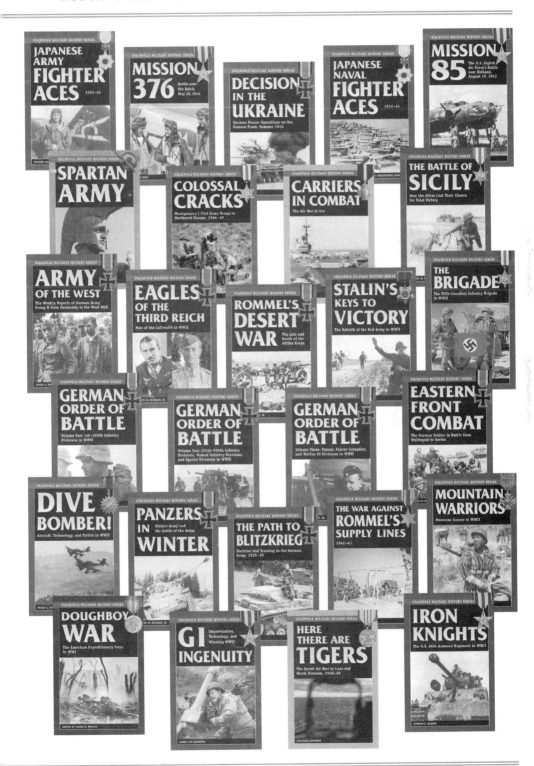

Stackpole Military History Series

Real battles. Real soldiers. Real stories.

Stackpole Military History Series

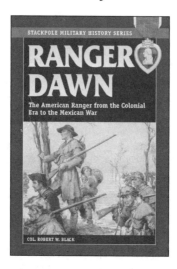

RANGER DAWN

THE AMERICAN RANGER FROM THE COLONIAL ERA TO THE MEXICAN WAR

Col. Robert W. Black

Ranger expert Robert W. Black adds a new chapter to his story of the American Rangers, beginning with the birth of the Ranger concept in the 1600s and tracking Rangers through the French and Indian War, the American Revolution, the War of 1812, the Texas War of Independence, and the Mexican-American War. For much of this period, Rangers were independent groups of citizen-soldiers under men like Robert Rogers, Francis Marion, and George Rogers Clark who patrolled, scouted, and made hit-and-run attacks in the wilderness of the American frontier. These early battles form an essential part of a Ranger legacy that continues into modern times.

Paperback • 6 x 9 • 384 pages • 9 b/w photos, 17 maps

WWW.STACKPOLEBOOKS.COM
1-800-732-3669

Stackpole Military History Series

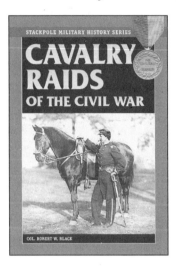

CAVALRY RAIDS OF THE CIVIL WAR
Col. Robert W. Black

In war, the raid is the epitome of daring. Usually outnumbered, raiders launch surprise attacks behind enemy lines to take prisoners, destroy communications, and seize supplies—in short, to cause as much disruption and confusion as possible. During the Civil War, these men marauded on horseback, stunning their opponents with speed and mobility. From J. E. B. Stuart's 1862 ride around the Union army to James Wilson's crushing raids in Alabama and Georgia in 1865, both Union and Confederate raiders engaged in some of the most adventurous exploits of the war.

Paperback • 6 x 9 • 288 pages • 18 b/w photos

WWW.STACKPOLEBOOKS.COM
1-800-732-3669

Stackpole Military History Series

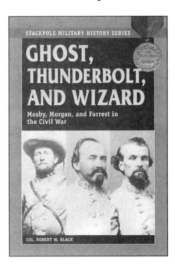

GHOST, THUNDERBOLT, AND WIZARD

MOSBY, MORGAN, AND FORREST IN THE CIVIL WAR

Col. Robert W. Black

Speed, boldness, and controversy marked the Civil War careers of this trio of Confederate cavalrymen. John Singleton Mosby teamed with J. E. B. Stuart to conduct the famous ride around McClellan's army in 1862. A year later, John Hunt Morgan led his gray raiders deep into Ohio, farther north than any other uniformed rebel force. Lacking military training, Nathan Bedford Forrest proved himself one of the war's best generals with his hit-and-run campaigns in Tennessee. Masters of scouting, raiding, and harassing the Union, Mosby, Morgan, and Forrest charged into history as pioneers of irregular warfare.

Paperback • 6 x 9 • 400 pages • 20 b/w photos

WWW.STACKPOLEBOOKS.COM
1-800-732-3669

Stackpole Military History Series

BEYOND THE BEACHHEAD

THE 29TH INFANTRY DIVISION IN NORMANDY

Joseph Balkoski

Previously untested in battle, the American 29th
Infantry Division stormed Omaha Beach on D-Day and
began a summer of bloody combat in the hedgerows
of Normandy. Against a tenacious German foe, the
division fought fiercely for every inch of ground and,
at great cost, liberated the town of St. Lô. This new
and expanded edition of Joseph Balkoski's classic
follows the 29th through the final stages of the
campaign and the brutal struggle for the town of Vire.

Paperback • 6 x 9 • 352 pages • 36 b/w photos, 30 maps

Stackpole Military History Series

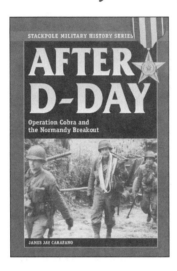

AFTER D-DAY
OPERATION COBRA AND THE NORMANDY BREAKOUT
James Jay Carafano

After storming the beaches on D-Day, June 6, 1944, the
Allied invasion of France bogged down in seven weeks
of grueling attrition in Normandy. On July 25, U.S.
divisions under Gen. Omar Bradley launched
Operation Cobra, an attempt to break out of the
hedgerows and begin a war of movement against the
Germans. Despite a disastrous start, with misdropped
bombs killing more than 100 GIs, Cobra proved to be
one of the most pivotal battles of World War II,
successfully breaking the stalemate in Normandy and
clearing a path into the heart of France.

Paperback • 6 x 9 • 336 pages • 31 b/w photos, 10 maps

WWW.STACKPOLEBOOKS.COM
1-800-732-3669

Stackpole Military History Series

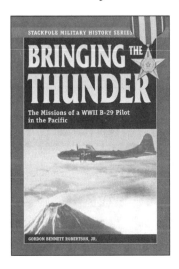

BRINGING THE THUNDER
THE MISSIONS OF A WWII B-29 PILOT IN THE PACIFIC
Gordon Bennett Robertson, Jr.

By March 1945, when Ben Robertson took to the skies above
Japan in his B-29 Superfortress, the end of World War II in the
Pacific seemed imminent. But although American forces were
closing in on its home islands, Japan refused to surrender, and
American B-29s were tasked with hammering Japan to its
knees with devastating bomb runs. That meant flying low-
altitude, nighttime incendiary raids under threat of flak,
enemy fighters, mechanical malfunction, and fatigue. It may
have been the beginning of the end, but just how soon the
end would come—and whether Robertson and his crew would
make it home—was far from certain.

Paperback • 6 x 9 • 304 pages • 50 b/w photos, 1 map

WWW.STACKPOLEBOOKS.COM
1-800-732-3669

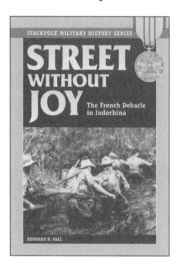

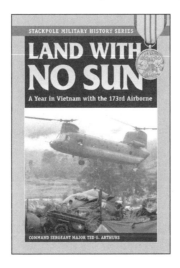

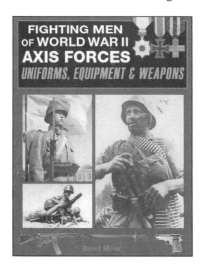
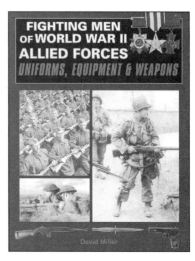